Let Us Alone

Let Us Alone

The Origins of Baltimore's Police State

MICHAEL CASIANO

© 2025 by the Board of Trustees
of the University of Illinois
All rights reserved
1 2 3 4 5 C P 5 4 3 2 1
♾ This book is printed on acid-free paper.

Cataloging data available from the Library of Congress

ISBN 978-0-252-04677-3 (hardcover)
ISBN 978-0-252-08888-9 (paperback)
ISBN 978-0-252-04832-6 (ebook)

Pa' Lucy, en paz descanse

Contents

Acknowledgments ix

Introduction 1

1 "This Modern Hades": Jails, Asylums, and the
Business of Punishment in Post–Civil War Baltimore 17

2 "Silk Stocking Aristocracy": Police, Reform, and the
Racialization of Crime in the Late Nineteenth Century 44

3 "With the Power of the Law": The Carceral Dimensions of
Charity, Social Science, and Public Schools 72

4 "If I Had Told What I Know": Drug Enforcement and the
Streets of Early Twentieth-Century Baltimore 100

5 "I Ask Mercy at Your Hands": The Case of Henry Alfred Brown,
Third-Degree Torture, and Black Grassroots Responses to
Judicial Inequality 131

6 "Policemen Were the Biggest Liars": Demystifying Public Order
and the Erosion of Black Privacy during the Roaring Twenties 164

Conclusion 193

Notes   199

Bibliography   233

Index   251

Acknowledgments

Writing a book is hard, lonely work. Along the way, one develops important relationships that provide respite from this loneliness. The following are just a few of the people who helped me finish this book.

This project began at the University of Maryland, College Park (UMD). I spent ten years there as an undergraduate and graduate student. I owe a deep debt of gratitude to everyone I worked with while I was there, including countless mentors and colleagues who became indispensable parts of my academic career and life. Thanks to my dissertation committee, Sheri Parks, Jan Padios, Christina Hanhardt, Mary Sies, and Randy Ontiveros, for shepherding the kernel of this project. The rest of the UMD American studies community, La Marr Jurelle Bruce, John Caughey, Robert Chester, Jason Farman, Jo Paoletti, Nancy Struna, Psyche Williams-Forson, Janelle Wong, Betsy Yuen, Julia John, and Tammi Archer, helped me understand what it meant to be in an intellectual community. Special thanks to Perla Guerrero, who read and provided feedback on portions of this book, Mary Sies, who championed my work and familiarized me with the world of academic publishing, and Patrick Grzanka, who introduced me to American studies and provided vital mentorship.

Thank you to my graduate school colleagues. Terrance Wooten has taught me so much about being a scholar, colleague, and friend. Additional thanks to A. Anthony, Bimbola Akinbola, Stephanie Akoumany, Tatiana Benjamin, Molly Benitez, E. Cassandra Dame-Griff, Jason Ezell, Dan Greene, Douglas x • *Acknowledgments*

Ishii, Robert Jiles, Ashley Minner, Tony Perry, Jessica Kenyatta Walker, Kevin Winstead, and Kalima Young.

After graduate school, I received a postdoctoral fellowship at Rutgers, the State University of New Jersey. Housed in the Department of History, I was a seminar participant in the Rutgers Center for Historical Analysis (RCHA). I would like to recognize the seminar's codirectors, Marisa Fuentes and Kali Gross. Under their tutelage, I received invaluable feedback that dared me to be more assertive in my writing and scholarship. RaShelle Peck, my partner at RCHA, made my time there enjoyable and productive. Thanks also to Miya Carey, Anna Hinton, Rachel Miller, and Johnny Bailey. Nicole Fleetwood, co-organizer of the Carceral Studies Working Group, has also provided me priceless mentorship and support over the years.

Now at the University of Maryland, Baltimore County, I cherish my colleagues, collaborators, and friends. The Department of American Studies has been a godsend as I navigated the publication of this book. Tamara Bhalla advocated for me in ways I probably still do not fully comprehend. Nicole King has inspired me with her tireless scholar activism. Sarah Fouts has waded through junior professorship with me. In American studies, I would also like to thank W. Edward Orser, Kathy Bryan, Ellen Gorman, Mike Hummel, Dabrina Taylor, Andy DeVos, Conor Donnan, Erin Minnigh, and Morgan Dowty. Outside of American studies, I thank my colleagues María Célleri, Keegan Cook Finberg, J Inscoe, Charlotte Keniston, Tania Lizarazo, Thania Muñoz, and Emily Yoon. You all fortified my resolve to finish this book even in the bleakest times. I would especially like to thank Keegan for her valuable friendship and thoughtful feedback on draft versions of chapters. To the Dresher Center for the Humanities, I give my sincerest thanks. Jessica Berman, Rachel Brubaker, Amy Froide, and Courtney Hobson have created resources, including indexing funds for this book, and avenues for me to present and workshop my research for years. To the participants of the book workshop that helped me finalize the initial revision of this book, I give special thanks. Melissa Blair, Nicole King, Michelle Scott, and Micol Seigel provided incisive feedback that helped refine my arguments and sharpen my prose. I applaud Micol Seigel, another incredible mentor, for providing me with academic and professional advice. To all my students, your support has energized and sustained me these past several years. Special thanks to Harrison DeFord who reviewed the data in this book and provided important corrections and context.

A historian is nothing without archives. To all the librarians, archivists, and volunteers who pulled records, transported offsite materials, and provided insight into my project, I owe you all an enormous debt of gratitude. I especially

Acknowledgments • xi

want to thank everyone at the Maryland State Archives and the Baltimore City Archives where I spent innumerable hours wading through mountains of documents.

Words cannot express how grateful I am to my incredible editor, Alison Syring. Alison picked this book up and ran with it. Her assurances and transparency throughout the process were comforting and encouraging. To everyone who helped with this book's production, including Leigh Ann Cowan, Megan Donnan, and Joyce Li, I give profound thanks. As a first-time author, I could not have asked for a smoother publishing experience. I would also like to recognize the anonymous referees whose suggestions made the book stronger. All errors in the final text are mine and mine alone.

I have been fortunate to work at an institution located five miles from where I grew up. As a result, I have had the privilege of being near my closest friends and family. To my dearest childhood friend, Chris Vaught, I give a million thanks. As kids, we encountered and navigated some of the persistent dynamics charted in this book. I would also like to thank Mason Brown, Andrew Cohen, Anjab Ghauri, Matt Lease, Sam Nassau, Orlando Nuñez, and Lealin Queen.

To all my siblings, Jennifer Almeida, Raymond Casiano, Jonathan Casiano, Hugo Lopez, Brian Valle, Giannis Valle, and Carlos Valle, thank you for supporting me all these years. To my mother, Lucy Figueroa, I miss you. To my father, Ramon Casiano, thank you for always being there when I need you. Thanks also to my stepmom, Lourdes Casiano, and my cousins, Amy Perez, Charlie Perez, and Johanna Nieves.

Finally, thank you to my wife, Priya Bhayana. You have been a fountain of positivity, a shoulder to cry on, and a motivator when I was feeling helpless. I love you. During the seemingly endless process of writing this book, you also gave me the greatest gift I could ever receive, Zoraida Luz Casiano-Bhayana, our Munchie.

Let Us Alone

Introduction

In May 1902, Baltimore police arrested Joseph Johnson, a Black man, for larceny. Police detained Johnson in the wake of a colossal manhunt for a Black cop killer that set the press ablaze with racial hostility. Given this backdrop, the press alleged that Black men's inherent instability had been activated by the murder and gestured toward the possibilities of a race riot.[1] As such, Johnson's threat was likely alarming. The man reportedly told his arresting officer, "We ought to make examples of a few of you funny policemen and then, maybe, you'd *let us alone*."[2] The sensationalist dailies took Johnson's proclamation as menacing, but the sentiment behind it echoed Black aspirations for the quiet enjoyment associated with civil life and an end to police harassment. In another story, the *Sun* reported that Northwestern District police received a letter that read, in part, "If you don't stop your police from treating us like dogs, we is up in this part of baltimore [*sic*] we can't do anything without being arrested."[3]

These pleas to be let alone spoke to daily life in early twentieth-century Baltimore. By this period, police had established a permanent and haunting presence in Black neighborhoods. They relied on discretionary public order statutes to arrest and incarcerate Black men and women at astronomical rates. Such targeted enforcement was meant to stymie what white racists described as "Negro rule," or the degradation of white society by potential Black advancement. The year before police arrested and confined Johnson to six months in the city jail, Black men and women accounted for 56 percent of all jail commitments,

2 · *Introduction*

which followed a broader trend of disproportionate rates of Black incarceration.[4] Johnson lived under the watchful eye of an increasingly bureaucratized police state that prioritized preemptive patrolling through consistent community surveillance. This constant presence prompted him and others to protest Baltimore's burgeoning police state—to be saved from the indignities of horrid treatment and to be "let alone." The police would not, however, let Black Baltimoreans alone—quite the opposite. Police power thrived on the ability to bother, to watch, to surveil, to detain, and to kill. This book documents how this power developed and crystallized over the course of six decades.

Let Us Alone: The Origins of Baltimore's Police State charts the institutional consolidation of the post–Civil War police state in Baltimore. It demonstrates how institutional coordination during the late nineteenth and early twentieth centuries organized and established municipal power in distinct but interrelated public and private sites, including jails, areas of political and social activism, public schools, street corners, courtrooms, and homes. The story woven throughout this book is tied together by two parallel and inextricable realities of urban governance in postbellum Baltimore. First, after the Civil War and well into the twentieth century, policing evolved from its relatively inefficient and vigilante-driven antebellum character into a modern and systematized paramilitary endeavor rooted in the suppression of populations and the maximization of capital. Second, given shifting political imperatives, Maryland's meager and ineffectual Reconstruction efforts, and the advent of Jim Crow, by the early twentieth century, Baltimore's policing apparatus became primarily oriented around the subdual of Black freedom. As such, this book narrates both the intensification of a punitive municipal state structure and the sedimentation of racialized policing in one of the country's largest commercial cities. Given this framing, the questions that guided the study include, as Baltimore grew in population, land mass, and administrative capacity, how did local government develop, justify, and frame its duties? What disciplinary mechanisms emerged to enforce these duties and how did they produce—and rely on—racialized and gendered constructions of city residents?[5] What can a broader conception of policing—that moves beyond merely considering the cops—allow us to understand regarding urban governance in the post–Civil War United States? What can an analysis of anti-Black policing at the turn of the twentieth century reveal about the persistence and character of racialized policing in the present?

In conceiving of policing beyond just cops, this study graphs the development of "police power" after the Civil War. This concept has become indispensable to contemporary studies of policing. Unlike much of the modern literature on policing, throughout this study, police power does not simply refer to the power of the cops. Instead, it relies on police power's use as a legal doctrine that undergirds the function of governing bodies, like cities. Police power vested cops with enormous paramilitary muscle. It also empowered cities to creatively and selectively create and enforce laws, programs, and other impositions on daily life. City leaders seized on the police power doctrine to bolster home rule city charters and justify state interference in everything from land use, pawning, and the organization of public space. Local government leaned heavily on police power to mediate conflicts among competing classes and protect the growing capital interests that propelled their cities into the twentieth century. This concept was rehearsed and exercised in the streets, negotiated in the courts, and administered in various sites of detention. Local government wielded police power like a bludgeon to categorize and manage what upheld—and what menaced—a deeply racialized conception of the "public good."[6]

As such, police power refers to everyday expressions of law enforcement. In this sense, law enforcement denotes any way a governing body restrains liberty in service of state imperatives to safeguard property, maximize capital, and organize populations. Indeed, the Supreme Court once defined police power as "the power of sovereignty, the power to govern men and things within the limits of its dominion."[7] Based on this capacious definition, police power can, and often does, refer to the cops. But it also refers to a host of other law enforcers. Magistrates, jail deputies, coroners, charity agents, school attendance officers, teachers, orderlies, private citizens, and other people or places augment and exercise state power by employing coercion, compelling behavior, and denying individual rights and freedoms. Police power, then, emerges as much in punitive expressions of state violence as it does in the banal administrative functions of urban bureaucracy—two poles that organize the analysis of this book.

In centralizing the role of the postbellum period in shaping the contours of police power's modern usage, this study contributes to currents in urban history and carceral history. It situates the emergence of the American city within the intersection of policing, politics, and urbanization. It adds to urban historical literature that theorizes the link between local confrontations among working people and state agents, as well as the concretization of urban governance at the turn of the century.[8] It does so through a pointed analysis of geographic, legal, and everyday manifestations of police power—what I refer to throughout as "sites of police power"—that hardened over the course of the late nineteenth and early twentieth centuries. These sites, governed from on high by various state actors, agencies, and emergent bureaucracies, organized daily life for city inhabitants through the administration of disciplinary and punitive measures rooted in the maintenance of a social order increasingly organized

4 · *Introduction*

around anti-Blackness. In engaging state formation, this study does not approach the state as an object; rather, the analysis prioritizes relations between people, places, and institutions that did not function or proceed in a tidy or straightforward way. While the state maintained power through assuming an impersonal and naturalized authority, its subjects experienced state power in profoundly intimate, everyday settings.[9]

Taking a cue from foundational studies of incarceration's relationship to state growth, *Let Us Alone* builds on analyses of nineteenth-century institutional dynamics wherein punishment gave way to disciplinary structures aimed at transforming citizens into productive, laboring subjects. The rise of commercial leisure and an assessed degradation of public morality proved so acute that early nineteenth-century penal reformers regarded the family and community not only as incapable of managing deviance but as the very *cause* of deviance. The creation of jails, prisons, and asylums signaled the emergence of a new set of social relations wherein a detached and paternal authority mediated community dynamics through force and institutionalization. Prison administrators sought to replicate systems of control within penitentiaries that inculcated hierarchy and compliance among inmates. These artificial spaces adopted organizational styles reminiscent of the family, the military, the workshop, the school, and the judiciary. Theorist Michel Foucault described this network as a "carceral archipelago" which delegated the management of deviance within a broad continuum of institutions, including courts, hospitals, almshouses, and public schools. This networked system of discipline formed the foundation of a modern punitive state. It also serves as the jagged but unmistakable throughline throughout this book. Capital growth, demographic changes, and increased state capacity propelled the management of so-called dependent populations, including children, the impoverished, and Black men and women, along interrelated sites of discipline.[10]

In parallel, the emergence of modern police forces in the mid-nineteenth century provided localities new, though unruly, agencies that buttressed state desires to pacify publics, punish the poor, and control crowds. European immigration, industrialization, labor unrest, and urbanization guided early policework which took on both coercive and administrative functions. After the Civil War, political bossism and underfunding created discontinuity in police operations, and several police departments, like Baltimore's, lost local control over their police forces. By the late nineteenth century, city and state governments attempted to reform the slipshod, disorganized, and corrupt municipal police departments of earlier decades with gradually bureaucratized police forces that emphasized crime prevention by establishing a permanent presence in working-class neighborhoods. Administrators believed that by stationing police in target areas, they could stop crime before it happened—a persistent assumption about preventive or "proactive" policing with uncertain results. Drunk men on sidewalks caused little personal harm to anyone. Their "crime" was lowering the perceived value of the streets on which they stood, not working in the formal economy, and potentially annoying passersby. None of these offenses were particularly injurious—or, indeed, offensive—but in their banality revealed the politicization of crime and the function of discretion in street policing. Baltimore's police followed this national trend. However, considering the racial politics and history of Baltimore and Maryland, policing more pointedly centered on institutional interventions into Black life. The Baltimore police served as the foot soldiers of white supremacy and Jim Crow, and their functions throughout this study became increasingly centralized on patrolling the color line.[11]

Contemporary scholarship of the post–Civil War carceral state proves useful in illuminating these dynamics. Historians in this tradition center Black and Brown men and women's encounters with various agencies, projects, and disciplinary regimes aimed at maintaining systems of racial hierarchy through incarceration, brutality, and corporal punishment. These carceral historians expand on police historians' preoccupations with the social construction and politicization of crime but deepen our understandings by accounting for the intensely gendered and racialized dimensions that attended these processes. For instance, in their studies of postbellum convict labor systems, Talitha LeFlouria and Sarah Haley detail how prison officials relied on presumptions about Black womanhood to justify disproportionate rates of confinement and brutal treatment in penal labor regimes. Such treatment serviced a larger consolidation of Jim Crow modernity rooted in a racialized and gendered social order that thrived on ideological justifications and defenses of anti-Black state terror.[12]

Drawing on this lineage, *Let Us Alone* melds urban historical emphases on the sedimentation of nineteenth-century state formation with probing analyses of how classed, racialized, and gendered administrations of discipline, punishment, and terror lay at the foundation of police power. It draws linkages between police departments, jails, reformatories, asylums, workhouses, and public schools to sketch the contours of Baltimore's elementary carceral state. A synthetic analysis of how these institutions worked in tandem heightens our understanding of the widespread nature of urban discipline and the centrality of police power in articulating the boundaries of both city space and the municipal agencies that managed it. As such, this book examines how intersecting disciplinary locations—sites of police power—continuously redrew the contours of

6 · *Introduction*

urban governance in post–Civil War Baltimore. While many carceral histories are police histories set in cities, this book is an urban history of policing. It tracks institutional change and growth over time to document how state organization and repression functioned to articulate a vision for Baltimore rooted in the preservation of an emergent and unmistakably racialized social order. Ultimately, this approach unites evolving notions and deployments of police power to understand how policing shaped the American city as a legal, social, and institutional entity.

Baltimore

Why is Baltimore the best city to provide a history of the consolidation of a post–Civil War urban police state? It both is and is not. Because policing is systemic, Baltimore *is* the best example—but so is every other city. This fact is made unmistakably clear by the continuities present in the outpouring of policing scholarship in recent years. As such, Baltimore's political leaders and city initiatives provided exemplary approaches to state formation in diverse realms of urban governance while contributing to and drawing from broader national currents.

Baltimore's nuanced history and character provide an analytical robustness that reveals how racialized policing impacted an urban community during the postbellum period. The city's geographic position as a "border city," in a state that served as a buffer between the Union and the Confederacy during the Civil War, has imbued it with a complex cultural, economic, and historical identity. Legal scholar Harold McDougall has detailed the paradoxical nature of Baltimore's developmental history, noting, "Baltimore is the southernmost city of the North, and the northernmost city of the South, its population and physical structure marked by the slave plantation, the merchant ship, and the factory."[13] While recent studies have emerged mining the depths of the city's history of racial dispossession, only two have focused extensively on the role of policing in the city, and no work has examined policing comprehensively after the Civil War and into the early twentieth century.[14] The city's position along the borderlands of the American North and South—as well as its perennial conflicts with state government—provide an investigative uniqueness that reveals the constructed and plenary nature of police power in stark detail.

During the period under review, Baltimore was the eighth most populous city in the United States. Even after the mass exodus of Black Americans to northern and midwestern cities in the early twentieth century, Baltimore's Black residents constituted a higher percentage of its total population than comparable cities that have received far more extensive treatments in urban and carceral history. In 1930, Baltimore's Black population accounted for 18 percent of its total, which outpaced New York's 5 percent, Chicago's 7 percent, and Philadelphia's 11 percent.[15] Additionally, given the city's history of enslavement, deeply embedded anti-Black racial hierarchy informed modes of policing and made Baltimore's Black population among the most policed in the country. Arrest rates illustrate this dynamic. By 1927, Black Baltimoreans accounted for 54 percent of all arrestees despite comprising 17 percent of the population.[16] Compared with other populous cities with significant percentages of Black Americans, Baltimore set an inauspicious standard for racialized criminalization.[17] When adjusted for population, between 1895 and 1929, Baltimore's Black rates of arrest, at best, doubled and, at worst, more than quintupled, white rates of arrest (figure 1). This reality should not be taken to mean that Black people engaged in more crime than their white peers because crime operates irrespective of arrests. It does, however, indicate disproportionate police activity in Black neighborhoods.

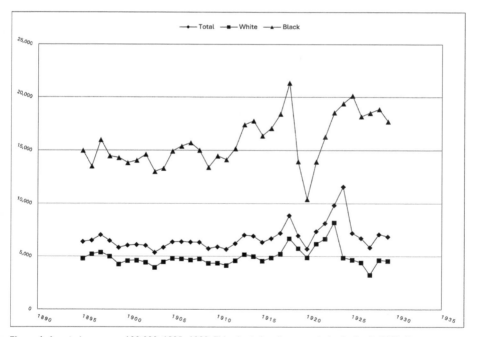

Figure 1. Arrests by race per 100,000, 1895–1929. This chart visualizes arrests beginning in 1895, the year the Baltimore police began to categorize arrests by race. Notably, in 1927, the Black rate of arrest more than quintupled the white rate of arrest as police deployed public order statutes to firm up the color line. Source: Board of Police Commissioner Reports, 1895–1929, Agency Reports and Publications, Baltimore City Archives.

8 · *Introduction*

Relatedly, Baltimore boasted one of the largest police forces in the country relative to the top ten most populous U.S. cities, none of which—besides Mobtown—were cities from the American South. For instance, by 1929, the state government had increased the size and density of the Baltimore police force to 2.4 police personnel per 1,000 residents. This per-capita density matched New York City and Detroit's extensive police forces and outpaced Chicago, Saint Louis, and Los Angeles's formidable police forces.[18] Many of these police departments were organized in the antebellum period which, in the South, coincided with the predominance of slave patrols. These patrols maintained prevailing racial hierarchy through seizures of educational contraband, everyday patrolling along plantations, and the apprehension of runaway slaves and their accomplices.[19] Moreover, white popular justice and vigilantism prevailed in the South where white men were empowered, as they were in Maryland, to detain suspected runaways. Indeed, historian Adam Malka argues that Baltimore provides a unique case study to understand the emergence of liberal policing as it combined the white vigilantism that typified punishment in the rural South with the creation of an organized police force in the style of the urban North.[20] Baltimore, a city in the dead center of the Eastern Seaboard, organized a police force in the style of the American North that counted among its functions the regulation of runaway slaves.[21] In the eight years during which the Baltimore police and the institution of slavery coexisted, cops arrested suspected runaways and their compatriots, had them committed to detention facilities, and held enslaved men and women for auction.[22]

The Baltimore police force *was* a slave patrol.

The Baltimore police's reign of racialized policing notably increased after the Civil War in large part because of Reconstruction's spectacular failure. Following the war, Maryland experienced consequential political realignments and the retrenchment of white supremacist control that disadvantaged Black Baltimoreans. Given Maryland's loyalty to the Union, conservative political leaders felt entitled to a quick adjudication of Reconstruction that would allow the state government to regain control over its civil and political processes with little federal interference. Democrats threw their support behind presidential Reconstruction which allowed wartime traitors to resume civic participation while permitting state legislatures to arbitrate matters of racial integration.[23] In Maryland, this enfranchisement proved significant as twenty-five thousand returning Confederates constituted a crucial voting bloc.[24] These ideals crystallized in the passage of a new state constitution in 1867 which denied Black Marylanders the franchise, as well as Maryland's symbolic refusal to ratify the

Fourteenth and Fifteenth Amendments. Obstructions to Black civil rights gave rise to a powerful Democratic machine as Republicans floundered for decades to gain a steady foothold in local and state politics.[25] The blip of Reconstruction in Maryland owed largely to the federal government's decision to allow the Free State control in overseeing postwar conciliation. Given this permissiveness, historian Barbara Jeanne Fields notes that Reconstruction in Maryland had a much shorter lifespan than it did in the former Confederate states.[26]

If Reconstruction was ineffectual at the state level, it was even less impactful at the city level. After the Civil War, emancipated Marylanders left the counties of their enslavement and headed to the Monumental City. According to historian Richard Paul Fuke, the city's postwar years saw an approximately threefold increase in Black householders. The lure of economic opportunity and an escape from the violence of the plantation made Baltimore a compelling landing spot. However, Reconstruction heralded market orthodoxies rooted in the valorization of wage labor, compulsory economic participation, and deracialized ideologies regarding access to the job market. As such, Black Baltimoreans' struggles finding employment, their difficulties navigating wage theft, and their problems accessing public relief belied the color-blind perceptions of the seasonal job market while justifying white supremacist conceptions of Black men and women's inability to adapt to urban life.[27] Given these and other repressive political realities, Black Baltimoreans experienced harsher disciplinary treatment from the city's burgeoning police state that resulted in disproportionate arrests, incarceration rates, and experiences of police violence.[28] Ultimately, Maryland's tepid loyalty to the Union's emancipatory cause ironically allowed the state and city governments to clamp down on Black citizens quickly after war's end.

Compounding the broader anti-Blackness that cohered during the postwar period was the state government's longtime insistence on circumscribing the city government's ability to self-govern. For instance, the Baltimore police was forged in a crucible of incongruity that generated a persistent power struggle between the state and city government. In the 1850s, Know Nothing mayors Samuel Hinks and Thomas Swann reorganized the Baltimore police into its modern form by combining disparate elements of the day and night forces.[29] Immediately upon this reorganization, the Know Nothing Party's political rivals sought to seize control of the police which both participated in election violence and allowed it to occur unaddressed. Street gangs, such as the Rip Raps, Plug Uglies, and Blood Tubs,[30] facilitated these efforts by attacking voters and coercing men to drunkenly vote for Know Nothing candidates through the process of "cooping."[31] In response to this corruption, during the 1860 state

10 · *Introduction*

legislative session, Democrats successfully passed measures that allowed the state government to seize control of the local police (and to subsequently install their own hired guns).[32] The city unsuccessfully appealed the law in the courts. Tellingly, the courts reasoned that the "City was a creature of the State," a common form of municipal organization in the nineteenth century.[33] This city-state relationship would become a source of political tension, negotiation, and debate as local government sought increased agency and latitude in urban matters through appeals to the police power doctrine.[34] It also distinguished Baltimore from its peer cities. Unlike most cities, Baltimore was independent from the surrounding county.[35] It became a veritable island whose economic centrality as a port city, its potentially outsized influence in state politics, and its large Black population, moved state government to put the clamps on whenever it could, including the denial of the rights and privileges associated with home rule.[36] Moreover, unlike its peer cities, the Baltimore police did not revert to local control. By 1900, state governments had revested Cleveland, New York, and Detroit with local control of their police departments.[37] As of this writing, the state of Maryland has still not reverted control of the Baltimore police to the city's residents, though grassroots efforts to accomplish this reversion are ongoing.

Augmenting its police force, Baltimore boasted one of the most efficient Charity Organization Society (COS) chapters in the country. Historian Michael B. Katz has noted that in the late nineteenth century, only Boston and Baltimore successfully implemented widespread friendly visiting programs aimed at privatizing poverty relief.[38] Baltimore charity agents, like Mary Richmond, became national figureheads in the charity movement—the movement that would develop and mold the vocation today known as social work. Their influence reframed the duties of policing and vested civilians with police power. They championed institutionalization in almshouses in lieu of cash relief, criminalized children through truancy crusades, and successfully exhorted police station houses to deny lodging to unhoused Baltimoreans. The influence of these reformers is perhaps best captured in one of Baltimore's most effective activists. Charles J. Bonaparte led the city's corps of reformers. During the late nineteenth century, Bonaparte deployed private detectives to root out police corruption and spy on Baltimore's working people. These formative experiences primed Bonaparte to accomplish what would become his enduring legacy: founding the Bureau of Investigation (later the Federal Bureau of Investigation [FBI]) in 1908. As a private citizen, Bonaparte's several clandestine investigations on the streets of Baltimore cultivated his interest and belief in the power of organized surveillance, a part of his biography largely ignored in the historiography of the FBI.[39]

Complementing its extensive police force and influential and efficient reform circles, the city's political and legal classes proved immensely creative in their execution of statecraft. To assert its local power and establish a distinct municipal identity from the overbearing grip of Annapolis, Baltimore became ground zero for experimental legislation to shore up the color line and test the limits of police power. Such legislation allowed local government to flex its autonomy and potentially challenge state control in the courts. In 1908, to regulate narcotics more comprehensively in Black neighborhoods, the city passed one of the first local ordinances that criminalized the *possession* of drugs. The ordinance's author, Colonel Sherlock Swann, knew the ordinance defied state law but passed it as an assertion—and test—of home rule. As expected, the court of appeals, the state's highest judicial body, assessed the ordinance's constitutionality and upheld it as a legitimate use of the city's police power. A lower court decision definitively defied the 1860 characterization of the city's subjection to state authority and asserted that the city's density provided justification to create specific laws that accounted for the unique character of crime (i.e., Black crime) in a populous urban area.[40] The decision buttressed the passage of more ambitious and far-reaching legislation, including the city's infamous racial zoning laws, which aimed to prevent Black families from settling in white neighborhoods.[41]

All told, Baltimore exuded contradictions by virtue of its interstitial geographic and cultural identity, its enduring battles against state control, its history of racialized policing, and its ambitious and effective reformers. A deep analysis of the endless confrontations that characterized the slow and unsteady growth of Baltimore's municipal power lays bare the nebulous, uncertain, yet extraordinarily robust affordances of police power.

Method

Illuminating the institutional implications of police power requires a focus on the strategies and tactics employed by intersecting disciplinary bodies that, through conflict, articulated a social order rooted in competing notions of propriety, morality, and urban duty. This process was by no means neat, and the nature of police power changed immensely during the period under review. The seemingly never-ending jurisdiction of the cops illustrated some of these changes. Over the course of this study, the Baltimore police assumed expansive functions that varied along a continuum of administrative necessity. Given this fact, this study draws on diverse sources to account for the disparate areas of municipal authority that comprised the branches of Baltimore's nascent police state.

12 • *Introduction*

Institutional archives provided insight into city and state government functions, particularly as they concerned the Baltimore police, courts, carceral facilities, and public schools. Reports, proceedings, and minutes from city agencies and police commissioners, criminal dockets, petitions, indictments, session laws, criminal records, and reformer publications proved invaluable for understanding the push and pull among municipal bodies as poor and working-class Baltimoreans became subject to processes of racialized criminalization. These sources also provided exhaustive quantitative data on rates of arrest, conviction, and incarceration that demonstrated broader anti-Black trends. Importantly, the data in this study do *not* purport to represent an accurate numerical representation of crime. Instead, it demonstrates police activity that targeted Black men and women. Other institutional archival material, such as census data, cartographic evidence, city directories, land records, and stenographic transcripts of court testimony, allowed for a deeper engagement with criminalized subjects' everyday lives and voices. Institutional archives proved necessary to both account for broader trends in policing and detention and to glean a semblance of insight into the everyday lived experiences of working-class men and women.

To understand the debates that accompanied the growth of police power, newspapers proved useful. Baltimore had an array of papers with numerous political bents. From the Democratic-leaning *Baltimore Sun*, to the Republican-leaning *Baltimore American*,[42] to the sensationalist *Baltimore Herald*, to one of the most widely circulated Black newspapers in the United States, the *Afro-American*.[43] The city's publishing establishment played a crucial role in both documenting and influencing social life and politics. Through close analyses of reporting, editorials, classifieds, exposés, and columns, this study situates the discursive construction of criminality in administrations of urban discipline.

In encountering the type of sources—indictments, news stories, criminal dockets, police records, and sociological studies—that fill out the vignettes in this book, overwhelming questions emerge that simply do not have answers in traditional historical evidence. To encounter criminality in the archive is to engage a deeply unidimensional and often racist set of materials that naturalized the supposed moral depravity of the people in question. Only recently have historians—specifically Black feminist historians—found profound insight into the lives of criminalized Black men and women. I draw from such scholars, particularly Hazel Carby, Kali Gross, Sarah Haley, LaShawn Harris, Cheryl Hicks, and Talitha LeFlouria, to guide my reading practices where possible.[44] These scholars have broadened historical understandings of the gendered and racialized dimensions of American institutional violence by centralizing the experiences of Black women whose designation as "criminal" has traditionally excluded them from African American urban and labor histories. And although this book's institutional focus does not allow it to provide—or even really attempt—an accurate or authentic representation of individual interiority, it nonetheless endeavors to situate everyday encounters and acts of resistance within the broader institutional development of urban governance in post–Civil War Baltimore.

Chapter Outline

In examining how policing undergirded the geographic and legal negotiation of Baltimore's growing police state, this book details how police power manifested in institutional priorities geared toward segregationist outcomes. That is, it details how the city itself *became* a site of police power. Police power symbolized an imprecise and contested terrain of urban governance. After the War of Southern Aggression, as cities morphed into modern municipal corporations and industrial strongholds, the search for order remained a central preoccupation. Several public and private groups had skin in the game. In their efforts to articulate and address urban social issues, the "public good" revealed a not-so-thinly veiled investment in white heteropatriarchal values that positioned the poor, destitute, nonwhite, and criminal as the problem that modern municipal structures strove to solve. The organization of this book into a chronological analysis of police power's various sites reflects police power's expansiveness and its progressively racialized application in Baltimore.

The first site this book visits is Baltimore's city jail. While much of carceral history focuses on prisons, jails provide an illuminating area of analysis that reveals the nuanced management of poverty under carceral regimes. As a location for short-term detention, the city jail purported to protect the public peace by confining poor men and women, or "bummers" as they were colloquially known. Bummers filled the city jail to the brim as government agencies and other groups, including the police department, the managers of the jail, police magistrates, and asylum officials, debated the proper disposition of public order cases. What became clear in the administration of the city jail was that policing was not a dispassionate enforcement of the law. Rather, city agencies all fought to profit from the confinement and labor of impoverished men and women. The seeds of racialized policing bloomed in the city jail as Black men and women, by the close of the nineteenth century, became the institution's primary inhabitants.[45]

The second site this book visits encompasses the meeting rooms, convention halls, and gathering spaces in which the city's reformers colluded and schemed to fundamentally alter structures of urban governance and policing. Taking a cue

14 • *Introduction*

from the foundational and voluminous studies of the Progressives, this analysis does not purport to sketch any neat cohesion among reformers who, in their various campaigns, often disagreed or otherwise did not overlap. However, in detailing the work of one of Baltimore's most notable Progressives, Charles J. Bonaparte, this foray into Progressivism engages how private citizen activism both contributed to and expanded state power. Bonaparte and his cadre of wealthy reformers agitated to reorient state functions, particularly those coordinated by the police, around the efficient and ethical regulation of elections, gambling, obscenity, liquor, and other purported social threats. Reformers hired private detectives, formed chapters of national anti-vice organizations, wrote home rule city charters, and stretched the limits of private civic activism to clean up city politics and enact lasting legislative changes at the local and state levels. In Baltimore, Bonaparte and his stable ousted the city's political machine, formalized civil services, and restructured the police force. By exploring these sites of political organizing, the importance of private citizens and their ability to assume state roles extended and complicated state power and its applications beyond just the cops.[46]

Such complexity emerged in full view in the third site of police power: the public school. In analyzing the school attendance officer, a precursor to school resource officers, the unruly marriage between private citizen activists and police became evident. Baltimore's "child savers," to quote Anthony Platt's useful terminology, created the problem of adolescent delinquency and prescribed its solutions. In Baltimore, the COS spearheaded many of these campaigns and waged them on multiple fronts. As charity agents advocated state intervention into the lives of the wayward poor—and justified their own "friendly" intrusions into people's homes—they made appeals to authority through the creation, citation, and dissemination of pseudo-empirical studies of impoverished people. Such studies relied on evolutionary theories of culture and heredity that contributed to and naturalized the supposed incapacities of foreign-born immigrants and Black Americans to function within civil society and take care of their children. Such seemingly robust empiricism (no matter its actual academic merit) justified campaigns to deny relief to poor Baltimoreans and to assume the paternal authority of the state to enforce truancy. Unlike reformers whose key directive was to reform policing and mold its functions around morals enforcement, the truancy campaign created civilian attendance officers who, backed by the full power and force of the law, assumed the authority to investigate, arrest, detain, and institutionalize children.[47]

The street constitutes the fourth site explored in this study. Open streets, sidewalks, and thoroughfares had always been a site of contention for public and

Introduction • 15

private policing. Cops scoured streets for inebriates as reform agents searched alongside them for disagreeable establishments and truant children. The key shift that made streets even more consequential in the early twentieth century were Jim Crow designs to orient city space around the protection of white property. Prevailing condemnations of Black people and the establishment of Black crime as a prime subject of political debate during the late nineteenth century marked a crucial turning point in Baltimore's policing objectives. Beginning in 1896, after reformers and Republicans ousted the Democratic machine, the subject of Black crime became a consistent and consequential political issue on which both parties stumped. This disorder—or "Negro rowdyism," as it was called—dovetailed with Southern alarmism around "Negro rule," or the possibilities of Black political power and culture decimating white cultural ideals, property values, and ways of life in the American South. These discourses led to targeted policing activities in interracial neighborhoods, particularly those abutting valuable commercial real estate and burgeoning white suburbs. Police waged campaigns targeting vice in interracial neighborhoods and advocated increased discretion in the regulation of Black crime. This advocacy convinced Maryland's high court to empower Baltimore's city council and police force to stamp out Black crime. As such, these crusades revealed how police power's deeply interpersonal encounters on street corners directly contributed to state growth and stretched the domain of urban governance.[48]

Building on the state's increased scrutiny over Black bodies, the fifth site of police power is the courtroom. Specifically, the U.S. district courtroom in Baltimore that tried the case of Henry Alfred Brown, a Black teenager who charged police with torturing him to elicit a confession for a murder he did not commit. Brown's case exemplified several overlapping dynamics that typified policing and the criminal legal system in the 1920s. Two are worth foregrounding. First, rising violent crime rates and unsolved murders undermined the police's capacity to protect urban publics. As such, the third degree, or the use of torture to secure confessions, became commonplace as cops and detectives tried desperately to get cases before judges with whom they often clashed. These efforts led to racialized murder conviction rates in a city that disallowed Black jury members. Second, the reemergence of the Ku Klux Klan, courts' hyper-reliance on capital punishment to mete out "justice" in cases involving white victims, and the enduring discourses that painted Black men as depraved predators primed publics who thirsted for what historian Douglas Flowe describes as "public racial justice." Despite—and perhaps because of—Black grassroots mobilization around Henry Brown, the court and federal authorities stood pat behind their decision to execute him. In this case, public racial justice negated

16 · *Introduction*

the good faith and eminently well-researched campaign advocating for Brown's commutation and asserted the state's prerogative to prosecute, condemn, and kill as an assertion of police power's grip over the Black body.[49]

The maintenance of such hierarchical organization underpins the sixth and final site of police power explored in this book: the home. In this case, the home refers to domestic spaces as well as the ideal of privacy that police routinely violated during the 1920s. As police, city officials, politicians, and reformers habitually advocated for broader latitude to invoke police power, policing tilted evermore toward surveilling, arresting, and detaining Black men and women. During this decade, Black Baltimoreans became just as likely, or more likely, to be arrested for non-traffic-related offenses as their white peers. The bulk of these arrests relied, like police power itself, on discretion. Public order policing, which harnessed vague statutes like disorderly conduct and public disturbance, filled police records yet masked more than they revealed. Through a close analysis of the city's Black newspaper, the *Afro-American*, this chapter illuminates to what exactly "disorderly conduct" referred and how it was policed. Based on stories, exposés, and printed petitions to the police commissioner, disorderly conduct referred to everything from keeping interracial company, complaining to police about brutalization, and protesting that police entered Black homes without just cause.[50]

1

"This Modern Hades"

Jails, Asylums, and the Business of Punishment in Post–Civil War Baltimore

In 1879, police arrested George Boston on drunk and disorderly charges. Boston, an itinerant laborer who belonged to a class of men that city officials and the press dubbed "bummers," petitioned to be discharged because the "commitment was not for being drunk and disorderly, but simply for being drunk."[1] Boston argued that state law did not allow police to arrest someone solely on suspicion of drunkenness. As such, patrolmen often arrested bummers under the pretense of disorderly conduct. Boston, however, contended that he had not acted disorderly and that the police used the looseness of "disorderly conduct" to arrest him for being drunk and *orderly*. This situation raised questions about the proper administration of punishment and what behaviors should be criminalized in the nineteenth-century city. What should police do about people like George Boston who acted drunk and orderly? Should it be illegal to drunkenly occupy public space if one did not threaten personal or commercial property? Was the mere existence of a bummer a threat to property values? In Boston's case, the Court of Common Pleas sided with the petitioner and let him go.[2] On the larger question of police discretion, the state legislature rethought the nature of discretion among the police force and eventually expanded police power to allow for the arrest of bummers like Boston and their commitment to the city's infamous city jail.

After the Civil War, Baltimore's city jail became a perplexing space in which the city mediated diverse and formative social conflicts that helped articulate the bounds and duties of its burgeoning police state. The building's infrastructure deteriorated, and the people who occupied it existed subject to the whims of emergent trends, policy changes, and political investments that shaped and characterized late-nineteenth-century urban governance and policing. It was a rarefied space around which bureaucrats, property holders, police, courts, and criminologists negotiated the powers and expectations of local government. In a strained quest to find order amid the city's growing capital inventory, profiteering magistrates, increasing population, and municipal retrenchment, the jail became a site whose key directive was to incapacitate vast swaths of poor people on short-term bases at the lowest cost possible. Jail administrators, staff, and the public came to slowly realize that incarceration at a mass scale could not rehabilitate; it could only cage.

Over time, the jail's primary inhabitants, the so-called bummers, came to represent the city's broader approach to maintaining public order. This class of occasional workers cycled in and out of the reserve army of labor—the transient results of a striated economic system—and grew in number every year. Their management represented a sobering reality about the criminal legal system during the Gilded Age: justice had very little to do with maintaining public order. Reshuffling the urban poor between police station houses, jails, penitentiaries, and asylums exposed bureaucratic aspirations to secure the revenue that accompanied fines and compulsory labor, as well as desires to eliminate what some elements of the citizenry considered annoyances from public spaces. None of these goals spoke to a detached application of the rule of law but rather emphasized competing governance philosophies that took as a given the inherent depravity of bummers and other presumed delinquent or dependent populations.

The various approaches, policy reversals, and conflicts that emerged as city agencies negotiated how to manage diverse—yet equally unruly—populations revealed both the city's investment in expanding its carceral capacity and moral presumptions regarding who deserved what treatment and why. Agencies and administrators perennially advocated the creation of new almshouses, reformatories, insane hospitals, and other sites of confinement.[3] Bummers, though chiefly confined to the city jail, spent time in these new facilities, too. Their management became a central conundrum that drove Baltimore's carceral expansion and forced the city to contend with systems of punishment. Whereas city jail officials insisted that the mayor and city council build additional annexes and workhouses to detain and employ bummers, opponents urged the city to reexamine a criminal legal system that made it illegal to be poor and made it profitable for various city agencies, especially the police, to throw bummers in jail at unconscionable rates. Why should the city make money off men's labor when their wandering and drunkenness posed no threat to others' bodily autonomy? Along the same lines, jail managers advocated transferring bummers to almshouses and asylums, particularly Bayview Asylum which the city chartered to provide relief to vagrants, paupers, and the mentally insane.

At the heart of these inquiries rested a tense negotiation that brought into question the duties of not just the criminal legal system but the city itself. During the nineteenth century, the power of the city and police power, which included the expansion, creation, and administration of detention facilities to promote public welfare, blurred. As sectors of Baltimore's citizenry came to expect and demand state interventions in previously under-regulated sectors, including the protection of private property, infrastructure, public morality, and the control of indigent populations, the city responded by exercising its police power to expand carceral capacity and regulate population groups in the service of the growing capital interests of the budding metropolis.[4]

In the process, abstract aspirations toward ensuring the rule of law and the public good obscured more craven motivations. Specifically, in the face of municipal retrenchment, aggressive public debt–financed enterprise, and the neglect of public services, including jails, police, and asylums, managers prioritized the efficient organization, reproduction, and survival of their agencies over servicing the populations under their purview.[5] These objectives manifested in revenue-motivated strategies aimed predominately at generating income through the affordances offered by the business of punishment. An analysis of bureaucratic restructuring in the wake of the Civil War reveals the kernel of what would become a persistent dynamic that typified policing and incarceration as much as it masked its basic character: institutions were organized around their own preservation. This goal often clashed with the dispassionate objectives of justice to which police and carceral facilities laid claim and made scapegoats of the poor, the sick, and the weary. Their exploitation within the criminal legal system exposed the socially constructed nature of crime while revealing how discretionary modes of criminal classification allowed carceral managers to shuffle the impoverished between institutions of confinement. Perhaps no institution was more illustrative of this dynamic than the city jail.

"A Place of Demoralization": Baltimore's First Jail

Jails remain relatively unexplored sites of historical analysis even though they predate the modern prison and constitute a key experiential site for working-class and poor people.[6] The jail, unlike the prison, began as—and continues to

20 • CHAPTER 1

be—a site of pure incapacitation. Eighteenth-century jails did not have rehabilitation in mind when they were constructed. They were unabashed storehouses for thieves, debtors, frauds, and other petty criminals. The institutions operated on fee-based systems, which meant that jailers' compensation depended on fees collected from poor or indebted inmates. The buildings themselves were relatively unsecured and allowed for easy commiseration among detainees. Indeed, historian Seán McConville refers to the organization of early jails as "locked-up anarchy." The nineteenth century heralded reforms to modernize the institutions. Rather than unsupervised and diverse populations of inmates, jail officials began to segregate detainees based on gender, age, and offense. They also attempted to implement penal labor programs to recoup the costs of jailing inmates. Local governments centralized jail operations, appointed governing bodies, and eliminated fee-based compensation in favor of salaried public employees. The U.S. penal system aspired to a two-tiered structure in which jails serviced petty misdemeanants and state penitentiaries serviced felons.[7]

As Baltimore's city jail attested, however, this organization proved overly ambitious. New crime categories created novel criminal classes, and building capacity could not neatly accommodate the increasing numbers of inmates into the city and state's jails and prisons, especially as legislative bodies reclassified criminal penalties to target and eradicate specific behaviors and lifeways. Officials scrambled to put inmates anywhere, including bakeshops, annexes, cellars, and other enclosures. In Baltimore, the city jail's history unfolded in profoundly illogical ways. Try as they did, jail officials could not make the city jail into a financially self-sustaining site of moral rehabilitation because the institution had never been intended to perform such functions. This reality did not stop the jail's administrators from trying, though. Baltimore's experience managing the city jail revealed the limits of urban governance as bureaucrats tried desperately to transform what was essentially a human cage into a well-oiled, money-making machine. Its management laid bare the crude calculus of the nineteenth-century municipal corporation, which pursued agendas rooted in generating revenue and managing the "dangerous classes"—those who, in their poverty, became criminalized as a condition of public order.[8]

In the early nineteenth century, Baltimore opened its first stand-alone jail. At the time of its completion, the jail sat just above the city's northernmost boundary and, thus, eluded the city proper. Designed by Robert Cary Long Sr., the jail was a modest and unimposing structure meant for short-term commitments.[9] Located next to the Maryland Penitentiary, this cloistered development of disciplinary institutions followed a national trend wherein crime control began to rely more—though not exclusively—on incarceration.[10] This led to an early prison boom as Pennsylvania, New York, New Jersey, Virginia, Kentucky, and Maryland all built penitentiaries to facilitate changing perceptions around criminal reformation.[11] Baltimore's jail served the populations of both the city and the surrounding county. In its early history, the jail confined debtors and runaway slaves. By mid-century, both groups, though still dominantly represented among the jail's population, had been joined in significant numbers by offenders of the public "peace." That is, drunkards, vagrants, and other petty criminals entered the ranks of the incarcerated. These inmates foreshadowed the postbellum codification of the supposedly idle class of bummers whose management would become the jail's chief concern. Officials believed that such offenders sought the creature comforts of incarceration—shelter, clothing, and food.[12] The jail population swelled as peace cases increased yearly admissions. In 1850, annual commitments totaled 2,242 with 26 percent coming from peace warrants.[13] In just four years, annual commitments increased to 3,139 with 39 percent coming from peace warrants.[14] Jail administrators, a loose assortment of unincorporated volunteers, could not keep pace as inmates overcrowded cells and the building began to fall apart—a pattern that would characterize new detention facilities that the city would ironically construct to make detention more humane. They bemoaned the nonsensical assortment of criminal classes held

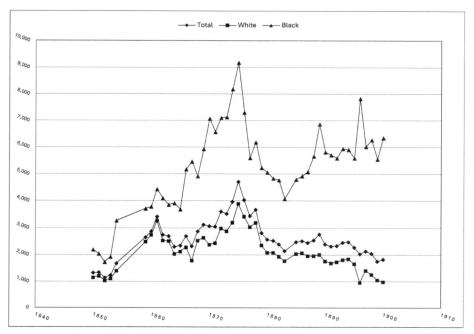

Figure 2. City jail commitments per 100,000, 1850–1900. Source: City Jail Reports, Department of Legislative Reference, Box 39, Baltimore City Archives.

in detention. Debtors commingled with vagrants, thieves, and runaway slaves. The latter constituted a "guilty" class by nature of their status as property.

To address the chaos that had transformed the jail into a mess of tangled populations, officials implored the state legislature to incorporate a dedicated agency to oversee day-to-day jail functions. In 1831, the General Assembly obliged and incorporated the board of visitors (BOV), a seven-man group tasked with supervising infrastructure maintenance, prisoner clothing and bedding, medical treatment, and labor contracts. The BOV represented an early advisory group for one of the city's sprouting institutions that allowed for spoils and patronage opportunities down the road. Regarding debtors, the state dictated that debtors could voluntarily engage in labor and recoup two-thirds of their production to pay down debt, while vagrants, freedmen, and slaves could be put to work involuntarily.[15]

Despite the BOV's increased scope, they continued to face challenges rooted in the capricious criminalization of the city and state's marginalized populations, including enslaved men, women, and children. In 1845, the BOV appealed to the state on the issue of runaways. State law dictated that "*any person* may arrest any runaway negro, and carry him before a judge or justice, and have him committed to the jail of the county."[16] This law deputized white Marylanders and vigilantes who spammed the jail with suspected Black runaways. This vigilante "popular justice" typified law enforcement during the nineteenth century and demonstrated how civilian policing formed a cornerstone of both regulation and assertions of racialized citizenship.[17] The BOV surmised that most of the Black runaways brought to the jail "have the chances in their favor of being free." Yet and still, following state statutes, after fifteen days in custody, the BOV bought classifieds in local newspapers detailing the physical descriptions of suspected runaways. Slave owners had sixty days after the advertisements' publication to claim the runaways and repay the jail for advertising and imprisoning them. In most cases, no slave owner appeared to claim the runaway. Although the practice represented a gross injustice that subjected free people to unlawful detention, the BOV couched its complaint in crudely economic language. They bemoaned the $6 they had to spend taking out ads for bogus runaway cases and the amount of money they had to pay to accommodate the detainees.[18] This economic logic led the BOV to steer suspected runaways to other detention centers around the city.[19] It also spoke to the broader drives of the nascent carceral system. Justice for the enslaved paled in comparison to the costs that threatened the institution's efficient administration. Preserving the dignity of the incarcerated was a fine goal if—and only if—the books were balanced first.

This emphasis on fiscal stability represented the city jail's core mission and signaled carceral orthodoxies to come. During the nineteenth century, municipal jailing relied, in part, on fee-based revenue arrangements. For instance, in 1854, 43 percent of the city jail's expenses were paid by various fees associated with holding federal prisoners and runaway slaves.[20] In attempting to shed expenses, jail administrators often reformed unfair practices to decrease operating expenses. In this way, the administration of the jail was not simply rooted in controlling crime; it also aimed to create a financially self-sustaining enterprise. The state of the facilities routinely challenged this goal.

The same year that the BOV appealed for an end to the fickle admissions of suspected runaways, they published a special report on the state of the jail. It had absolutely deteriorated in its four decades of use.[21] The board complained that the building had not been designed for long-term detention. The Maryland Penitentiary, a building located right next to the jail and built in 1812, was the intended detention facility for long-term convicts.[22] However, given the steady rise of debtors, suspected runaways, peace cases, and regular population growth, the city's carceral institutions began to wear down. The city government scrambled to find places to put individuals whose "crimes" constituted a set of unrelated economic and public behaviors as well as existential states that undermined the smooth and orderly progress of racial capitalism. While the jail had been envisioned as an institution in which each prisoner received their own cell to engage in the work of quiet reflection, by 1845, the jail accommodated ten to twenty prisoners per cell.[23] Their crimes? An inability to pay debts taken to survive, drinking alcohol in public, and being born Black. The BOV viewed the infrastructural conditions as inhumane and reported that such misery took place "within the walls of one prison, which should be a place of reformation instead of what we fully believe it now is a place of demoralization."[24]

In the following years, the BOV, other established and new government agencies, and the public advocated for the creation of more detention facilities. If buildings degraded, if individuals were imprisoned unjustly, and if magistrates indiscriminately confined too many people in the city's small jails and prisons, the answer was not to reform bureaucratic and legal procedures of punishment; it was to build new and bigger facilities. This pattern characterized local government's approach to the administration of discipline in the nineteenth century. When young boys became more prevalent at the jail, the BOV advocated for the creation of a House of Refuge.[25] When the new state constitution disallowed imprisonment for debt, the city government created the Trustees of the Poor (later the Supervisors of Charity) to oversee the almshouse and confine the impoverished and indebted as needed.[26] And when, despite the elimination of the jail's chief occupants in debtors, the building continued to fall apart and threaten inhabitants with contamination and contagious disease, the BOV asked for a bigger, better jail.

The city obliged. In 1856, architects Thomas and James Dixon designed a castellated gothic five-story structure. The builders stressed symmetry and proportion to convey a sense of stoic order (figure 3). The jail opened in 1859. It boasted 300 cells to accommodate a daily average of 178 prisoners. Each cell had an iron grated door and window to the corridors. Cells were arranged so inmates could only see the concrete wall opposite them. Prisoners used night pails for excrement which the jail staff dumped in the sewers. Drainage to the Jones Falls covered the city in the noxious odor of human feces.[27]

The new jail was erected on the same site as the old jail. The location allowed for the centralization of the city's expanding criminal legal system. The jail, penitentiary, and courts converged in the central city. The BOV's plan for the new jail was rooted in the philosophies of the Auburn system. That is, inmates were housed one to a cell. They spent their days in solitary confinement until they engaged in compulsory congregate labor. A central guardhouse allowed for wraparound surveillance.[28] While the jail's population rested at a comfortable 178 inmates per day as the architects and BOV planned the new structure, the year it opened, the average spiked to 230 daily inmates and 5,508 annual commitments, a record high. Officials noted that the increase represented an influx in peace cases. The closer the number inched toward three hundred, the more worried the BOV became. The jail was organized around a system of solitary confinement.[29] Like the old jail, however, the new jail's population would increase exponentially. By 1866, just seven years after opening, the daily average reached 305 inmates, dashing the ideal of solitary confinement.[30] The tide of rising commitments would not subside for another decade as yearly admissions increased steadily between 1865 and 1875 (figure 2).

The old jail's institutional history ominously foreshadowed the new jail's fate. Public order and economic cases would continue to rise and clog the facility. Overuse would lead to deterioration. The BOV and wardens would appeal to the city to reconsider processes of confinement and suggest detention in alternative facilities to provide relief for the flooded jail. Those alternative facilities, however, would face similar or worse mismanagement, deterioration, and collapse. Much of this advocacy took for granted the necessity of criminalizing impoverished city residents. As such, the question was not *if* the poor should be punished but *where* they should be punished. As the city searched for ways to efficiently manage diverse populations, and as interconnected yet

"This Modern Hades" • 25

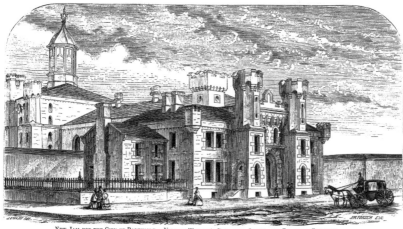

Figure 3. Line engraving for Thomas and James Dixon's plan for the city jail, ca. 1865. Source: Library of Congress Prints and Photographs Division, Washington, D.C.

competing institutional parties negotiated the seemingly limitless growth of Baltimore's population, capital interests, and boundaries, carceral expansion tore the dispossessed asunder. And while this system cast a wide net on who posed a threat to established public norms, the jail's primary inhabitants posed possibly the biggest threat by virtue of their indifference to normative standards of urban order: the bummers.

Bummers and the Business of Public Order

During the latter half of the nineteenth century, the city jail's annual admissions fluctuated by thousands. In 1867, the jail recorded 5,816 annual commitments. By 1874, this number doubled to 11,654. By 1883, total admissions fell again to 7,783 before ballooning back to 11,740 in 1889. These trends represented broader structural changes, including economic depressions, the formation of new detention centers dedicated to housing different groups, and evolving policing and legal orthodoxies that created new criminal classes, including the wayward young, the insane, and the purportedly work-hating bummers.[31]

Bummers constituted an economic group that most visibly occupied U.S. cities between the end of the Civil War and World War I. Elsewhere called "tramps," in Baltimore, these men were called bummers.[32] According to historian Eric

Monkkonen, American labor during this juncture required mobility, transience, and seasonal availability. Such conditions gave rise to what he characterizes as the "unknown thousands [who] spent portions of their lives following work, sleeping on the ground or in police stations and poorhouses."[33] Pathologizing discourses animated perceptions of such men whose lifestyles represented an unintentional anti-capitalist politic that power brokers attempted to deaden through forcible hard labor.

In the early 1870s, bummers became the use case that justified criminal legal reform and the erection of new buildings, annexes, and sites to detain criminalized populations. In 1873, bummers constituted 79 percent of jail admissions. The jail averaged 365 inmates over the course of the year—65 more than the facility was designed to handle.[34] To address bummer admissions and overcrowding, the BOV turned its attention to police magistrates who abused their fee-based payment compensation by liberally levying fines and sentences on poor men.[35] In its 1873 report, the board urged the legislature and city council to convert police magistrates into salaried employees.[36] Other reform organizations, including the Maryland Prisoners' Aid Association (MPAA), which was established in 1869 to deliver religious services and guide prisoners through the process of securing employment after their releases, echoed this sentiment, noting that most city jail commitments were poor men with no resources to pay the fines imposed by magistrates. Converting magistrates into salaried employees and removing their ability to commit bummers to jail would decrease total jail commitments.[37]

The practice of committing bummers to jail on petty crimes reflected the discretionary mode in which cops made arrests among the poor in the immediate post–Civil War era. Between 1868 and 1873, the most routine offenses for which police arrested bummers included breaches of the peace and intoxication. Within this five-year window, two-thirds of all arrests stemmed from these offenses.[38] The *Sun* surmised, "A large proportion of the fees of the station house magistrates accrue from arrests on the charge of being drunk and disorderly, about three fourths of which the city has to pay in consequence of the inability of the party arrested to do so. The expense to the city continues when the party is in jail, where most of them are sent."[39] Whereas the police defended such heavy-handed patrolling as a response to citizen desires to eliminate vice and public eyesores, some citizens protested the indiscriminate practice of targeting and arresting poor men. One reverend highlighted the hypocrisy of policing conventions which persecuted the needy while allowing the wealthy to rig local politics through corrupt machinery and graft. He questioned "why it was that the law is enforced against the weak and not against the strong; how it was that an obscure man is hung on circumstantial evidence, and a rich bully is set free, whose murderous deed is well known."[40]

In 1876, responding to the mounting pressure from city agencies, the press, and the public, the state legislature salaried magistrates and prohibited them from committing bummers to jail. The latter affordance became the exclusive provenance of the criminal court.[41] The reform paid off immediately. Three years after the state salaried police magistrates, drunk and disorderly arrests decreased from two-thirds of all arrests to one-half of all arrests.[42] This decreased emphasis on drunk and disorderly behavior helped reduce annual jail commitments in half from a peak in 1875 to a nadir in 1880 (figure 2).[43] Jail officials were particularly keen on this trend because the decrease provided a more reliable corps of prisoners. Rather than drunk and disorderly offenders who were quickly released and recommitted to maximize magistrate fees, the city jail's population stabilized with longer term commitments. Additionally, without the chaos of continuous new admissions, the city jail staff could turn its attention to different facets of the jail.

These developments revealed two key elements of incarceration that spoke to the nature of bureaucracy and law enforcement during the late nineteenth century. First, the sharp decline in peace arrests contradicted broader assumptions regarding the importance of enforcing public order. Surely, if the police were solely motivated by a desire to create a just and safe atmosphere in the city, the legislature's reformation of the magistrate system would not have had such a drastic effect on their enforcement of public order. Instead, the diminished potential of generating revenue off the backs of poor men decreased the importance of regulating public order. Second and relatedly, the decreased emphasis on public order arrests provided what seemed like a boon to the city jail's administrators whose own desires to generate revenue through convict labor were stymied by the cops' incessant confinement of unreliable and short-term detainees. During the brief window in which bummer admissions relaxed, city jail officials became hopeful that they could finally solicit contracts with private enterprises which had long interpreted the facility as bad for business. In both cases, public order rendered bummers the raw material for the reproduction and financing of public agencies. As such, bummer arrests were not objective enforcements of the rule of law or the dispassionate maintenance of the "public good." Rather, their arrests conformed to negotiations among city and state bureaucrats who jockeyed among one another to unlock the capital potential of their agencies and scale up capacity. And although the tide seemingly shifted in the city jail's favor, bummers proved much harder to manage than conceptual widgets for a convict labor contractor. Moreover, police administrators made

28 · CHAPTER 1

public order a key issue in hopes that magistrates could regain the power to detain bummers while also more forcefully exercising preemptive policing in poor neighborhoods. Both developments called into question the duty and function of policing.

Legally, the city government was bound to put "all persons convicted of offenses" to hard labor based on laws governing state and city penal institutions.[44] Despite this requirement and the supporting penal orthodoxies surrounding the rehabilitative capacities of convict labor, the legislation was a dead letter that officials had been attempting to resurrect at the city jail for years.[45] In its 1869 report, the BOV bemoaned the lack of work available for bummers and suggested that the city jail provided an ideal space of respite for vagrants and drunkards that discouraged them from productively contributing to society. With shelter, three meals a day, and no work, the prison population had no inducement to participate in the formal economy. No matter that, in the same report, the board asked for a liberal appropriation to make extensive repairs on a rapidly deteriorating, overcrowded, and hazardous building.[46] For the BOV, if inmates were made to labor while confined, they would be discouraged from seeking incarceration and encouraged to find employment in the formal labor economy.[47]

With these legal and moral mandates in mind, the late nineteenth century saw the BOV attempt to force the creation of a convict labor program at the city jail. Given paltry city appropriations, convict labor presented perhaps the only means by which to make the jail financially self-sustainable. The facility's deficiencies obstructed this goal and rendered the jail an unattractive place to do business. Because the jail, by nature, was meant to house petty criminals on a short-term basis and did not have dedicated workspaces, the BOV fared poorly in its efforts to attract contractors. Since sentenced inmates stayed at the jail for only a couple of weeks or months and bummers served only a few days, the board sought contracts that the unpredictable inmate population could fulfill. Although the reformation of the magistrate system provided a glimmer of hope for the BOV, an intensification in neighborhood policing again put bummers at the center of questions regarding the proper deployment of police power and the rights of citizens. Much of this increased policing came at the direction of the police board which adopted a preemptive approach to street policing to root out so-called ruffianism and prevent crime before it happened.

This policing approach proved controversial. In 1877, Mayor George P. Kane, a former police marshal,[48] declared that "the actual personal presence of a policeman is no protection against ruffianism." Kane believed that police were better suited to detect and capture criminals after offenses had been committed.[49]

The mayor's misgivings stemmed from the police board's tenacious requests to augment its corps of patrolmen and cover city neighborhoods with cops. The police received the second highest appropriation of any city agency behind public schools, and they wanted more.[50] Kane's positions on the impact of a large police force and their deterrent influence (or lack thereof) echoed broader debates regarding the effectiveness of the cops.[51]

For the police board, constant surveillance both lessened crime and protected private interests. The police board attributed much of its success to the growing detective bureau and the round-the-clock work of patrolmen. According to the board, the police provided year-round protection with the day patrol working thirteen-hour shifts and the night patrol working eleven-hour shifts.[52] Responding to Kane's assessment of the futility of preemptive policing, the board retorted, "Ruffianism, organized or individual, is kept cowed and upon its good behavior by the consciousness that it is under perpetual surveillance." For the police board, such surveillance was necessary because the city was growing. Suburban communities, high-value real estate, and rising commercial interests guided this deterrent policing philosophy and the police board's successful calls to erect new precincts in growing parts of the city. Although the legislature had reformed the magistrate system to decrease the number of bummers in the city's carceral facilities, the police board pressured the legislature to reverse the decision because of the high-value property to which bummers supposedly posed a threat. Specifically, they wished to both empower cops with broader discretionary powers to arrest bummers and revest magistrates with the authority to commit bummers to the city jail. The police board believed a reversal of the policy would address the newly emboldened bummers who defiantly occupied increasingly valuable city streets.[53]

Following this advocacy, the legislature emboldened the police board once again. In 1880, it reversed its previous decision regarding the jurisdiction of cops and magistrates and provided police wider discretionary powers. New legislation granted magistrates concurrent jurisdiction over drunk and disorderly cases with the criminal court, which meant they could once again fine and commit bummers to the city jail.[54] This legislation led to an intense spike in disorderly conduct arrests (figure 4).[55] The warden assessed that such enforcement "increased the number of prisoners known as 'Bummers' and 'Peace Cases' nearly fifty percent."[56] This decision demonstrated yet again that the administration of justice in the late nineteenth century represented the politicized compulsion of order rooted in revenue, and less so the objective enforcement of law and order.

While the policy placated the police board, commenters grew wary of the ever-increasing reach of the cops. In an 1884 editorial titled "Who Are the

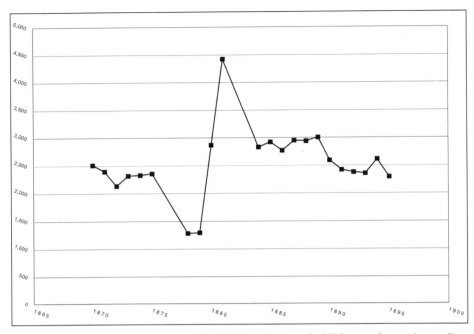

Figure 4. Disorderly conduct arrests per 100,000, 1870–95. Magistrates seized their renewed powers to commit bummers on disorderly conduct charges, which reached record levels. Source: Board of Police Commissioner Reports, 1870–95, Agency Reports and Publications, Baltimore City Archives.

So-Called Bummers?" a writer identified as "T. E. B." outlined how police harassment exploited the powerlessness of poor men. They criticized the convention of police officers targeting intoxicated people to secure fines that went directly into station house coffers. For T. E. B., "in other words, a terrible punishment is wreaked upon [a bummer] merely on account of his poverty." T. E. B. took issue with how the press characterized bummers as vicious and depraved, arguing that these attributions were "nothing more than lying slander." According to the writer, bummers were poor men who worked modest jobs and got caught up in a criminal legal system that profited from exploiting them.[57]

Moreover, the police's agendas clashed with jail officials' designs to optimize the city jail for hard labor. Years of overcrowding, the police department's renewed legal affordance to wage war on public disorder, and pending convict labor contracts led the BOV to desperately appeal to the city for more funding. They argued that if the city council provided capital to create workhouses and additional cell blocks, the revenue generated from satisfied convict labor contracts would lessen taxpayer burden in the long term. The city council remained unconvinced. The current jail, like its predecessor, had become a chaotic, incompetently administered storehouse for bummers who walked in and out of the facility every couple of days. The building was unsecured, and life inside was informal and underregulated. Getting contractors on board would be challenging.

The BOV tried to prove the jail's potential to coordinate a labor program by putting inmates to work on day-to-day operational tasks. They employed inmates in the kitchen, garden, stable, blacksmith shop, and laundry and sewing rooms. Bummers and those awaiting trial were not employed in favor of inmates who had already received sentences. To further expand labor capacity at the jail, the board asked for additional appropriations to purchase tools and equipment and hire more guards. The latter was necessary because, as prisoners began to fulfill roles that allowed them to move about outside of their cells, opportunities for escape increased. The board reported that on October 26, 1877, two prisoners, Thad Hall and Codger Williams, escaped the jail during the afternoon changing of the guards. As messengers, they were able to use the unguarded window to climb over the Madison Street wall.[58] Although the board attributed no blame to the officers on duty, they forbade the practice of allowing unaccompanied inmates to roam the facilities after nightfall.[59] This incident and several others motivated the BOV and jail officials to seek comprehensive infrastructural reforms. Such reforms would secure the jail. They would also make it a more attractive place for prospective labor contractors.

An unexpected turn of events fast-tracked the BOV's requests for more funding. On June 23, 1878, during his term in office, Mayor Kane died. Kane had opposed increased funding for law enforcement. His successor, Ferdinand C. Latrobe, forcefully advocated the creation of a convict labor program at the city jail. During his first year in office, Latrobe proudly reported that the facility had finally revived the 1860 dead letter statute that required inmates to engage in "hard labor" and "useful employment."[60] While the city jail did secure two contracts, as several officials suspected, the facility proved wholly unsuited to fulfill them.

On January 21, 1879, at a special meeting, the BOV received G. S. Griffith, a noted convict labor advocate, penologist, and manufacturer. Griffith proposed a five-year convict labor contract to produce carpets for his firm. After considerable debate, the board accepted Griffith's offer. Carpet weaving represented an ideal form of labor for the city jail's population because most inmates served relatively short sentences, and they could learn the skill quickly.[61] Under the arrangement, prisoners went uncompensated during a thirty-day probationary period. Afterward, they were given ten cents per day.

32 · CHAPTER 1

The board reserved carpet weaving exclusively for the "sentenced class," which constituted about one-third of inmates whose average prison sentence lasted three months.[62]

Whereas the sentenced class could pick up carpet weaving within that three-month window, bummers, who served much shorter sentences, presented a complication in the city's pursuit to make the jail self-sustaining. Because bummers served short sentences for innocuous crimes, the grand jury frequently requested that the criminal court release hundreds of them at a time to decongest the disintegrating jail. As labor contracts finally made their way to the city jail, however, officials pressured the grand jury and criminal court to discontinue the practice.[63] In the meantime, the BOV needed to find a trade that bummers could pick up almost instantaneously. They managed to strike a contract with Beebe & Co. to have bummers strip willow for baskets. The labor contract between the basket weaver and the jail read in part, "The Board will furnish said Beebe with the labor of 40 prisoners of the class known as Bummers." Beebe would pay the jail fifteen cents per man daily.[64] The contract experienced a rocky start. Since bummers were accustomed to receiving early releases, several of them simply refused to work and instead waited for their usual discharge. The BOV appealed to the criminal court to forgo its practice of releasing bummers early so that it could successfully "punish them into an observance of the rule requiring them to work." The criminal court complied, and bummers reluctantly began to strip willow.[65]

With these new labor contracts in place, the BOV advocated for massive reforms to both modernize the jail and impose stricter disciplinary measures on worker inmates. Under the stewardship of Warden J. F. Morrison, an aspirant political boss whose tenure at the city jail revealed the level of degradation the facility had experienced, officials managed to cobble together enough money to forestall the institution's collapse.[66]

In 1880, the BOV requested funding for uniforms, water tanks, electric lighting, and the construction of shared eating spaces.[67] Since the jail had finally secured labor contracts, the BOV also requested appropriations to expand the facility's manufacturing potential. Echoing criminologists, the board emphasized the monetary value of such an expansion as well as its moral reform capacities. They reported, "The amount needed for this expenditure appears large at first, but in a short while it would amply repay the city in increased earnings; and the moral effect which compulsory labor and enforced cleanliness will have upon the *habitues* of the prison would be great."[68] For the board, by infusing the jail with capital to develop manufacturing, the city was investing in both its fiscal growth and the moral stock of its residents. The same year, to communicate the soundness of this investment, Morrison submitted an uncharacteristically lengthy warden's report that outlined, in exhaustive detail, how the city jail's management proposed to maintain order among guards and inmates at the infamously dysfunctional institution.

Warden Morrison's report carefully anticipated potential critiques regarding the jail's deficiencies and how those issues would bear on discipline. For criminologists, the best way to pacify an inmate population was through solitary confinement. The city jail had been built on this presumption. However, since the number of daily average prisoners eclipsed the number of cells, the facility had involuntarily adopted an associative model.[69] Since solitary was not an option, Morrison fashioned a disciplinary scheme rooted in silence. Under the new rules, jail staff enforced absolute quiet among inmates during meals, marching, and work. Guards directed prisoners using a system of gongs in lieu of vocal commands. To diminish any semblance of conviviality among prisoners and guards, Morrison prohibited the exchange of goods, money, and conversation. If inmates desired information on attorneys, guards were instructed to give them the city directory.[70]

In addition to this disciplinary scheme, Morrison altered the city jail's organization. He divided the building into four cell blocks. The first was reserved for inmates awaiting trial, the second was reserved for inmates serving sentences, the third was reserved for women, and the fourth was reserved for bummers. A deputy warden oversaw the men's sections, while a matron oversaw the women's section. Prisoners were forced to abide by a system of bodily comportment that emphasized docility and hygiene. Upon admission, jail staff cleansed inmates of dirt and vermin. Guards forbade prisoner interaction, even among cellmates. Inmates were given a one-hour window in the afternoon to receive visitors. These meetings occurred under the supervision of a deputy warden, and additional grating was installed to ensure that visitors could not pass inmates liquor, weapons, or jail-breaking implements. At 6:00 p.m., inmates retired to their cells. At 9:00 p.m., after four strokes of the gong, it was lights out.[71]

While the warden reported that these regulations had created an orderly inmate population and more reliable guards, he equally emphasized the difficulties presented by the jail's infrastructural deterioration. He reported holes in the walls that leaked during storms, worsening masonry, an overtaxed and undependable system of steam heating, busted and leaky pipes, poor lighting and ventilation, an unpaved backyard that became a mud hole during heavy rains, and low walls around the jail that allowed for easy escapes.[72] These defects signified the wear and tear caused by thousands of men and women who had filtered in and out of the jail for two decades. These conditions would only get

34 • CHAPTER 1

worse as the city's demography continued to change and the police's discretion and jurisdiction broadened to patrol new environs.

In 1888, Baltimore annexed land from the surrounding county that doubled its size.[73] By 1890, the population had reached 434,439—an addition of over 100,000 residents in ten years. Given the new land and people, the police board appealed to the state for more funding for station houses, more cops to patrol expanding neighborhoods, and more communication and transit equipment, like patrol boxes and police wagons.[74] The police board defended its requests by detailing how capacious the police's duties had become. In addition to their express obligations to protect personal and real property, they assumed several public order functions that put them on the streets around the clock. They oversaw elections and mass political meetings, they patrolled thoroughfares to prevent and remove nuisances, they surveilled railroad stations to protect the city's chief enterprise, they enforced public morals by regulating Sunday laws, pawning, gambling, prostitution, public intoxication, and disorderly conduct, and because of trouble on the waterfront, they established a harbor police.[75] Affairs had become so chaotic that in 1887, the board recommended that the state grant it the ability to appoint "special policemen." Such a program had existed since 1880, but only the governor could appoint such officers.[76] The board hoped it could assume appointment powers to deputize civilians to patrol banks, factories, theaters, and other businesses.[77] Such an allowance would permit the police force to provide corporate protection for private businesses at no charge to itself while freeing patrolmen to focus on public order.

Arrest rates after the annexation reflected the police's emphasis on public order, and incarceration rates revealed the increasingly racialized carceral regime taking grip in the city. After the state legislated that police could arrest citizens on suspicions of drunkenness and rescinded prohibitions against magistrates, disorderly conduct and intoxication arrests began to increase. In 1889, the year after the annexation, those two charges accounted for 64 percent of all arrests.[78] And although police had not yet begun reporting the racial demography of arrestees, since most of these public order offenses landed arrestees in the city jail, jail admission trends provided a sense of how police placed disproportionate emphasis on surveilling and arresting Black men and women.[79] After the Civil War, the incarceration rate at the city jail increased steadily and reached its highest point in 1875. The Black incarceration rate at this apex was twice that of the white incarceration rate. Beginning in 1876, when magistrates were stripped of the ability to incarcerate city residents for breaches of the public peace, the incarceration rate decreased, as did Black and white rates of incarceration, though the relation was still disproportionate. Beginning in 1883, three years or so after the legislature revested magistrates with the capacity

"This Modern Hades" · 35

to commit bummers to the city jail, the total rate of incarceration began to increase gradually before trending downward in 1889. At this point, the city jail became a site driven by Black incarceration. While the white incarceration rate followed the overall downward trend in annual admissions, the Black incarceration rate trended upward. Several variables accounted for this disproportionate emphasis on Black incarceration. Chief among them was the proliferation of prevalent national and local discourses condemning Black criminality and political demagoguery concerning the effects of so-called "Negro rowdyism" on the body politic. Power brokers popularized this term in the late nineteenth century to promote the notion that Black men and women uniquely threatened public safety. It is no coincidence, then, that the Black incarceration rate at the city jail by 1900 was over six times the white incarceration rate (figure 2).

During the first half of the 1880s, the city jail's climbing commitments—specifically Black commitments—alarmed the BOV and Warden Morrison. The latter's appeals to the city council became more vociferous as he contended with policing agendas that prioritized punishment for low-level public order infractions and magistrates who liberally committed offenders to the city jail. A year after his lengthy report on the city jail's disrepair, the city council had made no headway in addressing the building's decline. In his 1881 report, Morrison rang the alarm bells. He warned that if the city continued to drag its feet, it might have to totally reconstruct the edifice—again. Every year, the jail's conditions worsened. Because of the spike in bummer admissions, these worsening conditions accelerated. The cell block designated for bummers overflowed to the point of unmanageability. It routinely averaged four hundred daily inmates. With only seventy-five cells allocated for their confinement, five to six bummers occupied cells reserved for two men.[80] The city council responded to Morrison's admonitions with piecemeal allocations that led to partial improvements, including the installation of electric lights and the incomplete pavement of the yard which still became a mud hole during heavy rain, albeit a smaller mud hole. Morrison reiterated his requests, particularly as they pertained to ventilation and safeguards against escape. On the latter point, he suggested the installation of iron gratings for dormer windows, grated transoms above large doors, grated doors in lieu of wooden ones, and a ventilation system in the jail's workshops.[81]

Given the city jail's conditions, G. S. Griffith decided not to renew his convict labor contract. Although Griffith touted labor as the only remedy to moral degradation, as it concerned his bottom line, the reformer valued profit over charity. After his contract expired, the MPAA, Griffith's prisoners' advocacy group, surveyed the jail. Its report confirmed much of what Morrison detailed. During the visit, the MPAA found 438 bummers crammed into 75 cells. Because of the crowding, jail staff placed some bummers in an overflow room above the

36 · CHAPTER 1

blacksmith shop. Even so, each cell in the bummer wing held four men. To create more space, the administrators looked to construct additional overflow space in one of the jail's cellars. According to the MPAA, "the darkness and insufferable heat and gases from the furnaces located here will indeed be a terrible punishment for those who are assigned to this modern hades."[82]

Countless stories detailing the jail's abhorrent conditions, as well as the police's continual harassment of bummers, led to critiques in the press. These critiques called for changes to the criminal code and opposed the erection of new detention facilities. One anonymous commenter suggested that a separate court be created to mediate drunk and disorderly cases, an altogether reasonable suggestion given the existence of police courts housed in jails like the infamous Tombs in New York.[83] Critics also suggested sending bummers far away to the House of Correction in Jessup, Maryland, which had a functioning labor program, instead of expanding labor capacity at the jail. Another writer criticized the legal system's criminalization of poverty, declaring, "In a word, let grand jurymen find out why simple poverty inflicts upon a man thirty days of brutalizing confinement, with other tortures unnecessary to name."[84] In addition to the legal system, these critiques questioned the motives of an emergent reformer class. Made up of temperance societies, poverty relief organizations, and anti-machine crusaders, bourgeois moralism guided wealthy private citizens who urged city agencies to aid them in subtending what they considered the civilizational threat posed by bummers and so-called pauperization. Fractured public sentiment highlighted larger debates surrounding law enforcement, police power, and the public good. Whereas the city's public agencies and reformer circles viewed the criminalization of bummers as necessary to satisfy monetary and moral ideals, other public commenters viewed the capricious arrests of bummers as punishment for poverty, a decidedly legal though difficult condition. On this front, the city jail managers agreed. Although motivated by pure self-interest, the BOV's new stratagem of advocating that bummers be confined to different facilities dovetailed with public sentiment regarding the arbitrary ways that law enforcement rendered them criminals in the first place.

Following persistent critiques regarding the ethical implications of imprisoning bummers, the BOV argued that bummers less resembled criminals and more resembled "idiots and insane people." They supported charges of bummer insanity by detailing how many of them, after binge drinking, became gripped by a debilitating mental delirium called *mania portu*. This delirium required specialized treatment unavailable at the jail. As such, Warden Morrison suggested that bummers be moved from the city jail to Bayview Asylum.[85] And although a compelling case could be made that bummers did not deserve the punishment of confinement at the city jail, the notion that they would face more favorable conditions at Bayview was dubious at best. Morrison seized on perennial questions of bummer treatment to reshuffle them to a different establishment following the typical and arbitrary conventions governing the institutionalization of poor and marginalized city residents. Bayview was certainly different in composition, but its tumultuous institutional history mirrored the city jail's and illustrated how, even under the guise of Bayview's altruistic charter, the city both struggled to figure out how best to store the impoverished and only had designs to accomplish as much.

"An Asylum, Not a Prison": Bayview Asylum and the Management of Indigence

Bayview Asylum opened in 1866. Located on the city's developing east side, it served as an almshouse for the poor, a hospital for the sick, and an asylum for the mentally unwell (figure 5).[86] Like the city jail, Bayview grappled with ever-increasing numbers of poor men and women, displaced by the acceleration of industrial capitalism and in need of refuge. During the late nineteenth century, insane asylums (and "insanity" more generally) gripped the national imaginary as grisly stories about brutal conduct, experimental treatments, and the dangers associated with going crazy proliferated public consciousness. The Association of Medical Superintendents of American Institutions for the Insane (AMSAII), later renamed the American Psychiatric Association (APA), noted that the combination of overfilled asylums, accessible and comprehensive census data, and sensationalist news stories about the brutal treatment of patients in the country's insane asylums fomented an overblown reaction to the supposed epidemic of mental illness overtaking the American public. Although the AMSAII did not necessarily reject the idea of a surge of insanity, it attributed the increase to more sophisticated classificatory standards and robust medical treatment.[87]

Whatever the case, Bayview became a crucial site of urban governance for Baltimore because unlike most insane asylums, the building served three distinct and often at-odds functions. It was a hospital, an insane asylum, and an almshouse.[88] As such, Bayview became a repository for people who had become impoverished in diverse ways, including through injuries, unemployment, scams, mental health complications, and other social and physical obstacles. Much like the city jail, throughout the late nineteenth century, city government and the Trustees of the Poor, the facility's managers, contended with complicated questions regarding the asylum's obligations to a growing citizenry. As stories of the asylum began to populate the local imaginary, questions arose regarding its function. Was it a space of refuge? An insane asylum? A prison? Despite Mayor Ferdinand Latrobe's firm declaration that Bayview was "an asylum, not a prison," the institution drew a fine line.[89] Since its inception, the trustees and other legally enabled parties—including the criminal court—could institutionalize "vagrants" and "paupers" against their will. Admittees could not leave without written consent. The asylum's managers expected all capable admittees to work. The asylum's staff meted out discipline through food deprivation, solitary confinement, or expulsion to different institutions, including the city jail. These rules applied in varied form to inmates classified as "insane." These inmates received treatment from a host of onsite physicians and medical students.[90]

Bureaucratic mismanagement, horrid stories, and external assessments led to increased sentiment that Bayview functioned more like an overcrowded and miserable prison than an asylum for refuge or an effective mental institution. During the 1870s, epidemics wracked the facility and led to hundreds of infections and dozens of deaths.[91] Like the jail, the asylum had barely opened before overcrowding and calls for improvements emerged. The trustees goaded the city to update the facility's plumbing, ventilation, and water supply.[92] Also like the jail, the trustees instituted a compulsory labor program. They reported, "The Board, impressed with the universally conceded truth, that 'idleness is the mother of evil,' have inaugurated a system of labor, compelling those who, on account of habits contracted, are unable to procure situations in respectable families, to spend a portion of each day in making carpet balls."[93]

While labor constituted the most common form of discipline, the asylum's staff were sometimes accused of brutalizing inmates. In 1874, officers reportedly manacled a patient suffering from an erysipelatous inflammation, a ghastly skin condition, during the inmate's transfer from Bayview to the Maryland Hospital for the Insane at Spring Grove. Dr. C. W. Chancellor, the president of Spring Grove, condemned Bayview's use of physical restraints and pled with the city council to redirect insane patients to his hospital, which had more resources and provided better treatment.[94] The local papers decried the brutality. The trustees denied the story.[95] After this calamity, Chancellor pushed to disallow Bayview from receiving certain patients based on the inadequate provisions and careless medical standards of the institution. He viewed Bayview's organizational structure as preposterous and believed that the curable insane should not commingle with the incurable, as well as paupers and the physically ill. Chancellor pushed to have curable cases redirected to Spring Grove and incurable cases steered to Bayview. The city council obliged in 1875 and continued to erect segregationist barriers as the so-called incurable were confined to the deteriorating facilities of Bayview while the so-called curable were sent to the tony suburbs at Spring Grove.[96]

Even though the new provisions should have alleviated congestion at Bayview, annual admissions to the insane department steadily increased. Given this surge, Mayor Latrobe supported constructing new buildings to accommodate the rising numbers of incurable insanity cases.[97] Bayview's physicians echoed this sentiment and noted that the reorganization of patients across local institutions saddled Bayview with only "idiots, imbeciles, epileptics, and chronics" who required special treatment, including mandatory labor. They suggested basket making, knitting, and weaving. For Bayview's physicians, "management often effects more than medicines."[98] In 1880, to build an Insane Department, the city council appropriated $50,000 for a fourteen-acre lot.[99] The following years saw the trustees clumsily shamble toward the completion of this wing. In 1884, the Insane Department was finally completed.[100] The governing logic that led to the creation of a larger Insane Department dovetailed with discourses that rendered certain urban dwellers as deviant while masking the ways that political presumptions regarding "curability" hid pseudoscientific and biologically racist modes of diagnosis. This dynamic is perhaps best illustrated by the arrival of one of Baltimore's leading medical experts, Henry M. Hurd.

In 1889, the Johns Hopkins Hospital opened down the road from Bayview. Hopkins's first superintendent was Henry M. Hurd, a psychiatrist and nationally renowned expert in mental and nervous diseases. Before arriving in Baltimore, Hurd served eleven years as the superintendent of the Eastern Michigan Asylum in Pontiac.[101] The Trustees of the Poor favorably reported that Hurd consulted on the construction of the additions to Bayview's Insane Department.[102] Before becoming superintendent of Hopkins, Hurd developed a reputation among the psychiatric community by publishing in major journals. Notably, Hurd's writings augmented and shaped debates on the racial and heritable character of nervous diseases. In an 1885 piece in the *Journal of Nervous and Mental Disease* titled "Race and Insanity," Hurd outlined how racial ancestry affected patients' susceptibility to insanity. For Hurd, the Teutonic races were likely to experience quiet dementia and systematized delusions rather than epilepsy or the more intense paretic dementia. Irish and German patients were likely to suffer from more pronounced and all-consuming mental illnesses, including chronic mania, irritable dementia, paralyzing dementia, and epilepsy. English-born patients, though susceptible to degenerative diseases, were, according to Hurd, more likely to recover from them because they possessed "more constitutional vigor" than German and Irish patients. Regarding curability, Hurd observed that native-born Americans were the most curable—a bizarre conclusion given that many native-born Americans were descendants of Irish and German immigrants. In this assertion, Hurd seemed to purport that nationality, a decidedly nonbiological category, bore directly on health. In any case, when it came to curability, native-born Americans were followed, in descending order, by English, German, and Irish patients. As it concerned patients of African descent, Hurd declared that they were "almost without exception incurable." So-called half-breeds, who possessed Indigenous ancestry, were slightly more curable than those of African descent because they were "better suited to our climate."[103] Such bogus science guided the administration of treatment in the city's medical facilities. Moreover, Bayview's increasingly poor reputation, which stemmed from the facility's own organizational deficiencies and its leadership's indiscretions, poised it to become a dumping ground for supposedly incurable foreign-born and Black patients who did not deserve the high-quality individualized treatment given at more well-resourced institutions in and around the city.

Bayview's managers did the institution no favors on this front. While the trustees coordinated the construction of new facilities, more evidence of maladministration came to light. Concerns emerged around ballooning annual expenditures, particularly as Superintendent Charles Carroll hired watchmen and turnkeys to police the facility. Carroll defended these new hires by stating that it was exceedingly irresponsible to hire inmates to conduct disciplinary duties. When inmates watched other inmates, whisky smuggling and other illicit activities became common. Indeed, in this arrangement, the inmates were quite literally running the asylum. Yet and still, the hires led to an official inquiry into the institution's finances that uncovered questionable, though evidently not "extravagant," spending.[104]

A more pressing concern emerged around the theft of inmate cadavers for medical experimentation. At Bayview, when inmates died, orderlies took them to the "dead house," a morgue. Before the institution released the body to a family member or other responsible party, physicians and resident medical students conducted postmortems if they believed they would advance the "cause of science."[105] If no party came forward, orderlies buried deceased inmates in an enormous pit behind the asylum. The pit was twenty feet wide and eight feet deep. Attendants placed the corpses in pine coffins and stacked them in rows separated by two feet of dirt. According to the *Sun*, the trustees had a tacit agreement with grave robbers, called "resurrectionists," who dug up these pits at night and transferred the cadavers to the city's various medical colleges. However, because of the resurrectionists' seeming green light to rob these graves, they became so emboldened that they began disinterring cadavers during the trustees' meetings. The horror of the practice and the disgust of the trustees led them to revise Bayview's burial practices.[106] They resolved to fill the pit permanently. Future corpses would be buried three per plot and sport a headstone with identifying information, including names and dates of death.[107]

Given Bayview's long history of mismanagement and poor standards of ethics and efficiency, several external bodies conducted routine assessments, and

"This Modern Hades" • 41

Figure 5. During the late nineteenth century, Bayview Asylum's administrative functions and duties articulated a wide array of social problems. Its management demonstrated the city government's investment in incapacitating—rather than rehabilitating—the city's indigent populations. Source: "Bay View Asylum and Alms House. 1895." Courtesy of the Maryland Center for History and Culture, MC3157.

many of them left the facility horrified. The grand jury, which was responsible for performing yearly evaluations of Baltimore's carceral facilities, regularly visited the asylum. They reasoned that since the facility oversaw poor and indigent populations, some of whom had been committed by the criminal court, it fell upon them to oversee.[108] Bayview's inclusion in the grand jury's rounds, among the city jail and Maryland Penitentiary, troubled Mayor Latrobe's vehement protestation that the institution was "an asylum, not a prison." Although technically true, city agencies and other bodies did not perceive the institution in such a clear-cut manner. In addition to the grand jury, officials from other mental institutions assessed Bayview. In 1892, E. N. Brush of Sheppard Asylum, a private institution in the bucolic countryside town of Towson, conducted another, more comprehensive evaluation. Brush found the novel arrangement of the hybrid almshouse, asylum, and hospital nonsensical. He recommended "abandoning the old asylum and its very undesirable connection with the almshouse" and starting from scratch. He further contended that "in caring for the insane, the institutional and custodial features of the asylum should aim to make

42 · CHAPTER 1

patients, not prisoners, of the inmates." Finally, he noted the deplorable state of overcrowding that led nurses and attendants to rely on almshouse inmates to help administer care for the insane.[109]

Despite the report's scathing findings, efficiency had long been a luxury at facilities like Bayview and the city jail. At best, these buildings offered short-term relief to systemically dispossessed people who perennially shuffled in and out. At worst, they functioned like storehouses for people beset by political and economic deprivation, overpolicing, and an urban government with no better options and no moral qualms about exploiting the poor. As more populations came under the microscope of city agencies, institutionalization continued to be the catchall "solution" that both diagnosed and managed social deviance.

Conclusion

During the last few years of his tenure, Warden Morrison managed to lobby for legislation that allowed him to offload bummers to Bayview. The poor shuffled in and out of carceral facilities, each more disgusting than the last.[110] He also lost another convict labor contract based on the practice's extreme unpopularity. During the latter half of the nineteenth century, a workingmen's movement combined tireless advocacy with legislative lobbying and made prison labor a risky reputational proposition for businesses.[111] Finally, after years of negotiating, Morrison secured funding for a woman's annex to free up space for bummers in the main jail.[112] With the annex complete and most, though not all, of his infrastructure requests implemented, Morrison abdicated his position as warden of the city jail after seven years of service. He stepped down because "he did not desire the place any longer, and that it was not now, nor had it been for a long time, suited to his taste."[113] In leaving the undesirable place behind, Morrison did what poor men and women could not.

In the latter half of the nineteenth century, Baltimore experienced urbanization that doubled its land mass and heavily augmented its population. Industry, capital, and wealth grew as workers laid miles of railroad tracks, builders filled empty lots with seemingly endless columns of rowhomes, and all manner of manufactories sprung up to produce cans, bottles, spices, steel, and other goods. Those who imperiled the city's broad responsibility to safeguard this process of urbanization became objects of reform and censure. City government erected dozens of buildings for debtors, the enslaved, the poor, the intoxicated, and the insane. New categories of criminality and deviance were created based in genteel standards and biological essentialism, shifting policing conventions afforded cops more discretion, and various institutional boards played high-stakes games of hot potato to offload throngs of desperate people between facilities. These buildings cast an altogether macabre picture—a medical student disinterring a cadaver from a mass grave behind a ramshackle mental hospital, ten intoxicated yet largely inoffensive men stuck in a small cell with one bucket for refuse, and a poor lodger conscripted to provide medical treatment to an ailing patient because of a facility's lack of resources.

These buildings were not just buildings. In their management of people identified as either criminal or sick, they constituted a major element of municipal capacity that, in turn, formed the elementary units of Baltimore's growing police state. Legislators, police officials, penal administrators, and asylum managers debated and determined both the existential threat of impoverished Baltimoreans and the disposition of their punishment or care. In so doing, bummers became the raw material for statecraft as police exploited them for funding, wardens and superintendents for labor, and hospitals for bodies. Within this matrix of human sorting, a key element of urban governance and policing became clear. Policing was not exclusively—and in many instances not even primarily—concerned with enforcing a politically neutral or objective rule of law based in ethical standards of accountability and good governance. Rather, policing, jailing, and the provision of mental health services were fueled by desires to reproduce or maintain the integrity and operation of burgeoning bureaucracies and institutions. The regulation of poverty and insanity became methods by which institutions, like the police, could generate revenue while presenting a glossy image to the public regarding their seemingly effective regulatory merits. This obfuscation, while effective for a time, came under scrutiny during the late nineteenth century. As private reformers organized better and more effective networks, police fell into their crosshairs.

Although private reformers supported public order policing as an example of good government, they did not trust the police and other wasteful bureaucracies to carry out such important urban duties. After decades of institutional mismanagement, reformers grew dissatisfied with the bureaucratic bloat and corruption in city government that stemmed from opportunism, spoils, machine politics, and unethical administrations of vital city services. Given the centrality of policing's various functions to the efficacy of state power, private reformers turned their attention toward city government itself. Through civic channels, private actors tossed their hats in the ring and attempted to unlock the potential of police power, reform police abuses, and rein in bureaucratic inefficiency.

2

"Silk Stocking Aristocracy"

Police, Reform, and the Racialization
of Crime in the Late Nineteenth Century

On October 30, 1895, six days before the general election, Roger Cull, the chairman of the Reform League, sent instructions to his Election Day watchers. "Your business at the polls on election day will be to watch the conduct of the police," Cull wrote.[1]

After several months of organizing ward clubs, protesting election judge appointments, strategizing over new legislation, and raising hell in the press, the time had finally come to knock the political bosses of Baltimore's Democratic machine off their pedestals. The Baltimore police proved to be the last line of defense for the unpopular machine. Economic depression, the national ascendancy of the Republican Party, and the collective organizing of an elite group of reformers fomented this unpopularity which opened the door for a political realignment that would allow crusaders to reframe the nature of policing in Baltimore and smash the bosses. The late nineteenth century signaled a national reckoning for political bossism. Several major machines, including New York's infamous Tammany Hall, faced significant challenges from Progressive reformers and moral crusaders. In New York, Charles H. Parkhurst, a clergyman and president of the Society for the Prevention of Crime and the City Vigilance League, challenged Tammany Hall's political influence by exhorting city leaders to investigate the New York police force. His efforts and those of other reformers materialized in the Lexow Committee in 1894. The committee found that the New York police had engaged in brutal and systematic misconduct.[2] Similar

"Silk Stocking Aristocracy" • 45

investigations into policing followed in other major cities, including Atlanta, Philadelphia, and Baltimore. Such methodical inquiries and alterations of local government became possible because of a sea change in national politics.

Given the severe economic depression caused by the panic of 1893, the Democratic Party, which had ruled politics in several major cities for decades, including Baltimore, lost ground in 1894. With solidly Republican councils, mayoral administrations, and governorships, urban reformers around the country—linked through national civil service and burgeoning Progressive reform networks—seized the moment to alter city charters, institute politically neutral and bipartisan oversight in bureaucratic bodies, and eliminate long-standing machine appointees from vital agency positions. And while public sentiment steered this political realignment, reformers, like bosses, yearned for power in ways that quickly disillusioned wary citizenries. All told, reformers did not destroy political machines in the late nineteenth century. However, they hobbled them and managed to institute lasting and meaningful governmental orthodoxies that reframed the function of urban governance.[3] Baltimore's experience was particularly illustrative of this dynamic.

Since the 1870s, Baltimore's Democratic machine controlled local politics. Until the Reform League challenge in 1895, that control remained ironclad. The so-called Ring coordinated political alliances, exploited the spoils system, and exercised broad influence over the Baltimore police. The Ring's bosses included Arthur Pue Gorman, a politician who rose through the ranks of Maryland politics and eventually became a U.S. senator, and Isaac Freeman Rasin, a secretive boss who exercised control from his relatively obscure position as clerk of the Court of Common Pleas.[4] In the surrounding county, J. Frederick Talbott, an ex-Confederate U.S. congressman, spread and buttressed the Ring's influence. Opponents referred to Talbott as Gorman's right hand in Baltimore County.[5]

To knock off this rooted political grouping, a reformer class emerged during the 1880s. Their emergence coincided with national currents in urban reform as white puritans sought to reorganize and professionalize inefficient city governments. In Baltimore, Charles J. Bonaparte embodied the movement. Bonaparte, a devout Catholic with time and money to spare, viewed the failures of urban government through interlocking religious, ethical, and political prisms. He viewed the saloon, the brothel, and other sites of popular leisure as integral to the consolidation of the Ring's political power. Through ward-level organizing, the Ring secured loyalty through promises of police protection for saloonkeepers, brothel owners, and bookies. In exchange, ward bosses intimidated Republican voters, installed Democratic election judges, and ensured elections for the Ring.

46 · CHAPTER 2

Given this loose yet efficient network, Bonaparte and his allies established several reform organizations to topple the Ring and construct a city in their own image. Locally, Bonaparte either helped found or served in an executive capacity in several groups which tackled elections, poverty relief, public immorality, and other social ills. Nationally, Bonaparte helped found the National Civil Service Reform League, which historian Ariane Liazos describes as a foundational coalition of translocal and regional reform organizations. These organizations identified systemic issues across U.S. cities and formalized strategies to oust bosses and develop bureaucratic standards of political neutrality and ethical governance.[6] Baltimore formed a crucial part of these coalitions with Bonaparte serving as a founder for many of them and as president of the National Municipal League in 1905. He left that position the following year to serve as secretary of the navy and then attorney general for longtime ally and friend Theodore Roosevelt's presidential administration. As attorney general, Bonaparte, drawing on his experiences as a local reformer that often saw him resort to private surveillance, founded the Bureau of Investigation—later the Federal Bureau of Investigation. Baltimore's elites did not just operate within the boundaries of the locality; their influence and ideologies permeated national reorientations and movements toward government surveillance and interventionist state authority.

Following these national movements, broad-based organizations grew and subsisted through the patronage and donations of wealthy white people.[7] Despite their outward pronouncements of politically neutral reform, working-class Baltimoreans, particularly Black residents, remained skeptical of the white bourgeoisie. In an editorial, the *Afro-American* wrote,

> The reformers rave against bosses; but there is not a more tyrannical class of dictators in American politics than they. Their idea of reform rises no higher than a desire to dictate, not the method of appointment of office, but the appointees themselves. Should this silk stocking aristocracy ever control the government, the appointees will be rich men's sons and college graduates only.[8]

The Black press had plenty of critiques for the Ring and the "silk stocking aristocracy" that challenged it. They viewed this power struggle warily. Ring control would perpetuate segregationist efforts in public conveyances and civil life but would at least maintain the working-class character of local politics. Reformer control would provide paltry and largely superficial Black participation in urban government while elevating the wealthy. As historian Daniel Czitrom has argued, common understandings of Democratic political machines and bossism have elided investigations into similarly corrupted Republican machines that existed during the late nineteenth century. Democratic machines largely thrived off the support of working-class white immigrants whose behaviors became subjects of reform for Republican bluenoses. These reformers created similarly organized and corrupted political alliances designed to supplant Democratic bosses and machines and exploit patronage systems.[9] As the *Afro-American* noted, neither of these options represented a radical alteration of urban life for Black people, though the Republican option might open avenues for Black men to secure political office—the best worst option.

Ultimately, the late nineteenth-century power struggle that dominated city politics hinged on the city's Black residents. While typically loyal to the Republicans—and, thus, the reformers—Black Baltimoreans became increasingly disaffected as the regulation of Black crime dominated political discourse. Democrats intentionally politicized race and crime to discredit their Republican adversaries. Nationally, crime became affixed to Blackness in criminological, sociological, and pseudoscientific literatures.[10] These presumptions guided Democratic political strategy. They charged Republicans with enabling "Negro rowdyism."[11] They reasoned that by allowing Black people to participate more fully in civil society, Republicans awakened the dormant disorder that only emerged when Black people were allotted a quantity of freedom. Democrats stoked the flames of white supremacy by engaging in panic discourses about supposed "Negro domination" and "Negro rule."

Taken as a whole, the reforms of the late nineteenth and early twentieth centuries represented a shift in local politics that reframed the nature of police power. While politicians and bureaucrats largely guided the development of urban governance in the immediate post–Civil War period, the Progressive reform movement saw the ascendance of private actors who turned the meeting halls, hotels, and homes that they met in into vibrant sites of political coordination and organizing—important and powerful sites of police power. Through this coordination, crusaders proved instrumental in remolding state power through political lobbying, shutting down local haunts, exposing police corruption, and agitating to get high-ranking cops fired. They instituted lasting civil service, charter, and police reforms. The struggle among reformers, politicians, and police revealed how murky the duties and powers of the city were.

"Crime Sown in Our Midst": The Society for the Suppression of Vice

During the late nineteenth century, public and private bodies ceaselessly negotiated state imperatives and duties. Many of these negotiations hinged on what police affordances the state could and should use to regulate morals-based "crime." As such, the reform movement of the late nineteenth century represented three important dimensions of police power. First, private reform bodies assumed state functions in civic capacities, such as petitions to the Liquor Board, and in questionably legal capacities, such as private investigations into the informal economy. In doing so, reformers engaged in state-making activities that did not necessarily assume police power but modeled it for the city's law enforcement agencies and legislators. Second, collective power among urban elites spanned across city borders and sustained a national coalition of Progressive reformers whose deep influence changed the trajectory of governance in U.S. cities. In the late nineteenth century, Progressives advocated that state bodies regulate the urban poor to temper morally injurious social practices that were often explained through paternalist and cultural evolutionary frameworks. Finally, the reform movement in Baltimore demonstrated the limits of policing. While the sheer volume of unpunished offenses and corruption catalyzed private bodies to tackle crimes that police let fall by the wayside, the police force as designed simply could not serve every aspirant master. Policing was not a deterministic process; it was a chaotic one. The work of Baltimore's chapter of the Society for the Suppression of Vice captured each of these dimensions of police power as reformers geared up for an uphill battle against the city's Democratic machine.

On February 22, 1886, the Ministerial Union of Baltimore, a group of pastors and clergymen, met to discuss the formation of a local branch of the Society for the Suppression of Vice (BSSV). While myriad social issues would come to define the BSSV's political advocacy, their initial meeting focused on eliminating lewd show bills on public thoroughfares. The holy men left the meeting determined to both advocate for prohibitive legislation on lewd advertisements and to organize a group of private citizens to lobby for social reforms to curtail what they perceived as the rampant desecration of public morals fueled by gambling, lotteries, tobacco, saloons, and bawdy houses.[12] In subsequent weeks, the Ministerial Union took out newspaper ads inviting "all male citizens" to a mass meeting at the YMCA to discuss forming the organization. Anthony Comstock, secretary of the New York chapter of the Society for the Suppression of Vice, attended the meeting and became an avid supporter of the Baltimore chapter in subsequent years.[13] Reformers formally incorporated the BSSV in December 1887 at a mass meeting where both Comstock and Samuel Colgate, president of the New York chapter, delivered fiery addresses highlighting the need for educated white men to hold government officials accountable to the ideals of public morality and to enforce police power vigorously. Colgate warned, "Legislatures, judges, and police will move no faster than you do." Comstock echoed these sentiments and provocatively charged, "Shall we see the seed of crime sown in our midst by means of vicious and pernicious literature, unclean exhibitions

"*Silk Stocking Aristocracy*" · 49

on the public stage and other insidious agencies, and make no efforts to drive the enemy back?"[14]

The BSSV followed Colgate and Comstock's lead, as well as that of famed New York reformer Charles Parkhurst who was known to deliver fiery sermons at Madison Square Presbyterian Church where he would publicly and influentially challenge the police and Tammany Hall in 1892.[15] The BSSV forsook the police and the bosses and endeavored to use the tools at their disposal as private citizens to stamp out public immorality themselves. They declared war on saloonkeepers and engaged in high-profile reform campaigns that brought public shame to city agencies. Guided by a persistent distrust of government organizations, the BSSV comprised one thread of a vast tapestry of private reform organizations that emerged in the late nineteenth century to clean up public agencies, professionalize government administration, and privatize some state functions. In 1881, the Charity Organization Society (COS) formed to challenge conventional forms of poverty relief, particularly the long-standing practice of providing shelter and alms at police station houses.[16] The COS, drawing on cultural evolutionary theories of survival, discouraged mendicancy through the promotion of industry, encouraged work in lieu of alms, and sought to "carry personal sympathy and advice into the houses of the poor" by conducting so-called friendly visits.[17] That same year, in response to rampant governmental corruption and the tenacity of political cronyism, reformers created the Civil Service Reform Association (CSRA) to dismantle long-standing patronage abuses.[18] In 1885, reformers formed yet another organization called the Reform League. This group focused on the fair administration of elections which the city's bosses had openly fixed for Democratic partisans since the 1870s. Historian James Crooks characterizes the Reform League's emergence as the "beginning of a sustained reform effort in Baltimore."[19]

These organizations moved in the spirit of urban reform that characterized the late nineteenth century. As cities gradually became the epicenters of American life, reformers contended with entrenched systems of political corruption that thrived off the distended, slapdash, and bloated organization of local government in the Gilded Age. And while several ideologies clashed in the creation and execution of reform coalitions, they overwhelmingly represented the interests of a group of wealthy, prudish, and highly educated citizens.[20] In Baltimore, what bound together the BSSV, the COS, the CSRA, the Reform League, and countless other national and local urban reform groups was the leadership of one man: Charles Bonaparte.

Charles's grandfather was Jérôme Bonaparte, Napoleon's youngest brother. In 1803, Jérôme met and married Elizabeth Patterson, daughter of the wealthy

50 · CHAPTER 2

merchant William Patterson, in Baltimore. The two had one son, Jérôme Napoléon Bonaparte, in 1805. After Napoleon forced Jérôme to abandon the marriage, Elizabeth returned to Baltimore where she raised her son alone. The young Jérôme and his wife gave birth to Charles on June 9, 1851. Bonaparte received his law degree from Harvard University in 1874. Afterward, he settled in his native Baltimore and began his law practice. Given the immense wealth he had inherited, Bonaparte did not actively pursue clients and, as a result, had more time than most to focus on volunteer reform efforts. A devout Catholic, Bonaparte considered the selection, duties, and comportment of public officials a moral question. Reflecting on local politics, Bonaparte believed that political bossism, election fraud, patronage, and morally reprehensible activities like gambling and prostitution were linked in a broad network of spiritual corruption. Amoral saloonkeepers and brothel owners sowed discord and coordinated fraud in voting precincts at the behest of ward bosses who worked in the service of political machines. To tackle such corruption, Bonaparte spearheaded a multifront campaign that targeted public morality, civil service, elections, and policing.[21]

Regarding police, the BSSV, of which Bonaparte was vice president, adopted a vigilante mode of regulation. They watched the watchers. Such an approach made private citizens into law enforcers, revealed the permeability of public and private state functions, and allowed the BSSV to expose the inutility of the cops. For one BSSV member, "it is a sad commentary on our police force that it is necessary to have a Society for the Suppression of Vice. The police is such a society, or should be, and I verily believe that if the men who are on that force were properly instructed in their duty, they would bring many to justice who now go free."[22] The BSSV's goal in exposing the ineffectiveness of law enforcement was not to undercut the police's capacity to punish crime but to support the expansion of police power into the dogged regulation of public morality. Indeed, while reformers despised machines and political corruption, they nonetheless revered—and eventually copied—the comprehensive organizational systems that such groups employed to activate citizens at the grassroots level.[23]

The BSSV began to develop such grassroots organizational systems in their war against saloons. In the spring of 1888, the BSSV organized a protest of 1,500 people at Saint Vincent's Catholic Church. The protesters denounced the prevalence of saloons a few blocks south of the church. According to one reverend, "there are . . . ten or twelve dives in the vicinity of the church. They are dens of iniquity, and crimes of every description are committed in them. They are . . . located on the main artery of the city, and are a standing disgrace. They cause property to depreciate in value."[24] This latter charge typified anti-vice lobbying and became the battle cry for segregationists over the next several decades. Two

"Silk Stocking Aristocracy" • 51

weeks after the public demonstration, the BSSV parlayed the momentum of their first major action into another public meeting where Summerfield Baldwin, longtime BSSV president, reaffirmed his dedication to destroying the dens of vice in the city, noting, "If the present laws are defective in that respect it would be the aim of the society to have the defects remedied, and protect the homes of Baltimore from being demoralized and debauched."[25]

To capture the extent of moral turpitude's effects on property and the police's negligence, John C. Rose, BSSV secretary, coordinated a citywide canvas to index the number of "objectionable places" and their locations. Rose revealed his findings at the BSSV's annual meeting. According to the secretary, in 1888, Baltimore had 2,903 so-called objectionable places. This number represented "ordinary" and "low" saloons, places that sold liquor on Sundays, bawdy houses, and gambling dens. Not surprisingly, downtown sported the highest density of such establishments which furthered the reformers' urgency. To protect the city's property interests, the police would have to regulate public morals.[26] Tellingly, the police would develop internal saloon censuses in subsequent decades that mimicked Rose's surveys. The police's adoption of this tool spoke to the permeable boundaries among public and private bodies in the development of policing strategies during the late nineteenth century.

In succeeding years, the anti-saloon movement adopted several strategies to stem the tide of places of ill repute. One strategy involved recruiting citizens to help them identify troublesome and well-hidden saloons. This type of deputization was a pervasive tactic that would help round out police power's functions (and functionaries). The BSSV frequently took out newspaper advertisements offering to assist Baltimoreans protesting the licensing or relicensing of saloons in their neighborhoods.[27] They, along with their compatriots, showed up to Liquor Board hearings in force—often packing boardrooms—to push through license revocations.[28] In April 1895, J. R. Slattery, a Catholic missionary, petitioned the BSSV to burn the liquor license of a saloon in the heart of Black West Baltimore. Slattery wrote Bonaparte that the police had raided the establishment and arrested almost two dozen Black men for shooting craps, that robberies and other crimes occurred there frequently, and that the marshal did not provide evidence collected during raids to the Liquor License Commission at the saloon's most recent hearing.[29] The last complaint became common, and reformers quickly realized that they could not rely on police officers to furnish appropriate evidence to shut down objectionable urban hangouts. They would have to do so themselves.

Additionally, the BSSV lobbied for policy reforms and advocated harsher legislative punishments for saloonkeepers. In 1893, the group urged the Supreme

52 · CHAPTER 2

Bench, the city's trial judges,[30] to alter their procedures for disposing of saloon cases. Standard practice dictated that saloonkeepers be tried before a grand jury *only* if they failed to pay their fines—fines that many could pay.[31] Punishment became transactional, and fines were just the cost of doing business. John C. Rose, who regarded saloonkeepers as the paramount bad actors in the city, believed they should be "dealt with along with all other sorts of criminals in the ordinary course of business of the courts."[32] This view represented reformers' broader investments in enforcing the public morals and expanding the bounds of police power. Instead of fines, imprisonment should regulate the saloonkeeper—a smalltime working-class business owner, often an immigrant, whose establishments besmirched the precious city that wealthy pedigreed citizens wished to clean up. He did not belong in his saloon—he belonged in the city jail.

Complementing legislative advocacy, the BSSV and similar organizations regularly developed and coordinated their own investigations to publicize vice and demonstrate that police were either incompetent, corrupt, or both. Reform organizations commonly relied on covert agents and private detectives to investigate homes and businesses when police refused or proved useless. In doing so, they assumed quasi-governmental roles. According to historian Jennifer Fronc, through use of organized undercover investigation, private groups had "made themselves part of the state by World War I."[33] Use of private detectives in major cities ballooned after the Civil War. While agents were usually able to blend in and maintain their cover, they often relied on their autonomy to double-cross their employers, furnish false testimony, or engage in the very extortionist practices that they were hired to investigate.[34]

The BSSV constituted one of several reform groups that emerged during the late nineteenth century to exert the collective will of a resourceful and influential class of private citizens. Led by the likes of Charles J. Bonaparte, Baltimore's reformer class participated in national reform movements aimed at orienting local government toward the disciplining of working-class and poor people. Historian Michael McGerr notes that late nineteenth-century Progressives considered themselves "the police of the world." Baltimore's reformers fell into this camp which sought to diminish individual agency among the wanting masses through the institution of coercive forms of state power.[35] They did so through private campaigns that expanded the umbrella of policing and through civic engagements directed at the suppression of the city's underground economy. By establishing a broad network of prominent and efficacious reform groups, crusaders caught the attention of the city's political class, especially Republicans who yoked themselves to Progressive causes to challenge the supremacy of the Democratic machine. The Ring had run politics in the region for two decades.

"Silk Stocking Aristocracy" • 53

While urban reform and bureaucratic professionalization largely prized political neutrality, the only way for reformers to enact significant legislative and political restructurings in the regulation of patronage and election fraud was to destroy the machine. Practically, this goal could only be achieved through a total Republican sweep in the consequential 1895 state and local election that changed the nature of policing and race relations in Baltimore City forever.

"By Smashing the Machine": The Election of 1895

The 1895 election came on the heels of several national developments that shifted the balance of political power in the United States. The panic of 1893 rocked American industry and banking. Uncertainty around American gold reserves and the failure of several large businesses and trusts, including the Philadelphia and Reading Railroad, the National Cordage Company, and the New York, Lake Erie, and Western Railroad, spurred the depression that resulted in ballooning unemployment, credit freezes, factory closures, and the dissolution of fifteen thousand businesses and six hundred banks.[36] The depression hit cities, the epicenters of American industrial labor, particularly hard. While national politics skewed Republican, local governments in many major cities tended to skew Democratic. The economic dispossession caused by the panic of 1893 opened a potential avenue for Republican victories in solidly Democratic cities. This possibility dovetailed with the work of reform groups who, though often nonpartisan, wished to oust machines from local government. Republican control would allow reformers to attack, dismantle, and hopefully, destroy bossism. Luckily, Baltimore did not have to navigate this electoral terrain blindly. The city had a model in New York. In 1893, New York Republicans, with the help of reformers, seized the state legislature. Republican control allowed for the creation of the Lexow Committee which investigated, publicized, and attempted to reform police abuses.[37] Baltimore's reformers similarly wished to alter corrupted local agencies and thus resolved to turn the city red like their New York peers had done two years before. They adopted grassroots tactics, including publicizing election abuses, keeping a vigilant watch of election supervisors and police officers, and more generally, using the bosses' strategies against them.

Bosses maintained power throughout the city by establishing networks in the frenzied and ever-changing wards which constituted one branch of the bicameral city council. To challenge these networks, at a November 1894 meeting of the Union for Public Good, for which Charles Bonaparte served as president, the group resolved to coordinate the creation and development of Good Government Clubs (GGCs) in wards where Republican victory was possible. The

54 • CHAPTER 2

CSRA, another of Bonaparte's groups, resolved to aid these efforts.[38] The idea of GGCs developed in New York. There, citizens established a collective of non-partisan district-based groups that actively sought the fair administration of elections.[39] Bonaparte drafted a constitution and bylaws for Baltimore's GGCs and passed them to Roger Cull who began identifying winnable wards with active citizens.[40] The constitution represented Bonaparte's broader multi-issue approach to urban reform. While most municipal reform movements around the country contained several complementary groups focused singularly on discrete issues,[41] Bonaparte did not separate one from the other. As such, the GGC constitution resolved to promote honest elections, protect public morals, ensure the punishment of crime, and secure the dismissals of corrupt officials.[42] While such lofty goals were impossible for one ward-based organization, they nonetheless crystallized Bonaparte's influence on the direction, investments, and ideologies of Baltimore's reformer class. By March 1895, the Reform League had cobbled together six GGCs in the city's twenty-four wards. Most were concentrated downtown. In May, Bonaparte directed Joseph Packard, the Reform League's board president, to organize the GGCs into a cohesive federation.[43]

As the GGCs took shape, the Reform League planned a mass meeting to rouse voters. With the election looming, the league needed to activate the public. While the Republican Party had Lloyd Lowndes and Alcaeus Hooper, candidates for governor and mayor, respectively, to speak at the meeting, they wished to attract more established speakers. Bonaparte and Rose both viewed Lowndes as a rather uninspiring gubernatorial nominee. To ensure the meeting's success, Bonaparte called in a massive favor to his counterpart in New York, Theodore Roosevelt.

In 1895, Roosevelt had begrudgingly left his post in the U.S. Civil Service Commission to accept an appointment as New York's police board president.[44] He took the job a year after the Lexow Committee began investigating and publicizing police abuses and ousting several high-ranking New York cops.[45] A rising star, Roosevelt had spent much of his political life up to that point fighting the Tammany Hall bosses.[46] Now a police commissioner, he sought to eliminate "delinquent coppers" and lessen Tammany Hall's grip on the police. Bonaparte learned a great deal from these experiences, especially as he contended with police obstruction at polling precincts in his own city.[47] In his invitation, Bonaparte asked Roosevelt to address police corruption and to eviscerate Arthur Pue Gorman during the meeting. Roosevelt agreed. News of his participation incensed voters who evidently stormed Republican enclaves in the city and threatened to "vote against any candidate who stood on the platform beside so straight-laced and bigoted a puritan" as Roosevelt.[48] These outbursts played into the Reform

"Silk Stocking Aristocracy" • 55

League's hands. Their platform sought to attract prohibitionists and faith-based organizations, who also desired expanded policing authority in the realm of liquor and morals enforcement.[49] In the same instant, the Reform League openly derided the largely immigrant saloonkeepers, brothel owners, and gamblers who formed the Democratic machine's base. The exertion of control over newly arrived working-class and poor European immigrants compounded desires for discretionary policing as cops targeted immigrant-controlled saloons and other establishments.

The reformers' political rally took place on October 15, 1895. The *Baltimore American* characterized it as the largest political meeting in Baltimore's history. Gubernatorial hopeful Lloyd Lowndes took the stage and delivered a speech that Bonaparte may as well have written. He echoed the reform platform and detailed plans for alterations in voter registration procedures, the elimination of the spoils system through the institution of merit-based selection criteria for public officials, and more rigorous examinations for police officers. These bureaucratic changes would create the systems of accountability that reformers saw as necessary to expand efficiency in policing. After Lowndes left the stage, Roosevelt stepped onto it to a deafening ovation. The crowd hooped and hollered for several minutes. On the question of police, Roosevelt noted New York's own issues with corruption.

He asserted the police's duty to secure honest elections.

An audience member bellowed, "You can't get that here!"

He asserted the police's responsibility to arrest repeat voters and intimidators at the polls.

Another audience member shouted, "The police are not built that way in Baltimore."[50]

He assured the deeply distrusting crowd that, although New York also dealt with police corruption, they had managed to right the ship—a dubious claim, if not an outright lie. Even though Roosevelt attempted to institute merit-based systems of appointment, Tammany Hall maintained its grip over the New York Police Department during and after his tenure.[51] Roosevelt attacked boss Gorman for obstructing the funding for naval ships because the senator had designs to secure the military contracts for his friends. The crowd hissed in disapproval. Roosevelt ended his remarks by proclaiming that all eyes were set on Maryland. The state had a chance to set a national example by ousting the bosses that hamstrung democracy. The crowd gave him another thunderous ovation.[52] Roosevelt's remark on Maryland's centrality represented the state and city's larger relationship to the country. Since the end of Reconstruction, Maryland voted solidly Democratic with the rest of the Southern states. Its largest city

56 · CHAPTER 2

was a Democratic stronghold. Its defection from its Southern cohorts could prove valuable on the national stage.

After the rousing success of the meeting, the Reform League turned to more practical matters. With the public firmly on its side, if the league could ensure a modicum of fairness at the polls, they could help the Republicans sweep the election and destroy the machine. To that end, Rose began working up a list of election officers to protest.[53] He consulted city directories to confirm residency requirements, he conferred with ward residents to dig up dirt on corrupt practices in previous elections, and he consulted the state laws governing election officials to justify his petitions. In October, Rose began spamming the Board of Election Supervisors with protests. In one protest, he implored the board to dismiss a judge who had managed to flip a precinct by throwing out twenty "blurry" ballots.[54] In several petitions, Rose protested judges who had been known to keep beer and liquor in precincts.[55] In others, Rose protested judges because of their employment by city agencies, particularly a group of street scrapers.[56] Rose's use of research and his mastery of civic processes again emblematized how private citizen organizing formed a crucial element of statecraft as reformers tipped the scales of corruption in public agencies. While these petitions struck at the heart of the matter—the smaller abuses that cumulatively constituted systematized corruption—none were particularly scandalous or newsworthy. To cause a stir, Bonaparte orchestrated a massive controversy that animated public discussion for several days leading to the election.

In early October, Roger Cull caught wind of a Democratic conspiracy to commit election fraud. William Jubb, a Black man, owned and operated a saloon in South Baltimore. The saloon sat a block from Hollins Market and two blocks from a massive industrial depot. Evidently, an unnamed and unidentified man witnessed a curiosity at Jubb's saloon. Several Black men—later identified as members of the Meadow Gang—entered Jubb's establishment. A white man, who was later fingered as John F. Ahern, a clerk who kept guard of the voter registration books at the Superior Court, met the gang members on the second floor of the saloon. Ahern allegedly gave each man a card with the name of a registered Black Republican. The men committed each name to memory and went to the precincts in which the voters were registered. They falsely represented themselves to the election judges as the registered Republican and asked that they be reregistered at a precinct on the other side of town in hostile neighborhoods. After the judges entered these changes, Ahern recorded them in the registration books.[57] While this story, if true, constituted a gross election abuse, it was transparently ludicrous. There were no witnesses who could credibly attest that Ahern, a high-ranking clerk who had access to the voter registration books, participated in this conspiracy. And the Reform League knew it.

"Silk Stocking Aristocracy" • 57

However, the league also knew that such abuses *did* happen, even if this one may not have. Given the difficulty of proving such activity, they opted to target Ahern and publicize the practice. In letters to Cull and Packard, Bonaparte ordered his on-the-ground envoys to have Ahern arrested. Given the election's proximity, Bonaparte felt that mass meetings and confrontational editorials had lost their fervor. To truly discredit the Ring—and shock voters—the public needed to witness a more severe action. Ahern's arrest, and the spotlight on the Ring's use of Black men in coordinating fraud, would make any potential legal consequences worthwhile. Bonaparte expected Ahern to post bail and never reach trial. In such an instance, Ahern would have recourse to file a convincing suit for malicious prosecution. Bonaparte did not care. He simply sought the sensation of the "mere fact of his arrest" and the Ring's implication in the scandal.[58]

On October 30, the criminal court issued a bench warrant for Ahern's arrest. The court also issued warrants for William Jubb, the saloonkeeper, and Bob Davis, the leader of the Meadow Gang. The police arrested all three that day. As Bonaparte expected, they posted bail, and the grand jury tossed their cases.[59] It did not matter, though. The stir revealed a malicious and contemptible election practice. The editors of the *Sun* eviscerated the Ring for employing so-called "crooked n——rs" to help them fix elections. These "sable henchman" operated local boozing and gambling haunts. They received protection from Democratic ward bosses in exchange for help on Election Day. They packed pistols and staged violent skirmishes at the polls to scare away voters. For the *Sun*, the white voting public should be "disgusted" by the Ring for providing legal cover for smalltime Black criminals.[60] Although Bonaparte, given his relatively positive relationships with Black Baltimoreans, did not likely intend for such vicious and racially condemnatory discourses to emerge from the Ahern debacle, he gladly took the anti-machine press that came with it.

Now with the election upon the city—and the Ring firmly on its back foot—the integrity of the election came into question. Under the gun, Marshal Jacob Frey promised a quiet and orderly election. After Cull organized his army of watchers, rumors began circulating that the cops would obstruct their ability to patrol the polls. Marshal Frey denied the allegations and noted that the police simply wished to ensure that the watchers did not clog up the precincts.[61] The Reform League remained vigilant and organized to stamp out abuses. In the days leading to the election, several hundred repeaters were "cooped" in saloons and lodging houses. These poor men came via train from surrounding cities, including Philadelphia, Wilmington, Norfolk, York, and Hanover. They slept on pool tables, in rolls of carpet, and on street corners. In exchange for cash and booze, they stormed embattled precincts to cast votes for Ring candidates.

58 · CHAPTER 2

The *Sun* speculated that the unprecedented volume of repeaters meant that the Democratic machine knew their days were numbered. The Reform League and its agents had shadowed the Ring's recruiters and tracked the repeaters' arrivals. On Election Day, the league instructed watchers to have repeaters arrested. Several Reform League lawyers waited at station houses to prosecute each case.[62] The Reform League kept to its word and had 291 people arrested for election-related crimes. In comparison, during the last major election, the police arrested a whopping zero people for election-related crimes.[63]

Counter to the marshal's promise, the election was not very quiet. Ring toughs, "or heelers," intimidated, beat, and shot several men, including Black voters and Reform League watchers. In one instance, a heeler whipped a Black voter in the back of the head with a belt. A group of white men descended on the man and kicked and punched him. In another case, a group of Black men arrived at a precinct to vote. A white crowd surrounded them. From out of the crowd, a gunshot pierced a Black voter's leg. The Black men fled with the white heelers in tow as they fired errant shots into the air. Leigh Bonsal, a Reform League watcher, enlisted the help of police to provide protection to Black voters who had been beaten or scared away from the polls. In one instance, a Black voter had been so traumatized that he refused the protection and opted to remain home.[64] Despite all this chaos, Marshal Frey held firm that the election had been peaceful.[65]

The Reform League's collective will, organizing, and resources paid off. Under the cunning leadership of Bonaparte, the unshakeable resolve of Cull, and the meticulous legal acumen of Rose, the Republican Party swept the election. They won the governorship, the mayoralty, and twenty-five of the thirty-three contested city council seats.[66] They rode this momentum into 1896 when William McKinley became the first Republican presidential candidate to win Maryland since Abraham Lincoln in 1864. Following the win, the Reform League's leadership, after several confrontations, turned its attention fully to the police. Cull found their comportment during the election reprehensible. He accused patrolmen of obstructing watchers from following repeaters at the polls. He attacked the police board for instructing cops to hinder watchers.[67]

For Bonaparte, the police board's inability to discipline the cops and control the rank and file made the agency both ineffective and menacing to the ideals of good government. After the resounding success of the election, Bonaparte reached out to Roosevelt. He let him know that the election, though a success, revealed persistent and troubling trends among the Baltimore police. He wrote, "Our Reform League watchers did excellent service; six or eight of them were assaulted, several pretty badly beaten, and one quite seriously injured. The

Police behaved very uncertainly, indicating that there was division or hesitancy among their superiors as to what they had better do."[68]

Like Roosevelt, who was overseeing the restructuring of the New York police following the Lexow Committee report, Bonaparte wished to systematically investigate and restructure the Baltimore police. As one of the clearest and most well-positioned agencies to enforce the dictates of the centralized and efficient state that reformers wished to see, the police force became a crucial site of alteration. Much like the BSSV desired that their existence become obsolete once police took seriously their vision of morals enforcement, Bonaparte and his reformers modeled idealized deployments of state power through private civic engagement and surveillance while simultaneously prodding the recalcitrant police force to satisfy those functions. To push the police further down this path, Bonaparte and his reformers parlayed their electoral victory into a comprehensive investigation of local policing. If the marshal believed that he had conducted an orderly election, perhaps it was high time to remove him from his post. To do so, the Reform League conducted an inquiry into the seedy corruption of urban gambling.

The Policy Wheel: The Politics of Police Reform

Late nineteenth-century police officers, if they had the protection of the political establishment, wielded power with little accountability. Lexow revealed that police in Tammany's stable received large sums of protection money, clubbed and beat the people they were meant to protect with no consequences, and participated in the scams of budding criminal networks. Police around the country adopted regulatory styles that emphasized quarantining, rather than eradicating, vice like sex work, drug use, and gambling. In the process, police collected protection money in exchange for cooperation. The magnitude of vice in late nineteenth-century cities was so extensive that eliminating it was a fool's errand. According to historian Robert M. Fogelson, "Contrary to the conventional wisdom, the police did not suppress vice; they licensed it."[69] In Baltimore, after the election of 1895, the Reform League could have chosen practically any illegal commercial vice to investigate. Given the overlap between election defrauders and gamblers, the league turned to the latter to justify their planned shakeup of the police department.

Policy was a simple and addictive game. Sometimes called "numbers," policy was named as such because of its similarity to risky insurance policies.[70] The game worked like a contemporary lottery. Players bet on "draws" by guessing combinations of numbers and writing them on a slip. Policy men collected the

60 • CHAPTER 2

slips and then drew a series of numbered balls from a wheel. Players got paid out if they guessed the numbers correctly. Policy men organized gambling in saloons, brothels, and other "dens of vice." On June 8, 1897, the *Sun* published a bombshell story that implicated the Baltimore police in providing protection to the city's policy men. Based on a report developed by the Reform League with assistance from the BSSV, the account outlined, in painstaking detail, how downtown police hid or doctored evidence to protect gamblers. Roger Cull, the report's primary author, framed the incident to both implicate the police in corruption and reveal what he and his collaborators considered the gross incompetence of the police's high-ranking officials.[71]

Cull's investigation proceeded as such: He employed and supervised four undercover agents, two white and two Black. The agents played policy in establishments widely known on the streets as "policy headquarters" where bookies conducted draws. The locations of these headquarters were particularly damning because they rested mere blocks from the Central District police station. The undercover agents played on a series of draws and kept their slips as evidence. By Cull's estimation, entering the policy headquarters was a piece of cake and "the police are either absolutely incompetent to deal with the crime or . . . their arrests are not made in good faith." The evidence Cull provided indicated the veracity of both charges. Cull's report detailed how the police often conducted "fake raids" which he described as "a raid on a number of policy men, generally at headquarters, in which arrests are made not for the suppression of the crime, but to deceive the public into the belief that the police are doing their duty." Cull charged that police made arrests they knew would not lead to formal charges and that through arrangements with bail bondsmen, the clique of uniformed police and policy men ensured that fall guys never spent significant amounts of time in jail. Additionally, Cull noted that his private agents easily gathered evidence that led to a genuine raid that resulted in the arrests of fifteen men.[72]

After Cull's report went public, the police board adjudicated the matter (figure 6). Three commissioners made up the board. The commissioners included Republicans D. C. Heddinger and W. W. Johnson and Democrat E. M. Schryver.[73] The commissioners' party affiliations were relevant in this case as questions surrounding their political motives shrouded the scandal. Onlookers presumed that reformers were staging the hearing to oust police leadership. They were right, but the public may not have known that for sure. The Reform League brought charges on three cops: Central District captain J. J. Gilbert and sergeants Edward F. Meehan and James F. Smith. The police board formally charged each with dereliction of duty and scheduled them for a hearing.[74]

During the first day of the hearing, Cull, a savvy lawyer, questioned the officers. He contextualized the emergence of his investigation by noting that during

"Silk Stocking Aristocracy" • 61

the 1895 election, the Reform League found that the same men posting bail for those charged with election infractions were posting bail for those charged with policy infractions. The seeming connection between election defrauders and policy men proved the organized and nefarious business of political, economic, and spiritual corruption that the Reform League and the BSSV sought to stamp out. Cull spent considerable time questioning the officers on the nature of fake raids and departmental policy regarding evidence. A fake raid at 102 North Frederick Street seemed particularly suspicious. Before patrolmen entered the policy den, they loudly struck the wooden boards covering the windows with axes. The noise tipped off the men inside, most of whom escaped out of another entrance. As if this blatant warning were not damning enough, the police

Figure 6. The Reform League compelled the police board to conduct a hearing on police negligence in the regulation of downtown gambling. Chief among the Reform League's concerns was the disposal of evidence. The police countered by reviewing policy cases in which sufficient evidence was supplied yet convictions were not made. Source: "Closing Scenes of the Police Investigation," *Baltimore American*, June 30, 1897.

62 · CHAPTER 2

failed to provide evidence from the crime scene to have the stragglers in the raid convicted.[75]

Cull noted that convicting someone for gambling required little effort. If police found someone in possession of a policy slip, they could easily have them imprisoned. Despite access to such paraphernalia, officers routinely failed to produce any evidence and allowed policy men to walk free. This failure to produce evidence became a point of contention among the officers. Captain Gilbert testified that before the Frederick Street raid, it was not departmental custom to produce paraphernalia before a grand jury. The captain further attested that because of the outcome of the raid, Marshal Frey issued a special order to require that police produce paraphernalia before grand juries. This testimony raised some eyebrows as there was no documentation to back up Gilbert's claims. The convoluted testimony—and the invocation of Frey's name—allowed the police board to summon the marshal, the Reform League's true target.[76]

Once on the stand, Marshal Frey noted that departmental procedure ordered that police supply evidence to grand juries when available and desired. Frey also noted that he had given the order to produce paraphernalia "a long time ago" and that Gilbert's ignorance on this front could be attributed to his relatively recent assumption of Central District command. The first day of the hearing ended with more questions than answers, and the trial dragged on for several days as the public watched with rapt attention as the Reform League exposed the extravagant corruption of the police force.[77]

Following adjournment after one of these long days, a reporter from the *Sun* approached William Colton, the officers' lawyer, for an interview. Colton assured the reporter that when the officers finally took the stand, they would be exonerated. Consequentially, the *Sun* quoted Colton who believed that the Reform League had forced a public hearing to "create widespread distrust in the uniformed police." He also believed that the Reform League had staged the trial to remove Frey and to "gratify private ends and accomplish personal results."[78] Incensed by Colton's comments, Commissioner Heddinger began the next hearing by haranguing the attorney. He accused Colton of impugning the integrity of the police board while prejudging—and encouraging the public to prejudge—the outcome of the case before the board heard all the evidence. Recent history was on Colton's side. Charles Bonaparte and his ring of reformers left no stone unturned and stoked public controversy to accomplish their ends. They also *did* want Frey gone.

After the tumult, Colton built the indicted officers' cases by calling on character witnesses and the officers themselves. He called on business owners who operated near known policy headquarters. They all testified that the officers

"Silk Stocking Aristocracy" • 63

hung around and entered the policy headquarters frequently. Major Douglas H. Thomas, president of the Merchant's National Bank and a firm supporter of the police, commended the officers' work and accused the Reform League of using policy to realize their political aspirations which included taking control of "the city, the state, the police board, and everything." Again, Thomas's charges were not entirely untrue. Central District officers then praised Captain Gilbert and the two other indicted officers.[79]

The police board levied its verdict on July 12, about two weeks after the trial's close. All three indicted officers were found guilty. The police board dismissed Gilbert and Meehan and transferred Smith to night duty. The police board considered the scandal so serious that in addition to dismissing these officers, they dismissed Marshal Frey. Even though not a defendant, the police board reasoned that, as marshal, Frey bore the ultimate responsibility for the executive administration of the police force. His failure to keep policy under control justified his dismissal.

These removals validated Colton's suspicions of foul play. The Reform League would not blush, though. After the 1895 election, they wanted Marshal Frey gone. Deputy Marshal Farnan ascended to the rank of marshal. In Heddinger's official decision, the police board president noted that policy menaced a key area, "a district representing at least seventy percent of the wealth of our city," and that Frey's failure to crack down on it meant that the marshal had no sense of policy's penchant to debase poor people and threaten children and property. Commissioner Johnson backed Heddinger and provided a fierier condemnation of the police by exalting the Reform League and the BSSV's good work. In his statement, Johnson affirmed that he believed that certain policy-related arrests were fake, that Central District police knew that policy headquarters existed and did nothing about it, that the conviction rate of policy arrests was suspiciously low, and that officers provided weak testimony and insufficient evidence to grand juries on policy-related cases. Johnson concluded, "The responsibility for this state of things, the evidence shows, rests solely on the police, and there is no escape from the conclusion that the central police authorities have been either unwilling or incompetent to deal with crime." Bernard Carter, counsel to the police board, resigned after seven years of service, citing the disreputable actions of Republican commissioners Johnson and Heddinger. He regarded Marshal Frey's removal as blatantly political. Captain Gilbert also questioned the police board's motives on his way out, noting that, had he greased the right wheels, he would still be on the force. Sergeant Meehan was less coy in his assessment of the trial, noting plainly, "I was dismissed because I was a Democrat."[80]

64 · CHAPTER 2

The Reform League's victory in the policy trial represented the immense power that private reformers wielded over municipal affairs. Their desire to remove the marshal from his post was an open secret that stemmed back to their public clashes during the 1895 election. While Democrats balked at the transparent scheme, reformers had won favor with the public, particularly when it came to restructuring the police department. The public perceived the cops as corrupt, inefficient, and incompetent. At the same time, reformers viewed the police as a crucial public agency whose centrality in organizing the chaos of urban life could not be overstated. While police power thrived on discretion, the present police department had perhaps revealed discretion's limits. As the 1899 election loomed and the Democrats strategized how to regain control over local and state politics, the regulation of Black crime became the keystone to the Democratic Party's strategy to resume political control in Baltimore City.

"Negro Rowdyism": The Racial Politics of Crime

As city leaders continued to jockey for control over the police force, the role of African Americans in political and civic life dominated national, state, and local politics. In Baltimore, Black leaders made political headway by securing elected office. In 1890, Harry S. Cummings became Baltimore's first Black elected official by securing a city council seat. During the 1895 election, J. M. Cargill won a city council seat in the eleventh ward.[81] Black Baltimoreans fought for civil rights through the organization of groups such as the Mutual United Brotherhood of Liberty, one of the first Black civil rights groups in the country, which operated between 1885 and 1891.[82] While Black people organized to realize political and social progress locally and nationally, white supremacists sought desperately to curtail this progress. In 1896, the Supreme Court passed its infamous *Plessy v. Ferguson* ruling, which upheld the constitutionality of racial segregation in public accommodations on a "separate but (un)equal" basis. This doctrine subsequently guided several crusades to regulate and disenfranchise Black Baltimoreans, including one that Charles Bonaparte played a key role in combatting.[83] Additionally, because of Black support for the city's Republican Party, Democrats, reeling from internal division, politicized Black crime to discredit their Republican opponents. In 1898, the term "Negro rowdyism" entered local political discourse to characterize Republicans as soft on crime. Democrats charged that Republican permissiveness emboldened Black city residents to commit all manner of public order and violent offenses.[84] With a new city charter and a wide-open political landscape, the racially encoded charge of "law and order" dominated city politics as Republicans and Democrats struggled for power at the turn of the century.[85]

In 1900, Baltimore's revised city charter went into effect. The charter, like many of its time, adopted a home rule ethos that vested more control in local government. The charter sought to weed out graft and address bureaucratic confusion that stemmed from the overlapping and competing jurisdictions of city and state agencies in areas such as public school administration, municipal elections, and the oversight of indigent populations. The charter did so by providing more power to the mayor. Under the new charter, mayoral term limits doubled, the percentage of votes required to override a veto increased, a five-person board of estimates wrested significant budgetary power in the mayor and his appointees, and city department heads and school commissioners became mayoral appointees.[86]

While the charter more clearly defined the relationship between the state and local government by centralizing power in the mayor's office, in his 1900 annual address, Thomas G. Hayes, a Democrat who became the first mayor to operate under the new charter, bemoaned the state's decision to maintain control of the police board.[87] Hayes felt that the arrangement had overrun its usefulness, removed the police board's accountability to Baltimore's citizenry, and stymied policing efforts that could more uniquely address Baltimore's problems.[88] During the 1900 legislative session, Hayes made the trip to Annapolis to voice his support for the inclusion of the mayor as an ex officio member of the police board. Under this proposal, the mayor's vote would be limited to financial decisions.[89] It ultimately went nowhere but represented the spirit of municipal reform which sought to bolster the autonomy and power of local government.[90]

Notably, Hayes—an aspirant political boss who rebuked the Ring's influence—served on the charter commission. During his mayoral bid, supporters applauded his anti-Black law and order pronouncements. One commenter approved Hayes's law enforcement aggressiveness and believed he would stamp out the current "Negro rowdyism" that had supposedly overtaken the city.[91] The election itself served as a symbolic backlash against the reformer class and the Republican administrations they had installed. According to historian Frank Richardson, the election of more Black Republican city council members during and after the 1895 election "disgusted the public."[92] Hayes and the Democrats fed on this disgust. Hayes charged that Black Baltimoreans possessed poor moral and mental education.[93] At the state level, John W. Smith, during his gubernatorial campaign, echoed this point in a Democratic primary debate on the "race issue" in Maryland. Smith downplayed the existence of racial inequality and

66 · CHAPTER 2

categorized racial anomie as an issue of law and order. "The Democratic Party ... proposes to put a stop to disorder, rowdyism, and crime. If that constitutes a race issue, then so be it."[94] Despite the city-state conflict over police control, one thing was certain: criminality in the expanding city had become affixed to the figure of the Black urban dweller, and city and state officials alike sought to reel in this supposed rowdyism through tough law and order policies and other measures aimed at curtailing the civic freedoms of Black people. As such, when reformers mounted another attack against the police board, Democrats came equipped with plenty of faulty, though persuasive, data to combat their accusations and stoke racial antagonisms.

After losing political ground during the election of 1899 in which Democrats resumed power of the mayoralty and governorship, reformers continued publicizing police corruption in a never-ending fight in the court of public opinion. In 1901, the *Baltimore Herald* published a front-page story titled "How the Police Are Helping the Machine." The story alleged that patrolmen, following Ring orders, were "arresting colored men upon the slightest provocation and very frequently without cause." Reformers charged that most of these spurious arrests occurred in districts with significant Black voting populations during voter registration.[95] This strategy coincided with broader disenfranchisement campaigns that typified Jim Crow. As legal challenges rooted in appeals to the Fifteenth Amendment made wholesale disenfranchisement legislation an unsure avenue for white governing bodies, new strategies emerged. These approaches included race-neutral laws that could pass Fifteenth Amendment challenges, including literacy tests.[96] Additionally, states and localities, like Baltimore, used discretionary policing to keep Black men from the ballot box.[97] To combat Republican charges of corruption, Democrats refocused the conversation to centralize the identities of the arrestees.

On October 28, 1901, Alonzo J. Miles, counsel to the police board, delivered an impassioned address before a packed audience at Hollins Hall. The *Sun* detailed the event and Miles's remarks in an exhaustive front-page story. At the mass meeting, Democrats dug their heels in on the subject of "Negro rowdyism." John Prentiss Poe, an attorney and Democratic loyalist who would later draft and fight for the passage of a Black disenfranchisement measure in 1905, said, "We must rise to the height of the occasion and resolve that the government of the state must remain in the hands of the white men of the state."[98] As such, the police and the legislature were engaged not in corruption but in a much needed reform to a corrupted system of voting that allowed a retrograde and socially injurious practice: Black suffrage.[99] The cops were not goons towing the line for

"Silk Stocking Aristocracy" • 67

white supremacists, they were the *real* reformers who would abet Democrats in forestalling "Negro rule."

Police counsel Miles organized his public comments at the mass meeting in Hollins Hall around the need to maintain Democratic control to guarantee police efficiency and public safety. He did so by extolling the virtues of the Democratic police board and criticized the supposedly alarming criminality that flourished under Republican leadership. For Miles, the current police board inherited a panoply of human degradation masquerading as a city. Booze corrupted innocent white women, brothels and bed houses enticed fornicators and destroyed property values, young people commiserated in horrid interracial dance halls, drug use proliferated among Chinese, Black, and immigrant residents, and the new moving pictures washed over a population of impressionable dopes. The Ministerial Union, which helped found the BSSV and took umbrage with all such moral debauchery, thanked the Democratic police board for "its efforts to enforce the . . . laws touching the morality of the community." Reverend Charles E. Guthrie, pastor of Strawbridge Methodist Episcopal Church and BSSV member, provided measured praise noting that the police board had taken definite steps in eliminating slot machines—the most recent gambling calamity to overtake the city—and noted, "This is not saying that *everything* is as it should be. But it *is* saying that the conditions affecting general lawlessness are much better than they were prior to the advent of the present board."[100] While reformers had certainly lost significant political ground, their campaigns had forced Democrats to adopt more clearly defined morals-based policing strategies. For groups like the BSSV, which had incorporated solely to get the police to enforce public morals, these developments were in line with their expectations for how a city and its law enforcement apparatus should function.

While appealing to the moral character of the current police board undercut Republican claims of corruption, Miles's most forceful evidence came through a comprehensive statistical comparison of Black crime rates under Democratic and Republican police boards. For Miles, "Republican speakers and newspapers tell you that the talk of negro rowdyism by the Democrats is a bugaboo intended and designed to prejudice the white man against the negro for political purposes." However, based on the rates of Black arrest under Democratic and Republican leadership, two things became obvious. First, Black crime and its menace to good morals and property was real and not embellished by Democrats for brazen political purposes. Second, Republicans were far too permissive in stamping out the rising tide of Black crime that would undoubtedly culminate in ruinous outcomes for the city.[101]

68 · CHAPTER 2

To prove these theses, Miles juxtaposed arrest statistics under two governors: Democrat Frank Brown and Republican Lloyd Lowndes. He did so by isolating eight crimes and their rates among Black Baltimoreans: assault, indecent assault, burglary, disturbing the peace, larceny, murder, profanity, and throwing missiles. In a bizarre development that undermined his argument, when aggregated, the number of Black arrests for these eight offenses under Democratic leadership was 27,930. Under Republican leadership, the figure was 34,175, indicating that Republicans, in fact, criminalized and arrested Black people just as well, if not better, than Democrats. Miles spun these figures, however, by presenting the increase in Black arrests under Republican leadership as the emboldening of the Black criminal class. He argued that "the negroes of Baltimore city became so much more bold, defiant and impudent while their masters were in charge that negro rowdyism increased to such an extent that 17 more of them were arrested every day of the Republican administration than there were under the Democratic regime." He further evidenced this claim by relying on anecdotal accounts published by the *Sun* in which the paper condemned Black men, particularly the Black boys that the editors dubbed "Sporty N——s," for indiscriminately hurling insults at white women and making them feel terror at the prospect of walking alone in public.[102] Such charges coincided with Jim Crow–era charges of Black men assaulting, raping, and harassing innocent white women whose virtue became a priority among segregationists.

The *Baltimore Sun*, which carried water for Democrats in the city, amplified Miles and the police board's message regarding Black lawlessness in a doom-laden editorial titled "Shall the Negro Rule?" The concepts of "Negro rule" and "Negro domination" fomented and justified segregationist efforts in the South and echoed among Baltimore's citizenry, many of whom absorbed it with rapt attention.[103] The *Sun*'s position drew on broader discourses of Black unfitness for civil life that permeated public discussions and drew on the afterlife of slavery to validate narratives of uncontrollability.

Such discourses were not new in Baltimore or indeed the nation. During the late nineteenth century, essentialist renderings of the various "problems" posed by Black freedom codified in debates regarding the so-called Negro problem.[104] Locally, William Cabell Bruce, a lawyer, Democrat, and future U.S. senator, penned a racist screed titled "The Negro Problem." Published in 1891, Bruce's condemnation of Black Baltimoreans echoed national conversations while decrying supposed biological and cultural traits of inferiority that rendered Black people unfit for civil and political life. Regarding biology, Bruce contended that the physiognomy of Black Americans, including "the wooly hair, the receding forehead, the flat nose, the thick lips, and the protruding jaw" created an "inveterate aversion" among

"Silk Stocking Aristocracy" · 69

white Americans that justified a separation of the races.[105] Regarding culture, Bruce asserted that laziness and complacency explained why Black Americans showed "little tenacity" in attempting to throw off the fetters of slavery.[106] Furthermore, Bruce argued that enslavement protected civil society from the depravity of Black people who, once freed, defaulted to their inherent childish, licentious, and unbridled predilections.[107] Bruce relied on these unevidenced conjectures to explain why Southern states voted solidly Democratic. Such political rigidity was necessary to subtend the imminent threat of "Negro domination."[108] This dog whistle resonated with Marylanders whose fears of Black political power materialized in state control of city agencies and other measures intended to dilute Baltimore's influence on state government.

Bruce's pamphlet did not go unaddressed. The same year it was published, Harvey Johnson, a Black civil rights activist and pastor, published "The Question of Race." The pamphlet, a transcription of an address Johnson delivered before the Monumental Literary and Scientific Association, took aim at Bruce's fallacious biological analysis, ahistorical arguments, and polemic tone. Regarding biology, Johnson found Bruce's litany of physical differences among races rather useless, noting, "[Bruce] does not stop one minute to notice that the existence of these differences found in the races is not the same thing as proving superiority and inferiority of race."[109] Johnson further remarked that Bruce and other white supremacists tended to paint African climates as deadly and inhospitable to the constitution of white men. Following the logic of biological superiority, Johnson questioned whether this reality challenged social Darwinist ideas to which white racists subscribed to diminish the fitness of Black people. If white people could not handle the weather of the continent from which Black Americans descended, perhaps, by their logic, white people possessed inferior physical endurance. For Johnson, this example was as ludicrous as Bruce's examples. Biology was simply not worth considering when examining racial matters. Regarding history, Bruce contended that Black Americans were seemingly content with enslavement given their irresolution in combatting it. To this critique, Johnson pointed to Harriet Tubman's Underground Railroad, Nat Turner's 1831 rebellion, John Brown's enslaved compatriots at Harpers Ferry, and numerous slave revolts. While Johnson found Bruce's individual points of dispute to be comically unsourced, he equally recognized that the tone and resonance of Bruce's polemic writing would undoubtedly appeal to the racist presumptions of his audience. The facts were irrelevant. Despite the lack of evidence or even footnotes in Bruce's pamphlet, Johnson lamentably noted that Bruce would "be largely quoted as authority on the past, present, and probable future degradation of the colored race."[110] He was right.

70 · CHAPTER 2

Bruce and his fellow white supremacists found an agreeable audience in publics intent on embracing strategies to limit Black freedom. The rationale behind these strategies was much less important than their successful execution. A decade after "The Negro Problem" was published, Bruce's preposterous yet effective prescriptions reverberated as Democrats fell in line to regain control of local and state government. In 1901, the *Sun*'s editors heartily echoed Bruce's assessments, going so far as to claim that Black and white Americans "were closer together in the time of slavery" and that "a single generation of freedom [had] almost destroyed [Black people]."[111] The editors condemned Republican "demagogues" for advocating Black suffrage and for betraying "their white friends and neighbors to gain political reward." For the editors, Black people were incapable of exercising the freedoms associated with civil life because they were a "child race" that had to "be developed under the tutelage and control, both socially and politically, of the whites." The editors defended their claims through appeals to academic and empirical authority. The 1901 annual report of the American Academy of Political and Social Science claimed that whites *had* to control the social and political development of Black people, who were presumably incapable of doing so themselves. To facilitate this process, the *Sun*'s editors urged Black people to repair their sullied relationship in the city by fully withdrawing from politics. Such an action was imperative "if the negro race [was] to escape annihilation."[112] In the meantime, anti-Black discourses justified oppressive policing and disproportionate rates of arrest and incarceration for Black Baltimoreans as Democrats regained control of politics in the city and state.

Conclusion

Late nineteenth-century Progressive reformers created national networks and coalitional bodies that advocated for broader state oversight over diverse areas of social life, including alcohol consumption, gambling, sex work, and other pastimes in the informal economy. As city governments negotiated and adopted new charters that provided home rule and expanded police power, reformers organized groups that engaged in state-making practices, including civic protests and street-level investigations into working-class behaviors and pursuits. Reformers gained traction by exposing corruption among electoral and policing bodies that thrived on political corruption. Despite their successes in these arenas, Progressives recognized the twin hurdles of decades of graft and the limitations of private civic power. Without political power, reformers' private protests would only go so far. The city, however, was rife with coercive agencies, backed by the full power of the state, that could adopt efficient bureaucratic

"Silk Stocking Aristocracy" · 71

systems, ideals of political neutrality, and a morals-based ethos that aligned with their broader Progressive designs.

To this end, Baltimore's wealthy elites organized to wage war against the social impediments that corrupted urban government and the working classes. Led by the likes of Charles Bonaparte, John Rose, and Roger Cull, Progressive organizations cropped up by the dozen. Some notable and influential groups included the Society for the Suppression of Vice, the Reform League, the CSRA, GGC, and COS. Largely self-funded, these groups either modeled what bourgeois policing looked like or sought to move against the city's ingrained political machine to knock them off their perches and install Republican politicians who would advocate for structural changes to city and state agencies. Prohibitionists and faith-based organizations joined with secular Progressive groups and rode the red wave that overtook the country in the late nineteenth century. They successfully ousted Baltimore's political bosses and installed a Republican mayor and city council that, in turn, ousted police leadership and demonstrated the vast power that private reformers could exert over local government.

Not to be outdone, the Democrats furthered their own vision of policing by seizing on national discourses that sutured Blackness to crime. Although Democrats lost at the ballot box, the popularization of race-based criminal analyses of crime trends provided a means by which they could, to quote Khalil Muhammad, "write crime into race" and win back political ground.[113] Moral panic surrounding Black crime stoked New South ideologies regarding so-called Negro domination and Negro rule, while also complementing purportedly empirical studies of Black crime that relied on anecdotal and pseudoscientific methodologies. In Baltimore, these Jim Crow developments manifested in increasingly draconian treatments of Black men and women, who, beginning in the 1890s, began to fill the city jail at vastly disproportionate rates. These policing trends dovetailed with public discussions surrounding "Negro rowdyism," which Democrats used to discredit Republicans' ability to subdue Black Baltimoreans' supposed predilection toward crime.

Although reformers squandered their moment of political ascendancy in the city, they continued to organize around institutional change. One organization in particular, Baltimore's chapter of the COS, curried massive influence in local and national reform circles by furthering the discursive and academic diagnoses of so-called dependent populations, including foreign-born immigrants and Black people. This knowledge informed their approach to the administration of poverty relief and their broader investments in expanding the coercive potential of urban government. It is to this group that we now turn.

3

"With the Power of the Law"

The Carceral Dimensions of Charity, Social Science, and Public Schools

In an 1898 issue of the *Charities Record*, the Charity Organization Society (COS), one of Baltimore's major poverty relief organizations, captured the consequences of lax juvenile regulation in the figure of the "Glass-House Boy." This boy represented a generalized immigrant or child of immigrants who toiled under the grueling conditions of the city's white-hot bottle factories. These boys sacrificed their educations to "grind off" glass and collect "fire-money." Because of the demanding work and their proximity to grown men, all the boys learned was to curse, shoot craps, and drink.[1] To combat the moral declension of children embodied by the glass-house boy, the COS joined a chorus of reform groups who supported disciplinary measures to regulate—and criminalize—truancy. In doing so, they transformed the public school into a site of police power in which the paternal authority of the state grew to encompass the identification, detainment, and institutionalization of children.

In their discussions of truancy, the COS and other reformers drew a causal link between school absences and crime. For them, idle children proved dangerous and, left to their own devices, would undoubtedly engage in delinquent behavior. Missing from such prognoses was a consideration of the conditions that typified urban childhood and schooling. Although reformers had well-meaning aims to provide all children decent educations, given the nature of the late nineteenth-century labor market, children from working-class families did not, in many cases, have the luxury to sacrifice work for school.[2] Moreover, conditions in many public schools were such that the educational environment available to poor children was anything but decent. Regardless, the "child savers," to quote historian Anthony Platt, theorized, criminalized, and cracked down on truancy because of its presumed link to crime.[3] In this way, while they suspected that truancy caused crime, in advocating for its criminalization, they *made* truancy a crime and poor children criminals. This chain of identification, theorization, and action characterized the approach of upper-crust and middle-class reformers who crusaded to inculcate genteel values in immigrants and Black people while propagating pseudoscientific theories regarding their purported dangers to the fabric of civil life.

Chief among Baltimore's poverty relief organizations was the COS. Its pool of directors, volunteers, agents, and supporters were influential private citizens who held profound amounts of wealth.[4] Indeed, some of the COS's biggest annual donors included businessman Francis White, who gave $100, reformer Charles J. Bonaparte, who gave $150, Judge William A. Fischer, who gave $250, and Olympian and investment banker Robert S. Garrett, who gave $500. Other notable donors included the president of Johns Hopkins University, Daniel Coit Gilman, noted prison reformer G. S. Griffith, and Mayor James Hodges.[5] In 1887, the COS reported that 82 percent of its operating budget came from these donations, interest on investments made using donations, and funds raised at balls, fairs, and theatrical performances. The remaining 18 percent came from labor performed by those receiving charity and government subsidies.[6] Private citizens invested substantial amounts of money to create a society in their own image. Doing so demonstrated both the power of the city's burgeoning middle class and its desire to move beyond mere advocacy through meaningful exercises of state power.[7]

The COS's approach centralized intervention into the lives of the poor. Agents, typically middle-class volunteer white women, conducted "friendly visits" that allowed them to assess the needs of families while also modeling an aspirant white urbanity. The COS expressed its goals in its periodical, the *Charities Record*. Within its pages, the COS participated in the production of what historian Alice O'Connor has termed "poverty knowledge," or the use of empirical investigation to explain poverty through an emphasis on the individual failings of the poor and a dismissal of the political and economic bases of inequality.[8] In Baltimore, reformers looked to urban sociology and provided glowing reviews of social Darwinist, cultural evolutionary, and white supremacist works emerging out of turn-of-the-century Great Britain and the United States. Baltimore's reformers participated in the evolution and stewardship of an international charities movement that formed a significant arm of Progressivism in the United

States. Reformers applauded work that downplayed the hostile and unforgiving nature of the contingent labor market and highlighted the centrality of human struggle in the development of a useful citizenry.[9]

In this vein, the COS's goal was to create a city in which dependence of all kinds—including dependence on government assistance, alms, or donations—slowly but surely dissipated. They commonly appealed to cultural understandings of race and ethnicity to explain how dependence manifested differently among groups in the city. These values buttressed ongoing national debates on race that had become a crucial element in city politics. For the COS and for other notable "experts," including psychiatrists and journalists, Blackness posed a distinct problem. This problem stemmed from the abrupt removal of slavery as a disciplinary institution. For these faux experts, during enslavement, Black people were forced to abide by a certain moral code that regulated their cultural proclivities and directed their energies toward productive labor practices. According to historian Talitha LeFlouria, "These 'experts' rationalized that the *gift* of personal autonomy excited the dormant criminal sensibilities of the Negro, which were kept intact by slavery."[10] Race science underpinned the COS's prescriptive value system and reinforced prevailing Jim Crow ideologies.

The COS applied paternalist understandings of working-class deficiency to legislative and municipal reform efforts, including the regulation of beggars, peddlers, and children. On the last group, the COS published countless treatises on the relationship between truancy and crime. These treatises joined a cacophony of voices, groups, and legislators who sought to pass compulsory education laws and limit the abuses of child labor. A noble effort to be sure, the campaign revealed the COS and its allies' ideological commitment to the punishment, management, and institutionalization of dependent populations, as well as a developing—though contentious—relationship between private reformers and police. In all, the COS's popularization of paternalist and white supremacist urban sociology, coupled with the materialization of these theories into the growth and emboldening of disciplinary structures like civilian police, legitimized the goal of more expansive policing and helped enlarge the breadth of police power.

At the turn of the twentieth century, as Progressive liberalism and administrative volume shifted the nature and capacity American government, interventionist programs into the urban poor's daily lives were typified by policing, incarceration, and other exercises of state power.[11] These programs, by and large, replaced informal and direct monetary relief with noncash state intermediations into poverty relief. Progressives reasoned that deprivation made worthy citizens and would test the mettle of those struggling at the bottom rungs of the

American economic order. If relief proved necessary, it should come in the form of institutionalization, not cash assistance. Within this tapestry of poverty relief, Baltimore's charity agents operated in dual capacities as the administrators of assistance and the moral arbiters of who deserved it. For them, the efficacy of relief varied based on the recipient's cultural characteristics and perceived ability to succeed. In this way, charity agents participated in the creation and dissemination of race science that helped to consolidate binary understandings of racial identity during the early twentieth century.[12] Moreover, as administrators of poverty relief—and as agitators against public relief—the charities movement established a foothold in the city's forming police state. In their various crusades, charity agents–cum–social workers occupied a formidable policing function. In Baltimore, the COS embodied these dynamics like no other.

"Five Awful Faces": The *Charities Record* and the Carceral Logics of Poverty Relief

Established in 1881, Baltimore's chapter of the COS formed part of a broader international charities movement that aimed to eradicate poverty by indoctrinating refined family standards in the wayward urban poor.[13] The concept of charity had deep religious roots in eighteenth-century American colonies. Clerics reasoned that poverty allowed wealthy men the opportunity to find salvation through their voluntary philanthropic relief.[14] The expansion of Sunday schooling and benevolent societies in the mid-nineteenth century further buttressed this tradition of religious voluntarism.[15] While the charities movement would become increasingly secular, the premise that wealth redistribution should be voluntary remained a keystone of the crusade. By the 1840s, major U.S. cities had all established gradually more bureaucratized poverty relief organizations, including the Association for Improving the Condition of the Poor in New York City, the Union Benevolent Association in Philadelphia, and the Ministry to the Poor in Boston. Each organization took a miserly stance on cash relief and instead opted for moral training, home visiting, and in-kind relief. While these U.S. antecedents certainly paved the way for the emergence of a centralized charity movement, the COS, among the most far-reaching charity organizations in the world, originated in London in 1869. The COS movement gained steam internationally and attracted practitioners in France, Germany, and Russia. International practice and theory informed American poverty relief efforts through scholarship and the widespread deployment of home visiting, or "friendly visiting" as it was called in the United States.[16]

In 1877, Englishman Stephen Humphreys Gurteen founded the first American COS in Buffalo. According to social worker Verl S. Lewis, the precept that guided early COS work "held that deprivation was the essential incentive if the poor were to be kept at work." This principle tied the emergent nineteenth-century carceral state together as jails, prisons, asylums, and social welfare organizations all advocated for work as relief and rehabilitation. Chapters of the COS emerged shortly after Buffalo's incorporation in cities like Baltimore, New York City, and Indianapolis. By 1893, there were COS chapters in over one hundred American cities. In addition to the denial of cash relief, the COS used friendly visiting to establish seemingly benign cross-class connections among (mostly white women) volunteer agents and poor people. The COS and other charity organizations contributed broadly to the project of carcerality through the elimination of public outdoor relief in favor of both indoor relief and private outdoor relief. That is, instead of providing poor people with food, clothing, and financial support, the COS advocated institutionalization in almshouses, inns, hospitals, and other facilities where discipline could be meted out through compulsory labor. Otherwise, for families receiving monetary support, friendly visits and other forms of scrutiny became standard practice.[17]

Visiting became a cornerstone in the development of "scientific charity." Given widening economic and social stratification, COS chapters embraced friendly visiting to create familiarity among social classes, Americanize foreign-born immigrants, and streamline private almsgiving. Visitors assumed a paternal role in poor life by monitoring impoverished families' behaviors and distributing alms based on agents' perceptions of their worthiness. According to historian Michael B. Katz, the "visitor was to be at once a sympathetic friend, an official, a teacher, and a spy."[18] What made this movement "scientific" was the presumption held by charity figureheads like Josephine Shaw Lowell, Mary Richmond, and Stephen Humphreys Gurteen that poverty relief had a set of irrefutable and broadly applicable principles and that social scientific inquiry and research should form a major part of charity agents' educations and outlooks. Moreover, charity agents stewarded a hazy yet ultimately productive relationship between public and private bodies. Since public indoor relief and private outdoor relief formed the core of charity organization, groups that oversaw public relief facilities and private volunteer organizations maintained close, if fraught, relationships. Ultimately, sleek relief procedures, municipal coordination, and the development of social scientific scholarship drove charity organization's mission to forestall the "pauperization" of the country's working poor. Baltimore stood out within this movement as a profoundly impactful and active chapter with broad influence over municipal governance.[19]

Baltimore's COS chapter was one of few that maintained a regularly published independent journal, the *Charities Record*. Initially edited by General Secretary Mary Richmond, a bastion of modern social work, the *Charities Record* circulated among Baltimore's Progressive elite.[20] It cataloged trends in urban social science and economics, reported on the work of the COS's various offices and agents, and indexed known vagrants through the dissemination of a "Cautionary List," a litany of habitual beggars circulated among elite Baltimoreans to deny beggars alms. One of the *Record*'s recurrent concerns was the difference between poverty and pauperism. Whereas poverty represented a temporary economic state in which people found themselves battling to survive, pauperism represented a dangerous way of life in which the detritus of society basked—drinking, begging, and scamming their way through life. The *Record*'s various engagements with urban sociology and the way the COS used that knowledge as a tool to surveil and understand poor people provided a window into the organization's values and how those values guided the administration of poverty relief and the implementation of social services during the late nineteenth century.

While popular reporting identified the opportunistic beggar and recidivist as a "bummer," the COS applied the somewhat more refined term "pauper" to characterize seemingly vicious and reform-immune poor people. In an 1887 address, Amos Warner, a COS agent, detailed the society's perspective on pauperism. Undignified in their poverty, paupers represented "an inferior sort of parasite" who could make do with scraps. For Warner, five key elements caused pauperism: vice, crime, disease, hereditary incompetence, and indiscriminate almsgiving. Regarding heredity, Warner encouraged "a consideration of the race tendencies." He detailed the disproportionate alms given to Black and foreign-born Baltimoreans relative to their population. He reserved a marked vitriol for Black paupers, noting, "a colored pauper, when fully developed, is one of the most hopeless cases a friendly visitor ever tried to energise."[21] Warner's conception of Black life dovetailed with popular notions that cast Black people as culturally unsuited to urban life. His imputations were not unique; instead, they echoed prevailing racist ideologies that penalized Black Americans relative to their white and immigrant peers.[22]

In another example, reformer and COS agent Helen Pendleton penned an essay that appeared in a special collection of the journal *Charities* titled "Negro Dependence in Baltimore." This special issue, called "The Negro in the Cities of the North," boasted such high-profile contributors as Booker T. Washington, Mary White Ovington, W. E. B. DuBois, and Franz Boas. Historian Khalil Muhammad characterizes its publication as "the moment when the North officially

78 · CHAPTER 3

became the universally accepted proving ground of African American fitness for citizenship in modern America."[23]

Pendleton, who came to Baltimore by way of West Virginia, was an active COS member, serving as an agent in the organization's Northwestern District and as an attendance officer for the Baltimore School Board.[24] Pendleton's contribution spoke to the commonly held belief among the period's New South ideologues and reformers that Black men and women's antisocial behaviors were an unintended consequence of emancipation. The abrupt removal of this institution explained why sexual promiscuity, criminal activity, and unemployment—the key attributes of the so-called Negro rowdyism that had become a political dog whistle in local politics—were tied to Black communities. Nationally, reformers seized these discourses to construct deviant ideologies that justified disproportionate criminal punishment, compulsory systems of labor extraction, and gendered and racialized terror.[25]

Pendleton interpreted the perceived cultural propensities that Black working-class women had supposedly developed in American cities through the prisms of enslavement and emancipation. For her, crime, vice, and immoral behavior stemmed from the dependency Black women had developed during enslavement. Informed by her white, Southern, and middle-class outlook, Pendleton abstracted the Black working-class urban woman into two generalized tropes: Aunt Sarah and Fighting Mag.[26] In the first figure, Aunt Sarah, Pendleton identified the Black woman domestic—a charity case, who, in receiving handouts from employers, became, along with her family, disincentivized to become a prolific member of her community. Aunt Sarah was a "relic of slavery,"[27] a matriarch wholly disinterested in becoming socially independent and more than happy to readopt the structures of enslavement in her new urban setting. Pendleton argued, "The people to whom [Aunt Sarah] belonged in slavery times are dead, or their children are out of town; but she adopts any sentimental lady who becomes interested in her, and manages to scrape along until illness overtakes her, or her benefactors move away or grow tired of her."[28] Aunt Sarah's lifestyle led her children and spouse to become listless and muted their desires to attain education or employment. Pendleton's "Aunt Sarah" caricature condemned the Black woman domestic worker and relied on behavioral and pseudo-psychological evaluations culled during her friendly visits that failed to account for Black women's economic possibilities in a hostile and segregated labor market. This tendency characterized many of the period's reformers who condemned felonious domestic servants whose thefts might more realistically be interpreted as desperate actions undertaken to augment the paltry wages afforded by housework.[29]

Opposite Aunt Sarah was Fighting Mag, an immoral and young Black woman whose loose sexuality and violent nature traced to the "untaught, misguided freedom" available to her in the city.[30] Fighting Mag and girls like her were sexually hyperactive and, in cases of unplanned pregnancy, routinely had their "illegitimate babies 'put away'" either by leaving them with another mother or by disposing of them in some other, unspeakable manner.[31] Pendleton's latter charge contributed to prevalent associations between Black women and infanticide that failed to consider both the trauma of childbirth within the context of intense poverty and social isolation and the burden carried by Black working-class women charged with the act for whom all-white juries and the court of public opinion had no sympathy.[32] The attribution of "misguided freedom" to the caricature of Fighting Mag again reinforced the conventional gendered and racial logics of the time: the present consequences of emancipation included a unique inability for Black working-class women to possess and exercise the full privileges associated with American citizenship. This inability to cope with the newly encountered "largeness of their freedom"[33] led to maladaptive behaviors that menaced both the health of the city and the capacity for the exceptional Black residents among them to thrive.

Pendleton's theories of Black social dependence relied on cultural assessments to draw a link between the elimination of slavery and the current state of Black working-class women's supposed unruliness. Indeed, historian Charles Crowe understood this brand of Southern Progressivism as a key institutional force in suppressing Black freedom, noting, "Even the Progressive movement itself served mainly to provide new occasions for racial aggression in the Southern search for a system of social control to replace slavery."[34] Although perhaps an extreme calculation of Black life in Baltimore, even Pendleton's moderate contemporaries relied on similar ascriptions of pathology to interpret the city's persistent social problems within a prism of comparative racial analysis. Such analyses resulted in moral conclusions that disavowed Black urbanites in favor of the more palatable and familiar foreign-born white immigrant.[35] Whatever the case, the fact of poverty pointed to a broadscale moral corruption among the urban poor that the COS worked dutifully to theorize and manage.

In this vein, at the 1897 National Conference of Charities and Correction, Daniel Coit Gilman, president of Johns Hopkins University and a nationally renowned reformer, applied a race-neutral lens to pauperism and elucidated five injuries that paupers wreaked upon cities. He waxed poetic on the "five awful faces" of the "hydra" that befell the poor and working classes: disease, intemperance, crime, vice, and ignorance.[36] Gilman, and the COS at large, believed that pauperism posed a grave challenge to urbanization that was distinct from mere

80 · CHAPTER 3

poverty. On the one hand, pauperism indicated a patently urban condition in which vice and crime consumed men and women and prevented them—and the city and nation—from realizing their full potential. These squalid and wretched people required tough intervention, oversight, and sometimes institutionalization. Gilman juxtaposed pauperism with poverty, which represented a lack of resources, not a lack of trying. Gilman's militant depiction of pauperism mirrored the degree to which reformers and social scientists within the COS's orbit perceived and theorized the condition of the idle poor.

The *Charities Record*, the Baltimore COS's in-house publication, did much of the heavy lifting on this front by engaging emergent trends in urban sociology. The COS dutifully and comprehensively covered these trends in the "Library" section of the *Charities Record*. Every issue, the COS provided reviews of popular—and sometimes controversial—works that presented lessons to its readership on the theory and practice of delivering relief to the needy. For the editors, "Some knowledge of practical sociology, as well as of economics and civil government, is coming to be recognized as a requisite for the best citizenship, and an essential part of a liberal education."[37] Regarding the latter, the COS highlighted works that aligned with twentieth-century American liberalism and placed the onus of success on individuals while diminishing, though not totally ignoring, the impacts of environmental and structural barriers. This emphasis on individualism worked to repudiate the salience of social classes, discredit socialist politics, and naturalize economic hierarchy.[38] The COS romanticized the "struggle" of daily life and consigned certain groups to failure based on their presumed cultural, social, or hereditary incapacity to overcome this struggle. State interventions into daily life, especially police, carceral, and institutional impositions, propped up this ideology and aimed to correct and punish individual failings.[39] As such, the "Library" expressed broader national and international currents in Progressive liberalism, as well as the local attitudes of Baltimore reformers. These attitudes did not simply reside in the realm of imagination; they materialized in the COS's crusades against beggars and truancy.

The COS interpreted deviant pastimes and behaviors, such as gambling and pornography, as markers of depravity that would either naturally destroy the indulgent or fester and grow into abhorrent and dangerous lawlessness. The COS lauded Charles Richmond Henderson's *Introduction to the Study of the Dependent, Defective, and Delinquent Classes*. Henderson, a professor at the University of Chicago, would go on to hold leadership positions in the National Conference of Charities and the National Prison Association. In its review of Henderson's work, the COS joined him in condemning inebriates and advocated treating

"*With the Power of the Law*" • 81

paupers as if they were insane—a current that animated debates around the proper detention of bummers. They also emphasized Henderson's characterization of gambling as a direct cause of crime and pauperism that contributed to "all of the impulses which lead to rape, theft, arson, robbery, and murder."[40] In another "Library" section, Amos Warner imparted a glowing review to Benjamin Kidd's *Social Evolution*. He echoed Kidd's suggestion that the "uncontrolled intellect" found among the pauper class necessitated a "super-rational" intervention that could accomplish the "perpetual weeding out of the unfit." This sentiment was rooted in white supremacy and emphasized "the primary importance of selection in race improvement, or even in the prevention of absolute decadence."[41] Kidd, an Englishman, though dismissive of biologically deterministic justifications of racial superiority, nonetheless believed in the supremacy of white people, particularly the English, when it came to "social efficiency."[42]

Whereas urban sociology valorized rugged individualism and the triumph of the human spirit, some segments of the urban poor subscribed to a collectivist politics that located the source of human struggle in the consolidation and abuses of capital. To that end, many of the COS's charges flirted with or fully subscribed to socialist and communist value systems. On this front, the COS, though critical of the idle rich, vehemently pushed back. Rather than a public redistribution of wealth, the COS championed an approach to charity that relied on appealing to the sympathy of the rich while decreasing government intervention in the administration of poverty relief and vesting those powers in the hands of private groups. While the COS believed in providing relief to the poor, it believed that inculcating the poor with the values of thrift and hard work would weed out the paupers and promote competition, a central feature of capitalism that was key to the COS's intellectual ethos.

To that end, in a review of English critic Leslie Stephen's *Social Rights and Duties: Addresses to Ethical Societies*, the COS embraced the author's repudiation of socialism by noting that "some sifting of men is essential to social health, and that involves competition." Such competition ensured that people played the social roles for which they were "best fitted" and that "each individual . . . be able to give sufficient reason for existence."[43] This latter perception again echoed the COS's romanticized characterizations of struggle that proved altogether ironic given many COS agents' relative lack of struggle. In another rejection of socialism, the COS took up the edited collection *Aspects of the Social Problem*, compiled by English philosopher Bernard Bosanquet, husband of English COS leader Helen Bosanquet. In what the editors characterized as the clearest rejection of socialism, they cited, "The abolition of the struggle for existence, in the sense in which alone that term applies to human societies, means, so far as [we] can see,

82 · CHAPTER 3

the divorce of existence from human qualities; and *to favor the existence of human beings without human qualities is the ultimate inferno to which any society can descend.*"[44] The COS's absolute intolerance for paupers led them to not just criticize their ways of life but to position their very existence as a threat to humanity. This eugenic orientation exalted struggle as that which would gradually eliminate the unfit and create the ideal conditions for urbanization.

The COS institutionalized the theories developed in its "Library" section in their charitable relief programs. On the front page of an 1898 issue of the *Record*, the COS articulated its general principles and what it considered Baltimore's most pressing needs. The COS enumerated the following three values:

1. To put one family beyond the need of charity is more useful than to tide twenty over into next week's misery.
2. We have no right to make our alms a temptation to the poor; we must not teach men that it is easy to live in idleness.
3. The misery of a large city is only curable in so far as we strive *personally* to remove its causes.[45]

The COS's values reflected their tightfisted approach to the administration of direct monetary relief. They believed that indiscriminate giving caused men and women to lapse into idleness, which led to a host of social issues, especially crime. Based on their glowing reviews of cultural evolutionary literature, such giving also stripped the needy of their humanity through the elimination of struggle. The latter constituted a key facet of existence, and as the COS emphasized on several occasions, people had to justify their reason to exist by demonstrating a willingness to persevere through financial hardship. The COS's moralism disallowed a recognition that what they called "pauperism" was just that—a way of life that provided an avenue for poor men and women to endure the hardships attendant to industrial capitalism. The COS considered thrift among all classes a central facet of progress. This value stressed private rather than public relief and often put the COS at odds with public agencies, especially the police.

"Addicted to Begging": Charity and Policing

During the late nineteenth century, Progressive reformers looked to the state to provide heft to their campaigns. Although their ideological perspectives varied, Progressives, for the most part, valued associative forms of engagement across class, ethnic, and racial lines. For instance, friendly visiting, though blurring the line between the punitive and the altruistic, constituted one such associative

"With the Power of the Law" • 83

mode of engagement. Given reformers' reliance on various institutions of local government, including police, asylums, public works, housing agencies, waste disposal, and others, reformers realized that they needed to harness, shape, and ideally direct the powers of the state.[46] Doing so would be difficult given the graft and partisanship that organized municipal government. Charles Bonaparte and the Reform League's crusades against the bosses and the police provided insight into the deeply entrenched political corruption that typified Baltimore's social and civil services. As such, many Progressives staged challenges against local agencies to both further their specific reform agendas while simultaneously molding state power to conform to their plans.[47] One of the Baltimore COS's specific reform agendas, upending direct monetary aid and indiscriminate relief, required the cooperation of a historically uncooperative police department. In their clashes, the COS and the Baltimore police negotiated the contours of police power and the responsibilities, limitations, and effectiveness of the police state.

The relationship between the police and the COS had always been tense, particularly concerning the police's habit of housing lodgers in station houses and the lax regulation of street begging. Regarding the former, police departments around the country administered lodging to poor people in what historian Lawrence Friedman has called a "primitive welfare program."[48] In 1893, the Baltimore police accommodated 39,976 lodgers, mostly white men, in station houses across the city.[49] By 1895, this number had fallen to 100. The police board attributed the precipitous decline to citizen activism and the incorporation of the Friendly Inn Association, a federation of charity organizations that managed two lodging houses: the Friendly Inn and the Wayfarers' Lodge. The managers of these lodging houses required labor as a precondition for accommodation.[50] Both the police and the COS found the arrangement optimal. This shift corresponded with national movements to eliminate station house lodging. In 1893, famed photojournalist Jacob Riis completed an investigation on the matter in New York. Published in the *Christian Union*, Riis noted that the cramped living quarters were "hotbeds for typhus fever." New York, like Baltimore, eliminated the practice shortly thereafter.[51] In doing so, the police ceded a central and long-standing police function to civilian reformers who assumed and deployed this state utility.

Street begging posed another problem altogether. Rather than convincing police to cease a practice like lodging, the COS and other charity groups had to convince police to proactively enforce petty crimes that they had not meaningfully administered in decades. This issue was not unique to Baltimore. Across the country, reformers found that morals-based legislation was not difficult to pass or identify. However, its enforcement proved problematic without

84 • CHAPTER 3

persistent and organized civilian agitation.[52] In 1887, the COS publicized their dissatisfaction with the dead letter laws that governed begging and peddling. Concerning begging, in 1860, the General Assembly empowered police to arrest "habitual beggars" and bring them before the criminal court. The court then decided, based on the beggar's history and reputed crimes, whether to dismiss, imprison, or institutionalize them.[53] Beggars could forestall arrest by securing a peddling license. If secured, peddlers could sell notions and small wares on public thoroughfares. Although the mayor could revoke licenses at any time, they carried an indefinite term.[54] The COS applauded reforms that eliminated indefinite terms on peddling licenses.[55] However, police scantly enforced them.[56] In response, the COS pressured the police to prioritize the regulation of street begging. In 1897, three COS representatives met with the police board to enter a formal complaint regarding nonenforcement. Based on an independent investigation, the COS alleged that many street beggars lived in "comfortable circumstances" and begged simply out of opportunism and low moral character. They found that young beggars routinely accosted well-to-do couples until the couples paid to simply eliminate the annoyance of the interaction. They also found that beggars hid behind saloon doors until the wee hours of the night to assault and rob intoxicated men.[57]

The police took these complaints to heart and began regulating peddling and begging. The ensuing press did not conform to the COS's characterization of "vicious" beggars. In one instance, police arrested David Meyers, a blind Black man, who, accompanied by a young boy, sold lead pencils and matchbooks to passersby. In another case, police arrested George Hawkins, a seventy-two-year-old Black man, for peddling matches. The court committed Hawkins to Bayview Asylum and left his bedridden wife to fend for herself. The police also rounded up a host of beggars. One beggar wore a card around his neck that indicated that he was blind. He had gone blind after enduring an explosion while working on the railroad. Hardly a work-hating pauper, the man represented countless victims of industrial capitalism's dangerous consequences and the lack of worker protections that prevailed. Police arrested another man, who was both paralyzed and deaf, for habitual begging. The criminal court dismissed the charge.[58] In a letter to supporters sent shortly after the publication of these arrests, the COS's executive committee made clear that they did not support "unkindness" to those stricken by "unavoidable misfortune." They asked supporters to contribute to a pension fund that the organization would use to distribute money to disabled men and women caught up in their war on street begging.[59] The COS, in characterizing the published instances as unfortunate circumstances, did not engage an environmental or structural analysis

"With the Power of the Law" • 85

of urban poverty. The gears of industrial capitalism churned the disabled and elderly asunder. In Baltimore's chaotic commercial and industrial economy, such populations became problems whose solutions lied in piecemeal donations, institutionalization, and arrest.

Even after police began indiscriminately arresting street beggars in larger numbers, the COS remained vigilant. Like the Reform League, their eyes remained trained on cops. The COS pounced whenever the police backtracked on one of their deals. In one instance, the COS accused the police of "lavishly" providing aid to a couple known to the organization as runaways who had each abandoned their partners. In providing financial aid to the couple, the COS accused the police of supporting criminals, writing, "In this particular case, we have the spectacle of law-breakers being tenderly coddled by the Baltimore [police]." The COS suggested that police rely on plainclothes officers to patrol the city and "clear the streets of beggars."[60] On January 12, 1898, a coalition of charitable organizations, including the COS, the Association for the Improvement of the Condition of the Poor, the Saint Vincent de Paul Society, the Hebrew Benevolent Society, and the German Society, wrote to the police board to protest their continued, though much diminished, administration of alms. The statement characterized the police's actions as excessive and noted the prevalence of charitable societies in the city. The coalition wrote, "We feel justified, therefore, in saying that all who are in need in Baltimore can be properly taken care of by the agencies whose special duty it is to provide for their needs." The police board conceded and agreed to halt direct relief, functionally emboldening private citizens to exercise police power that had been the police's duty and jurisdiction for decades.[61]

The police were not the only organization with which the COS collaborated to war on beggars. They also maintained a relationship with the city's newspapers. In the same issue detailing its correspondences with police, the *Record* reported that it had reached an agreement with the papers to suppress the names, addresses, and dramatic details of stories involving paupers. According to the COS, such suppression was necessary to avoid lending free publicity to scams. The organization highlighted one instance in which a husband and wife attempted to con a newspaper into publishing their name and address. The ploy was intended to entice charitable persons to bring donations to their doorstep. The wife allegedly contacted the paper and said that she had been deserted by her husband and needed money to feed her children. The paper published the story without identifying details. This omission led readers to send donations directly to the newspaper's offices. Upon receiving the donations, the editor purportedly reached out to the COS which had been actively working on removing

86 · CHAPTER 3

the couple's children from their custody. The COS informed the editors that the woman had not been deserted; rather, she and her husband refused to work. Because of this refusal, two of their children had been "rescued," and the COS was working on sending their third child to out-of-state relatives. The COS applauded the paper for reaching out to them instead of the scamming couple because it allowed them to divert donations away from the couple and into the relocation of the third child.[62]

Despite positive reports that the dailies had become allies in the COS's crusade against pauperism, a few years later, the COS published another editorial defending itself from an attack by the *Baltimore Sun*. The *Sun*, a Democratic paper, had little love for the busybody reformers whose desires to seize state power rang a recreant bell. The paper lambasted the COS for ordering police, who had become the COS's allies, to have a woman arrested for begging. The paper highlighted the danger present for poor people when speaking to COS agents in public. Bridget Ragan, a fifty-year-old mother of one, had appealed to the COS for relief and was turned away multiple times. Ragan's husband worked as a stevedore but had been out of work with an injury suffered on the job. Ragan attested that because of her husband's unemployment, they had fallen behind on rent and their child was starving. After the COS denied them relief, she turned to begging. While out begging one day, she recognized a COS agent. She explained her family's situation and asked him for help. The agent immediately had her arrested. He testified before a judge that he had reviewed Ragan's COS file and found her undeserving of aid. The judge dismissed the case and contended that she did not constitute what the law considered a habitual beggar.[63]

In its February issue of the *Record*, the COS defended itself from the *Sun*'s story alleging that it had known about Ragan for six years. According to the COS, Ragan and her husband had moved to Baltimore from Albany. Her husband left behind a wife and several children. In Baltimore, the COS claimed to have found work for the husband and to have coordinated the family's relocation after they were forced to vacate their home. After working with the family for some time, the organization became privy to the fact that Ragan was begging in public with her child. To address this lapse into moral improbity, the COS reached out to her church. When that tactic failed, the COS had her committed to Bayview Asylum. After her release, Ragan continued begging, which caused the organization to condemn her.[64]

Ragan's case crystallized the COS's governing ideologies and its approach to poverty relief. The COS's justifications for denying Ragan aid echoed editorials and book reviews that characterized pauperism as a pox on civil society. The society interpreted Ragan's decision to beg with her child as a moral failing.

"With the Power of the Law" • 87

She simply could not overcome the struggle of urban poverty in a way suited to liberal standards of thrift, hard work, and a profound endurance in the face of hardship and adversity. As such, Ragan required state intervention and discipline. Instead of cash relief, she was promptly sent to Bayview, a site of public indoor relief and institutionalization organized by confinement and compulsory labor. Ragan's familiarity with and appeal to an agent on the street broadly represented the associative—and surveillance—function of charity agents who combed the streets, entered people's homes, and familiarized themselves with habitual and "vicious" beggars like Ragan, a mother of one with no money to eat. This latter characteristic, the spy role of the charity agent, could be seen quite clearly in the *Charities Record*'s "Cautionary List" on which Ragan may well have fell.

The COS proactively engaged in the criminalization of poverty by routinely publicizing the names and aliases of habitual beggars on the "Cautionary List." Each name was accompanied by some identifying characteristics, including age, hair texture and color, address, race, and the tactics each person used to elicit sympathy. This system of indexing paupers paralleled the Baltimore police's daily lookout sheets. The parallel is not a coincidence. Chapters around the country collaborated with police on the creation and maintenance of their pauper databases.[65] The COS instructed its subscribers and friendly visitors to avoid giving alms to each person listed. Further, they foregrounded each installment of the "Cautionary List" with a standard disclaimer that asserted, "One way to help all persons to live honestly is to make it more difficult for them to live otherwise."[66] One representative entry read,

> Catrup, Mrs.—Auburn hair mixed with grey, tall, large frame, about sixty. Sometimes gives the name of Mrs. Goldsborough, and begs money for certain poor families. Uses the names of prominent citizens, saying they have contributed.[67]

Catrup landed on several lists and deployed a strategy that seemed to work well enough that the editorial staff released a general caution regarding the invocation of COS agents' names and the names of other well-known citizens. The COS warned members against beggars who lied about being acquainted with the COS as part of their plea to wealthy Baltimoreans, who they often tracked down in city directories.[68] Using their familiarity with Baltimore's wealthy elite, poor men and women begged in flusher parts of the city and sometimes name-checked people like Mary Richmond, William Cabell Bruce, and other well-regarded movers and shakers.[69]

As an example, among Charles Bonaparte's personal effects were dozens of letters to and from COS agents inquiring about poor men and women. In one letter, a COS agent named A. L. Sears responded to Bonaparte's inquiry regarding a Black woman named Amelia Cromwell. Cromwell lived with her husband, grandson, and daughter Josephine who was sick with a stomach tumor. Sears characterized Cromwell as "addicted to begging" from both private individuals and on the streets. The COS began a file on Cromwell in 1888. During an 1895 visit, Sears found Cromwell and her husband "too inferior to work longer for their support." Additionally, Josephine's health had taken a turn for the worse. Sears requested that Amelia and her husband enter Bayview and that Josephine enter a hospital. They rejected the requests. A few months later, the COS district board notified Amelia that, given the lack of family support, the COS would only respond to further requests for relief by institutionalizing them. Shortly after they had issued the ultimatum, Sears encountered her begging on the street. The agent promised to have Amelia put away if she continued begging. Ultimately, Sears discouraged Bonaparte from providing money to cover the family's overdue rent because Bonaparte "would certainly be annoyed."[70] This declaration reflected a broader attitude among COS agents toward the urban poor. The elderly, the infirm, the supplicant, and the disabled were not products of a mammoth and historically unseen system of capitalist dispossession; they were an annoyance. Cultural evolutionary theory suggested that time and circumstance would eliminate such annoyances.

The COS's administration of poverty relief coincided with its broader moral and intellectual ethos. The society believed that pauperism stemmed from personal failings. Stratified labor markets, low wages, disability, and other obstructions played little role in the perpetuation of extreme poverty as industry accelerated along and the city became jam-packed with poor and working people. Given this assumption, the COS engaged in practices and reform efforts intended to obstruct and punish men and women who sought desperately to make enough money to tide them over into the next day. The agents corresponded with wealthy elites and expressed disgust with beggars and peddlers whose mere existence they characterized as an annoyance. For the COS, if the public made these people's lives as difficult as possible, they would either get jobs or die—two natural and acceptable outcomes. After all, not everyone was suited to the "misery of a large city." However, the COS's ability to police relied on its capacity to tap into and harness state power. In most cases, the COS collaborated with existing agencies to access state resources and compel morals-based enforcement. In others, like compulsory education, the COS and other Progressive reformers angled to assume state power. And they succeeded.

"A High Type of Citizenship": Compulsory Education and the Creation of School Attendance Officers

At the turn of the century, various Baltimore charity and reform groups agitated for the passage of a compulsory education law. The city joined a national movement that looked to institutionalize such laws and attack the scourge of truancy and child labor. The history of compulsory education dated back to colonial Massachusetts when, in 1642, the colonial government appointed "selectmen" to monitor parents and ensure that they were delivering proper religious, educational, and civic instruction to their children. Although not a compulsory education law per se, the statute represented the first systematized state intervention into youth education in the United States. In 1852, Massachusetts continued to trailblaze the compulsory education movement by passing the first modern compulsory education law in 1852. In 1863, Washington, D.C. followed suit and then Vermont in 1867. By the late nineteenth century, most states had compulsory education laws on the books. Like peddling legislation, enforcement of compulsory education laws was lax. Historian Michael S. Katz notes, "[The] last quarter of the nineteenth century witnessed a plethora of compulsory attendance laws and a paucity of enforcement mechanisms." A lack of infrastructure and a reliance on citizens to police other parents' children made the laws practically unenforceable. However, as Progressives agitated to harness state power to abet their crusades, they reinvigorated efforts to either pass or resuscitate compulsory education laws. More education funding, reliable school censuses, and increased southern and eastern European immigration provided the means and justifications reformers needed to home in on compulsory education. Additional funding allowed for the creation of parental schools to detain truant children and place immigrant children in public schools—the primary sites of assimilation. The employment and training of attendance officers, many of whom approached their positions with missionary zeal, centralized enforcement in a dedicated cohort of civilian busybodies that both created the problem of truancy and juvenile delinquency and administered its solution—the investigation and punishment of thousands of American children.[71]

While most states had passed compulsory education laws by 1900, Maryland did not have one. In fact, many rural states adopted compulsory education laws much later than states with large metropoles, primarily because education operated differently in the countryside. Many legislatures in rural states felt that such laws were unapplicable to their states' ways of life.[72] However, reformers viewed Baltimore, a large metropolis that contained half the population in a

90 · CHAPTER 3

deeply rural state,[73] as needing a compulsory education law to chip away at both child labor abuses and truancy. On the former issue, reformers considered the predominance of child labor a grave social issue that should be eradicated by the federal government.[74] The federal government did not tackle the issue until the passage of the short-lived Keating-Owen Act of 1916. In the meantime, education reformers focused on truancy.

To this end, in 1898, Mary Willcox Brown, secretary of the Henry Watson Children's Aid Society, delivered a speech before the Maryland Conference of Charities and Correction. She argued that truancy increased crime. Brown based these observations on statistical reports developed by penologists who interpreted widespread illiteracy among inmates as proof that a lack of education caused crime. Drawing on complementary observations from other charity-based organizations around the country, Brown arrived at a series of recommendations to curtail truancy, including the creation of attendance officers, the chartering of parental or ungraded schools, the maintenance of censuses of truant children, and most importantly, "the vigilance of the public to watch the enforcing of the law."[75] The last recommendation echoed the attitudes of groups like the Reform League and the Society for the Suppression of Vice which placed the onus on private citizens to see through enforcement and monitor the police. At the same conference, public school teacher Rose Sommerfeld echoed Brown's remarks. Sommerfeld located the roots of truancy in home life, including harsh environmental realities, which she characterized as claustrophobic and socially deadening. Like Brown, she recommended a compulsory education law that emphasized institutionalization in parental schools as a method of discipline and deterrence.[76]

These ideological currents materialized in collective action and legislative advocacy. In 1899, the Baltimore City School Board and reformers made their case to the mayor and city council. The school board, headed by Joseph Packard, a Reform League veteran, detailed the causes of truancy by appealing to administrative difficulties and the supposed cultural predispositions of the diverse student population. It asserted that poor teaching discouraged students from attending class. Although later evidence would confirm that poverty and sickness far outweighed instruction in fomenting truancy, if the voluminous staff resignations are any indication, the school board frequently scapegoated its teachers. The school board also alleged that "heredity, environment, and the natural inclination of the child" presented challenges in regulating attendance. Echoing the COS's comparative approach to racialized and inherited traits, the school board alleged,

"With the Power of the Law" • 91

> Speaking generally, it may be said, children of German parents attend school the best, and make the most of their opportunities; those whose parents are colored attend the worse, and secure the least benefit from the schools.[77]

Although attendance numbers may have reflected racial distinctions, the school board failed to account for the horrific states of Black schools, of which there were few, and the relative economic advantages of German immigrants compared to Black Baltimoreans. Indeed, in the same report, the school board asked for better accommodations considering the odious state of Black schools.[78] They would have perhaps better captured the dynamic if they said, "those whose parents are colored attend the [worst schools]."

While the school board appealed to the city for a compulsory education law, reformers lobbied the state legislature for a similar one. In March 1900, Florence E. Peirce, a reformer who made her way to Baltimore via Boston, the birthplace of compulsory education, delivered a fiery speech titled "The Child at School" to a reform group called the Progress Club. The speech drew from her COS-sponsored investigations into school attendance. Foregrounding parental responsibility, Peirce informed the crowd that "in many instances parents do not take the school life of the children and its ultimate effect upon character into serious consideration." She noted that "if the parent disregarded his [*sic*] obligations, it [becomes] necessary for the State to pass those laws which would produce by their enforcement a high type of citizenship." Truancy menaced this idealized citizenship which Peirce, like many others, connected to crime. She contended that the "majority of shiftless husbands and tramps were men who had been sent out to work [instead of to school] in childhood." To combat the crime associated with truancy and to discipline parents who could not manage their children, Peirce, drawing from similar regulations in Boston and New York, advocated a comprehensive truancy plan that would deputize civilians with the city's police power and establish a corps of attendance officers.[79]

These precepts guided a 1902 compulsory education law drafted by the Good Government Club,[80] a Progressive organization that boasted such high-profile members as William Cabell Bruce, former state senator and future U.S. senator, and James H. Van Sickle, superintendent of city schools. The proposed law required every child between the ages of eight and twelve to attend school regularly and every unemployed child over twelve and under sixteen to do so as well. It established a series of misdemeanor fines, including fines for parents whose children were identified as truant and fines for businesses that employed children. It also proposed the establishment of attendance officers, appointed by the school board, and empowered to "arrest without warrant any child between

92 · CHAPTER 3

8 and 16 years of age found away from his home and who is truant from school." Arrested children could either be returned to their parents, to school, or, if the child was deemed incorrigible, brought before the juvenile court and sentenced to detention in a parental school. Attendance officers would also be empowered to visit businesses that employed minors and request to see proof that all employed children were over twelve years old.[81] The governor signed the bill into law on April 8, 1902.[82]

After the law took effect, the school board held a special meeting to appoint their allotted corps of twelve attendance officers.[83] The school board appointed Florence Peirce chief attendance officer and instructed the Committee of Rules to prepare a set of guidelines for the program.[84] The school board adopted these guidelines on January 14, 1903. Attendance officers answered to the assistant superintendent of public instruction, John E. McCahan. They patrolled eleven districts, charted out by the school board. Each school involved in the program maintained a register where officers checked in and out. Officers were to regularly visit schools and investigate attendance records and teacher complaints. If unable to identify a truant student, officers were directed to engage McCahan who would apply to the juvenile court for an arrest warrant. Each attendance officer was outfitted with a special badge and the text of the compulsory education law, printed in both English and German.[85] Later, in 1907, the school board supplied officers with one written in Yiddish to patrol the substantial Russian Jewish population that settled in the city.[86]

With their organization set and their badges in tow, the attendance officers kicked off their truancy crusade by looking into the attendance records of children in their respective districts over a three-month period.[87] After gathering this information, the truancy crusade came to an abrupt halt. Although the compulsory education law provided a way to institutionalize children in parental schools, Baltimore did not have any. One city council member warned that the absence of a disciplinary institution dedicated to reforming truant children could increase truancy because children knew the city did not have a way to punish them.[88] This statement was ridiculous considering the panoply of reformatories in Baltimore geared toward disciplining children. In fact, in one of its first reports to the school board, attendance officers stated that they had institutionalized a student in the House of Refuge.[89] Moreover, the juvenile court sentenced multiple truant children to correctional institutions, including Saint Mary's Industrial School.[90] Yet and still, reformers sought desperately to create a stand-alone parental school.

After the attendance officers' first month of work, John McCahan proudly reported that thousands of truancy cases had been investigated. He noted that the

"With the Power of the Law" • 93

absence of parental schools was to be handled, in the intermediary, by placing truant children in "ungraded classes"—separated from their peers—at their current schools.[91] In 1902, McCahan, in preparation for the return of truant children, conducted a one-month pilot of ungraded classes. Since truant students would have fallen behind on basic reading, writing, arithmetic, and morals, ungraded classes had to cater to the specific needs of each pupil. For one month, teachers identified and removed students who had fallen behind on material from their first- and second-grade classes and placed them in ungraded classes. In these classes, students thrived in an atmosphere that foregrounded individualized attention. McCahan ascribed their success to the fact that "slow, dull and troublesome children" could not cope in a normal classroom environment.[92] McCahan's assessment emphasized the individual failings of students rather than the inhospitable conditions of public school classrooms. This outlook animated the assistant superintendent's approach to the attendance officer program.

Over the course of its first two years in operation, the program resulted in tens of thousands of investigations into truant children, most of which were resolved by returning children to their parents.[93] In 1903, attendance officers investigated 24,698 cases. In contrast to the assumptions that guided the creation of the program—namely that irresponsible and apathetic parents neglected their children to lives of crime—the officers found that the chief causes of truancy were sickness and poverty. In the latter case, students either had to work to help their household or did not have shoes to walk to school. Parents and teachers had mixed reactions to the program. Parents either welcomed attendance officers for finding their children or greeted them hostilely. In both cases, McCahan noted the police authority that the attendance officers had assumed. He reported, "The parents are now accustomed to meet the Attendance Officer at the door with the power of the law behind him [*sic*] to perform the duties which they formerly assumed belonged entirely to themselves." These deputized civilians, with their badges and power to detain children, became all too familiar state agents. As McCahan shrewdly noted, the state's paternal authority operated quite literally in the regulation of school attendance. Whereas it had been the sole duty of parents to get their kids to school, the state now stepped in to compel the duty. And while the program seemed an excellent success, McCahan reported dissatisfaction from teachers. The program placed considerable burden on them to supply attendance officers with adequate information, and teachers simply were not paid enough to shoulder additional work.[94] School reformers' designs to expand and assume state discretion through the harnessing of police power had worked. Parents now lived in fear that local government might take their children away from them for missing school.

94 · CHAPTER 3

Now that the attendance officers had developed a reputational police authority, the school board pushed for the creation of a parental school. Nationally, parental schools represented key enforcement mechanisms for compulsory education laws, and Baltimore's experiences mirrored and buttressed these national trends. Chicago pioneered the parental school and the administration of juvenile delinquency. By 1889, Chicago reformers had successfully advocated the creation of a corps of attendance officers to direct compulsory education enforcement. However, without a parental school, the attendance officers resorted to moral suasion to persuade children to attend school—a tactic that yielded minor results. As such, they sought more dogged enforcement provisions. After a decade of advocacy, the Illinois General Assembly passed legislation in 1899 that established both a juvenile court and parental school provisions. Regarding the latter, the legislature required the state's larger cities to create separate schools for truant children. The legislation also empowered officers and civilians to petition the juvenile court in cases of suspected truancy. Between 1899 and 1906, Chicago's superintendent of compulsory education reported a record high 2,807 prosecutions. In 1902, Chicago opened the doors of a boys-only parental school. In 1919, a separate building opened to house girls. Taken together, these two buildings constituted the Chicago Parental School. Although conceived as an institution for truant children for whom little disciplinary recourse remained, over time the Chicago Parental School became a storehouse for hundreds of children who had not violated Illinois's compulsory education law. As historian Tera Eva Agyepong notes, the juvenile court began to treat the Chicago Parental School as a "dumping ground" primarily for Black children who endured heinous and violent treatment. The close entanglement of the juvenile court and the Chicago Parental School spoke to the increasingly criminalized management of public schools, which Baltimore not only mimicked but actively sought.[95]

Building a parental school in Baltimore required delicacy. The school board did not wish to build what seemed like a reformatory or site of punishment. Indeed, McCahan, despite the badges, police authority, and numerous applications to the juvenile court, maintained that the parental school was "in no sense to be classed with penal institutions."[96] McCahan's clarification echoed Ferdinand Latrobe's declaration over a decade earlier that Bayview Asylum was "an asylum, not a prison."[97] In both cases, city agents grappled with public perceptions of disciplinary programs and institutions that adopted carceral logics, structures, and strategies. Their declarations spoke to the elasticity and continual negotiation of police power. Although a parental school was certainly not a prison, the attendance officer program deputized civilians who assumed

"With the Power of the Law" • 95

state power to identify, detain, and confine children. They were not the police, but they exercised police power.

Responding to continual pressure, including protests from the Supervisors of Charities,[98] the city council eventually passed an ordinance in June 1904 providing for the establishment of a parental school. The ordinance gave the school board ample discretion by requiring that it site the school in "some convenient locality" and that it assume "authority to make all rules and regulations for the confinement, maintenance and instruction" of truant children. The ordinance also enabled the school board to contract with other detention facilities instead of or in addition to leasing a new facility for the parental school.[99]

After two years of advocacy, the school board established a temporary parental school. Using its power to contract with institutions, the board partnered with the Henry Watson Children's Aid Society to lease part of its building at 1205 Linden Avenue. The contract allowed the school board to house up to ten white boys at a time.[100] Assistant Superintendent McCahan outlined the regulations that governed the new institution. The managers prohibited boys from seeing their parents except for brief visits on Thursdays. Boys were allowed recreation time, but "their daily routine [would] be the routine of a mild reformatory." Boys received individualized instruction from Annie E. Brennan, a public school teacher who had experience overseeing ungraded classes. The boys engaged in manual training, including iron work and chair caning. Additionally, though the ordinance only allowed the school board to detain truants for one school year, McCahan noted that their punishment would last as long as it took them to satisfy the school board's criteria for reform.[101]

The school board managed the parental school on Linden Avenue until 1906. Afterward, to accommodate more pupils, they leased a colonial-style mansion on Gilmor Lane.[102] The mansion stood in the austere developing suburbs in the northern part of the city.[103] Removing the boys from the city allowed the school board to show them "a better life than that in which [they have] been buffeted." The mansion scaled three stories, contained sixteen rooms, and was surrounded by plentiful open space. Brennan continued teaching the boys who, in addition to instruction, kept house and tended to a chicken coop and garden.[104] In addition to the parental school, the school board instituted twenty ungraded classes in schools around the city.[105] During 1907, the parental school confined thirty-six truant boys.[106]

While the school board and reformers managed to make headway in their efforts to stamp out truancy, the public and other education professionals questioned their tactics. In one *Sun* editorial, the editors outlined what they perceived as the competing and irreconcilable philosophies of school reformers. They captured these approaches in three generalized types of reformers. The first type viewed child laborers as the products of avaricious and improvident parents and unethical employers. These reformers misunderstood and were "jealous of human rights," such as the right to work. The second type believed that "equality" signified identical school experiences for all children. The editors took umbrage with this idea, sardonically noting that in these reformers' views, "The colored young gentleman from the back alley is entitled to as good an education as the son of the millionaire and must vindicate his right by taking the same courses and using the very same books." This misguided notion ignored the realities of racial hierarchy and downplayed the usefulness of skills-based education. Finally, the third reformer, who aligned with the editors' idea of a rational perspective, emphasized the importance of trade schools in allowing children of different socioeconomic and racial backgrounds to realize their "practical callings," or to know their place in the racialized, classed, and gendered pecking order. These reformers understood that select children were better suited for the factory, which, in some cases, could present a much better environment for children both educationally and morally. The editors concluded, "Equality is alright, but it is not vindicated by spoiling the boy's or girl's career as a useful citizen."[107]

Although the *Sun*'s view reinscribed white supremacist views of social hierarchy, they nonetheless dovetailed with other reformers' perceptions about the costs of the school board's idealism. Robert Fawcett, a perennial critic of the school board who participated in efforts to oppose the creation of a Black school in Northwest Baltimore,[108] printed and delivered dozens of circulars to the House of Delegates in 1904. In the circulars, Fawcett detailed the deteriorating conditions of school buildings. He scolded the school board for overworking, harshly disciplining, and harassing teachers. According to Fawcett, these conditions emerged from a curriculum rooted in the "silly ideas of old women."[109] Fawcett undoubtedly referred to women like Florence Peirce, Mary Willcox Brown, and other education reformers whose crusades emerged from well-meaning desires to keep kids in school. Their tactics, however, revealed the degree to which absences reflected broader structural disadvantages. Yet and still, for reformers, the buck stopped with parents and students, no matter the social, economic, or political hurdles that beset poor families.

Not everyone blamed parents and students, however. Dr. H. Warren Buckler, a Health Department official who served as chief of the school hygiene division,[110] situated the roots of truancy in the disgusting and learning-averse conditions of the city's public schools. At a parental meeting, Buckler challenged reformers' emphasis on parental malfeasance, arguing, "Much of the truancy reported in the schools is due to the [deplorable] conditions that prevail. Some

"With the Power of the Law" · 97

of the children labor under disadvantages, become indifferent and their pride is hurt because the teachers rebuke them."[111] He further elaborated his assessment at another parental meeting by noting that children's difficulties at school were often misidentified and remediated through harsh punishments that failed to address the actual causes of their troubles. He argued that children were often dismissed as stupid, inattentive, and indifferent when they were suffering from undiagnosed physical ailments, including blurry vision, adenoid inflammation, and dental anguish, as well as mental distress from the repugnant environmental setting of the public school. Buckler concluded that administrators were quick to use "the rod or the discipline of the reformatory" and ignore the underlying structural issues that prevented successful learning.[112] For Buckler, private reformers' philosophies on discipline failed to address the everyday lived realities of students contending with inhospitable school environments and perhaps struggling with learning disabilities.

The truancy crusade showcased how disciplinary governance emerged through collaborations among private agencies, state and local governments, police, and the criminal legal system. Reformers relied on pseudoscientific evidence, noting the supposed causal link between truancy and crime. They leveraged both social science and their privileged positions among Baltimore's elite to advocate for legislation that effectively deputized citizens through an expansion of state power. This expansion allowed civilians to surveil, arrest, and detain children. In that way, to quote McCahan, civilian attendance officers were vested "with the power of the law."[113] The logic of this crusade misidentified the root causes of truancy while simultaneously traumatizing children and their parents through punishment. The unforgiving realities of a classed and racialized job market, as well as an awful and similarly striated public school system, contributed to truancy in ways that demanded overhauls of both sectors of urban life.

Instead of structural changes to the education system, though, the truancy crusade followed a familiar pattern that characterized policing at the turn of the century. Private interests, through invocations of morality, lobbied legislative bodies and police to criminalize actions that menaced idealized aspirations of good citizenship and robust public life. Reformers alleged that truancy caused crime and corrupted the next generation of citizens. Their solution: criminalize truancy. Whereas their hunch about truancy's relationship to crime lacked the meaningful context of urban life's complex travails, the institutionalization fomented by attendance officers no doubt created criminals out of children. In other words, by seizing on the disciplinary powers of the state, reformers created new crime categories and enforcement strategies that unquestionably caused—indeed, *created*—crime.

98 · CHAPTER 3

Conclusion

In Baltimore and the nation, the turn of the century witnessed how wealthy urban elites weaponized their considerable influence in city government to coordinate both an enlargement of state power through policing and a distribution of police power to civilians who fulfilled quasi-police functions. Ideological currents in the social sciences and charities movements informed these developments. Progressive liberalism, which filtered association among classes through an individualist lens that romanticized and normalized human struggle, guided reformers' crusades to access, shape, and in some cases, assume state power. Cultural evolutionary theories regarding the relative capacities of racial and ethnic groups hierarchized poor people based on perceptions regarding heredity and culture. Such theories contributed to discursive condemnations of Blackness as well as the parsimonious administration of poverty relief and other social services. Given perceptions regarding certain racial and ethnic groups' disproportionate dependence on public relief, organizations like the COS assumed a philosophy of deprivation that minimized direct relief and mutual aid in favor of institutionalization and punishment. In this way, the charities and Progressive reform movements proved instrumental in extending the police state through the miserly and disciplinary administration of social welfare.

Like election, gambling, and civil service reformers, social welfare and public school reformers adopted policing strategies to promote and further their causes. As police handed lookout sheets to their patrolmen and kept biometric case files on perpetrators, the COS published Cautionary Lists to their subscribers. These lists indexed so-called deviants into typologies that allowed agents to identify unworthy beggars and coordinate discipline as needed. Michael B. Katz might interpret the Cautionary List as a tool to support the "spy" dimension of charity work.[114] Surveillance formed a cornerstone of such work as agents familiarized themselves with habitual beggars and petitioned police officers to institutionalize them at Bayview or any of the other countless reformatories, jails, prisons, or asylums in and around the city. When police failed to fully execute reformers' desires, they looked to other methods. Notably, school reformers managed to institute a long-lasting attendance officer program that displaced the necessity of police officers through the deputization of civilians. School officials, though wary about perceptions regarding the punitive dimensions of the program, nonetheless touted the program's success by emphasizing the recognition on behalf of parents that attendance officers came to their doorsteps propped up by the full weight of the law.

All told, reformers were not cops. They were, however, integral to the expansion and augmentation of the police power of the state. Contemporary carceral scholars refer to such actors as "soft police," seemingly benevolent and noncoercive entities, like social workers, whose intentions seem—and in many cases *are*—pure, but whose impacts buttress disciplinary systems of deprivation, paternalism, and police power.

While the truancy crusade focused mostly on saving white and foreign-born immigrant children from lives of crime by making them juvenile delinquents, the COS, reformers, and city politicians had also developed and contributed to long-standing diagnoses of Baltimore's supposedly unruly Black citizenry. After decades of handwringing over the threat of Negro rule, white racists concluded that Black Baltimoreans were immune to reform in any meaningful way. In fact, given reformers' assimilationist aspirations for newly arrived European immigrants, the proximity that the city's Black and immigrant populations shared made the suppression of Negro rowdyism even more important. By the turn of the twentieth century, the suppression of Black crime largely guided the construction, articulation, and deployment of police power in Baltimore as institutional actors sought to shore up segregated geographies and drive a wedge between interracial sociality. Police officials, jail administrators, social scientists, and myriad state actors turned their attention toward stamping out so-called Black disorder. As they shifted their focus toward this subject, so now do we.

4

"If I Had Told What I Know"

Drug Enforcement and the Streets
of Early Twentieth-Century Baltimore

"I could not tell you that," Alverta "Sweetie" Bailey said from the stand.[1]

Sweetie Bailey was born in Maryland in 1886. She grew up in a neighborhood east of downtown called "the Pot." At thirteen, she lived as a boarder in a cramped alley house and attended school. After finishing her studies, Bailey tended house as a domestic worker and moved to 256 North Chestnut Street—a home located on a small but bustling street in the middle of what the press dubbed the "Great Cocaine Way" for its centrality in the city's early twentieth-century drug trade.[2]

In 1908, state's attorney Albert Owens subpoenaed Bailey, the reputed "Cocaine Queen" of Baltimore City, to testify against Will Dull, a notorious druggist from the Pot who supplied Black men and women with coke to sell on street corners. During her testimony, defense attorney William S. Bryan grilled Bailey regarding the contents of a basket that she had allegedly transported. Already facing charges from another cocaine-related case, Bailey refused to talk. During cross-examination, she pled ignorance:

> BRYAN: What happened to the basket in the store?
> BAILEY: I set the basket down and somebody taken it but I don't know who, because I was scared, I did not know who it was took it.
> BRYAN: What did they do with it?
> BAILEY: I could not tell you because I was not watching.[3]

"If I Had Told What I Know" • 101

Bailey's testimony enraged State's Attorney Owens. He interjected during Bryan's cross-examination to read the court sworn statements that Bailey had made to the grand jury before the case. Bryan, shocked, protested that the state could not attack its own witness. The judge overruled him and briefly suspended the case against Dull to allow Owens time to question Bailey. The judge referred to the bizarre detour as "an inquiry on the part of the Court as to the administration of justice." Dull's defense attorneys stood and watched as the state's attorney decimated his own witness.[4] The state later used that testimony to convict Bailey for perjury. They sentenced her to one year in the Maryland Penitentiary. Will Dull, the pharmacist on trial who supplied the coke, walked scot-free.

Owens's attack on Bailey represented institutional rejections of established systems that state actors sought to replace with newer—and sufficiently punitive—modes of controlling working-class Black men and women in turn-of-the-century Baltimore.[5] For Owens, the criminal legal system served as a tool to punish. Legal convention came second to meting out discipline to an insubordinate Black woman whose constitutional protections against self-incrimination proved inconvenient and obstructive to the state's broader goal of disciplining Black people. During the early twentieth century, politicians, reformers, and social scientists approached the subject of Black criminality through the lens of cultural and hereditary prisms that buttressed Jim Crow projects, including racialized policing, housing segregation, voter disenfranchisement, and battles over public accommodations.[6] As the years after 1895's consequential election demonstrated, Black criminality offered city and state Democrats a key issue on which to stump and regain political power. In Maryland, the strategy was a colossal success as politicians captured Blackness's presumed threats to civil society as "Negro rowdyism." Between 1900 and 1936, Democrats held control of state government for thirty-two years. Increasingly racialized rates of arrest reflected their solution to the "Negro problem" as the state government, who controlled the Baltimore police, appointed Democratic cronies to the police board. Under their administrations, policing in Baltimore oriented around racialized crime control. While Republicans fared nominally better at the city level, this period witnessed intensive institutional and disciplinary impositions on Black life that received bipartisan support from the city council and mayor's office, particularly in the realm of public order policing.

As such, this chapter turns its attention to an important site of police power—the street. The streets that women like Sweetie Bailey walked about in search of livelihoods more fruitful and autonomous than domestic work or laundering, two key industries for Black women.[7] While Bailey balked at Jim Crow

102 · CHAPTER 4

expectations regarding how she should sell her labor, institutional responses to the informal economy were swift and repressive. Police, social welfare agencies, and local government negotiated the nature and reach of state discretion every day through confrontations on street corners, public thoroughfares, and other areas of intimate encounter. As charity agents spotted and institutionalized beggars, peddlers, paupers, and children, uniformed patrolmen scoured the streets for drug dealers, inebriates, prostitutes, pickpockets, and other actors for whom the street provided avenues to sustain a livelihood or, at the very least, a social life. City elites and middle-class reformers proved instrumental in guiding this street-level patrol. They clamored for crime mitigation and the removal or reformation of what they considered depreciating land uses like brothels and crime-ridden neighborhoods. Reformers' influence on police and their assumption of crucial state functions heightened comprehensive regulations of public life, sometimes to the chagrin of police officials who considered such regulation overzealous at best, and a waste of time at worst.[8] As historian Kelly Lytle Hernández notes, such public order policing revealed which groups had a "right to *be*" in public—to exist outside and comfortably under the discerning gaze of the state.[9]

Taken together, the flourishing anti-Black policing that typified early twentieth-century Baltimore, political and reformist investments in such policing, and Jim Crow campaigns that sought to consolidate racial order propelled police campaigns against drug use, commercial sex, and liquor consumption. These campaigns politicized and publicized so-called Black "dysfunction" on city streets en route to strengthening the locality's police power. They also allowed police to test and develop novel and emergent policing technologies that indexed biometric data and anonymized detectives and plainclothes police officers as they spied, watched, and surveilled Baltimoreans.

"The Cocaine Habit": The Racialization of Drug Use

During the late nineteenth and early twentieth centuries, drug dealers began to pop up on Baltimore's streets and peddle coke to interested passersby. They moved clandestinely in and out of stash houses that masqueraded as banal retail establishments and pocketed good money. While Baltimore's drug dealers were predominately white, press coverage in the city—and across the South—ascribed cocaine sale and use to Black Americans. These ascriptions invoked politicized and decidedly nonmedical assessments of cocaine's effects to drum up moral panic and seize on white fears of racial violence. While national narratives about drug use made it seem as though a cocaine epidemic gripped the country, drug consumption in Baltimore was a relatively mild concern compared with other substance-based crimes, such as public drunkenness. The police's own records showed few drug-related arrests. Yet and still, newspapers burst at the seams with stories about Black drug dealers, Black coke addiction, and the corrupting influence of Black drug use on foreign-born whites and city property.

As such, Baltimore's early twentieth-century drug enforcement campaign signaled three key developments regarding the advancing police power of the city. First, while gambling and other criminal activities already invited police surveillance and justified cops' use of bodily search and seizure, drug panic provided an urgency that the police board seized on to advocate for even broader discretion in street policing. They argued that policing city streets required greater impunity to identify, search, and convict drug dealers. In their appeals to state government and the courts, police officials accentuated the uniqueness of patrolling city streets and exhorted the courts to reflect this distinctiveness in their rulings. In a rural state with one of the country's largest cities, Maryland's state government and court system had to recognize that Baltimore required exceptional treatment, particularly in the administration of law enforcement. Extending greater home rule powers to Baltimore's mayor and city council would both bolster local government and allow the police to patrol with fewer constraints.

Second, the drug enforcement campaign and its resulting legislative precedents regarding the city's police power had immense ramifications on the negotiation of Jim Crow neighborhood politics. As frightful stories and reports emerged from the thicket of the city's interracial neighborhoods, the "Negro menace," embodied by the Black drug dealer, activated segregationists who pointed to Black criminality as an infectious influence. This influence, they argued, had the capacity to degrade Black Baltimoreans' southern and eastern European immigrant neighbors, particularly Italian, Russian Jewish, and Czech arrivals, for whom many nativists had little love in the first place. For nativists, those neighborhoods needed to be patrolled, cleansed, and cordoned. To prevent spillover into well-to-do white neighborhoods and developing suburbs, white Baltimoreans championed racial zoning and targeted police enforcement. Taken together, this pairing formed the bedrock of Jim Crow segregation in Baltimore City.

Finally and perhaps most importantly, while Baltimore's foreign-born white immigrants remained firmly embedded in the informal economy and often shared space and drug revenue with Black men and women, prevailing discourses cast Black people as disproportionately involved in fomenting the so-called cocaine evil. For instance, to describe Sweetie Bailey as the "Cocaine Queen" of Baltimore City belied the reality that she was a petty dealer who made $5 a week in service of a white druggist whose influence on cocaine traffic was far more profound. However, Sweetie Bailey personified national moral panic surrounding Black women's supposed incapacity to handle urban life.[10] Moreover, institutional condemnations of Black people reflected Jim Crow ideologies that buttressed separate and unequal treatment. Whether it came from reformers who opined that Black "dependence" was anathema to social progress or from newspapers that toed party lines and propagated Negro rowdyism discourses, ideological constructions of Blackness in early twentieth-century Baltimore often proved useful for city officials who sought more local power to police and protect the color line.[11] Missing from the extant historiography of Baltimore's Jim Crow foundations is a key use case that stoked racialized moral panic and justified the expanded scope and breadth of local government: cocaine.

Derived from the coca leaf, cocaine proved a versatile agent upon its emergence in the late nineteenth-century United States. Practitioners and businesses took advantage of the drug's medical, therapeutic, and recreational properties through incorporation in topical anesthetics, lozenges, and remedies used to treat asthma, catarrh, and other sinus-related ailments. Some tonics, wines, and soft drinks even contained cocaine.[12] On the street, dealers and users called the drug "coke." Commenters called addicts "coke fiends," "whiffers," "snowbirds," and "leapers." Users ingested the drug both hypodermically and through inhalation. Distribution relied on strong connections between druggists and street dealers.[13] The latter received coke from druggists in bulk quantities that they would "whack up" into smaller packets, or "decks." Dealers sometimes diluted these decks with white powders, including magnesia, powdered sugar, and acetanilide, to increase supply and profits. If druggists wished to forgo the process of employing dealers, they could sell the drug from their storefronts using any number of codes to veil the transaction. In one *Sun* exposé on drug trafficking, the reporters noted that asking for a "trip to heaven" was code in some druggeries for a deck of cocaine.[14] In other instances, drug users could deploy specially marked receptacles to signal that they wanted coke.

During the early twentieth century, recreational drug use became a familiar feature of urban leisure and the urban underworld.[15] Based on medical and journalistic efforts, cocaine was broadly associated with Black people, particularly in cities with large Black populations. For instance, Dr. John Young Brown, the superintendent of City Hospital in Saint Louis, claimed that Saint Louis and Memphis were the cocaine epicenters of the United States.[16] The *St. Louis Post-Dispatch* published innumerable stories that highlighted the drug's supposed social effects and suggested enforcement mechanisms to regulate Black drug

"If I Had Told What I Know" • 105

use. In 1902, the paper reported that Mississippi boasted "thousands" of Black drug users and that "the negro succumbs quicker to [cocaine's] seductions than a white man."[17] In 1904, legislators in Oklahoma devised regulatory mechanisms for cocaine use and suggested the creation of a public registry to catalog habitual users.[18] In 1905, police in East Saint Louis alleged that two-thirds of the shootings and cuttings that occurred there could be traced directly to the cocaine habit. The story, like many to come, demonized Black women at all levels of the economic spectrum. It alleged that Black women schoolteachers as well as poorer Black women were similarly susceptible to coke's tantalizing allure.[19] Such stories underscored cocaine's gendered racialization during the early twentieth century. Southern ideologues couched medical diagnoses in larger social and political warnings. They claimed that in cities with significant Black populations, cocaine activated Black criminality in ways that demanded invasive interventions. Indeed, historian David Musto has detailed how Southern whites scapegoated cocaine to stoke fears around racial unrest.[20]

Comparative racialization agitated the moral panic around cocaine use. While press accounts linked Black men and women with cocaine's ills, white people did coke, too. Popular characterizations often contextualized white cocaine use within a sordid and interracial underground economy that corrupted white virtue. After years of reporting on Black cocaine use, the *St. Louis Post-Dispatch* bemoaned the spread of cocaine's allure to "society women."[21] In a 1908 exposé, the paper ran an alarmist piece that characterized cocaine as a step beyond other recreational drugs. Specifically, the editors detailed the growing prevalence of so-called Tennessee Parties in New York's Tenderloin. The name "Tennessee" came from the common drugstore order of "ten-of-c," or ten cents worth of cocaine. Traditionally, New York's drug scene was synonymous with opium, a popular drug that emerged in the United States as a recreational activity after the Civil War. Toward the end of the nineteenth century, opium became associated with an emergent bohemian subculture as well as the profligate and idle rich due to its high price.[22] In reporting on New York's Tennessee Parties, the *Post-Dispatch* detailed how high society men and women had become jaded by the relative weakness of recreational drugs like opium and found that cocaine reactivated the thrill of drug use. The editors emphasized the torridness of New York's black and tans where "Negro orgies" and other interracial affairs occurred as Black and white men and women passed around decadent atomizers filled with liquid cocaine and rose water.[23]

Yellow journalism fueled these national narratives. Southern ideologues seized on Black drug use to draw an explicit connection between urban leisure and supposed Black corruptibility. The link between cocaine, Blackness, and

106 · CHAPTER 4

crime justified ever-increasing police and governmental interventions into Black life. Moreover, the terror of interracial drug use and sex in commercial vice districts shadowed every subsequent story as impressionable white people were said to fall victim to the influence of unscrupulous Black drug peddlers and users. Baltimore's drug war bore all these national features but differed importantly in the extent of its regulation. By the end of the city's war on drugs, narcotics *possession* had been illegalized at the local—rather than state—level in a development that would change policing in the city forever.

The Baltimore dailies took an active role in reporting and supporting drug enforcement efforts. As early as 1903, the *Sun* reported on the "growing evil" of narcotic use.[24] Three years later, after voluminous reporting on recreational drug use, Maryland's attorney general drafted legislation to make drug convictions easier by placing the burden of proof on the accused rather than police or prosecutors. The accused would have to produce evidence of a prescription from a licensed druggist or else face heavy fines. Additionally, druggists could not knowingly sell to addicts. The *Sun* opined that the law would "protect the negro population from the cocaine habit." While scant evidence showed disproportionate drug use among Black people, popular discourses drew a direct line between Blackness, coke, and crime.[25] The same year that Maryland passed its drug law, the federal government passed the Pure Food and Drug Act, which required that products containing cocaine, opium, and alcohol be marked "dangerous." According to historian Andrew W. Cohen, its passage marked the "beginning [of] the era of direct federal regulation of domestic life in the United States."[26] While state and city governments continued to operate relatively autonomously in their unique wars on drugs, the Pure Food and Drug Act foreshadowed more stringent regulations on commercial vice from the highest level of U.S. government. Depictions of rampant urban disorder and municipal police forces' difficulties regulating drug use no doubt informed the federal government's gradual involvement in local affairs.

Dramatic accounts of police raids filled newspapers and stoked latent fears of the volatility of Black criminals and interracial neighborhoods. In one story, the police ransacked a house suspected of selling coke after a woman emerged with a suspicious package. The package contained the drug and a strange piece of paraphernalia. The instrument was a glass and rubber tube. The user filled the glass end with cocaine, inserted it into a nostril, and blew on the rubber end to shoot the powder deep into their nasal cavity. Such propulsion evidently increased the rapidity of the drug's effects. Police arrested the proprietor of the drug den, along with nine other Black men during the raid. In another instance, the police set up a white druggist by hiring a Black informant to buy coke without a prescription. The police and detective bureau used this strategy to great effect by sending countless Black men into pharmacies as undercover agents to entrap druggists.[27] The police also began deploying plainclothes officers to catch drug dealers in the act. According to one story, "The policemen [were] part of the plain-clothes brigade Marshal Farnan has out waging war against the cocaine evil."[28] The reliance on plainclothes officers reflected policing activities on public streets. Because cops had to catch drug dealers in the act of illegally distributing narcotics, uniformed patrolmen became virtually useless. The street, then, became a site of clandestine surveillance that plainclothes officers anonymized themselves on when staking out illicit private establishments or cracking down on underground transactions.

While onlookers lauded the progress of plainclothes cops, officials considered fines, the primary punishment for drug dealing, too lenient. The grand jury sought more breadth for imprisonment given that offenders easily paid fines with drug profits. They suggested imprisonment for sellers and penalties for people found in possession of illegal drugs.[29] Colonel Sherlock Swann, the president of the police board, characterized the state law as "going to war with an enemy and firing eggs against the other side's bullets." While Swann's "Colonel" honorific was purely commemorative, his use of militarized language captured his law enforcement attitude.[30] As one of his first major campaigns in office, Swann planned to aggressively pursue harsher penalties for cocaine traffic, even if it meant potentially destabilizing the already tenuous relationship between the city and the state regarding matters of policing. Swann intended to pass a local law regulating narcotic traffic while the state legislature was out of session. Using the police power provisions of the 1898 city charter, Swann believed the law could stand up to scrutiny in the court of appeals.[31] Swann seized on the police power doctrine to stage a potential challenge to state control over municipal policing and lawmaking. For such a precedent-setting challenge, the police would need a convincing use case. The racialization of cocaine, coupled with racial conflagrations in the country at large, made drug enforcement the perfect case in point.

At the turn of the century, news stories on coke's medical and physiological effects expressed the nature of drug use in markedly social and political ways. These slippery prognoses invoked the dangers of Black unmanageability or attributed Black unrest to cocaine use. Such ideological diagnoses were not unique to Baltimore. In a 1906 Atlanta dispatch to the *Sun*, the editors recounted how the city's race riot that year could, in part, be attributed to "the remarkable increase of the cocaine habit among negroes."[32] White responses to the Atlanta riot bore several parallels to Baltimore's cocaine battle. In Atlanta, crusades

108 · CHAPTER 4

against vagrancy and vice found renewed life as Southern ideologues exploited the riot to justify closing Black saloons and establishing an even more invasive presence in Black social life. Alcohol spurred the supposed Black disposition toward drunken rowdiness. Lest another riot break out, access to booze, white Atlantans argued, had to be restricted.[33] Moreover, much as cocaine—a public health issue—became fodder for the criminalization of Black social life, white Atlantans employed similarly nefarious discourses in their characterizations and treatments of tuberculosis (TB). A communicable virus capable of affecting all people, physicians relied on cultural prescriptions to characterize TB as a "Black virus" that Black people passed onto white people. In this framing, Black people were perpetrators of disease while white people were their victims.[34] A similar dynamic came to characterize cocaine in Baltimore. Since cocaine was a relatively new drug with few commonly understood attributes, the press, physicians, and law enforcement took analogous pains to characterize coke as a "Black drug." Ample yellow journalism contributed to this myth and reinforced discourses of Negro rowdyism that police and segregationists used in their efforts to augment state power and defend their crusades.

In writing about cocaine, the press, much like the charities and reform movements, sought "expert" opinions to lend empirical weight to their contentions. For instance, in a 1906 piece titled "Baltimore's Negroes Are in the Thrall of Cocaine," *Sun* reporters interviewed three supposed white experts on the issue of Black cocaine use in the city. The first expert, a judge, estimated that Black offenders accounted for 90 percent of cocaine addicts. Responding to the startling nature of this figure, the judge noted, "It is a large, but, according to my observation, a conservative estimate of the number of criminal colored people using the drug." According to another judge, "the indulgence of cocaine by uneducated Blacks is responsible for half of the assaults of these beasts upon white women." Moreover, a "moderate" estimate of the percentage of Black people in the city who used cocaine was 70 percent. The third expert, the city jail physician, estimated that the percentage of female prisoners on the drug, which represented the largest demographic group popularly considered users, rested around 20 percent. When asked to speak on the vast discrepancies present in the numbers given by the two judges, the physician speculated that self-reporting and varying definitions of "addiction" contributed to the dissimilarities.[35] The press's reliance on law enforcement officials' assessments of Black drug use offered readers authoritative perspectives. Although their estimates were vastly dissimilar, this appeal to authority reinforced white fears regarding rape, public disorder, and crime that garnered national significance as distinctive elements of Black disorder in the urban imaginary. While the *Sun* did not have to contend with the facts of the issue, the archive affords us some clarity.

According to city jail reports, by 1908, the physician had begun enumerating drug addiction statistics in his annual report. That year, the physician provided treatment to twenty-four patients for drug addiction, mostly white men addicted to opium and morphine. He treated more detainees for asthma, heart disease, and TB than he did for drugs.[36] Black men and women did not receive treatment for cocaine addiction. While cocaine use might not have affected users negatively enough to require medical treatment—a damning rebuttal to the judges' allegations of brutish uncontrollability regardless—a more likely explanation is that the judges' racial animus colored their perceptions. Or perhaps they just lied. Whatever the case, no credible corroboration of the purported epidemic of Black cocaine use exists in any official government publication.

Although cocaine's symptoms and rates of use dramatically varied from account to account, for the city's "experts," there was no question that coke caused crime. Indeed, this attribution was perhaps cocaine's only consistently cited feature. The *Sun* boldly opined that the drug was "the direct cause of much of the current lawlessness among the colored people." In the early stages of panic over cocaine's psychoactive effects, specialists in nervous and mental diseases noted that "much of the insanity and nervous derangement prevalent is noticeably due to the drug habit and crime is often directly traceable to the impulse." Prevailing discourses filtered the connection between crime, insanity, and cocaine through a prism of racialized and gendered assumptions. One commenter reasoned that "the practice of cocaine using is confined at present almost exclusively to the colored population and to degraded white women. To narrow it down more, it may be said that the practice is confined to the criminal element, but when this is asserted it practically means exactly what the first sentence did."[37] In identifying both the "colored" population and "degraded" white women as the city's primary drug users, the editorialist propagated unsubstantiated perceptions of women's drug use—rooted in anti-Black and misogynist sentiments—that explicitly situated their supposed proclivities as the source of the lion's share of crime in the city. The press continued to push the party line of Negro rowdyism which supposedly spurred the present upsurge of criminal behavior fueled by the cocaine evil. What is more, the press highlighted the seemingly contagious effect of Black cocaine use on white working-class women and, in so doing, parroted segregationist ideologies regarding the ruinous consequences of integration.

Continuous news stories on cocaine-related crimes in interracial neighborhoods bolstered these perceptions, while longer exposés profiled the nature of cocaine addiction in thickly descriptive accounts. Both contributed to broader presumptions about Black people—specifically Black women—who the press characterized as violent and unruly. On June 21, 1902, on the last page of the *Sun*'s morning edition, there appeared a small but powerful story titled, "Cocaine and Beer Cause Trouble." In it, reporters detailed how Henrietta Woods, a twenty-two-year-old Black woman who the police later identified as a prostitute, created a commotion on Chestnut Street. According to the story, Woods shattered a beer glass over the head of one woman and a lampshade over the head of another because she "couldn't get enough beer to wash down a quantity of cocaine." Woods then reportedly threw another beer bottle in the direction of a patrolman who detained her.[38] Despite the paper's contention that Woods assaulted no less than three people, the patrolman took her to the Central District station house where the magistrate charged her with one count of making "loud and unseemly noises." For her actions, the magistrate fined Woods $50 and committed her to the city jail.[39] Despite the story's likely sensationalism, Black working-class women's violent actions regularly appeared in newsprint to provide credence to the idea that they both used cocaine more frequently than any other group in the city and that doing so led them to stir public disorder and commit wanton acts of physical violence.[40]

Three years after the publication of Woods's activities on Chestnut Street, the *Sun* published a much longer story with the subhead, "Nearly Every Negress Arrested Is a Victim of the Drug." The story documented what it considered a common cocaine narrative. In it, an abstracted Black woman managed to procure some coke after borrowing ten cents from a friend, typically on Chestnut Street, also called the "Great Cocaine Way." She probably bought it from a druggist or drug dealer, who often worked for a druggist. Once the woman's body absorbed the drug, she became enraged and created an uproar that ended in violence or some other crime. Police would arrest and imprison her. Tucked in her cell, the woman's "shrieks and yells, curses and blasphemies" shook the station house. Unable to control herself, she became erratically despondent and energized. She could dance the entire night without a break—a victim of the "largeness of her freedom."[41]

This characterization of the unbearable weight of freedom spoke to broader discourses that masked white social critiques of Black life behind pseudo-medical diagnoses of cocaine's effects. For instance, one editorialist claimed, "Many [cocaine users] are rendered frantic, and public disorder and breaches of the peace are constant results."[42] In articulating the consequences of the drug's consumption, onlookers focused on the social and political consequences of drug use, which they linked to Black civil unrest and violence. The equivocation of the drug's symptoms reflected a political investment, not in discovering the medical nuances of cocaine but in condemning its users. In one editorialist's estimation, "Whisky is bad, opium is worse, more destructive of the moral nature, more ruinous; cocaine seems simply to annihilate. It is swifter than any of the others and kills morals, character, mind, and body together."[43] Whereas some viewed the drug as responsible for producing "mad" and "crazed" users who became hell-bent on creating public disturbances and fomenting race riots, this commenter viewed the drug as an agent of annihilation that destroyed ambition, created listlessness, and encouraged laziness. The paradox here—that some attributed the drug to rage and others to listlessness—did not so much illuminate the medical effects of cocaine as it pointed to the biases implicit in commenters' opinions on the cultural proclivities of Black people.

Although there is medical merit to such disparate prognoses, the context in which these varying reports emerged coincided with moral panics associated with Black urban settlement and crime.[44] The line of reasoning that emerged in popular discourses assumed that disruptive behavior and cocaine were intrinsically linked—one no doubt led to the other. While the outward expression of these discussions used the terminology and seemingly objective approach of medicine, the overtly political conclusions reproduced common condemnations of Blackness. The period's reform literatures and other prominent academic denunciations of Blackness furthered similar theories and contributed to the panic that gripped cities. In these discussions of cocaine's symptoms, commenters arrived at what was becoming codified at the time as the nature, not of cocaine use, but of *Blackness*. Such treatments cast the drug as the root of social ills in Baltimore's working-class communities while presenting absurd yet effective falsifications regarding the problem's extent.

Much of the cocaine-related journalism that appeared during the early twentieth century covered interracial neighborhoods located just outside of downtown. On Bath Street, near City Hospital,[45] the *Sun* branded one neighborhood "the Meadow," home to the Meadow Gang. Much more infamous than the Meadow, where Henrietta Woods committed her alleged assaults (or perhaps made some loud noises), rested "the Pot," sometimes called "the Jungle."[46] This neighborhood formed the core of the broader "Cocaine Belt," which sat just south of present-day Old Town and east of downtown. After countless stories, the Pot became the epicenter of white racial fear—an interracial, disorderly, cocaine-filled site of bygone civilization where Black men and women corrupted degraded white immigrants. On May 31, 1908, in a piece titled "Quiet Region of Homes, and Later a Resort of Bad Men, 'The Pot' Is Now the Center of the Cocaine Trade," the *Sun* described the neighborhood residents as "beautifully indolent," noting that "they all remind you of a bunch of overgrown children."

112 · CHAPTER 4

Such descriptions echoed New South ideologues who justified stringent regulations of Black life based on the assumption that Black people constituted "an infantilized and separate species" lacking the ability to self-govern.[47]

Given these presumptions, the neighborhood's condition did not surprise onlookers. Teeming tenants with unstable employment filled unkempt and deteriorating houses and did nothing to maintain them. A neighborhood of renters, the paper conveniently omitted that maintaining collapsing properties did not fall to tenants. No matter. Such conditions proved the existence of the ongoing "race suicide" the paper perceived among Black Baltimoreans. This assessment enforced cultural evolutionary theories of the relative fitness for civil life that the Charity Organization Society and social scientists believed Black men and women lacked. The streets and sidewalks ran amok with "little half-dressed pickaninnies," "lounging men," and "dirty hucksters." Saloons dotted the blocks. These haunts served as gathering spaces for the immoral "Potters" who frequented them rather than attending church or school. It hadn't always been this way, though. In the "good old days," the Pot served as home to respectable white working families whom these incorrigible Black hucksters and white ethnic victims replaced.[48] This interracial composition likely contributed to the community's namesake. The Pot boiled over with the unnatural and reprehensible shared lifestyles of poor Black and foreign-born people. As segregationist fervor raged on, the Pot served as a cautionary tale for the inevitable results of racial intermingling. The neighborhood became a scapegoat in the popular imaginary whose existence validated sweeping "protections" in racial zoning laws and strategies.

This intermingling went beyond merely living in the same area. In the Pot, foreign-born white and Black residents sometimes lived on the same block and even sometimes in the same homes.[49] While the majority of the Pot's inhabitants were Russian Jews and Black people, there were notable Italian, Austrian, and German clusters. Russian Jews dominated Exeter and Aisquith Streets, while Black residents occupied most of the residences on Chestnut Street and the small dwellings on Hull's Lane, Half Moon Alley, and Necessity Alley. A site where race mixing was—at the very least—a begrudged reality, the Pot presented living opportunities for outlier minorities, including some Cubans and Bolivians. The Pot's racial and ethnic integration made the neighborhood a menacing possibility for well-to-do whites, who had at this point developed a reputation for intimidating potential Black residents or forming protective societies to prevent Black settlement in their neighborhoods—tactics that ensured that parts of the city remained heavily segregated and sheltered from the perceived corruption of Negro rowdyism which stewed in places like the Pot.[50]

"If I Had Told What I Know" • 113

Amid this voluminous reporting, which scapegoated Black men and women through appeals to academic authority that validated presumptions regarding Black crime's supposed detrimental effects on public morality and residential space, two highly visible figures emerged. These figures were Daniel "Big Dan" Waters and Alverta "Sweetie" Bailey. Even though neither had much access to cocaine—they relied on a white druggist for it—the press characterized them as masterminds of the cocaine trade. The profiling of these two Potters' identities, much like the description of Henrietta Woods, cited prevailing associations of Blackness and crime. A close analysis of their public representation reveals the tactics that the white press deployed in the construction of the Black criminal. Allusions to certain details of the Potters' identities spoke volumes about normative interpretations of what constituted a productive and moral citizenry. Their deviations no doubt animated and justified disciplinary and segregationist zeal as whites became incensed by the prospect of living, like their Russian Jewish and Italian counterparts, in areas where Negro rowdyism prevailed.

Big Dan Waters was born in Maryland around 1870. His local origin did not stop the press from curating Waters's public image to coincide with stereotypes associated with Afro-Southern migrants. The press described the thirty-nine-year-old Big Dan as a saloonkeeper–turned–drug dealer and a "hoodoo" practitioner who carried a conjure bag filled with quicksilver and rabbit's feet. Big Dan's corner was located at the intersection of Low and Chestnut Streets. The pink packaging of his cocaine decks distinguished his sales. In a piece written in May 1908, the *Sun* detailed, in dramatic fashion, the police's raid of Big Dan's home. During the raid, the cops found a safe which held "$16.90, a package of powder which [was] believed to be cocaine, and a 'conjure bag.'"[51] A sketch of Big Dan accompanied the story (figure 7).

The press's sensational characterization of Big Dan relied on tropes typically associated with Afro-Southern migrants to elicit fear and fascination from city readers. By emphasizing Big Dan's "hoodoo" practice, the paper condemned what they considered a pagan and blasphemous form of folk magic. Black Americans regularly practiced supernaturalism to navigate the harsh realities of life under Jim Crow. According to historian LaShawn Harris, believers of hoodoo relied on spiritual practice, in part, to "prevent and navigate race, gender, and class discrimination." While Big Dan likely relied on hoodoo as a meaningful everyday practice, white and some Black bourgeois onlookers regarded hoodoo as a "manifestation of [the] Black southern culture and African primitivism" associated with the poor, the uneducated, and the criminal.[52] Big Dan's relationship with hoodoo served to further criminalize him and communicate a superstitious practice synonymous with con artists and Afro-Southern migrants.

Additionally, Big Dan's transition from a brick-and-mortar saloonkeeper to a drug dealer lent credibility to the idea that Black men preferred the seediness of the underground economy to the "dignity" of poor-paying and racially discriminatory work in the conventional labor economy. Big Dan represented an alien interloper whose desire to live as a "bad man" spread a civilization-threatening evil in the city's slums. His press sketch lent a Black face to this evil.

While Big Dan became synonymous with Black masculine criminality, Alverta "Sweetie" Bailey, a twenty-three-year-old domestic worker reared in the Pot, became synonymous with Black working-class women drug dealers. Police first arrested Bailey for selling cocaine on May 6, 1908. Sadie Harris, one of her patrons, gave her up to authorities.[53] After receiving the tip, police alleged that they apprehended Bailey as she transported fifty-three decks of cocaine that she had received without a prescription in a covered basket. Once in police custody, Bailey "peached"—or snitched—on Big Dan, who had given her the coke. The police promptly arrested Big Dan and charged him with fourteen counts of selling cocaine without a prescription.[54] Although just a petty dealer in the employ of Waters and a white druggist named Will Dull, the public came to

Figure 7. A photo of Daniel "Big Dan" Waters that appeared in a *Baltimore Sun* article detailing the raid of his home. Source: "'Big Dan's' Safe Opened," *Baltimore Sun*, May 29, 1908.

"*If I Had Told What I Know*" • 115

know Sweetie Bailey as the "Cocaine Queen." A reputed mastermind, Bailey's actual involvement in drug trafficking was small and purely practical. As a domestic worker, Bailey made $2 a week. When she began selling drugs for Will Dull, she started earning $5 a week. Waters and Bailey struck up an arrangement wherein Bailey would access a locked bureau in the back of a cigar store, divide the cocaine found inside into decks, and sell each deck for twenty-five cents. She would then return the profit—subtracting her $5 cut—to Waters.[55] Although press coverage of Bailey focused on highlighting the supposed depravity of working-class Black women, reading along and against the grain, there is much to be gleaned from the woman the press dubbed the "Cocaine Queen."

Bailey, employed like many Black working-class women as a domestic laborer, abandoned her job and more than doubled her weekly salary as a drug dealer.[56] Keeping house, while a popular occupation among working-class Black women who could not find work elsewhere, paid poorly. To make ends meet, Bailey began dealing drugs and raised her standard of living immeasurably. Additionally, Bailey challenged prevailing understandings of Black working-class women's easy victimization by refusing to be incriminated by her coconspirators, all of whom were men and many of whom were in law enforcement. From the city jail, she accused Waters of selling cocaine without a prescription and Will Dull of providing bulk quantities of cocaine to Black drug dealers. Moreover, Bailey's intimate knowledge of police racketeering kept her out of jail and allowed her to determine her own destiny. In response to a reporter who probed her about a mysterious benefactor who bailed her out of jail, Bailey reportedly said, "Well, I don't know much about that. It's probably because I kept my mouth shut when some policemen were before the Police Commissioners. If I had told what I know they would not be wearing brass buttons."[57] Bailey, like so many other Black women who peached on corrupt cops, sought justice through self-preservation and weaponized knowledge to advocate on her own behalf.[58]

In the midst of her cocaine woes, Bailey insisted, "I am out of jail and I don't want to go back." She leveraged her knowledge of the police's indiscretions to advocate for her freedom. This opportunity was made possible by the direct and oblique encounters that Black men and women experienced navigating city streets and coming into frequent and intimate contact with police. As much as police watched suspected criminals, working people watched them, too. Bailey used the information she culled from her encounters to engage in acts of what historian Sarah Haley calls "Black feminist refusal," or "the rejection of psychic and social domination" at the hands of law enforcement. Although these everyday actions did not have the capacity to radically alter the criminal legal system, they nevertheless challenged, temporarily stymied, or functioned as exertions

116 · CHAPTER 4

of individual will in the face of brutal repression.[59] The press coverage of the Pot, its Black residents, and its drug dealers dovetailed with Progressive thought concerning the irregular and antisocial lifestyles that distinguished Jim Crow modernity. The reproduction of Big Dan's police sketch provided a literal face with which the *Sun*'s readers could associate the cocaine evil. Sweetie Bailey's defiance of authority and her characterization as opportunistic and duplicitous buttressed national and local understandings of the dangers of Black freedom. At both levels, the intensification of police power in poor neighborhoods was seen as warranted and necessary. The *Sun* heralded Big Dan's and Sweetie Bailey's arrests as "the most important capture[s] so far in the crusade against cocaine."[60] This sentiment was short lived. As Bailey had refused to go down without dragging Big Dan and Will Dull with her, she similarly refused to let the Pot's beat cops off the hook. From jail, she peached on several officers. Her testimony led to the biggest police scandal since the policy hearings of 1897.

In May 1908, the police board suspended five white cops on charges of negligence (figure 8).[61] They based the charges on testimony provided by incarcerated Black men and women, including Sweetie Bailey. The complainants alleged that the officers protected the sale and distribution of cocaine in the Pot in exchange for bribes—an eminently standard transactional arrangement that coincided with national policing conventions in which cops provided cover for vice in exchange for kickbacks.[62] As was its custom, the police board adjudicated the matter internally.

The cops' hearing began on June 6, 1908. Police board president Sherlock Swann, grandson of Thomas Swann, the man who signed the law that formalized Baltimore's modern police force, presided over the affair. On the first day of the trial, over a dozen witnesses testified. Most of the witnesses lived or operated in the Pot. The witnesses accused the officers of looking the other way when they bought or sold cocaine, receiving hundreds of dollars from Will Dull in return for police protection, alerting dealers to police activity in the neighborhood, recruiting dealers for Dull, and even steering Black voters away from the polls on election days. In response to the allegations, the officers' counsel mounted a defense that relied on demonstrating that the witnesses were untrustworthy. During cross-examination, counsel forced Potters to admit to past criminal offenses. They also made light of the Potters' unique speech habits and lifestyles to magnify a distinctive Black vernacular that whites generally interpreted as dishonest or untrustworthy. Over the course of the trial, Potters admitted to acts of larceny, assault, domestic violence, perjury, and even "fussing."[63] The defense swayed Swann and the police board who were predisposed to view the witnesses as unreliable.

"If I Had Told What I Know" • 117

Figure 8. As five police officers were accused of aiding and abetting cocaine traffic in downtown Baltimore, suspicions arose regarding their complicity in fomenting, rather than quelling, cocaine use. Source: "Has It Reached 'The Finest'?" *Baltimore Sun*, May 27, 1908.

After three days dominated by the public incrimination of the Potters, Swann brought the case to an abrupt end. The defense had not even argued its side.[64] Swann quickly delivered the verdict. The police board acquitted all five officers, immediately reinstated them to active duty, assured them that they would receive payment for the period of their suspension, and tasked them with "cleansing" the immoral conditions of the Pot within thirty days of their acquittals. Commenting on the abrupt nature of the acquittal, Swann said, "Although we heard the statements of some of the witnesses before the trial, we heard a different side of the case. We didn't know the witnesses were the class of people they proved to be."[65] Swann refused to hear any additional testimony from the Potters.

Notably, Governor Austin Crothers, the man who appointed (and offered to reappoint) Swann to his post, found the police board's judgment in the case

118 • CHAPTER 4

unsatisfactory. Crothers felt that Swann should have been less permissive on matters of police misconduct—a consistent sticking point during the rest of Swann's tenure. After announcing his retirement from the police board, in a hastily scrawled note buried in his personal papers, Swann reflected,

> If findings of Board was thought bad judgement [Governor Crothers] should have said so and not reappointed board. . . . Unfair to let me retire if work was unsatisfactory. . . . No fair minded man could find the officers guilty on such testimony.[66]

On the last point, Swann was partially right. Perhaps less "fair minded" than racist, an all-white jury did acquit Will Dull, the true mastermind of coke selling in the Pot. Like the police board hearing, Potters, including Sweetie Bailey, comprised many of the witnesses in Dull's case, and the defense counsel similarly exploited the jury's prejudices to sway them toward lenience for the druggist. Yet and still, Crothers's admonitions reflected a broader shift in national and local politics wherein systematized civil reform, standards of accountability, and municipal responsibility came to the fore—at least superficially. While Swann's administration of the Baltimore police left much to be desired, his enduring legacy contributed to these broader political currents.

During the trial, Swann drafted an ordinance intended to stamp out the cocaine evil once and for all. Popularly called "Swann's Cocaine Ordinance," the law made it illegal for any person or entity to "sell, furnish, give away, or have in his, her, their, or its possession" any regulated narcotic.[67] The ordinance penalized drug possession for the first time in Maryland. States like Massachusetts and New York would follow suit in 1910, and the federal government would finally intervene with the passage of the Harrison Act in 1914 which banned cocaine and opiates.[68] Alarmist stories, theories, and reports accompanied its passage. Black men and women had become symbols of dysfunction, addiction, and gross indulgence; they simply could not handle the freedom of the city and resorted to drugs and booze to cope. Or so the story went. Despite voluminous yellow journalism, over the next three years, police arrested eighty-one people under Swann's Cocaine Ordinance. Of these, seventy-two, or 89 percent, were men and 60 percent were white.[69] These statistics countered popularly disseminated narratives that Black people—particularly Black women—had fallen victim to cocaine use in panicking numbers. One story went so far as to allege that "99 out of every 100 negro women" abused cocaine, a stunningly inaccurate but persuasive statistic.[70]

Baltimore's cocaine crusade typified broader trends in policing, neighborhood politics, and the racialization of crime. Cops combed poor neighborhoods for evidence of wicked conduct and criminal activity. The street became a site of everyday encounter among cops and working people that resulted in corruption, disproportionate rates of arrest for Black men and women, and potential brutality. The plainclothes officer became uniquely important to street-level patrolling as cops anonymized themselves and scoured suspected drug haunts. Journalists publicized the seediness of urban streets and constructed an imaginary in which the wanton disorder of interracial neighborhoods stemmed from the corrupting influences of Black men and women—in this case, drug dealers and users. Such scrutiny fed national and local narratives regarding the supposed depravity of Black men and women as the press quoted "expert" opinions regarding cocaine's purported capacity to increase instances of rape, racial unrest, and public disorder. Moreover, accounts gestured toward the corruptibility of foreign-born immigrants, many of whom participated in cocaine sale and consumption. This reality did not lead to a similarly virulent condemnation of foreign-born white immigrants; instead, the press and segregationists used white lapses into what they considered Black habits to fortify Jim Crow ideologies and justify segregationist crusades. The cocaine evil signaled a potentially catastrophic outcome. If local government did not have the capacity to organize residential space and cordon white neighborhoods, Baltimore would become a city of Pots. Luckily, Swann's Cocaine Ordinance provided a powerful tool with which to tackle this issue.

"General in Terms but Very Ample": Swann's Cocaine Ordinance and the Expansion of Police Power

On July 11, 1908, Howard Nelson, a Black man, entered William Rossberg's pharmacy on the 900 block of Frederick Avenue. Nelson asked Rossberg for six decks of cocaine. Rossberg obliged and charged Nelson $1.50 for the drugs. Just then, detectives blew through the doors and put Rossberg in handcuffs. The druggist became the most high-profile victim of Swann's Cocaine Ordinance.[71]

The criminal court charged Rossberg with nine cocaine violations, including selling without a prescription and possession.[72] Rossberg did not accept his punishment quietly. His attorneys challenged the ordinance's constitutionality. The Baltimore police was a state agency. They enforced state laws. The 1906 state drug law, which Swann found lacking, did not criminalize drug possession and carried laxer fines. Given the ordinance's excessive penalties and the Baltimore police's subordinate position to the state government, Rossberg's attorneys argued that it violated the Maryland Constitution which protected against excessive fines and cruel treatment. State's attorney Owens countered that the city's 1898 home rule charter provided broad latitude for city officials to legislate in the interest of the public peace through its police power provisions.[73] The judges of the Supreme Bench sided with Owens.

In their decision, the Supreme Bench noted that cities around the country had to contend with issues of urban density, lawlessness, and dysfunction that required harsher penalties and severer measures than statewide legislation could anticipate or adequately address. Such considerations often led to the vestment of wider authority in local government. This dynamic constituted a central feature of police power which the judges described as "general in terms but very ample." Rather than provide precise parameters to such an undefinable concept, the judges characterized police power as any measure taken to ensure the "safety, health, and good morals of a community." Given an infinite number of perspectives, this definition functionally included any and every measure. To narrow this scope, the judges invoked a standard of "reasonableness." While police power provided theoretically limitless power, the intention behind its use presumed that local government would not invoke it oppressively or unreasonably. When applied to narcotic possession, the judges found Swann's Cocaine Ordinance eminently reasonable. After all, statutes in Maryland and around the country made possession of much less harmful paraphernalia, including policy slips, oysters, and gill nets, illegal in some cases. On these grounds, the judges of the Supreme Bench and, later, the court of appeals upheld the constitutionality of the ordinance. The criminal court sentenced Rossberg to one day in jail and assessed the druggist a $100 fine.[74]

The court's decision elated Colonel Swann and Marshal Farnan. They planned to immediately apply the precedent to regulate the possession of other dangerous and illegal objects, including razors and guns. State's attorney Owens applauded the decision for allowing the city broader latitude in the exercise of home rule. He noted, "The decision is of value, as it establishes the right of the city to absolute home rule on all matters of police regulations."[75] The decision was not only a coup for the police department; it also provided segregationists with a new tool in the fight for racial zoning. In upholding the cocaine ordinance, the court affirmed the city's extensive power and duty to mediate urban conflict through interventions in public and private life. Chief among these conflicts was where people lived. Milton Dashiell, one of the architects of racial zoning in the country, frequently referenced the *Rossberg* decision while campaigning for the passage of the United States' first racial zoning ordinance which prohibited Black and white residents from living on the same blocks as they did in the Pot.[76]

The decision bore a lasting impression on policing and urban governance in Baltimore. Built on a drug war that demonized Black men and women through overblown prescriptions of deviance, addiction, and social unrest, the ruling provided legal weight to the police's invasive and discretionary capacities to stop and search people suspected of having illegal things on them on city streets. The decision proved important for Swann's career and legacy, though he had only been in power for a few months. While he rode the *Rossberg* wave for a time, his Democratic loyalties prevented him from fully embracing much of the anti-vice advocacy foisted on him by Progressive Republicans who exhorted him to apply the same energy he had applied to cocaine to policing liquor and sex work. Privately, Swann considered such policing a "disgrace" that took "officers from regular work."[77] Publicly, Swann, the man who toppled the artificial cocaine epidemic, was expected to expand his crusade and tackle other urban vices. Taken as a whole, Swann's tenure stood in the borderlands of old-style machine-based policing that protected political allies while punishing foes and the broader civil service reform movement that idealized apolitical bureaucratic efficiency. Although he struggled greatly with the administration and necessity of vice policing, he did manage to streamline policing identification, surveillance, and street-level enforcement in ways that continued to expand the police's already broad ability to control, seize, search, and index human bodies. The cocaine crusade reverberated for the rest of Swann's tenure as he reluctantly took aim at sex work, Sabbatarianism, and other forms of commercial urban leisure.

"Facing the Masks": Surveillance, Sex, and Alcohol

In March 1909, the police arrested William F. Downs, a stock clerk, for embezzling thousands of dollars from city coffers.[78] The arresting officers turned Downs over to the Bureau of Identification (BOI), a department established in 1900 to develop and coordinate fingerprinting, biometric, and photographic technology. Downs refused to allow the BOI to take his biometric data and challenged the police's ability to do so in the courts. The complaint reached the court of appeals which upheld the police's right to photograph offenders because such photographs, fingerprints, and bodily measurements enabled police to identify repeat offenders and fell within the purview of the department's police power. Given the court of appeals' ruling, the criminal court ordered the warden of the city jail to turn Downs over to the marshal for identification.[79]

The precedent established in Downs's case emboldened the ever-expansive breadth of surveillance that typified the police's ubiquitous control over the human body at the turn of the century. As plainclothes cops combed the streets for drug dealers in simpler and more direct approaches, the police force adopted the latest policing technologies to index offenders, anonymize detectives, and collect demographic information that contributed to the development of criminal

122 • CHAPTER 4

typologies.[80] Reformers influenced such tactics by, in many cases, modeling how effective private undercover surveillance could be in apprehending moral offenders of gambling, liquor, and prostitution laws. Indeed, historian Jennifer Fronc has detailed how such private undercover investigation served a crucial function in extending state and police power during the early twentieth century.[81]

In police station houses, cops adopted modern surveillance technologies to modernize their operations. Some of these techniques included photography and biometric standards of identification that became commonplace among municipal police departments around the country.[82] The BOI, which police used to catalog arrestees, build cases, and identify fugitives, spurred many of these technical advancements.[83] The bureau maintained a photography room to take portraits of offenders and used implements to measure suspects' body parts. Using the Bertillon system, which relied on anthropometry to index offenders' forehead, nose, head, and ear measurements, as well as identifying marks, scars, and tattoos, the police developed databases of offenders. In 1904, the department adopted the Henry classification system of fingerprinting, which refined fingerprint classification through use of "ridge counting" and "ridge tracing."[84] Finally, the BOI, through use of an electric Neostyle mimeograph, printed and distributed daily "lookout sheets" with individualized descriptions of suspected criminals, lost and stolen property, and missing persons.[85] One representative entry to the lookout sheet read, "Lookout for 17 five gallon empty milk-cans, one bed comfort with flowers, a broom with blue handles."[86] The lookout sheet remained a staple of policework in Baltimore until well after mid-century, if not longer. In the 1950s, the lookout sheet became the "persons wanted" daily brief. The chief inspector distributed the brief which contained precise descriptions of wanted persons.[87]

After recording offenders, the BOI sorted them into groups that corresponded with criminal classes on which they wished to keep tabs. One such class, "Dishonest Servants," cataloged mostly Black women domestic workers who stole from their employers. Given paltry wages and the desperation engendered by the pressures of urban life, Black women domestic workers resorted to all manner of redress, including collective organizing, quitting without notice, or stealing.[88] Each identification sheet contained the smallest minutiae of offenders' body types.[89] In one arrestee description, police cataloged Hattie Woodbridge, a twenty-one-year-old Black woman domestic worker who lived in West Baltimore. She stood five-foot three-inches tall and weighed 110 pounds. She had black woolly hair, brown skin, a slender build, adhering earlobes, and a burn scar on her right wrist. Mary J. Burke, Woodbridge's employer, called the police on her and her roommate Kate Vincent. Police identified Vincent as a "Mulatto"

"If I Had Told What I Know" • 123

born in Indian Territory.[90] The criminal court charged the two with the theft of linens, spoons, forks, pitchers, cups, saucers, and plates. The all-white jury found both women guilty. They sentenced Vincent to two years in the penitentiary and Woodbridge to four.[91] It was both women's first offense. Woodbridge's and Vincent's experiences revealed the racialized and gendered biases of the criminal legal system. Their harsh punishment no doubt stemmed from a desire to bolster racial hierarchy and put Black working-class women—particularly those who kept house in white residences—in their place at the bottom of that hierarchy. Their experiences with the BOI also revealed the emphasis that Swann placed on keeping pace with advancements in criminal surveillance and professionalizing police operations.

As Swann spurred this process forward, surveillance became one of his central focuses. Under his tenure, the BOI was active as never before, significantly increasing the number of arrestees photographed, measured, and fingerprinted.[92] Additionally, Swann determinedly researched ways to strengthen the department's surveillance operations and stay on the cutting edge of policing trends. In 1909, to empower and encourage citizens to contact police, Swann's police board produced a pamphlet titled "Information for Citizens."[93] The police distributed the pamphlet to ensure that civilians knew the locations of call boxes and station houses. This device encouraged the citizenry to become involved in law enforcement processes while deploying the department's new technology. Swann also drummed up relationships with other municipal police departments. This proclivity was not unique to Swann as police chiefs, detectives, and specialists, like BOI officials, worked across geographic boundaries to stay apprised of new policing trends, technologies, and strategies. For instance, one of Swann's relationships resulted in the adoption of a novel detective strategy that presaged the two-way mirror.

In March 1908, Commissioner Theodore Bingham invited Swann to examine the New York police's newest detective strategy.[94] Swann entered an assembly room where he encountered one hundred detectives wearing white muslin masks. The detectives conducted the daily lineup and closely analyzed forty prisoners.[95] Bingham relayed the importance of the masks, noting that, in some cases, "crooks . . . would have themselves arrested upon some pretext or another just for the chance of studying the faces of the detectives."[96] The mask strategy addressed the creative and oblique tactics men and women used to spy on the cops. Criminals flipped the top-down gaze of the police state to engage in their own form of looking and to identify and informally catalog the identities of cops and detectives.[97] The masks, then, allowed detectives to preserve their anonymity in a constantly evolving conflict among police and civilians.

Swann, enamored by the idea of masked detectives, returned from New York determined to institute a similar process in Baltimore. He believed that the new mask policy (i.e., "facing the masks") would allow more comprehensive and sophisticated detective work. In the past, to preserve detectives' secrecy, they would rarely interface with detainees. Instead, they relied on photographs and Bertillon measurement data. Now detectives could analyze prisoners in the flesh and familiarize themselves with their embodied features.[98] The police board formalized the policy in July 1908. Detectives sported masks "of the ordinary white dominoes, with muslin covering the lower part of their face[s]."[99] Swann was so proud of the police's advances in criminal identification that he invited Governor Crothers to tour the BOI, have his "mugg" taken, and witness the masked spectacle firsthand (figure 9). Crothers lauded the masked detectives and expressed his adoration for the professionalization that Swann had spearheaded.[100] Each of these developments compounded state power by allowing police and detectives to blend into public spaces and surveil suspected criminals with little fear of being identified themselves.

Figure 9. Detectives don their masks to examine a suspect. Source: "The White Masks Inspecting a Prisoner at Detective Headquarters. Circa 1908–1910." Courtesy of the Maryland Center for History and Culture, PP8.585.

"If I Had Told What I Know" • 125

In addition to new surveillance practices and technologies, the department continued to use tried-and-true tools and approaches. During day-to-day policing, patrolmen relied on a comprehensive system of signal boxes that allowed officers to communicate with station houses and ask for backup and horse-drawn patrol wagons to transport offenders without having to face the wrath of potentially angry mobs.[101] These patrol boxes and transport wagons strengthened the neighborhood-level police presence on public streets by allowing patrolmen to remain on their beats without having to personally escort suspects to precincts.[102] Uniformed patrolmen relied on old-fashioned intimidation and harassment to instill fear and demand deference from civilians. Although the police board rarely addressed the complaints that resulted from such encounters, some caught their attention. Most of the complaints that they entertained came from well-to-do white citizens who they held in higher regard than working-class immigrant and Black residents who routinely encountered and protested police violence. In one instance, Henry Bergman, a white bookkeeper, complained about a patrolman who mean mugged him on a train car. When Bergman asked what the problem was, the patrolman replied, "You look like a bad actor, if you don't watch out I'll lock you up."[103] Although the patrolman likely only wished to intimidate Bergman, the threat was not an idle one. In 1909, the police booked sixty-one people on "suspicious character" charges.[104] Even though they investigated Bergman's complaint, the police board did not discipline the officer. This encounter represented emergent patterns in police-civilian relations. As cops became more firmly embedded in the social life of the city, interpersonal acts of intimidation, backed by the tacit threat of violence, typified civilian life. Although impossible to quantify each of these types of encounters given their sheer magnitude and the police board's unwillingness to systematically investigate complaints against officers, the complaints for which there were investigations provide a glimpse into police-civilian relations on city streets.

For instance, in April 1909, Leigh Bonsal, a white lawyer and reformer, petitioned Colonel Swann on behalf of two friends, Robert and Cornelius Brown, both Black men. They had been caught in a dragnet at a busy intersection where patrolmen arrested dozens of Black men. Bonsal, quite naively, suggested that the police board give the arresting officer, a patrolman who had only been on the force for two months (i.e., a "probationer"), a slap on the wrist for treating his clients roughly. The police board refused. Irate, Bonsal tore into the commissioners. He criticized their decision to excuse a gross injustice as an "honest mistake." He wondered rhetorically if efficiency and duty factored into their vision for the police at all. He snarled that the police board condoned street-level activity whose "evident purpose [was] intimidating the whole negro population."[105] The dragnet appeared that way because the police *did* endeavor to maintain public order by targeting Black men and women on charges of disorderly conduct and disturbing the peace. The street was a site of confrontation where the impunity of police power manifested in the seemingly arbitrary use of force that was nothing short of intentional. Cops policed the color line, regulated overblown charges of Negro rowdyism, and instilled intimidation under the seemingly race-neutral goal of upholding the public good. What became clear in these racialized policing conventions was that busy intersections in bustling parts of town were not for Black folks and that cops had both the power and penchant to steer them to different parts of town.

As patrolmen worked to control crowds, intimidate, and establish an obvious police presence by walking streets with their badges and uniforms on full display, the plainclothes officer sneaked around the city to gather intel and respond to complaints from wealthy business owners. They staked out saloons and brothels and gathered evidence for potential raids. The police board generally focused on establishments about which influential reformers, prominent businesses, or trade associations complained. For instance, in September 1909, the Old Town Merchants and Manufacturers Association protested the presence of a bawdy house near a cluster of commercial interests on Gay Street. They believed that the women who exited the bawdy house in loose fitting clothing and who "street walked" on the main thoroughfare posed a threat to their businesses and to the property values of the area. The police board obliged the association and stationed a plainclothes police officer to surveil the house and assess the looseness of women's dresses.[106] Such preemptive and undercover policing reinforced the cops' express duty to protect private property while positioning women's forms of "suggestive" dress as anathema to that goal. Policing strategies also demonstrated how plainclothes officers established an omniscient yet hidden presence on the streets. They spread fear by watching, assessing, and springing into action when identifying a potentially "loose" woman. Such monitoring represented the gendered logics of policing as commercial sex and red light districts became the preeminent social problem of the early twentieth century that public and private interests collaborated to address and quell.[107]

While the street became a site on which uniformed and plainclothes officers could advance the police board's various agendas to shore up the color line and control women's agency, it also became a site on which they themselves were disciplined. This dynamic spoke to an inherent contradiction in the structure of the police force. The patrolmen and detectives charged with enforcing morals-based policing often belonged to the very class of people they were supposed to punish. This contradiction represented an age-old tension that kept wealthy reformers on their toes. For them, working-class patrolmen proved incapable of accomplishing their lofty goals of ordering society along a moral order that renounced base indulgences like promiscuous sex, boozing, and populist entertainment. Patrolmen drank liquor on the job, solicited sex from prostitutes, and abetted drug trafficking. During Swann's tenure, the police board tried officers 454 times. A large chunk of these trials involved workplace conduct, including tardiness, improper patrolling, or losing a weapon. The police board dished out few acquittals. Most officers faced some form of discipline, such as fines, demotions, or fewer days off. In extreme cases—or in cases of repeat offense—the board dismissed officers. Between 1908 and 1909, the police board either dismissed or forced the resignations of thirty-one officers. Patrolmen and probationers accounted for most of the dismissals, which generally stemmed from more egregious offenses. Police captains and other superior officers caught patrolmen in the act of drinking, allowing prisoners to escape, and mouthing off. For graver transgressions, the police board masked the particularities of their indiscretions under the charge of "unofficerlike conduct."[108]

Often, this charge referred to a sex-related indiscretion. For instance, on October 25, 1909, the police tried and dismissed two patrolmen. The first, James Hardesty, received two counts of unofficerlike conduct. While on active duty, the uniformed patrolman entered Riley's Hotel, a popular meeting place for Irish associations like the United Irish League and the Hibernian Club. Hardesty indulged in liquor in the company of several women, likely sex workers. In another instance, the police board charged Patrolman George W. Hisley with five counts of unofficerlike conduct. Police spotted Hisley exiting Laura Brown's house in the heart of Black Baltimore. Brown, a transplant from Illinois, ran a manicure business out of her home on the 1100 block of Brighton Street. The narrow street housed several Black laundresses and porters. Hisley frequented Brown's house to pick up Minnie Raabe, a sixteen-year-old white domestic servant. Northwestern District officers caught wind of Hisley's tryst and followed him and Raabe as they met several times around the city. The police board suspected that Hisley met Raabe for "immoral purposes," which likely meant that he had solicited her sexual services.[109] In Hisely's case, the watchers watched the watchers as cops trailed their own to ensure that officers did not bring scandal to a department in an active war against prostitution.

Although patrolmen and probationers faced the brunt of the police board's wrath, on occasion, superior officers came under scrutiny when the parties to their corruption peached on them. Sadonia Young, a Black laundress, operated a bawdy house out of her home on 510 Tyson Street. In the heart of downtown, the humble alley house bordered high-value land uses which increased the likeliness of daily police encounters. One of Young's charges—or "inmates," as they were called—was Annie Jones, a white girl. Police raided Young's house and arrested her. The criminal court charged her with abducting, enticing, and harboring Jones as well as with keeping a bawdy house. Much as Sweetie Bailey refused to let cops off the hook, Young dragged exploitative officers into the ordeal. During her testimony, she implicated Sergeant Frank Plum for accepting her money in exchange for protection. An official police board investigation uncovered six such arrangements between Plum and bawdy house proprietors, three of them Black women in the same area.[110] Plum's role in providing protection to matrons scaled all the way up the chain of command to Captain Bernard J. Ward. In Sadonia Young's case, Ward provided protection by transferring patrolmen who bothered her business to different posts. After uncovering that Ward had either willfully ignored or actively protected brothels and saloons in his district, the police board dismissed him.[111]

Such rampant misconduct constituted an inherent tension of metropolitan policing that administrators tried futilely to eliminate. During Swann's commissionership—and far beyond—the police force was awash in corruption. Upon assuming his post, Swann, quite naively, lectured patrolmen on the importance of temperance and duty.[112] His admonitions fell on deaf ears. After his tenure, Swann reflected that policework constituted a constant fight that proved both impossible to win and exceedingly unpopular.[113] Rather than try to stamp out corruption, his strategy shifted toward containing it. Police focused their attention on vital city resources and protecting their own image. That meant protecting downtown and ensuring that scandals like the ones brought on by Alverta Bailey and Sadonia Young were quickly quashed. Most of the high-profile calamities that beset the police department occurred in the Central District, the most prized in the city.[114] Its location on the waterfront, the presence of several banks, trust companies, theaters, opera houses, hotels, and stores, as well as its role as the city's transit and trade hub, made it both an important area to police and a spot ripe for public order violations, sex work, and drinking.[115] Well-to-do whites who had escaped the rough-and-tumble central city for developing suburbs on the urban periphery still frequented the Central District to indulge in high society leisure.[116] Wealthy Baltimoreans entered downtown by passing through neighborhoods with rich populations of working-class Black, Chinese, and foreign-born white immigrant residents like the Pot. Given these competing interests, and despite boasting the second smallest land mass and the smallest population, the Central District contained the highest number of daily patrolmen. This corps of officers attempted to preempt any affronts to the city's nexus of wealth and property by occupying and patrolling interracial neighborhoods to ensure that the inhabitants' influence did not spill over into the bustling downtown.[117]

Conclusion

During the early twentieth century, Baltimore's streets became the stage on which the city's police power was rehearsed and negotiated. They were occupied by all manner of at-odds identities, including drug dealers, sex workers, uniformed cops, plainclothes officers, and detectives. They served as arteries that connected Baltimore's growing real estate interests. This reality made them vital sites of compulsory surveillance as segregationists and police officials attempted to organize the chaos of urban density to fit their desired outcomes. As such, police sought more discretion to police residents. It was not enough to catch criminals in the act of crime; police required access to the body. In advocating for this discretion, police cravenly rode a wave of racial panic to make cocaine the justification to sell their case for broader impunity to state authorities.

At the turn of the century, cocaine had become a staple of working-class urban leisure. Muckraking journalists and other commenters employed bogus medical and pseudoscientific observations to advance claims that the drug unleashed the latent violence of the city's working-class Black residents, particularly Black women. Newspapers carried voluminous stories documenting violent ordeals and public order incidents supposedly fueled by the "cocaine evil." Cocaine regulation concretized complementary carceral systems and logics of governance that typified early twentieth-century Baltimore, including white supremacist Progressive theories of Black culture, the press's role in fomenting racist moral panic, policing as an everyday fact of working-class life, and the police board's continued war against so-called Negro rowdyism. The precedent established in the *Rossberg* decision that litigated the constitutionality of Swann's Cocaine Ordinance dramatically increased the latitude of the city's police power. Segregationists seized on *Rossberg* to defend prohibitions on Black housing access by scapegoating working-class slums in the public imaginary as the inevitable results of the interracial housing patterns that had typified the city for decades. This ordeal signaled the centrality of racialized policing to Jim Crow urban governance. Black men and women became the preferred and primary targets of Baltimore's police, and there was no turning back. Baltimore's Black residents would become progressively more likely to be arrested than their white peers as policing adapted around regulating Black life and protecting white property.

Relatedly, street policing necessitated technological investments and undercover investigation. Crowd control, identification, and the creation of databases demanded more sophisticated approaches. The patrol box, the police wagon, the photography room, the white muslin mask, fingerprinting, and other surveillance and identificatory technologies expanded police efficiency and enlarged the breadth and reach of the state. Plainclothes officers combed the streets looking for drug deals, suspected sex workers, and even their own compatriots. Police-civilian relations changed because of such watchfulness and, in many cases, suspected criminals kept a keen eye out for cops. Such sousveillance allowed for small acts of resistance, including supplying information to the police board that led to misconduct proceedings and the occasional dismissals of cops. Surveillance occurred from the bottom-up and the top-down on Baltimore's streets which served as vital sites of state formation and negotiation. And while streets allowed for a modicum of resistance, another site of police power, the court, provided a different dimension to police power's workings and a more public and organized site of resistance that activated Black Baltimoreans. It is to the court that we now turn.

5

"I Ask Mercy at Your Hands"

The Case of Henry Alfred Brown, Third-Degree Torture, and Black Grassroots Responses to Judicial Inequality

On the evening of January 14, 1921, Kenneth W. Riley left the Naval Academy grounds and headed to downtown Annapolis. Riley had been at the academy for seventeen months as a pharmacist's mate second class. Downtown, he briefly chatted with a friend before catching a movie. Afterward, he hit a soda fountain for a sundae. Around 10:00 p.m., Riley returned to the Naval Academy. On his way back to his quarters, he heard a groan.

Then another groan.

Riley followed the noises over a hill and saw an umbrella, a muff, and a white glove on the ground. Frightened, he slowly approached the groans. He discovered a body, someone he knew. The woman, Harriet Kavanaugh, a nurse at the Naval Academy, lay semiconscious. Blood and vomit caked her clothing and hair.

"Oh Lord," she moaned.

Riley rushed to get help. He and a colleague brought Kavanaugh to the hospital on a stretcher.[1] Surgeons assessed the nurse and found that she had suffered a depressed skull fracture and other head wounds. She had been hit with a blunt object several times. The surgeons attempted surgery, but she had hemorrhaged too much blood. She died the next morning.[2]

Three days later, Harriet M. Kavanaugh was laid to rest at the naval cemetery. A military escort accompanied her casket. Her colleagues and friends came out in droves to commemorate her life.[3] Authorities had no clue who killed her. A naval board of inquiry began investigating the matter but possessed few leads.

132 · CHAPTER 5

The same day that Kavanaugh was laid to rest, the Baltimore police arrested Henry Alfred Brown, a nineteen-year-old Black naval mess attendant.[4] The police booked him on charges of desertion, a routine offense. That year, the Baltimore police arrested 133 people for desertion—they returned 123 of those arrestees to the custody of whatever military branch they had left.[5] Brown was no different. The commander and master-at-arms[6] of the USS *Cumberland*, a naval training ship for Black mess attendants, traveled to Baltimore to retrieve Brown. They took him back to Annapolis.

Shortly after his arrival, the board of inquiry questioned Brown regarding his whereabouts on the night of Harriet Kavanaugh's murder. He told the board he had briefly been in Annapolis that day to retrieve some personal items but returned to Baltimore shortly thereafter.[7] Regarding Brown's arrest, the Washington, D.C.–based *Evening Star* noted, "It is understood that there is nothing more against Brown at this time than the fact that he is a deserter and that he had been a patient at the hospital at one time."[8] As the facts of the case unfolded, Brown's culpability never convincingly moved beyond this circumstantial connection.

However, after several days in police custody, a rattled Brown confessed to the murder. He alleged to have done so after experiencing the third degree—a shorthand for police torture—at the hands of the Baltimore police.

Henry Brown's experience with third-degree torture illuminated the subterranean and progressively private operation of police power in the 1920s U.S. city. Police exercised their monopoly over force to rearticulate and bend due process in the name of law and order. While police power vested state agents and governing bodies with the ability to determine what constituted a "legitimate" use of force, this legitimacy need not (and often *did not*) correspond to "legal" uses of force. In the early twentieth century, police relied on discretionary statutes—and took cover behind institutional protection—to violate due process on the streets and in station houses where they routinely beat confessions out of potentially innocent suspects. National increases in arrests for violent crimes during the 1920s led to a more systematized use of the practice as publics sought justice no matter the cost.[9] Guilt and innocence became secondary concerns if *someone* paid the price. During the 1920s, Black men increasingly became scapegoats in murder cases. They endured third-degree torture as calls for law and order, coupled with broader agendas to maintain racial hierarchy in diverse areas of social life, coalesced in Black men's experiences of disproportionate arrest, incarceration, and lynching rates around the country. Regarding violence, historian Douglas Flowe has coined the term "public racial violence" to detail how such routine and flagrant demonstrations of cruelty and torture were "often deliberately advertised as visible expressions of racial authority."[10]

The public secret of police violence troubles prevailing and foundational treatments of the rise of the modern carceral state. While some scholarship points toward the emergence of a carceral system based in the removal of the individual from society, the presumption that public torture's disappearance or diminution accompanied this systemic shift is overstated.[11] As Henry Brown's case demonstrates, Black people were vigilantly attuned to police torture which they understood as rampant and central to policing. What is more, such flagrant brutality is not an aberration within the context of policing but the very essence of it. As Micol Seigel has argued, "violence work," the application of force that state officials use to express and legitimize the power of the state, is an indispensable feature of policing.[12] Violence is not the exclusive provenance of the police—that is, officers wearing badges. It materializes in multiple sites, including the military, the station house, and the courtroom. All three of these sites, particularly the latter, are crucial to Henry Brown's case. As such, this chapter, while keying in on one instance of police brutality, draws parallels between Brown's experiences, the broader consolidation of Baltimore's police state, and national trends in third-degree torture. From the conduct of police officials, to the contested nature of "truth," to the flagrant violations of due process, to the Black grassroots responses to state-sponsored violence and injustice, Henry Brown's case offers a glimpse into the evolving nature of Baltimore's police state during the 1920s when brutalization became a fact of life for Black residents. The contemporary resonances of this case ring clearly and poignantly well into the twenty-first century.

"Excessive but Misguided Zeal": The Third Degree

At the turn of the twentieth century, the third degree became a central element of police work that built on the cops' desires to control and seize the bodies of suspected criminals. As drug enforcement, the development of identificatory technologies, and conventions of street policing showed, the police clamored for power over individuals to such a degree that due process and other protections steadily eroded in the administration of discipline. The police, the politicians who appointed police leadership, and the courts that judged the so-called reasonableness of such strategies coalesced around a vision of policing in Baltimore that allowed cops discretion to identify and detain suspects more easily. Police found support among segregationists who benefited from expanded police power. Policing in Black and interracial neighborhoods solidified the color line,

134 · CHAPTER 5

protected white property, and kept a supposedly unmanageable population in line. The third degree fit into broader currents of policing by allowing the criminal legal system to deliver "justice" during a period of rising violent crime rates and poor police conviction rates. Getting suspects to trial was difficult, and the written confession functioned as a golden ticket for inept cops.

For cops, the third degree referred to nothing more than the third step in a police officer's duty of apprehension. The three degrees of police work included arrest, detention, and interrogation.[13] For historians and the public, this rather procedural depiction of the third degree obscured the violence that typically accompanied interrogation. Historians attribute the origination of the third degree to New York detective Thomas Byrnes, who served the New York police during the late nineteenth century. Although the act of beating confessions out of prisoners had existed for decades before Byrnes's tenure, the detective popularized the practice in its modern form. Byrnes often beat, starved, deceived, and isolated prisoners to force confessions.[14] While Byrnes routinized the practice in the late nineteenth century, at the turn of the century, metropolitan police departments began systematically employing furtive physical, emotional, and mental torture to elicit confessions from potentially innocent suspects. In one case, the Chicago police subjected a suspect to fifty-two hours of questioning before he finally confessed to murdering a policeman. The young man hanged himself in his cell afterward.[15] In another instance, a man accused of robbery alleged that New York police officers grabbed him by the throat and threatened to kick and choke him to death if he did not confess. At trial, the judge left the veracity of the confession up to the jury—a common convention—and it sided with law enforcement.[16]

Similar tales began to pepper the dailies. The third degree became a national curiosity. The National Theater in Washington, D.C. mounted a play based on Charles Klein's novel *The Third Degree* for a week in 1909. In it, a young man awakened after a night of binge drinking to find a dead man in his apartment. In a review, the *Washington Post* noted, "[Klein] shows that a man in a semidazed [sic] condition may be made to submit to a stronger mind than his own, and through this hypnotic influence admit a knowledge of things of which previously he had no knowledge."[17] Such hypnotic suggestion shrouded the practice in mystery while raising questions as to its legality. Residents of the nation's capital described the rash of third degree incidents as the "American Inquisition" and a threat to the essence of democracy.[18]

As news stories, cultural production, and victims' complaints animated the popular imagination with portrayals of concealed, mysterious, and illegal interrogation methods, police defended the third degree as nothing more than good police work. One writer contended, "To-day the third degree is psychological, and the conscience of the prisoner himself causes him to fall upon his knees, and, admitting all, cry for mercy."[19] Police argued that sophisticated examination techniques would lead to higher conviction rates in instances of murder and other violent crime. Despite victims' detailed stories of harsh physical torture, police rarely admitted to the brutalization of suspects and did not consider prolonged and arduous "grilling" sessions as an infringement of due process. This stance echoed the increased latitude afforded police at the turn of the century. Discretion formed a major element of policing, and police officials championed more invasive street policing and access to biometric data. It followed, then, that they also sought and defended vicious interrogation procedures, particularly given the shifting sands of violent crime rates.

The emergence of widespread third-degree abuses coincided with rising violent arrest rates and public exhortations to ameliorate violence, particularly murder. Because a lack of material evidence often led to dismissals, acquittals, and cold cases, detective bureaus sometimes sought confessions to help get suspects to trial. As murder arrest rates increased (figure 10) and public panic over racial conflagrations and high-profile assassinations led to calls for justice, police began to rely on the third degree.[20] Such rough treatment seemingly paid off in racialized rates of conviction for murder. Between 1917 and 1923, the Baltimore criminal court presided over 223 murder cases. Of these, Black Baltimoreans served as defendants before all-white juries 118 times, or more than half of the time. Over the course of this seven-year sample, Black defendants were convicted 67 percent of the time, while white defendants were convicted 49 percent of the time (figure 11).[21] The police seemed to have become better at detecting crime—a reasonable assumption given the substantial resources and identificatory advancements at their disposal. Equally reasonable were suspicions—and quite more than suspicions—that the Baltimore police, like police departments around the country, violated due process to compel confessions, particularly from Black Baltimoreans for whom all-white juries had little sympathy.[22]

Scandal compelled journalists to question local police forces regarding their use of the third degree. In 1910, Colonel Sherlock Swann denied that the Baltimore detective bureau employed physical violence on detainees. Swann did, however, admit that detectives "sweated" detainees, a police tactic that trounced due process by subjecting suspects to untold hours of harsh interrogation.[23] A. J. Pumphrey, captain of the detective bureau, had a storied career among the Baltimore police for his ability to elicit confessions on cold cases through sweating. In one instance, proprietors of a confectionary store found Caroline Link, a white woman,

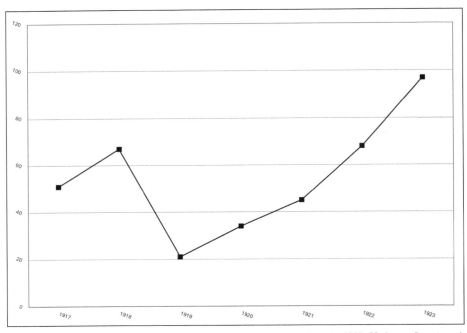

Figure 10. Murder arrests, 1917–23. Source: Board of Police Commissioner Reports, 1917–23, Agency Reports and Publications, Baltimore City Archives.

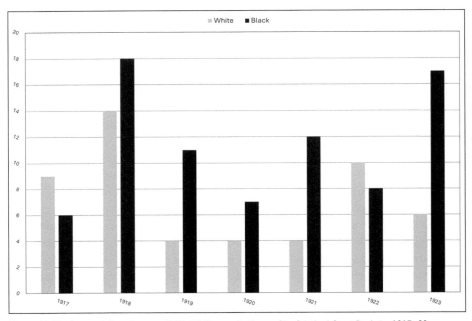

Figure 11. Murder convictions by race, 1917–23. Source: Baltimore City Criminal Court Dockets, 1917–23, Maryland State Archives.

"I Ask Mercy at Your Hands" • 137

dead in their store. Few clues, leads, or witnesses could explain her death. In fact, police and physicians believed she had fallen and died because of a head wound. A subsequent postmortem indicated the possibility of murder. Pumphrey believed that Black boys known to the police committed the act. Despite scant evidence, Pumphrey and his detectives detained Charles Jones, a twelve-year-old Black boy. After a four-hour sweating session conducted by Pumphrey, the marshal, the deputy marshal, and four other detectives, Jones confessed. The court sentenced the twelve-year-old to fifteen years in the Maryland Penitentiary.[24] In murder cases with scant evidence, police "grilled," "sweated," and tortured Black men and boys. The racialized nature of the third degree represented broader trends in Baltimore's evolving police state as Black people became ever more likely to be arrested and imprisoned than their white peers.[25]

In the 1920s, as police fought to keep pace with organized crime rings and maintain racial hierarchy as Afro-Southern migration led to ballooning Black populations in the urban North, the federal government took a comprehensive look at municipal policing. In 1929, President Herbert Hoover convened the National Commission on Law Observance and Enforcement to investigate police abuses. Known colloquially as the Wickersham Commission (after Attorney General George Wickersham), the commission published fourteen reports that probed officer conduct, detention centers, and the third degree.[26] The Wickersham Commission found that police violated due process through protracted questioning, threats, intimidation, physical abuse, illegal detention, and denial of counsel.[27] Denying counsel proved particularly effective because suspects often did not know—or had been persuaded to waive—their constitutional protections against self-incrimination. The concept of a confession itself operated in a legal gray area. Since the Fifth Amendment protected suspects from self-incrimination, federal courts grappled with admitting forced confessions into evidence.[28] Without them, though, cases like Henry Brown's would have no evidence and no resolution. During a period of increasing violent crime, publics wanted results—the suspect's guilt was a secondary concern. The Wickersham Commission found that the "excessive but misguided zeal" spurred by civic outcry encouraged police to produce _anybody_ to account for a crime that would satisfy the public's thirst for justice.[29]

And that is what two Baltimore police detectives did in 1921.

"Take Me to the Baltimore Jail": The Confession

Henry Brown's culpability hinged on a confession. Confessions had murky legal foundations but nonetheless represented the spirit of socialized justice that typified American jurisprudence at the turn of the century. As legal historian

138 · CHAPTER 5

Michael Willrich has noted, the administration of justice in the early twentieth century embraced socially responsive forms of legal execution that engaged the pressing social and political problems of crime.[30] Tough law and order values stemmed from social agendas that valorized orderly societies, moral uprightness, and the management of hereditarily unfit people. Progressive reformers propelled this brand of social justice. As courts reviewed more cases and punished suspects at a greater clip in the first three decades of the twentieth century, some of the social values that drove courts and Progressive court reformers stemmed from latent and blatant eugenic ideals, particularly in the 1910s and 1920s.[31] As such, courts became sites in which prevailing social antagonisms, including and especially racial ones, animated the legal administration of crime. In the case of Henry Brown—and countless other third-degree victims—this dynamic manifested in the court's acceptance of coerced confessions. Ignoring the unconstitutional methods by which such confessions were secured, courts also tended to overlook the dubious legality of the confession itself, a form of self-incrimination that, when coerced, became questionably admissible. The technical and legal foundations of courts, in many cases, became secondary to the efficient and socially "responsible" forms of judicial disposition, especially in Brown's case which involved a dead white woman. The court's socialized form of justice echoed the police's mandate to maintain racial order regardless of their discretionary limits. For Henry Brown, the Baltimore police pulled out all the stops by assigning two infamous police officers, Peter Bradley and Henry Hammersla, to the case. Using violence to compel the confession, the officers similarly engaged in a sociopolitical administration of justice that ignored and openly flouted due process.

Peter Bradley served the Baltimore police for thirty-three years. He became a detective in 1903 and developed a reputed expertise in profiling the "hobo" criminal class. In 1904, he participated in a series of raids that led to the apprehension of a band of safecrackers known as the Yeggmen. He received a commendation for meritorious service for his role in the raids and earned several more commendations in the following years.[32] His peers characterized Bradley as a "master detective," who had an uncanny ability to solicit confessions.[33] Given his reliability, Police Commissioner Charles Gaither ordered Detective Bradley to Annapolis on Tuesday, January 18, 1921. Gaither instructed Bradley to choose a partner to aid the investigation into Henry Brown.

Bradley selected Harry Hammersla to accompany him. Hammersla had a checkered past. Scandal characterized his career. In 1902, the Anti-Saloon League caught Hammersla attempting to dig up dirt on two of their private detectives. He evidently did so to scare them off the scent of saloonkeepers

"I Ask Mercy at Your Hands" • 139

that the private investigators had been scrutinizing and to whom Hammerlsa provided protection.[34] In 1903, the police board briefly dismissed Hammersla from the force on multiple counts of insubordination.[35] In 1905, as whispers of the third degree began to emerge, Hammersla, along with several colleagues, "sweated" a Black man named William Henry Jones for hours until he admitted to killing an elderly night watchman. The court struggled with the admissibility of the confession. The judge, in a move that would become common in American courts, left the veracity of the confession up to the jury, who found Jones guilty of first-degree murder. He was executed.[36] In 1910, the police board again investigated Hammersla for charges that he extorted $100 from a wealthy broker.[37] And so on. Hammersla's rap sheet rivaled those of many career criminals in Baltimore. Together, Bradley and Hammersla provided expertise in detective work and the solicitation of confessions. Both had familiarity with sweating and likely had experience with far harsher interrogation strategies unrecorded in the police's archives.

Baltimore's finest arrived in Annapolis at 5:00 p.m. and surveyed the Naval Academy grounds, presumably looking for clues. They left that night without seeing Brown. They returned the next day and requested a closed-door meeting with Brown. After one conversation, the Baltimore police detectives managed to do what the naval board of inquiry and the Department of Justice (DOJ) could not. Henry Brown signed a confession for them on the spot.

According to Brown's signed confession, he had traveled to Annapolis on January 14, 1921 to turn himself in for desertion. Upon arrival, Brown met another Black seaman who dissuaded him from surrendering. Convinced, Brown supposedly went off to find someone to rob. When he could not find anyone, he decided to surrender after all and resumed his path back to the Naval Academy. He encountered Harriet Kavanaugh there. Seeing an opportunity to finally commit the robbery he had abandoned and, in fact, had had no intention to commit in the first place, Brown grabbed a piece of loose iron pipe and hid behind a tree. Thoroughly hidden, Brown emerged and struck the nurse on the head once with the pipe, fracturing her skull in three places. He then grabbed the fallen women's pocketbook, kept the $8 inside, and tossed the evidence. He headed downtown and spent the money before traveling to Baltimore that same Saturday night.

The confession sounded far-fetched and overcomplicated—a fact that Brown's supporters later seized on to advocate for him. Brown's incoherent actions, including his immediate susceptibility to the suggestion that he rob someone instead of surrendering for desertion, echoed racist presumptions that prevailed during the period regarding Black men's supposed uncontrollable susceptibility to crime.[38] It did not read like the actions of a Black teenager on the lam for desertion. Instead, it read like a document clumsily put together by white racists that would activate an all-white jury's prejudices against Black criminals while also corroborating the rest of the unaccounted-for physical evidence in the case.[39] In the confession, Brown's exact knowledge of the murder weapon and where Kavanaugh's pocketbook had been thrown made the prosecution's job a piece of cake. The fact that nobody saw Brown in the act also made the prosecution's case simpler because they did not need to locate eyewitnesses.

According to detectives Bradley and Hammersla, extracting the confession was simple. They deployed "religious talk" and moral suasion. They also benefited from Brown's delirium. He had been kept awake for several days.[40] When the commander of the *Cumberland* brought Brown to the detectives, he trembled from anxiety and sleep deprivation. Brown feared a potential lynch mob and reportedly told the detectives, "Gentlemen, if you'll take me to the Baltimore Jail instead of to Annapolis, I will tell you the truth." The detectives assessed Brown to be an "awfully bad n——r" and were convinced that he was "one of the most coldblooded criminals they ever met." Brown reportedly confessed in exchange for the detectives' word that they would prevent his lynching—a foreboding omen.[41]

After securing the confession, DOJ agents transported Brown under cover of darkness to Baltimore.[42] Since the murder occurred on federal property, the U.S. District Court presided over the case. On February 2, Brown appeared before U.S. Commissioner J. Frank Supplee. Brown had yet to secure legal counsel.[43] Unrepresented, Brown used the hearing to recant his confession. He told Supplee that he had not been in Annapolis when the murder took place. He had been in Baltimore, and he had witnesses. He further alleged that he had only confessed after days of torture. According to Brown, while confined in the brig of the *Cumberland*, he had been kept forcibly awake, had a rope tied around his neck, had been threatened with lynching, jabbed in the ribs with a bayonet, shackled around the wrists, and beaten across the back. Additionally, when the Baltimore detectives arrived, they menaced him with a blackjack and, knowing of his anxieties of being lynched, had threatened to turn him over to the ship's crew to be hanged.[44] Brown's story did not sway Supplee. He confined Brown to the city jail without bail. A federal grand jury then charged Brown with first-degree murder.[45]

Brown's retraction caused a firestorm in the press. Detectives Bradley and Hammersla denied Brown's accusations.[46] Simultaneously, charges that Brown had been subject to the third degree began to crop up in the press. The authorities involved in Brown's torture seemed uninterested in hiding their activities. According to a *Washington Times* article, DOJ agents admitted that Brown had been brutalized and that he was "on the verge of a breakdown" when turned over to the Baltimore detectives. Moreover, the *Washington Times* indicated that the DOJ had other suspects in its crosshairs.[47] Agents close to the case corroborated Brown's charges against authorities.[48]

Despite ongoing investigations into other suspects, the U.S. District Court rushed Brown's case to trial. The pressing social and political implications of a white woman's murder in a Southern state whose political apparatus and citizenry demanded racial retribution influenced law enforcement to pursue prosecution despite suspicions on other suspects. Brown faced the brunt of not just the legal system but also the social and ideological orientation of a police state that sought justice no matter the deficiencies in its investigations. For Henry Brown and countless people like him, justice was not blind but fully perceptive and quick to judgment. Newspapers in Baltimore, Washington, D.C., and Buffalo (Kavanaugh's hometown) reported frequently on the proceedings. The *Sun* anticipated "a quick trial of Brown ... if no unexpected obstacle develops."[49] Brown's fate seemed sealed from the start. His trial began on March 28, 1921.

"Leave Half of Him Down There": The Trial

John C. Rose, an esteemed judge and noted social reformer in Baltimore, presided over the case. Rose had earned a stellar record as a public servant. In the late nineteenth century, he served as secretary for Baltimore's chapter of the Society for the Suppression of Vice. He worked in partnership with Black reformers to shut down saloons in Black neighborhoods. In 1895, he served as general counsel and second-in-command to Charles J. Bonaparte's Reform League. Rose proved instrumental in coordinating the league's surgically precise decimation of the Democratic machine. The subsequent resurgence of the Republican Party provided Black Baltimoreans new avenues into local politics.[50] Members of Baltimore's Black political class grew to respect and trust Rose's judgment, particularly after he presided over a 1917 case that deemed residential segregation unconstitutional. After his death in 1927, Warner T. McGuinn, a decorated lawyer who argued that segregation case before Rose, wrote a sterling obituary in the *Afro-American* for the late judge. He noted that "in [Rose's] Court, all men stood equal before the law."[51] Brown could not have been assigned a better judge.

United States attorneys Robert R. Carman and George W. Kieffner helmed the prosecution.[52] August W. Schnepfe, a real estate lawyer, defended Brown.[53] The whole case came down to the confession. Would Rose toss it, or would he leave it up to the jury?

142 · CHAPTER 5

The prosecution first called several witnesses to demonstrate that Brown and Kavanaugh could have been at the same place at the same time. On January 14, 1921, Henry Brown and Harriet Kavanaugh were in Annapolis—that much we know. Brown boarded the W. B. A. Electric Railway at 6:00 p.m. in Baltimore. He arrived in Annapolis at 7:00 p.m. According to Brown, he had gone to Annapolis to retrieve some personal belongings from the *Cumberland*. His confession, which he later retracted, purported that he had gone to turn himself in for desertion. That night, several acquaintances and coworkers testified to seeing Brown. Stewart Green, a fellow mess attendant on the *Cumberland* and part of the shore police, was on patrol duty that night. He reported seeing Brown at a cabaret around 9:30 p.m. Brown came in, noticed Green, and left when he spotted Green's patrol leggings. While Brown did not deny seeing Green, he testified seeing him at 7:10 p.m., shortly after arriving in Annapolis. The *Cumberland*'s commanding officer, Lieutenant Raymond Smith, said this sighting would have been impossible because he had confined all the mess attendants to the ship after they had staged a rebellious demonstration.[54]

Kavanaugh's whereabouts were somewhat clearer than Brown's, though the testimony regarding the timing of her activities was similarly inconsistent. The Naval Academy grounds were protected by watchmen who manned the entry gates. Watchman Samuel Hardesty, Gate No. 5's guard, reported that Kavanaugh left the Naval Academy grounds at 5:00 p.m. A jeweler, Peter Corosh, testified that Kavanaugh came to his shop to retrieve a pencil that she had had engraved for a coworker at around 7:30 p.m. Watchmen Hardesty saw her return to the Naval Academy at 8:00 p.m. She left again shortly thereafter and returned at 9:25 p.m. At this point, the story got messy. According to Robert Pinkney, an acquaintance of Brown, the two crossed paths in the street. Brown asked Pinkney for the time. Pinkney said it was 9:25 p.m. If Hardesty was correct in his recollection, Kavanaugh was still alive. If Pinkney was correct in his testimony, Brown was walking about the streets of Annapolis while the nurse was returning to her quarters. Although it is eminently possible that Hardesty and Pinkney were mistaken, there existed a reasonable doubt. Judge Rose, assessing this testimony, instructed the jury, "If [Brown] was on the street at 9:25 and Herdesty [*sic*] was right, this man could not have committed the murder."[55]

The prosecution could not convincingly place Brown at the scene of the crime. Everything rode on the confession. If Schnepfe could get Rose to toss it, Brown might avoid hanging. To do so, the defendant would have to sway the all-white jury to both believe that he had been tortured and to care. A tall order.

Henry Brown took the stand. According to the mess attendant, Lieutenant Smith and John Boteler, the master-at-arms, detained him on January 17 in Baltimore and brought him to Annapolis. The board of inquiry questioned Brown regarding his whereabouts on the night of the incident. He arrived in Annapolis at 7:00 p.m. to retrieve some belongings and left on the next train back to Baltimore. After this initial interrogation, the board of inquiry released Brown to Lieutenant Smith who tossed him in the brig of the *Cumberland*. Brown spent Tuesday confined in his cell with shackles on his legs and wrists. Lieutenant Smith sent Stewart Green to Brown's cell. A considerably larger man, Green beat Brown mercilessly and demanded that he admit to killing Kavanaugh or else. Green took a rope from his hammock, tied it around Brown's neck, and cinched it to a pipe. He pulled the rope taut to asphyxiate Brown. He pulled the rope over and over, all the while punching and kicking Brown. Other mess attendants participated in the brutality, including Robert Pinkney who testified to seeing Brown the night of the murder. One allegedly threatened to stick Brown with a bayonet.[56]

During the abuse, Green told his victim, "Brown, they are going to kill you down here on the ship and you better say what I say." Green then relayed the details of Kavanaugh's murder—how she crossed a bridge on the Naval Academy grounds on her way to the nurse's quarters. How an assailant grabbed a galvanized iron pipe from behind some cannonballs and waited behind some trees. How the assailant sneaked up behind the nurse and bludgeoned her in the head. How the assailant grabbed the fallen woman's pocketbook and scaled a wall to escape the campus grounds and avoid detection at the watchmen's gates. How the assailant ditched the pocketbook containing $8 somewhere on St. John's College campus, a liberal arts university near the Naval Academy.[57]

Brown refused. Green persisted. Brown testified, "He told me to say that I killed Miss Kavanaugh because it would get him out of trouble and me out of trouble and save my neck."[58]

Why would Green be in danger if Brown did not confess to the murder? Green's motives and position in the incident remain confusing. Perhaps Lieutenant Smith enticed Green to beat a confession out of Brown to settle an existing conflict between the two. Brown had also overheard Smith giving Green orders to beat him within an inch of his life.

"Don't finish him up. Leave half of him down there," said Lieutenant Smith.[59]

It is possible that Smith sought to force Brown's confession and that he used Green because the two had an existing antagonism and because Green faced disciplinary consequences for allowing Brown—a known deserter—to escape when he saw him at the cabaret.

All these possibilities—and several others—exist in the ambiguities of Smith's and Green's testimonies, which were a garbled mess. Smith had evidently confined Green and a fellow patrolman, Samuel House, as prisoners on

144 · CHAPTER 5

the ship for allowing Brown to escape the night of the murder.[60] Until Green received a trial date, he would remain in custody on the *Cumberland*. Schnepfe questioned Green's legal standing on the ship. How, if Green was a prisoner, did he end up in Brown's cell? Green could not recall a reason, though he did confirm hitting Brown—a startling admission that corroborated at least some of Brown's claims. Green downplayed the abuse and said he had been in the brig with Brown for only five minutes. Smith, when asked how Green had ended up in a cell with Brown, noted that Green was a prisoner at large on the ship. He had ordered Green to the brig the same night that the master-at-arms had confined Brown but did not specify in what cell he should be kept. Smith chalked up the mistake as a communication error. When asked how long they were together, Smith said ninety minutes. When asked why he finally removed Green, Smith said, "If I had kept him in the brig he would have done bodily harm to Brown, it would have been a very bad thing."[61]

Although Green and Smith could not manage to square their stories, they both (mostly) denied Brown's testimony. What is more, Brown stumbled during his testimony in ways that the judge and jury likely interpreted as dishonest. On a few occasions, Judge Rose curtly rebuked Brown for mixing up dates. "Get it straight," Rose warned. While such inconsistencies may have indicated dishonesty, it is possible that they stemmed from the effects of the brutality that Brown experienced. According to Brown, the *Cumberland* crew had not just beaten, choked, and threatened him; they had also kept him forcibly awake the night before the Baltimore police interrogated him. This detail made it to popular press accounts, though law enforcement denied it during the trial. Notably, during cross-examination, one of the men who participated in Brown's torture made a grave error. Sherman Faulkner, a watchman, entered the brig after Green had finished beating Brown. According to Brown, Smith had sent Faulkner to keep him awake. During cross-examination, Faulkner told Schnepfe that he had been placed in the brig "for the purpose of keeping Brown awake." Faulkner's admission stunned the prosecution. On redirect examination, Carman scrambled and asked Faulkner to clarify several times that he had *not* been sent to keep Brown awake.[62] For a receptive jury, the watchman's admission may have been a bombshell turning point in the case that lent credibility to Brown's story. For Brown's jury, the admission was forgiven as a slip.

While Green, Smith, and Faulkner flailed on the stand and provided damning and incoherent testimony, the *Cumberland* crew paled in importance to the prosecution's star witnesses: the men who secured Brown's confession.

Peter Bradley, the hefty and imposing mustachioed Baltimore detective, took the stand. He did not hide his utter contempt for Brown. During his testimony, he often referred to Brown as "this boy," a diminutive and racially encoded infantilization that spoke to his white supremacist outlook. Far less encoded were Bradley's frequent references to Brown as a "n——r" in the press. His racial animus undoubtedly colored his perceptions of Brown's guilt, or perhaps assuaged any shame or ethical sticking points that may have arisen as he and Hammersla threatened the young man with a blackjack.[63]

On Wednesday, after having been kept awake the previous evening, Lieutenant Smith brought Brown to Bradley and Hammersla. The two detectives talked to Brown for an hour while Smith stood watch at the other end of the room. Bradley painted the ordeal as massively routine and simple. After an hour, Bradley coaxed the confession out of him. After admitting to the murder, Brown then guided Bradley, Hammersla, Smith, Boteler, and a few others through the Naval Academy grounds and showed them how he coordinated the nurse's murder.[64]

While Bradley alleged that his detective acumen extracted Brown's confession, the latter forwarded a different version of events. According to Brown, Smith and Boteler brought him before the detectives after Sherman Faulkner had kept him awake all night. Brown told the detectives his side of the story—that he came to Annapolis to retrieve some belongings and headed back to Baltimore shortly thereafter. One of the detectives replied, "Now, N——r, you are lying. You want to tell me the truth. I am saving your neck. . . . Because these officers will take you back to the ship and murder you down there, hang you up by your feet and neck, liable to burn you up." Even though Brown felt weary, he refused to confess. Bradley pulled out a blackjack. He glanced back at Smith and said, "Have you got an empty cell down on the ship they can put him in so they can beat the life out of him?" Brown stood pat. Hammersla punched him in the jaw and said, "N——r you are lying." Smith, from the back of the interrogation room, offered, "Let me shoot that n——r." Brown, afraid for his life, finally consented to confess. According to the nineteen-year-old, "They forced me to say yes and I had to say yes else they were going to take me back on the ship and beat me and hang me by my toes."[65]

Given Brown's testimony, Schnepfe moved to strike the confession from evidence. Rose denied the motion and left the matter up to the jury. Whether Rose knew it or not, he had just condemned Brown to death.

Rose's ruling functionally empowered the jury to decide who they trusted more—a nineteen-year-old Black deserter accused of killing a defenseless white woman, or several white police officers and servicemen. One after another, these men took the stand and the trial slipped away from the defense. Bradley reiterated Brown's flawless recollection of the events of the murder, including

146 · CHAPTER 5

where Kavanaugh was struck and where the assailant threw her pocketbook. He also testified that Brown confessed, not only to the Baltimore detectives but before the naval board of inquiry. Commander Edward Washburn, the convening authority and senior member of the board of inquiry, organized a hearing after Bradley and Hammersla extracted Brown's confession. The board provided Brown with counsel. Brown, in thick detail, noted all the particulars of the murder as he had to the Baltimore police. Schnepfe moved to strike the confession. Rose overruled him. Commander Randal Jacobs, another member of the naval board of inquiry, took the stand and detailed the similarities between the signed confession given to the Baltimore police and Brown's confession before the board. Schnepfe moved to strike the confession. Rose overruled him.[66]

The prosecution rested its case.

Although the material witnesses placing Brown at the scene had not panned out and the *Cumberland* crew let slip some critical evidence that undercut the prosecution's case, law enforcement all consistently detailed the nature and particulars of Brown's confession. This sterling consistency owed either to an honest recollection of events or from Brown's assertion that they had drafted the confession and coached him on the details.

The defense called one witness—Ray Foggy, a mess attendant stationed on the *Cumberland* who had been on watch duty the night Brown had been beaten. Foggy had been told to bring Stewart Green and Henry Brown to Lieutenant Smith's private quarters. Smith ordered that the two be placed in the brig together. Although Foggy could not see what transpired in the brig, he heard Brown's shrieks. Foggy screamed into the room and told Green to cut it out. At one point, a petty officer opened the cell door. Brown spilled out and asked why they were beating him. The petty officer said that Lieutenant Smith ordered it. Crew members were ordered to beat Brown but not kill him—half of him should be left down in the brig. Brown emerged from the brig bloody. The crew took him to Lieutenant Smith's quarters again—for what, Foggy did not know. Green, a "prisoner at large," returned to his quarters and went to bed.[67]

After Foggy's testimony, Rose gave the jury its instructions. Perhaps convinced by Foggy's recollection, he struck the confession extracted by the Baltimore police. He maintained, however, the confession given before the board of inquiry. Both confessions were identical, so this decision provided little help to Brown.

After twenty-two minutes of deliberation, the all-white jury found Brown guilty of first-degree murder. Rose denied Brown's motion for appeal. He condemned Brown to death by hanging on June 2 at the Baltimore city jail.[68]

"I Ask Mercy at Your Hands" • 147

Henry Brown's case demonstrated broader dynamics in racialized criminal justice and the function of courts. Regarding the former, Black people's exclusion from juries created a racial imbalance that vested condemnatory legal power in white citizenries. Baltimore's Black newspaper, the *Afro-American*, took umbrage with this convention and noted that in cases wherein Black men and women were excluded from jury service, "practically, the man [*sic*] is tried by a jury of *superiors*."[69] Given the racial reckoning that Brown's case would spark, this type of conventional and systematized racism proved far bigger than just the young man's case. It spoke to deeply entrenched forms of white supremacist social organization that denied Black people the rights and privileges associated with civil life. Moreover, the court's decision to uphold the signed confession despite clear admissions from the *Cumberland* crew that Brown had been kept awake and beaten, as well as conflicting testimony regarding his whereabouts, spoke to the court's compulsion to convict as a social responsibility rather than an impersonal and objective administration of justice. The rushed trial, the abandoned inquiries into other credible suspects, and the retention of the confession represented the court's desire to convict in the interest of the white polity. However, Baltimore's Black political class would not accept the decision so easily. In their examinations of the case, they found the court's decision rushed and lacking proper investigation. In the spirit of Progressive reform, they conducted their own investigations. And although Rose condemned Brown to hang on June 2, he did not. A fractured, though effective, collective emerged to fight for the young man's life while navigating the complexities of Black politics in Maryland. Laura Wheatley, an Afro-Southern transplant to Baltimore City, led the movement against police brutalization and joined a broader movement of Black women across the United States who spearheaded persistent campaigns for Black freedom.[70]

"Justice before the Law": The Citizens Committee

In 1878, Henry and Mollie Dickerson birthed their second eldest daughter, Laura. Laura's father, Henry, was born into slavery on a plantation in Raywick, Kentucky—a small town an hour south of Louisville. After the Civil War, he moved to Louisville to work as a farmhand. Laura's mother, Mollie, had five kids and worked as a domestic servant. In 1880, the family settled in Saint Louis, Missouri. There, Henry found steady and relatively well-paying work as a railroad porter. They moved back to Louisville where Laura worked as a public school teacher. After her father passed, Laura moved her mother and youngest

148 · CHAPTER 5

sister, Bertha, like so many of their Afro-Southern peers, to a bustling urban center: Baltimore. In 1906, Laura Dickerson married Dr. Edward J. Wheatley, a physician who lived in a three-story walk-up in Baltimore's lively westside.[71] Armed with the lessons she learned living in radically different areas of the country, Laura Wheatley became a disruptor in Baltimore's Black activist circles, particularly in the local branch of the National Association for the Advancement of Colored People (NAACP) where she rose through the ranks and became a fierce advocate for Afro-Southern migrants.

For instance, in November 1920, Wheatley coordinated with the Charleston branch to locate the parents of Ruth Virginia Brown, a twelve-year-old girl who had been abducted from her home, brought to Baltimore, and raped by a white couple.[72] She also brought the case of a twenty-two-year-old man named Fred Washington, who had fled a white lynch mob in Bainbridge, Georgia, to the Baltimore branch. Seeing the ordeal as part of its obligation to redress racial discrimination, Wheatley believed the local branch would help Washington secure employment. The branch refused. Incensed, she arranged travel for the young man who had relatives in Jersey City. After the ordeal, Wheatley wrote a strongly worded letter to James Weldon Johnson, executive secretary of the NAACP, condemning the local branch's callous leadership.[73]

Wheatley's resolute commitment to the Baltimore branch, coupled with her determined efforts to mold the branch's activities around redressing the injustices experienced by Afro-Southern migrants and everyday Baltimoreans, ruffled feathers. She bumped heads with branch president James A. B. Callis, who consistently refused to allocate time and resources to Wheatley's crusades. For Callis, the branch needed to tend to the membership which grew impatient every day the latest issue of the *Crisis* was delayed. Members came to officers' doorsteps and overflowed the branch mailbox with angry complaints about their missing magazines.[74] The Baltimore branch struggled to keep its head above water and could not fulfill its operational duties let alone pursue the types of campaigns that Wheatley considered its central duty.

Wheatley remained undeterred. She continued pursuing justice for the unjustly treated. It was hardly surprising, then, that a meeting with Henry Brown, the young Texan on death row for a crime he may not have committed, galvanized Wheatley to organize a Citizens Committee to fight on his behalf. Until this committee took an interest in the case, Brown's attempts to escape execution had proven futile. He reportedly wrote to First Lady Florence Harding requesting that she appeal to her husband on his behalf. The first lady refused.[75] When Wheatley joined the fight, she immediately reached out to the Baltimore branch of the NAACP to galvanize the membership around Brown. They again refused her crusade.

"*I Ask Mercy at Your Hands*" • 149

The campaign would be hard.

Wheatley joined Emma Truxon, a social worker, and Boston Allen, a reverend, in the fight for Brown's exoneration. Allen, who had first taken notice of the case and secured Brown's counsel, informed Truxon who reached out to Ovington Weller, a Republican senator from Maryland, to request a meeting with the attorney general.[76] As the campaign gained steam, Wheatley insisted that any mention of their efforts in official NAACP publications and the *Afro-American* exclude reference to the local branch.[77] All publicity should highlight the grassroots labors of the three volunteers. And these labors were certainly newsworthy. Weller satisfied Truxon's request, and the Citizens Committee received a meeting with the president. On May 28, they traveled to Washington, D.C.

At the meeting, the Citizens Committee went over the case with a fine-toothed comb. While the prosecution could not produce a single witness to definitively place Brown at the scene of the crime, the committee found several Baltimore residents who had seen him when the murder took place. A few issues prevented their testimony. First, the committee noted that Schnepfe, a competent lawyer, was white. He did not know—or did not bother—to engage Black Baltimoreans who could build Brown's alibi. Second, the witnesses in question were hesitant to testify. Brown had evidently been at a brothel when the murder took place with a Stella Brown, who refused to corroborate his story for fear of self-incrimination. Not only did they keep a disorderly house and engage in sex work; they also harbored a military deserter. The heat from testifying could backfire and impact their livelihoods.[78]

The Citizens Committee wrapped up its presentation and headed back to Baltimore. In the following days, they sent affidavits and letters from residents and witnesses who corroborated Brown's alibi and implicated the police in using intimidation to steer witnesses like Stella Brown away from testifying on his behalf.[79] Regarding the former, Zachariah Jackson, a resident from the northwestern part of town near where Brown had been staying, testified that he saw Brown with Stella Brown at 10:00 p.m. on the night of the murder. If Jackson was correct, Brown must have caught a train from Annapolis before Kavanaugh was murdered. Moreover, Jackson's testimony lent credence to Brown's assertion that he had been with Stella Brown the night of the murder—a fact she denied to keep her business out of the incriminating affair. What is more, Jackson claimed to have confronted Stella Brown for what he viewed as her cowardice for allowing Brown to hang to protect herself.[80] Despite Jackson's testimony, Stella Brown's actions were likely not the result of cowardice but instead the results of a well-founded fear of incurring the wrath of local police. According to J. Steward Davis, Brown's new attorney and general counsel to the Citizens

150 • CHAPTER 5

Committee, the Baltimore police routinely intimidated Black witnesses to either compel or discourage them from testifying. In a letter to Harry Daugherty, Davis recounted an instance in which police arrested a man who refused to testify. They booked him on a vagrancy charge and had him incarcerated in the House of Correction. Two witnesses, Annie Rhuebottom and Rhoda Simms, alleged that the same happened in Brown's case. They were privy to the fact that Northwestern District police had threatened Stella Brown with incarceration if she corroborated Brown's alibi.[81]

Given the sheer magnitude of the Citizens Committee's labors and the evidence brought forth which potentially corroborated Brown's alibi and summoned doubt regarding the criminal legal system in Baltimore, the attorney general simply could not ignore the shakiness of the case. Two days before Brown's scheduled execution, the condemned man received a surprising respite. President Harding granted Brown a thirty-day stay of execution.[82] The Office of the Pardon Attorney, seemingly convinced by the Citizens Committee's evidence, filed a formal petition to Harding and took up the case.[83] An initial assessment revealed that Brown had not been properly informed of his right to appeal for a stay of execution. The attorney general's office also found discrepancies in the testimonies of the prosecution's witnesses.[84] These inconsistencies likely echoed Judge Rose's own assessments during jury instructions that the witnesses placing Brown at the scene of the crime had riotously inconsistent testimony that raised significant (and reasonable) doubt. After further investigation, the attorney general recommended another stay of execution, which President Harding granted. Brown's life had been spared until August 1.

This second evasion of state-sanctioned murder turned an open-and-shut case into a matter of intense public scrutiny. Some of Maryland's white population and Baltimore's loudest newspapers wanted blood. Their exhortations for Brown's hanging demonstrated both a desire for mob-style justice that preserved the racial status quo and an intense fear of the effectiveness of Black collective power. White newspapers, particularly the *Sun*, ran countless stories and scathing editorials on the developments of Brown's case, as well as several other exposés that highlighted Black crime in other parts of the city and state. Wheatley found this outpouring reprehensible, noting, "Our white press is like a red flag waving before a bull on the Negro question here."[85] For the Citizens Committee and their supporters, Brown's case represented a grave injustice that revealed police corruption and brutality, the inherent racism of the judicial system, and a disregard for due process that disproportionately affected Black Americans. For many white citizens and news outlets, the case represented

"I Ask Mercy at Your Hands" · 151

nothing more than a Black man's attempt to get out of paying the price for a crime to which he had already confessed.

Beyond Brown's case, the public discourse surrounding his potential exoneration revealed the degree to which Blackness had become sutured to violent crime in white racist imaginaries. Brown's circumstances exposed the *longue durée* of "Negro rowdyism" discourses that led to the consolidation of Baltimore's racialized criminal legal system at the turn of the century. The bloodthirstiness with which white onlookers conducted themselves also spoke to racialized execution trends in Baltimore. Between 1844 and 1873, no Black people were executed in the city. Black rates of execution spiked and followed increased rates of arrest and incarceration after the Civil War when free Black people became a "problem" that only brutal repression could fix. From 1873 to 1923, thirteen people were executed in Baltimore's city jail. Eleven, or 85 percent, of them were Black, including one Black woman who was accused of poisoning her husband. Black men were hanged on charges of murder, rape, and assault, which followed a national trend.[86] In addition to executions, in cases where suspects were not sentenced to death, they often still experienced corporal punishment in the form of lashes.[87] As such, in Henry Brown's case, much of Baltimore and Maryland's white public was animated by complementary compulsions to protect white women's safety and enact routinized and brutal violence, whether through lashes or the noose. Black activist challenges to these systemic assertions of racial order posed a grave threat to racial hierarchy. These sentiments materialized in the press.

In the *Sun*'s column, "Ezekiel Cheever and the Breakfast," the pseudonymous Cheever characterized President Harding as an incompetent who continually interceded at the last minute and sardonically declared, "Hangman, spare that Ethiopian." Such practice made Brown "a monthly tenant of this world who at the last moment may have his lease canceled and be cast out into space." The columnist took aim at the "colored gentry" for organizing around the case and attempting to reframe perceptions regarding Brown. They believed that Brown's guilt was undeniable and efforts to prove his innocence were either manipulative acts of political convenience—in Harding's case—or menacing expressions of Black political power.[88] Not all white publications took as firm a stance on Brown's guilt. The *Baltimore American*, one of the *Sun*'s chief competitors, in a dispatch to a paper in Kavanaugh's hometown, cautioned patience, noting, "Until reasonable doubt of his guilt is removed there ought to be no clamor for hurrying the execution along."[89] Moreover, the Citizens Committee included a clipping from the *American* to make their case for an independent investigation

152 • CHAPTER 5

to the pardon attorney. In the clipping they chose, the *American* editors temperately wrote, "A man ought to have fair play whether he is rich or poor or white or black."[90]

While the white press had mixed reactions to the case, the Black press stood firmly behind Brown. The Associated Negro Press (ANP) sent dispatches to Black papers across the country. In one story, the ANP applauded the Harding administration for granting reprieves and reexamining the case. The organization remained hopeful that the attorney general's office would recommend executive clemency based on their own publicized assertions that the prosecution relied solely on circumstantial evidence and a potentially bogus confession.[91] A man should not hang with such thin proof. In Baltimore, the *Afro-American* continued providing publicity to grassroots efforts while abiding by Wheatley's wish to omit reference to the Baltimore branch of the NAACP. On July 12, after the first reprieve, Wheatley, Truxon, and Allen organized a meeting at the Bethel AME Church on Druid Hill Avenue. Sixty people attended the event. Allen appealed to the crowd for continued support based on their independently collected evidence. According to Allen, since their initial inquiries in the brothel, two additional men had come forward who said they saw Brown in Baltimore on the night of the murder. They were willing to testify on the condemned man's behalf but did not know how to get their evidence to the proper authorities. The organizers collected $21.65 to help fund their efforts. They also noted that although evidently aware of the case, the national office of the NAACP had not taken it up.[92]

This latter assertion was partially true. Laura Wheatley had sent letters to James Weldon Johnson requesting support, but he had not responded. His silence was deafening. It was not altogether unexpected, though. The national office relied on local branches to maintain standing committees, including a Legal Redress and Legislative Committee, to handle such matters.[93] Local affairs should be handled locally because branches had more intimate knowledge of the political landscapes of their cities and towns. When the national office received a complaint concerning a legal injustice, they promptly forwarded it to the closest branch and provided legal support only in the most extreme circumstances.

This stance stemmed from both a desire to cultivate autonomous local branches and because, frankly, the national office was busy. In 1921, their capacity was consumed by lobbying efforts associated with a congressional antilynching bill, the provision of legal aid to the victims of the 1919 Elaine massacre in Hoop Spur, Arkansas, the coordination of fundraising efforts to provide aid for victims of the 1921 Tulsa race massacre that decimated a thriving Black

"I Ask Mercy at Your Hands" • 153

commercial district, a public relations campaign to combat the resurgence of the Ku Klux Klan, the organization of the association's second Pan-African Congress, efforts around Haitian liberation after U.S. occupation in 1915, and getting thousands of issues of the *Crisis* out the door.[94] Yet and still, after several unanswered letters and another hard-fought reprieve for Brown, Wheatley, who had been iced out by her local branch, wrote Johnson, "I was disappointed not to receive at least a word of encouragement from you."[95] She would have to keep waiting.

In the meantime, the Citizens Committee, specifically Emma Truxon and J. Steward Davis, continued collecting evidence and new leads from Baltimore and Annapolis and sending them to the Office of the Pardon Attorney to aid its investigation.

As the Citizens Committee continued these efforts, Henry Brown's case reached a new level of public exposure when Albert C. Ritchie, the newly elected and ardent state's rights Democratic governor of Maryland, publicly sparred with Attorney General Harry Daugherty over Brown's fate. The Baltimore dailies devoted voluminous newsprint to catalog the back-and-forth. Ritchie requested that Daugherty and Harding arrive at a speedy resolution. While cagey on his stance, the governor invoked the safety of white women to gesture toward Brown's guilt. He wrote, "I owe it to the sense of security to which the people of this State, particularly the women of Annapolis, are entitled to draw your attention to the very great importance of disposing of the case at the earliest moment that is possible."[96] As the Wickersham Committee would later identify as a systemic response to public pressure that undermined the criminal legal system, Ritchie reacted drastically to white calls for execution. He wanted someone to hang, and Brown had already confessed. The legitimacy of the confession was not Ritchie's problem. In the same issue, the *Sun* stoked fears over white women's safety by highlighting that "the special consideration shown the negro murderer of a white woman tends to encourage the commission of other crimes and outrages by negroes, and especially crimes against women." In characterizing Brown's reprieves as "special consideration," the paper obscured the eminent possibility that Brown was innocent. The *Evening Sun* assumed a much harsher tone and argued that executive clemency encouraged crime. The paper ominously suggested that long delays in the execution of the death penalty aroused "contempt for the law in the minds of many good persons and [led] often to lynchings." The paper warned that "lynchings have gone out of fashion in Maryland, in spite of many horrible crimes in recent years. It would be a terrible pity if a mistaken sympathy for a negro murderer should revive the practice."[97] By the *Evening Sun*'s implication, Brown had been right to worry about

154 · CHAPTER 5

a lynch mob while trapped in the brig of the *Cumberland*. Moreover, the paper bolstered perceptions of Black criminality and reiterated white public support for the execution of nearly a dozen Black men and women since the Civil War.

Daugherty's offices stood pat, though. They believed that Brown received an unfair trial and that he should have been granted an appeal. More damning still, after reviewing the case, the attorney general's office concluded, "There was some doubt as to whether anything the witnesses said should be believed." Daugherty himself wrote Ritchie that Brown had been "convicted entirely upon circumstantial evidence."[98] A third reprieve seemed imminent. This possibility incensed Ritchie who, in another widely circulated letter, ceased mincing words. He fully adjudged Brown guilty and described Kavanaugh's murder as "one of the most brutal in the history of the State." He warned of political violence and exhorted the attorney general's office to grant no additional stays of execution. At a Democratic State Central Committee meeting, Ritchie reportedly railed against the president who he believed only investigated the case to appease Black voters.[99] Daugherty responded to Ritchie by again highlighting the conflicting testimony and Brown's unconstitutional treatment. He further emphasized the shaky foundation on which the prosecution's case rested. The primary evidence against Brown was his confession. Given questions surrounding the confession's legitimacy, the attorney general reasoned that "where a man is convicted upon circumstantial evidence expedition is by no means as important as careful and thorough investigation to see that no mistake is being made in the execution of the condemned."[100]

To that end, James A. Finch, a lawyer with the Office of the Pardon Attorney, conducted an independent investigation with the help of the Citizens Committee. Finch revisited the crime scene in Annapolis and met with the prosecution's witnesses. Finch reportedly found their conflicting testimony during the meetings alarming. He also met with Brown and witnesses in Baltimore who were willing to testify that they saw Brown on the night of the murder. The *Sun* reported that "local Federal officials who talked with Mr. Finch are of the opinion that Brown will not be executed."[101] Based on Finch's investigation and after Harding could be peeled away from the golf course, Brown received a third reprieve until August 31 and narrowly escaped the gallows for a third time.[102]

Despite these seemingly positive signs, Laura Wheatley was worried. A few days after Brown's third reprieve, she sent the national office another letter. For the third time, Wheatley explained Brown's situation to James Weldon Johnson. A nineteen-year-old Black man, without friends, family, or money, was being "railroaded to the gallows," and only a few people were doing anything about it. She suspected that Black Baltimoreans did not rally around the case much

"I Ask Mercy at Your Hands" • 155

because John C. Rose, the sentencing judge with an unimpeachable judicial record, had gained the trust of Baltimore's Black citizenry. Indeed, in Governor Ritchie's appeal to the attorney general, he invoked Rose's reputation to note that there existed no "possibility of racial or other prejudice" in Brown's treatment.[103] Wheatley counted herself among those who trusted Rose, but she believed he had gotten this one wrong. The lettered ended, "I trust that this experience will encourage others to take a deeper interest in seeing that Colored men get JUSTICE before the law."[104]

Wheatley's next action marked a significant turning point in the Citizens Committee's campaign. Since both the local and national branches of the NAACP offered no support and since the committee had trouble rousing grass-roots backing, she sought new allies. She appealed to her congressional representative, J. Charles Linthicum. Linthicum reached out to Daugherty's office. He forwarded Laura Wheatley's findings which outlined *Cumberland* officials' vendettas against Brown, discrepancies in the pocketbook produced at trial, and at least six witnesses who could corroborate Brown's alibi. He implored the attorney general to consider the evidence and act accordingly. Based on Linthicum's letter, the Just Government League, a group of white women suffragists, publicly criticized Governor Ritchie's recklessness. Although appalled by Kavanaugh's murder, they found the case against Brown extremely weak. In an editorial, the league emphasized the attorney general's public statements concerning the circumstantial nature of the evidence against Brown. They wrote, "Innocent men have been hanged before when a scapegoat was wanted."[105] Wheatley's letter roused both an elected Democratic official to raise interparty doubts and a league of white women—the mythologized victims of the whole ordeal—to side with Brown, the alleged killer. Given these developments, the backlash that followed likely shocked Wheatley.

In his letter, Linthicum characterized Laura Wheatley as a "very influential citizen" perhaps to lend credibility to her findings.[106] However, the press took this invocation as a threat rather than an appeal to respectability. The case's lead prosecutor, Robert Carman, publicly responded to Linthicum in the *Evening Sun*. He expressed deep suspicion and even anger at Wheatley's characterization as "influential." The district attorney wrote, "If the woman is bright and knows what she is talking about, that is all right. . . . But I fail utterly to see what bearing the fact that she is influential has on her efforts to secure a review of the Brown case." While Carman scantly addressed the evidence of the case, he harped on the ascription of influence, again noting, "But I should like very much to know what Mr. Linthicum means when he says that Mrs. Wheatley is an influential citizen."[107] Carman's indignation revealed the degree to which Black men and

156 · CHAPTER 5

women's growing political influence stirred animosity and fear among white Marylanders. The city's white political establishment, from politicians to police, expected deference from Black Baltimoreans and Marylanders alike. In highlighting Linthicum's use of the term "influential," Carman discredited Wheatley and the Citizens Committee while avoiding a substantive engagement with the legal questions of the case. In doing so, Carman revealed that white supremacy thrived on justice that propped up state imperatives to maintain racial order. A police state rooted in the maintenance of capital relations and white racial hierarchy could not bend to the eminently reasonable and well-argued position of the Black bourgeoisie. Whether Henry Brown was guilty or not was beside the point. The legal system could only maintain its authority and centrality in broader segregationist and anti-Black projects if Brown hanged. Wheatley's ability to encourage Linthicum to break ranks was the last straw. And Wheatley's small but mighty committee knew this.

Although Carman deployed craven rhetoric to attack Wheatley and invoke the boogeyman of Black collective politics, J. Steward Davis, the lawyer running Brown's defense, fumed at Wheatley for a different and more calculated reason. The Citizens Committee's strategy from the outset hinged on maintaining an all-Black defense and forsaking public support from white politicians and lawyers. The Citizens Committee angled to avert public charges of politicization. In remaining politically neutral, they hoped that their actions could not be distorted as anything but legal due diligence. After Linthicum's letter became public, Davis publicly attacked Wheatley likely because he knew the case for Brown crumbled the moment the letter was published. In a harsh dispatch published in the *Afro-American*, Davis severed all ties with Wheatley, writing, "I insist most emphatically that I prefer your hatred rather than your good will for if I had your good will I never could trust it." Davis further characterized Wheatley's actions as a betrayal of their exhaustively crafted defense strategy. He noted that in the past, Wheatley had suggested engaging prominent white figures, like former Maryland attorney general Isaac Lobe Straus.[108] The Citizens Committee had nixed these suggestions every time in favor of an all-Black defense. As damage control, Davis penned an editorial for the *Evening Sun*. He denounced Linthicum's letter and Wheatley's actions and claimed that he, Allen, and Truxon had played no part in contacting the congressman. He wrote, "The defense deprecates as much as anyone else that said letter was sent; inasmuch as the defense has been scrupulously solicitous that no pressure other than that of reason be brought to bear upon the Department of Justice at any time." He also wrote James Finch, the agent working the case for the Office of the Pardon Attorney, a letter to the same effect. For their parts, Allen and Truxon were

"I Ask Mercy at Your Hands" • 157

reportedly perturbed that Linthicum's letter had given the prosecution and the white press ammunition to diminish the legal robustness of their findings.[109]

As the Citizens Committee dealt with the fallout from Linthicum's letter, James Weldon Johnson finally responded to Wheatley. He apologized for the lapse in communication. Her letters had been misplaced. He commended the committee's work and pledged to provide publicity from the national office.[110] This promise of support came just after the Office of the Pardon Attorney finished its investigation into the case.

On August 8, 1921, three weeks before Brown's scheduled execution, James Finch forwarded his recommendation to the attorney general's office.[111] Throughout the process, Finch and the Office of the Pardon Attorney had gained the trust and adulation of the Citizens Committee. Indeed, in a letter to Finch, Laura Wheatley raved, "Our committee has the confidence to trust this case with God and YOU."[112] The feeling was mutual. Finch, in his report, described Wheatley as "a very intelligent, educated, and refined colored woman . . . in whose judgment and veracity I have entire confidence."[113]

Finch's extensive report examined elements of the trial and subsequent investigations to square away puzzling details in an error-laden case full of contradictory and doubtful testimony. In examining the evidence gathered by the military, the government, the Baltimore police, and the Citizens Committee, Finch took issue with the naval board of inquiry. The board of inquiry's findings were never brought before the jury during the trial despite their availability. What is more, after Brown's confession, the board of inquiry abandoned promising leads and suppressed elements of their investigation that cast doubt on Brown's guilt. As such, the jury was not privy to one sailor, identified as M. Jones, who was missing from the _Cumberland_ during the window of time in which Kavanaugh was killed. When Lieutenant Smith informed the crew that a murder had taken place on the Naval Academy grounds, Jones attempted to escape the ship and was sent to the brig as a prisoner. Upon examination, Jones had what appeared to be flecks of blood on his shoes. Moreover, half a button from a peacoat was found near Kavanaugh's body. Jones wore a peacoat. Brown did not. Finch judged the fact that the jury did not hear any of this evidence as improper due diligence.[114] Moreover, in his review of the case, Finch uncovered that another of the board of inquiry's chief suspects, Roland Casey, was spotted entering the Naval Academy grounds moments before Kavanaugh had entered.[115] The Citizens Committee had long suspected Casey and submitted two affidavits from people who knew him and alleged that he had been hired to kill Harriet Kavanaugh.[116] While Finch did not assess that any of this evidence was enough to convict either man or exonerate Brown, he did find

158 · CHAPTER 5

the material evidence and witness testimony compelling enough to conclude that they "should be investigated further before Brown is permitted to hang."[117] Moreover, the jury should have known that the board of inquiry collected such evidence, and the defense should have been permitted to call on Jones and Casey to testify at trial.

Although Finch found the trial recklessly administered, he did find the confession compelling enough to convict Brown. Indeed, Finch concluded that had he been on the jury, he would have moved to convict the accused. Finch wrote, "I have . . . no reasonable doubt of Brown's guilt."[118] Brown's alleged walk-through with the Baltimore police detectives and board of inquiry sealed the issue for him. According to a stenographer, who Finch evaluated as largely indifferent to the outcome of the trial, Brown led the detectives and officials around the Naval Academy grounds and showed them the exact locations of pivotal evidence. Since the stenographer had nothing to gain, Finch believed she was telling the truth, and that Brown had conducted the walk-through without coaching. Despite Finch's certainty on this front, he also wrote, "Of course, another person could have committed the crime and it would not be surprising to learn that someone else committed it."[119] This statement seemed to stand in direct conflict to his assertion that there was no reasonable doubt of Brown's guilt. Perhaps this tension is what led to Finch's final recommendation. For months, the Citizens Committee worked with Finch by collecting evidence, submitting affidavits, and ensuring that the Office of the Pardon Attorney had access to all the information it needed to make an informed decision. Their legwork paid off. Though Finch believed he would have voted to hang Henry Brown and that there was no reasonable doubt of his guilt, he ultimately expressed doubt in his recommendation. He concluded that "there is a very real possibility—not a probability, but a possibility—that a mistake might be made" in upholding Brown's death sentence.[120] As such, Finch recommended a commutation for Brown. Instead of death by hanging, the young man should face life imprisonment. Finch forwarded this recommendation directly to Harry Daugherty, and that is where his work, the Citizens Committee's work, and Brown's life was ultimately ignored and invalidated.

After a public feud with Governor Ritchie, Daugherty reviewed Finch's report, considered his recommendation, and made his own to President Harding. Like Finch's, Daugherty's report seemed to suggest that Brown's guilt was doubtful. He reiterated his position that Brown had been "convicted wholly upon circumstantial evidence."[121] Regarding the confession, the attorney general noted, " . . . there is not the slightest reason for suspecting him of the crime except his own admission which was *certainly induced*."[122] Daugherty conceded that the treatment was reprehensible but that, ultimately, Brown could have just told the truth anyway. Given this callous assessment, Daugherty ignored Finch's recommendation and advised President Harding to deny Brown's petition for executive clemency.

After receiving Daugherty's recommendation, President Harding rejected Brown's petition and ordered his execution to take place on September 1. In their assessment, the *Sun* editorial board believed that the Citizens Committee's resort to "politics" had failed to tip the scales of justice.[123] The *American* reported that Harding remained unconvinced by the discrepancies raised by the Office of the Pardon Attorney's investigation.[124] Davis speculated that Linthicum's letter proved a major turning point but remained nonetheless baffled at how quickly and precipitously the situation had changed.[125] Wheatley believed Harding had never planned to commute Brown's sentence in the first place.

A U.S. marshal delivered the news to Brown at the city jail. He reportedly received the final decision stoically.[126] Shortly afterward, Brown called on Laura Wheatley. She went and spoke to him a final time. She noticed that he was distant. Perhaps his hearing was impaired. It took him a long time to respond to her questions. When he did, the answers seemed rushed and off-topic (figure 12). She noted, "He answers for politeness before he realizes what was said to him." Wheatley's husband, a physician, thought an alienist should have assessed Brown's mental state before the trial.[127]

Figure 12. The only known image of Henry Alfred Brown, sporting the naval uniform he wore for months. Originally published in the *Afro-American*, Laura Wheatley bundled it, along with several other clippings on the case, in a letter to James Weldon Johnson. She attached a piece of scratch paper to the photo noting that "this picture looks nothing like him." Source: "Third Degree Victim," *Baltimore Afro-American*, February 11, 1921. Courtesy of the AFRO-American Newspapers Archives.

160 · CHAPTER 5

In a last-ditch effort to save Brown, Wheatley sent another letter to James Weldon Johnson. She pled with the executive secretary to put pressure on President Harding. She felt the Citizens Committee had been played. Harding had extended an olive branch to the Black citizenry in Maryland by granting three reprieves but ultimately kowtowed to the virulence of white racism. Perhaps that was his plan all along. Wheatley speculated, "So as usual the Harding administration has made another unsuccessful stab at trying to please all concerned and satisfying none."[128] Johnson could likely relate. The NAACP had mixed results during Harding's limited time in office. After his election, he expressed support for hiring Black staffers in cabinet offices and putting together an interracial commission to investigate race relations in the United States. He spoke up after the Tulsa race massacre and supported Leonidas Dyer's anti-lynching bill. His stance proved duplicitous on other pressing race questions, including debt peonage, systematic voter disenfranchisement, the segregation of federal agencies, and U.S. occupation in Haiti.[129] Harding had loads of symbolic support for Black social issues but took few material steps to realize solutions to those issues.

Wheatley saw the case as an opportunity to hold Harding's feet to the fire. In her letter to Johnson, she enclosed a five-page comprehensive memo of the evidence the Citizens Committee had gathered over the last three months. It raised several questions about the prosecution's case. How did Henry Brown scale the Naval Academy wall? This fact proved convenient for the prosecution because it explained why the gate watchman could not identify him that night, but Brown seemed physically unable to commit such an athletic feat. Why did Peter Corosh, the jeweler who engraved a pencil for Kavanaugh and who saw her take money from her pocketbook, not testify as to the authenticity of the pocketbook? Upon further investigation, the pocketbook presented in court was too small to fit the pencil that Corosh engraved. In fact, Corosh provided an affidavit in which he categorically stated, given the incorrect pocketbook presented at trial and the improper amount of money attributed to Kavanaugh, that he believed Brown did not commit the murder.[130] What happened to three of the key witnesses? Kenneth Riley, who found Kavanaugh's body, Susan Oblender, who testified that she had entered the Naval Academy grounds at a time inconsistent with the time specified by the gate watchman, and Lieutenant Raymond Smith, the reviled commander of the *Cumberland*, were all transferred out of Annapolis. Finally and most importantly, why were the witnesses who could provide testimony as to Brown's whereabouts barred from the stand? Several Black men and women came forward and none of them were allowed to provide testimony.[131]

"I Ask Mercy at Your Hands" • 161

Wheatley submitted the memo and implored Johnson to consider sending it on behalf of the Citizens Committee—and under the auspices of the NAACP—to President Harding. Johnson responded favorably to the request. The breadth of evidence the committee collected impressed him. He vowed to use the NAACP's resources to do everything possible to have Brown's sentence commuted. In the meantime, he counseled Wheatley to mobilize the committee and begin a petition drive to secure the signatures of "as many influential citizens, both white and colored, as possible."[132] Johnson had clearly not read about the Linthicum snafu. The same day he responded to Wheatley, Johnson fired off a letter to the attorney general requesting that the office reconsider granting Brown executive clemency based on the Citizens Committee's findings.[133] The national office was all in.

But it was too late.

Brown had already been executed.

Conclusion

On August 28, 1921, Henry Alfred Brown, in his last-ditch effort to escape the gallows, penned a letter to President Harding. It is one of the few pieces of archival material to catalog Brown's voice and, as such, is reproduced here in full without alteration,

Baltimore City Jail
August 28, 1921

Dear Mr. President, I am to be Hanged on thursday September 1st Mr. President Spare my life and commute my Sentence. I am innocent of the crime as charged against me in the name of the good Lord ask his mercy for me of the poor Colored boy. Dear Mr. President I ask mercy at your hands. May God bless you and your family.

Henry A. Brown.[134]

The president ignored Brown's letter, and on September 1, 1921, guards escorted him to the bakeshop of the city jail where the gallows had been erected. Standing atop the scaffold, the teenager uttered his final words:

I thank the public, both black and white, for all they have done for me. I know how I got into this trouble, and the man who got me in knows. Some day you all will know. I am going to meet my God. I'm not afraid to die. I know God will take care of me and I want you all to pray for me.

162 · CHAPTER 5

The executor sprung the trap at 7:49 a.m. Brown died shortly thereafter.[135]

While it is impossible to know who killed Harriet Kavanaugh, over the course of Brown's arrest, interrogation, trial, condemnation, reprieve, and execution, revelations regarding the case provided substantial and reasonable doubt concerning his guilt. Brown served as an early use case that demonstrated the effectiveness of third-degree torture at the beginning of a decade where it would reach untold heights. The tactic would only become more commonplace in subsequent decades as public spectacles of cruelty and murder perpetrated against Black people became increasingly private and staged in secluded station house rooms or, in Brown's case, the brig of a naval ship.[136] Although the attorney general and his office expressed significant misgivings about Brown's trial, the collective will of the state's white political establishment, including high-ranking politicians and influential news outlets, appealed to the safety of white women to rush Brown's execution.

Although just one case, Brown's experiences in the courtroom and as a subject of public debate regarding the nature of Blackness and racial politics illuminated several key facets of Baltimore's burgeoning police state. First, the story of policing in Baltimore had been one of increased discretion for police officials, including cops, judges, and politicians. As Colonel Swann battled for police to have greater access to the bodies of individuals, national trends in policing sought even greater protection for cops and detectives who deployed violence to compel suspects to confess to crimes. The third degree stretched the so-called reasonableness of police power to its near breaking point, though courts, in accepting confessions secured through violence, validated its use and tacitly endorsed the practice. This compulsion melded with broader judicial trends in which courts became sites of *social* justice rooted in Progressive ideologies around the ruinous effects of crime. Judges like John Rose, a Progressive champion in Baltimore, subscribed to such ideals and likely weighed the social costs of Brown's exoneration against a legal and ethical interpretation of the case. Rose himself believed the material witnesses were unconvincing and even tossed one confession. Ultimately, Rose's decision to keep the second confession was a profoundly political one that allowed for the court to condemn and murder a Black teenager suspected of killing a white woman.

This reality pointed to the second important dynamic that Brown's case illuminated. In mediating conflict and sustaining its imperatives, the state exercised its right to not just police but to kill. In Baltimore, state-sanctioned murder followed Southern trends as post–Civil War executions and punishments disproportionately affected Black people well into the twentieth century. Such executions tended to stem from charges of murder, rape, and assault, particularly in cases where Black men were the perpetrators and white women the victims. Brown's case typified these dynamics and set off a reckoning in Baltimore and Maryland where the symbolism of Brown's hanging became much more important than finding out who killed Harriet Kavanaugh. White dailies thirsted for blood and even threatened that lynching could come back "in style" in Maryland if Brown was let off the hook. These public remonstrations reinforced the Negro rowdyism discourses that undergirded the city's racialized criminal legal system and revealed the degree to which white supremacist ideals of Black deference and submission underpinned white racial attitudes and policing.

Finally, Brown's case illuminated the state of Black politics in Baltimore, especially in reference to police and judicial reform. While women like Laura Wheatley fought tooth and nail alongside her supporters to exonerate Brown, these supporters were few and far between. Black organizations like the NAACP contained multitudes as Black organizers negotiated pragmatism, respectability, radicalism, and all manner of approaches to pressing racial issues. While Wheatley embraced a more radical orientation, her dismissal of pragmatism revealed how white supremacy manifested in repudiations of effective Black mobilization that challenged police power's capacious affordances. The white legal and political establishment, as well as the press, railed against the "influence" wielded by the supposed Black "gentry." These sites of police power expected submissiveness from Black men and women and reacted ferociously when faced with effective expressions of Black political power in the adjudication of racial conflicts within key institutional spaces like the courts. White disciplinary institutions wielded power with impunity and doggedly defended their ability to brutalize, torture, and kill Black people. Brown's case foreshadowed what Black Baltimoreans' experiences during the 1920s would be like as police power expanded its jurisdiction, discretion, and brutality to historically unseen heights.

6

"Policemen Were the Biggest Liars"

Demystifying Public Order and the Erosion of Black Privacy during the Roaring Twenties

On the evening of March 7, 1929, Helen Harrison went out for a night on the town. She traveled to one of West Baltimore's hottest spots, the New Albert Auditorium. A popular space, the auditorium hosted everything from basketball games, to boxing matches, to balls, to cabarets, to dances. Inside, Black Baltimoreans shimmied, wringed and twisted, and snake-hipped until the wee hours of the night. On this Thursday night, the auditorium hosted a dance. Harrison approached the entrance where police stood guard. Ticket in hand, Harrison asked a patrolman if she could wait at the entrance until space freed up. The patrolman lashed out at Harrison and "called her a name which characterizes only lewd women of the street." Harrison immediately went to the Northwestern District precinct to report the officer. The cops responded to her request with handcuffs and booked her for disorderly conduct. When Harrison's friend came to post bail, the police arrested and booked him for disorderly conduct, too. After the fact, Harrison appealed to the police commissioner. He did nothing.[1]

Harrison's encounter with the Baltimore police typified Black life in the 1920s. She and her friend accounted for 2 of the 7,629 disorderly conduct charges levied against Black people in 1929. Black men and women accounted for 53 percent of all arrestees charged with disorderly conduct that year despite comprising only 17 percent of the population. Police under the new police commissioner's command engaged in targeted public order enforcement that resulted in vastly disproportionate Black arrests for both disorderly conduct and disturbing the

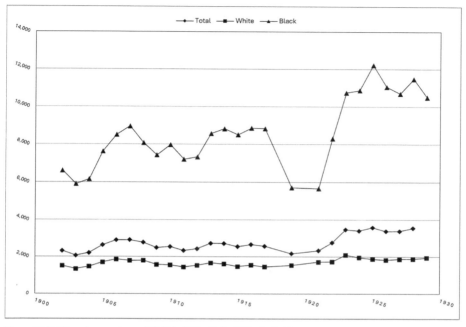

Figure 13. Public order arrests per 100,000, 1902–29. In 1898, the Baltimore police introduced a new arrest category, "disturbing the peace," in their annual reports. The legal distinction between disorderly conduct and disturbing the peace was largely superficial. As such, this graph includes total and racial arrest rates for both offenses under the category of "public order." Source: Board of Police Commissioner Reports, 1902–29, Agency Reports and Publications, Baltimore City Archives.

peace (figure 13).[2] Police concentrated their efforts in the Northwestern District to maintain a preemptive and intimidating presence in calcifying Black neighborhoods.[3] As new segregationist methods, including residential segregation ordinances, the city's first zoning code, and restrictive covenants, codified the color line, the cops maintained Jim Crow.[4] Beat patrolmen routinely harassed, profaned, and brutalized Black people.

Harrison's ordeal represented another crucial reality of policing—the obfuscatory nature of discretion. Harrison and thousands of Black Baltimoreans were booked on the same charge, but not all of them were arrested for trying to attend a dance. Some were arrested for clogging up sidewalks, others for suspicion of having interracial sex. As such, this chapter balances institutional police records alongside what historian Kelly Lytle Hernández calls the "rebel archive"—in this case, the *Afro-American*.[5] By focusing on the *Afro-American*'s reporting, this chapter fills in archival gaps that traditional historical inquiry might ignore for lack

166 · CHAPTER 6

of evidence. In Baltimore's police records, annual reporting did not enumerate how many police committed murder, brutality, or harassment in any systematic or transparent way. Even if it did, given the intimacy and ephemerality of police encounters, the data simply could not capture the magnitude of police violence. Moreover, internal minutes of official police proceedings, particularly under Police Commissioner Charles Gaither, proved undetailed and sparse. As such, this chapter relies on reporting from the *Afro-American* to provide a glimpse into the everyday lived realities of policing in the city and demystify the panoply of behaviors that constituted public "disorder."

Culling from the newspaper's most heavily reported stories during the 1920s gives context to the decontextualized and nonspecific charges of disorderly conduct that police typically deployed to mask their capricious law enforcement activities. As previous chapters have demonstrated, police advocated for and exploited the boundlessness of police power to regulate social life and its attendant activities, some of which were not illegal but nonetheless challenged prevailing racial hierarchy and white supremacist expectations. In the 1920s, police intensified this style of policing by using discretionary public order conventions to crack down on consensual interracial sex and to invade Black private spaces, particularly the home.[6] Historian Rashad Shabazz notes how, in the 1920s, compulsions to police interracial sex manifested in increased police power which led to an enlargement of police personnel and door-to-door searches in Black communities.[7] This dynamic bore out locally as Black Baltimoreans felt Jim Crow's everyday incursions evermore intimately and disproportionately.

The chief enforcer of this mode of outsized policing was the city's first police commissioner, Charles Gaither, who emboldened his men to wreak havoc in the streets. A former National Guard general, Gaither brought his expertise in occupation and marksmanship to the police force. He flippantly ignored civilian petitions, refused to engage Black citizens in their calls to diversify the police force, and even defended cops who murdered city residents.[8] Gaither's management of the force spoke to the increasing latitude of police power. Although it had never been purely bound to the letter of the law, police under Gaither's tenure patrolled the streets with highly flexible discretion wherein police committed the crimes they had at least been superficially tasked to prevent. They broke into private residences. They tailed and detained interracial couples. They even murdered people in their own homes. Gaither defended his patrolmen at every turn. It is no wonder that the decade culminated in the convening of the Wickersham Commission, which produced extensive reports detailing the alarmingly violent, corrupt, and lawless activity of municipal police.[9] What follows is the Baltimore police's contributions to such conditions.

"The General": Baltimore's First Police Commissioner

The 1920s proved to be a hugely transformative moment in American history. The decade began with the "noble" yet ultimately failed experiment of Prohibition and ended with a stock market crash that threw the country into the Great Depression. The decade saw the ratification of women's suffrage as well as the liberating and excessive cultural pursuits codified under the moniker of the Roaring Twenties. Automobile manufacturing intensified and cars flooded city streets. Municipal bodies scrambled to adapt to the new—and often dangerous—form of transportation that became increasingly attainable to working people. Afro-Southern migration continued as Black populations swelled in urban centers while Black people maintained and developed new forms of cultural expression.

In Baltimore, between 1920 and 1930, the Black population increased as never before. During that decade, Black Baltimoreans came to comprise 18 percent of the total population—their highest representation up to that point. The city itself grew because of a 1918 annexation that increased its landmass threefold.[10] Given these national, state, and local changes, the Baltimore police were due for major structural transformations. State and city officials sought to streamline the police department by altering its managerial structure while also beefing up the number of beat cops to keep pace with the city's accelerated development and the new challenges of policing traffic, Prohibition, and public morality.[11] In the process, the 1920s saw the intensification of discretionary public order policing that disproportionately affected Black residents. The increase in patrolmen also led to more instances of police brutality, which became a common topic of reportage and critique in the pages of the *Afro-American*, the third largest Black newspaper in the United States. During the 1920s, *Afro-American* historian Hayward Farrar argues that "the *Afro* became more radical in its pronouncements on racial and economic problems, calling for the creation of a more egalitarian and racially desegregated society than it had before."[12] The *Afro-American* spent the decade organizing against police violence and the consolidating color line that confined Black homeownership to discrete parts of the city. The editors targeted much of their ire at the police's new head honcho, the city's first police commissioner.

By 1920, Baltimore still relied on an outmoded three-man police board to supervise the force. New York had abandoned its board in 1901 and Boston in 1906 in favor of a sole police commissioner. Although Baltimore attempted to reorganize the police board in 1900, the legislature produced a tepid bipartisan reform that failed to eliminate the board itself.[13] More substantive reforms came in 1920 when the General Assembly passed two major acts to address issues of local control and the overly complicated structure of the police board.

168 · CHAPTER 6

The first reform was the abolition of the police board. Colonel Sherlock Swann, former police board president and current postmaster of Baltimore, publicly supported the change. According to Swann, the police commissioner should operate independently for the sake of good police work.[14] Swann's sentiments echoed prevailing feelings which justified swift action. On April 9, Governor Ritchie—with very little controversy—signed a bill into law that abolished the police board and replaced it with a sole police commissioner. Instead of the two-year term served by past commissioners, the new commissioner served a six-year term subject to termination based on misconduct or incompetence but otherwise renewable indefinitely. The new police commissioner would earn $10,000 annually, making the appointee one of the highest paid government officials in the state.[15]

As the installation of a sole police commissioner passed through the General Assembly with little disagreement, the question of local control remained fraught. Who would appoint the commissioner—the mayor or the governor? Since 1860, Baltimore's mayors had consistently criticized state control over the police department to little avail. When the issue emerged during the 1920 legislative session, it proved a partisan affair. Republicans favored a shift to local control while Democrats favored a referendum that would allow voters to decide if the current arrangement should change.[16] Opponents of municipal control feared that, just like the Know Nothings in the 1850s, the police could be corrupted by city politicians to do their bidding. Opponents stressed that police had to be insulated from politics. To many, that meant state control was optimal.[17] This line of argument ignored the present reality that the police board was explicitly politicized in the requirement that members of both political parties be represented on the board in a way that vested de facto decision-making power in whatever political party won the governorship. This arrangement caused the city's Black citizenry to voraciously support local control. Whereas Democrats and other white commenters contended that a governor-appointed police commissioner would somehow disentangle the police from political suasion, the *Afro-American*'s editorial board argued that gubernatorial police appointments were often made to pay off "political debts" rather than benefit Baltimoreans.[18] Moreover, although Black residents continued to develop and harness formidable electoral and political power in Baltimore, that power became diluted at the state level. Black Baltimoreans had a much better chance of swaying the mayoralty in a city in which they comprised a significant political bloc than the governorship in a state where they comprised a smaller percentage of the electorate. Vesting police control in the governor stifled Black Baltimoreans' ability to advocate for meaningful structural changes in policing.

"Policemen Were the Biggest Liars" • 169

Although Republicans supported a bill to transfer appointment powers from the governor to the mayor, Democrats were unwilling to compromise and preferred the current arrangement. In the previous half century, there had only been two Republican governors of Maryland, both ousted after one term. The current governor, Albert Ritchie, was a Democrat and would hold the office for the next fifteen years. Although Democrats certainly could not know of Ritchie's perennial electability, their control over Annapolis was proven. While they held dominion over the governorship, their control over the mayoralty was less ironclad. The current mayor of Baltimore, William F. Broening, was a Republican. As such, Democrats refused to entertain a transfer of appointment power during the 1920 session. The compromise they reached was a referendum that would allow the citizens of Baltimore to choose. And lest the citizens elected to transfer power to the mayor, the change would not take effect until 1923—after Broening's term expired.[19] The referendum appeared on the 1920 election ballot where 73,894 votes went to maintaining state control and 61,732 votes went to local control.[20] That referendum and subsequent ones failed.

After the electorate affirmed the governor's power to appoint the police commissioner, Governor Ritchie tapped General Charles D. Gaither to serve as Baltimore's first police commissioner. Gaither, nicknamed "the General," was a retired brigadier general who had served in the Maryland National Guard. Ritchie lauded Gaither's extensive military record, noting his service in the Spanish-American War, the Mexican Border War, and most recently, World War I where he served as commanding officer of the National Guard forces at Camp McClellan in Anniston, Alabama. Ritchie emphasized Gaither's military accomplishments to highlight his ability to lead a corps of men, and Gaither brought his military background to bear on his administration of the Baltimore police. This dynamic mirrored fundamental realities about policing. A paramilitary endeavor, colonial occupation strategies and military logics molded—and continue to mold—American policing.[21]

General Gaither assumed office during a period of municipal and police transformation. Two years before his appointment, the police arrested 12,929 more people than they had the year before. This spike owed largely to the recent annexation and a marked increase in traffic violations. Given these upsurges in landmass and arrests, the state legislature conceded that the city had not been provided a "sufficient number of patrolmen . . . to properly patrol this new territory." As such, they approved the appointment of one hundred additional police officers to coincide with Gaither's assumption of office.[22]

In his first annual report to Governor Ritchie, Gaither articulated his plans to hire the new patrolmen judiciously and to reorganize the enlarged force's

170 · CHAPTER 6

patrol shifts. Before Gaither's tenure, patrolmen worked in three complementary divisions with regular schedules. Gaither found the arrangement inefficient and, in one of his first major actions as police commissioner, renamed patrol units "platoons." He had each platoon work eight-hour shifts that rotated every six weeks. He ordered district captains to gradually implement the new system over the course of the year.[23] In addition to organizing the police into military battalions, Gaither, an accomplished marksman, organized a "Revolver Team" that sent the department's best marksmen to National Rifle Association competitions. Gaither hoped such internal competition would distinguish his police force and promote an appreciation for marksmanship among the increasing corps of patrolmen.[24] Between assuming office in 1920 and the end of the decade, Gaither managed to increase the size of his aspirant urban army by 534 employees.[25] His use of militarized techniques and his access to more resources spoke to the expanding power of the police state and the increasing sophistication of the police's paramilitary function in American cities. Gaither self-consciously created an occupying army. And his chief goal was the enforcement of Jim Crow, spatially and psychically.

Between 1920 and 1929, nontraffic-related arrests remained steady at approximately fifty thousand per year. Despite the continuity of arrest figures, racialized rates of arrest changed dramatically. Black men and women, though they settled in the city in larger numbers than they had in previous decades, still constituted a significant minority of the population. However, under Gaither's tenure, their representation among arrestees increased dramatically. When Gaither assumed office, Black people accounted for 27 percent of all arrests. Although still disproportionate based on population, this number was lower than the average of the previous decade. However, as Gaither's reign continued and as heavier platoons began swarming Baltimore's streets, Black men and women became just as likely to be arrested for nontraffic-related violations as white men and women. During the latter half of the decade, the arrest rate for white and Black people was approximately even. In 1927, Black men and women were even more likely to be arrested than white men and women and comprised 54 percent of all nontraffic-related arrests—an inauspicious historic feat.[26]

The police reforms and institutional reorganization that characterized Gaither's assumption of office, though promoted as steps toward a less politicized police department, in fact allowed for the opposite. While the former police board was stacked to benefit one party, there at least existed a minority opinion. With the change to one commissioner, Gaither took unilateral control over executive-level decision-making. What is more, since the referendum on local control shored up Annapolis's control over the Baltimore police, Democrats

"Policemen Were the Biggest Liars" · 171

would determine the appointment of the police commissioner far more often than they would not. Indeed, Gaither served as police commissioner for the entirety of Governor Ritchie's fifteen-year tenure in office. Gaither's enlarged police platoons ran roughshod over Black neighborhoods, leading to more arrests, by percentage, than at any time in the city's history. As such, the *Afro-American* spent the entirety of Gaither's tenure holding the police commissioner accountable and publicizing his misdeeds and those of his officers. The paper criticized him for selectively enforcing the law, for fostering a police culture that normalized the harassment, brutalization, and murder of Black people, and for emboldening white supremacists. Although their record was mixed, the *Afro-American* managed, through public pressure, to get Gaither to relent on some key issues while making little to no headway on others.

"A Seemingly Necessary Investigation": Extending Police Power

What is eminently clear when looking through the police's records during the 1920s is that Black men and women were arrested for public order charges at astronomical rates (figure 13). What is unclear and in fact masked by these data is for what. What were cops arresting Black people for? What types of disorder and disturbance constituted arrestable offenses? The editors of the *Afro-American* addressed this question by detailing the treatment and brutality that Black Baltimoreans experienced at the hands of the cops. In doing so, they looked to ensure that the newly appointed police commissioner and his roving army administered its duties in ways that upheld the letter of the law. The *Afro-American* illuminated routine beatings, shootings, and capricious arrests. Disorderly behaviors manifested in several ways, including violence, domestic disturbances, and other activities that might be seen as reasonable grounds for arrest. However, the *Afro-American* also reported on several instances in which Black residents were harassed, detained, beaten, or shot for looking suspicious, contradicting overzealous patrolmen, or for simply existing inside of their own homes. All told, the 1920s signaled a distinctively racialized enlargement of police power and the reach of the state. Police violence, brutal treatment, and lawlessness typified roving untrained platoons. In Baltimore, the police force was larger than ever before, and the Black press sought to keep them honest.

During Charles Gaither's first term as police commissioner, the *Afro-American*'s editors filled the paper's pages with stories detailing police violence and harassment against Black men and women. In one story, a man named Emanuel Williams was shot by a police officer for purportedly acting "in a suspicious manner." Even though Williams proved to be a bootlegger, the newspaper considered that revelation largely beside the point. The editors questioned "whether policemen [were] justified in shooting suspicious persons on the street who have not been caught in the act of committing a crime." Gaither backed the patrolman, who he contended was firing a warning shot. The commissioner considered the fact that the shot hit Williams an unfortunate but justifiable outcome.[27] In another story, the paper condemned a patrolman who civilians caught making improper advances toward women. He invoked his status as a police officer to intimidate and coerce them. While Gaither forced the patrolman's resignation, the fact of its interracial character likely contributed more to his decision than the patrolman's abuse of power. Gaither's stance on interraciality evolved over the course of his tenure until he supported transparently illegal arrests to punish interracial sociality.[28] Both stories demonstrated broader dynamics that the *Afro-American* portrayed as systemic abuses. The cops' itchy trigger fingers spelled peril for Black Baltimoreans, particularly if "suspicion" was the only threshold for lethal action. Moreover, racialized gendered terror typified Black women's everyday experiences with the police.

In a story involving a brutal arrest, a patrolman detained a Mrs. Rose Chandler for disturbing the peace. Her arresting officer, Alvin Burke, viciously beat her unconscious in broad daylight. While Burke defended his actions by alleging that Chandler resisted arrest, a group of witnesses refuted him and contended that she was only trying to change her dress before going to the station house because Burke had ripped it apart. Gaither defended the officer's actions by noting that Chandler had a history of defying police and had been arrested on charges of "dope addiction and peddling."[29] Black men and women remained under ever-increasing police scrutiny on public sidewalks, in places of leisure, and in their own homes. The all-white police force, in their everyday interactions with Black residents, demanded deference from the growing Black population who had laid claim to city space and who were wont to fight back. In Chandler's case, the officer's actions revealed the degree to which Black bodies remained vulnerable to the scrutiny and violence of city police—a continuation of racialized dynamics that intensified at the turn of the century.

In another arrest involving excessive force, a patrolman beat a man named Henry Simuels for failing to obey orders to the officer's satisfaction. Simuels had left his home and bumped into a friend who engaged him in conversation. When a patrolman told the two to move along, Simuels reportedly "did not move as quickly as [the patrolman] wished" and was placed under arrest. The patrolman escorted Simuels to a patrol box to call for a police wagon. According to the *Afro-American*, "When Simuels attempted to step into the patrol [wagon] . . . the officer struck him over the head with his night-stick knocking him to the

"Policemen Were the Biggest Liars" • 173

gutter. He then beat him in the face with his stick knocking out several teeth." In response to the officer's brutal actions, Simuels retained J. Steward Davis, an activist attorney who routinely petitioned Gaither on matters of police brutality, to request that Commissioner Gaither discipline the arresting officer. At the officer's hearing, the patrolman alleged that Simuels cursed at him and had attempted to choke him. Witnesses on the scene refuted the officer's claims and contended that Simuels had complied with his commands. In the end, Gaither charged the patrolman a $10 fine. The *Afro-American* editors considered the fine a weak resolution that reinforced the police's ability to brutalize Black men and women with impunity while also holding a monopoly over the truth.[30] The patrolman's slap on the wrist demonstrated how police operated with license based on the tacit and explicit support of their bosses. This dynamic made police accountability both an object of reform for Black lawyers and activists and an obstacle toward bettering police-civilian relations.

Even though the police's executive officers had the ability—and responsibility—to reprimand patrolmen for misconduct, cops were likely to elude discipline when committing heinous and potentially fatal acts of violence against Black people. In March 1921, the marshal reported that James Scott, a Black resident of the Southern District, had been "shot and seriously wounded" by a patrolman during a skirmish. The marshal sided with the officer who alleged that Scott had resisted arrest and assaulted the patrolman. The patrolman faced no discipline.[31] A few months later, the police department received a formal complaint, which an attorney filed on behalf of a white witness who saw a patrolman errantly fire at John Parker, a Black resident of the Northwestern District. Gaither elected not to discipline the patrolman and instead lectured him on "the necessity for the exercise of the greatest care at all times in the firing of revolvers."[32] Errant shots would spell catastrophe for Black Baltimoreans in the years to come, though Gaither would never back down on the importance of lethal force and marksmanship training for his police army.

Street policing and brutal arrests typified legal and extralegal assertions of police power in public. Augmenting this routine terror was the imperious disregard for Black private residences and activities. During Gaither's reign, Black men and women experienced white mob violence, illegal home entries, and the suppression of interracial conviviality. Police power was not simply confined to the regulation of public life; its tendrils slithered through keyholes, violated property rights, and punished private behaviors.

Regarding Black homes, police routinely looked the other way when residences were vandalized. They also contributed to the diminution of Black privacy by entering homes without prompting. Thomas Reddick, a Pimlico

174 · CHAPTER 6

resident, reported that white vandals routinely attacked his home and those of his neighbors. According to Reddick, the vandals hurled bricks through the front windows while no one was home. On one occasion, they broke into Reddick's cellar and stole half a ton of coal. When asked if the police were of any help to him, Reddick noted that they would not act unless he could positively identify the vandals. In other words, they would not act unless he did their job for them.[33] In another instance, the police themselves terrorized a man in his own home. Samuel Bolden, a West Baltimore resident, was aroused at 5:00 a.m. by the sound of footsteps. He woke to find two police officers flashing lights in his face. The patrolmen had evidently seen a man enter Bolden's house. When they could not find the alleged man, they left. When Bolden appealed to Gaither for an investigation, the commissioner responded, "I am sorry you feel offended at the intrusion, but I really do not seen [sic] that there is any harm to find fault with the officers for making a seemingly necessary investigation."[34] While police protected property above all, not all property was created equal. Gaither's platoons violated the sanctity of Black homes, trounced due process, and defended their actions through the impenetrable self-legitimization of police power.

William Jones, an *Afro-American* editorialist, connected the routine intrusion of police officers in Black residences to broader national agendas that aimed to regulate interracial sex in the service of maintaining segregated geographies.[35] Jones did so by critiquing the double standard present in the state's flippant dismissal of Prohibition on the grounds of personal freedom. Marylanders rejected Prohibition for its unconstitutionality but frequently ignored Black personal freedom and their Fourth Amendment protections. In his "Day by Day" column, Jones highlighted this double standard to point out the hypocrisy inherent in deploying the rhetoric of "freedom" while the police—a state agency run by a state official—systematically violated the freest space in modern America: the home.[36]

As an example, Jones recounted an incident in which patrolmen spotted an interracial couple on the street. The patrolmen witnessed a white man and a "fur-coated race girl" stop in a Black neighborhood and enter a house. Suspecting a sexual affair, the cops trailed the couple and entered the house. What they found inside was not some lewd affair but a party. The man was speaking with another man in the kitchen, while the woman had gone to the second floor of the house. Jones railed on the officers' actions and used the discourse surrounding Marylanders' attitudes toward Prohibition to emphasize the racial double standards inherent in law enforcement:

We have a hot tempered disgust for the average interracial "affair," not because it is an "affair," but because of the sneaking manner in which it is done; but we cannot but have a more distasteful disgust for the kind of policing and the law machinery which talks "free state" where prohibition is concerned, and prostitutes the sanctity of homes, trying to regulate morals by laws where the races are concerned.[37]

Jones's column detailed a common police abuse—the consistent and illegal violation of Black privacy—while connecting the practice to the self-reputed "freedom" that Baltimore and Maryland lawmakers grasped to justify their dismissal of established law. In Maryland, "freedom" was conditional and rooted in racially dissimilar standards of justice.

These contradictions typified the evolving and ever more racialized police state in Baltimore. The 1920s heralded the highest number of patrolmen, the most anti-Black rates of arrest in the city's history, and the sentiment among the Black press that police used and abused their power to explicitly curtail Black freedom and prop up Jim Crow imperatives. As wayward shots from untrained pistols punctured purportedly suspicious people and as police officials emboldened patrolmen to exert excessive and brutal force through lax discipline, Black residents witnessed the erosion of their privacy, their rights, and their freedoms. The *Afro-American*'s comprehensive and dutiful reporting captured these flagrant violations through consistent coverage. During the decade, the paper exhaustively covered two stories that, in their specificity, illuminated broader systemic dynamics. The first, the story of a suspected interracial affair, clarified how police strategically used the capacious definitions of public order to arrest Black people for eminently legal activities. The second, the tragic story of a civilian murder, demonstrated the rank-and-file patrolman's expectations of Black submission to wanton authority, as well as the police's explicit support of extralegal Jim Crow violence. Taken together, these ordeals crystallized the Black press's centrality in realizing a semblance, however small, of police accountability. We turn to both stories in turn.

"She Was Innocent": Policing Interracial Sex

The early twentieth century was marked by profoundly racialized and gendered forms of sexual regulation. During this period, the enlargement of local government, the ever-shrinking distinction between public and private spheres, the rise of a profoundly racist Progressive reform movement, and the geographic implications of local interventions into commercial vice typified life

176 · CHAPTER 6

on U.S. streets. With urbanization came vice districts that emerged in downtowns across the country. Liberal sexual customs replaced doctrinaire Victorian pearl clutching as foreign-born European immigrants, U.S.-born whites, and Black men and women engaged in commercialized leisure, interracial sex, and sex work. Dance halls, speakeasies, black and tans, brothels, saloons, and other local haunts peppered urban areas. As segregationist fervor gripped cities and Jim Crow sounded the alarm bells of miscegenation, sex work became the preeminent social evil of the early twentieth century. Progressive reformers, private detectives, vice commissions, and private citizens conducted investigations, raids, and other forms of repression to eliminate these districts. Although middle-class whites kept vice alive through "slumming," or the act of engaging in sexual tourism, the regulation of sexuality revealed police power at work. A constellation of institutional and disciplinary bodies mediated conflicting values around public and private sex and ultimately created new criminal categories and modes of regulation that expanded the legitimacy and breadth of local government.[38] As historian Anne Gray Fischer has argued, policing urban sexuality in the twentieth century formed a foundational and crucial use case for police power, which operated using logics rooted in white supremacy and discretion.[39] The story that follows represents how police seized on public order laws to regulate interracial sex.

On the evening of August 3, 1925, James A. White, a Black dentist from Harlem Park, drove a group of friends home. The thirty-two-year-old had come to Baltimore by way of North Carolina with his wife, Mary.[40] He set up a dental practice so successful that the *Afro-American* described him as "one of the most prominent and successful dentists in the city."[41]

As White cruised along Madison Avenue, Patrolman Frank Picha ordered him to stop. Picha, a beat cop in the city's embattled Northwestern District, had been honored for meritorious service the year before.[42] Despite his record of praiseworthy accomplishments among the police department's management, he had developed a reputation among Black residents for routinely unprofessional and violent conduct. Rumors circulated about his recent transfer to a different beat, and some Black residents suspected him of graft.[43]

After White complied with Picha's command to stop the vehicle, the patrolman jumped on the running board of the car and shined his flashlight into the passenger's seat. Picha wanted to know whether the passenger, Myrtle Phillips, was a white woman. She was not. James White vehemently protested Picha's actions. The patrolman called White a "smart n——r" and arrested both White and Phillips. He took them to the station house where Magistrate Frederick A. Rohleder charged White with disorderly conduct and let Phillips go. According

"Policemen Were the Biggest Liars" • 177

to Rohleder, it fell within the purview of police power for cops to investigate the racial identities of women passengers.[44] After his release, White retained the services of J. Steward Davis. The incident highlighted the draconian administration of law enforcement in the Northwestern District which had the highest concentration of Black people in the city. According to the *Afro-American*, "General opinion is that it is the worst administered district in the city."[45] Moreover, the fact that White was charged with disorderly conduct and therefore punished for riding in the same car as a white woman—a legal if abhorrent practice to white racists—spoke to the breadth of public order policing and the archival uncertainties inherent in analyzing it. Relatedly, Phillips's avoidance of a charge obscures the trauma and harassment she experienced at the hands of police. Although not charged with a crime, she was nonetheless detained, arrested, and taken to a police precinct.

Davis swiftly submitted a complaint to Gaither. In it, he noted that "there is nothing in the statutes nor decisions of Maryland that gives an officer the right to accost a citizen for no other reason than that of the officer's suspicions of his companion's race." White's counsel strategically conceded that the complaint was not a referendum on the policing of interracial friendships or romances. Since that subject would likely put the police on the defensive, the lawyers reminded the commissioner that both people involved in the controversy were Black. This strategic move echoed Davis's strategy during Henry Brown's case. For him, challenging the color line incurred the wrath and righteous indignation of fragile white racists; he preferred to advocate without destabilizing conventions of Jim Crow social life. To that end, Davis emphasized the dangerous precedent that the case could set based on the complexities of colorism, noting, "Yet the fact remains that if officers are permitted to insult every colored citizen whose femal [*sic*] companion's complexion may be fair, there are thousands of Negro gentlemen who would accompany such ladies at their peril." Additionally, White's counsel appealed to the dentist's reputation, noting that he was a "gentlemen of the finest type," who possessed respectable employment, paid taxes, had a family, and did not have a criminal history prior to the incident.[46] In doing so, Davis hoped to forestall charges of Black lawlessness or cultural predilections toward criminality that could diminish his client's case.

However, as Laura Wheatley faced backlash for her supposed "influential" position among Baltimore's citizenry, white rank-and-file patrolmen exercised aggressive treatment toward the Black middle class based on their economic position. The *Afro-American* argued that in recent years, police officers—especially those in the Northwestern District—had demonstrated increasingly violent tendencies toward Black people, regardless of economic stature. In fact, upon

178 · CHAPTER 6

discovering White's pedigree, Patrolman Picha seemed even more incensed. Picha purportedly grew furious over White's invocation of the influence he wielded as a Black professional.[47] This anger illuminated broader expectations of Black power under Jim Crow, which cultivated a racially and economically striated social environment. Black people's influence and agency attacked the very fabric of these conditions and therefore inspired the ire of white patrolmen, officials, and judges.

Davis's complaint ended with a request for a full investigation and hearing where White could offer testimony. Magistrate Rohleder, perhaps taken aback by the aggressive response to a routine stop and the defense's rebuttal to his contention that policemen could and should determine the racial identity of women passengers in cars driven by Black men, attempted to clarify his ruling. White had been charged with disorderly conduct, which the magistrate said came because of White's verbal protests against Picha and the invocation of his "influence" as a prominent member of Baltimore's Black professional class. He also conceded that there was no law prohibiting Black men and white women from riding in cars together. Indeed, if such a law existed, it would deeply impact the chauffeuring industry. Rohleder, in a demonstration of legal gymnastics, noted that the situation was so highly irregular that it caused a disturbance disruptive enough that, as a patrolman, Picha simply *had* to investigate. Rohleder conveniently omitted the fact that Picha instigated the disturbance.[48]

The *Afro-American*'s editorial board connected White's violent treatment to broader national trends in policing, particularly use of the third degree, which it had covered extensively since Henry Brown's case, and the rampant dishonesty that characterized municipal police departments. The editors suggested that if cops and detectives could not build strong cases without beating suspects into "semiconsciousness," they should find other jobs. Additionally, the editors criticized the police's habit of providing false testimony to secure convictions. They quoted a late Baltimore judge who purportedly believed that "policemen were the biggest liars appearing in his court." The judge remarked, "I would not believe a one of them if he swore on a stack of Bibles." The editors connected these routine practices to White's ordeal, noting that to defend his arrest of the dentist, Picha "lied without conscience." Given Picha's actions and reputation among Black residents of the Northwestern District, the editorial board demanded his dismissal from the force. Furthermore, if the issue was structural in nature—that is, if the police's administrative and executive management promoted Picha's behavior—then a much more thorough investigation into the department was necessary.[49] The *Afro-American* wanted accountability even though policing in the 1920s thrived on immunity. This contradiction made Gaither's response all too predictable.

Even though White's counsel and the editorial board provided compelling evidence that Picha acted excessively and brutally, Commissioner Gaither disregarded all of it. He denied White a hearing and exonerated Picha. In a letter to Davis, Gaither responded to the attorney's request for a hearing by noting that the Baltimore police were, first and foremost, committed to nondiscriminatory policing. Furthermore, in White's case, Gaither asserted that no prejudice had been exhibited. According to his officers, Picha demonstrated integrity in his position. Gaither contended that White's car had flickering lights which merited a stop. Picha's next action, forcefully ascertaining Myrtle Phillips's racial identity, was justified since the Northwestern District had "generated complaints of improper association of white women with colored men." For Gaither, these complaints warranted inquiry, no matter what the law said. Gaither further alleged that White's invocation of "influence" constituted disorderly conduct. Picha was well within his rights to arrest the dentist because of broader attitudes surrounding interracial sex and his refusal to submit to Picha's authority.[50] Gaither did not need the law or lawyers to tell him how to police.

The *Afro-American*'s editors were incensed. The editorial board decried Gaither's decision to deny a public hearing and found his justification wholly inadequate. Gaither failed to address why Phillips had been arrested and taken to the station house with White in the first place. She, by all accounts, did nothing wrong.[51] William Jones devoted most of his "Day by Day" column to discussing Phillips's innocence and vicious treatment. He criticized the department's unwillingness to at least take accountability for the patrolman's transparently illegal actions. He attributed the silence around Phillips's arrest to the systemic culture of blind support that ran through the police department, noting,

> There seems always a tendency on the part of the police department to shut its eyes to facts and condone the acts of officers, but in this case, there is added the wanton disregard of the sanctity due the most humble woman in this city whatever the offense of her companion. SHE WAS INNOCENT.[52]

In detaining, brutalizing, and providing no respite for Phillips, the police reinforced their imperious and unjust treatment of Black people. In the Northwestern District, the cops' refusal to prioritize justice over the force's esprit de corps created a culture wherein police could and did cover for one another even in cases where they acted with dishonesty and violence. Magistrates validated this behavior by providing legal justification in the slippery and flexible interpretations of disorderly conduct and public disturbance.

News of the petition's failure shocked James White, particularly considering that Gaither made the decision based solely on police officials' words. He

180 · CHAPTER 6

stressed that beyond the arrest, he and Phillips had suffered humiliation at the station house and that there was much more to the case than what Picha and the station house staff had provided. Given Commissioner Gaither's diminution of White's integrity by characterizing him as disorderly and insubordinate, White offered to submit to a lie detector test. He also suggested that perhaps lie detectors, created a few years before this incident, should be used more often.[53] Indeed, at the root of this incident lay an intractable and deep-seated contestation over truth to which the police laid authoritative claim despite countless instances of malfeasance, corruption, and provable lies that emerged from their ranks. Ultimately, Picha's exoneration stood, and the patrolman did not face disciplinary action.

James White's and Myrtle Phillips's ordeal provided insight into key facets that shaped the relationship between the Baltimore police and Black city residents during the 1920s. Although the police claimed that they had legally stopped White for flickering headlights, the magistrate confirmed that the "disorder" stemmed from Myrtle Phillips's white-passing appearance. Municipal police cracked down on interracial leisure, commingling, and sex. During the 1920s, the police's word carried more currency than that of the people they patrolled—a dynamic that persists in the present. The Black press, organizers, lawyers, and other Black residents contended daily with a law enforcement apparatus that harassed and brutalized them while claiming ownership to the truth and exercising the ability to deny due process through systems of self-regulation. Because the police department largely relied on vague public order statutes to defend arbitrary arrests, appealing to the law proved futile. As Gaither noted, the Northwestern District police had received complaints about interracial companionship and were investigating instances thereof regardless of what the law allowed or prohibited.

This latter admission spoke to the culture of discretionary patrolling that continued to characterize street policing in the 1920s. Police routinely regarded Black people with suspicion. They disproportionately arrested Black men and women on public order charges. The year Picha accosted White and Phillips, police arrested 8,334 Black people for disorderly conduct—a figure that accounted for half of all such arrests.[54] Perceived slights to police authority became grounds for "disorder" as cops came to expect, demand, and forcefully extract deference from civilians. This expectation came largely from a site of insecurity as cops self-consciously sought to firm up the color line and check the overreaching "influence" of Black professionals like James White. According to historian David Taft Terry, "Police brutality came to function as a control—as an expression of the outsized power racism afforded the white community and

"Policemen Were the Biggest Liars" • 181

that community's desire to see its vision of the racial norm maintained."[55] That desire ran so deep that sometimes Black people lost their lives at the hands of police. Shoring up the color line, expectations of servitude, and institutional reassurances that superiors would defend even the most heinous actions coalesced in the tragic case of Charles Williams.

"God Man, Help Me, I'm Dying": Policing the Color Line

Charles Edward Williams was born on May 30, 1876, to George, a sailor, and Mary, a laundress (figure 14). When Charles was three, his family lived at 34 Little McElderry Street next to Belair Market. Whereas the Williams family traced its roots to Maryland, many of their fellow Black neighbors had come to Baltimore by way of the deeper South, and many of their white neighbors had immigrated to the country from Russia and Bohemia. Census documents typically identified Charles and his parents as "Mulatto."[56] Charles began work at a young age and spent his life employed in various trades, including day labor, packing, and clerking. At age twenty-one, Charles married Bessie, and the couple lived with his widowed mother on 502 North Eden Street, a few blocks away from his childhood home. By 1910, Mary's second husband had passed, leaving her a widow again. What is more, of her eight children, only one—Charles—remained alive and helped her make ends meet by working as a grocery wagon driver.[57]

In the 1920s, given zoning regulations and the creation of planned white suburbs on the city's periphery, Black housing near downtown became denser as Black population growth outpaced white population growth in the central city.[58] The decade saw glimpses of white flight as population decompression occurred in seventeen of the city's twenty-eight wards, all of them downtown.[59] The decade also saw the consolidation of Jim Crow neighborhoods as overwhelmingly Black wards, especially wards 14 and 17, solidified and drew the color line in bright red ink on Baltimore's residential landscape.[60] Targeted police enforcement, particularly in the Central and Northwestern Districts wherein the majority of Black Baltimoreans lived, made each day an unsure one. Would a confrontation escalate after a patrolman demanded that people move along? Would worries of an interracial tryst end in handcuffs? Would police assess someone suspicious enough to open fire?

Within this context, Charles and Bessie sought more than they had come to know in the city's downtown neighborhoods. The Williams house stood two blocks west of the Pot, a sobriquet given to an acutely visible vice district which was infamously plastered about the city's white newspapers for its purported exemplification of Black dysfunction. Their life there coincided with increased police oversight of saloons, sex work, recreational drug and alcohol use, and other indulgences that characterized downtown life. In 1914, after spending decades living in an area overrun with slaughterhouses, coal yards, stables, police, and other loud and odorous land uses, Charles and Bessie moved to 929 North Chapel Street.[61] Although still an alley house,[62] the home was located in a primarily residential neighborhood that stood a stone's throw away from the growing Johns Hopkins Hospital.[63] The area spared them many of the irritations of downtown life, and although not as racially homogenous as West Baltimore, the demography contained an eclectic mix of residents. Located in the seventh ward, the neighborhood was mostly native white, though foreign-born immigrants and Black residents comprised a substantial portion of the population.

Figure 14. Charles Williams, then living at 929 North Chapel Street, was murdered by Patrolman Charles Urban. Source: "Extra!!!! Police Kill Two in Their Own Homes," *Baltimore Afro-American*, October 28, 1921. Courtesy of the AFRO-American Newspapers Archives.

"Policemen Were the Biggest Liars" • 183

Even so, the couple's 1914 settlement in a mostly white neighborhood coincided with rampant segregationist fervor both locally and nationally. In 1910, Baltimore's city council inauspiciously revolutionized Jim Crow by passing the country's first residential segregation ordinance. Even though unenforceable because of a combination of Black legal activism, political incompetence, and their patent unconstitutionality, the series of racial zoning measures aimed to prohibit Black settlement on white blocks and vice versa.[64] Faced early with the question of constitutionality, the measures' champions sought legal cover in the precedent-setting *Rossberg v. State of Maryland*, a court of appeals decision that upheld the enforceability of Swann's Cocaine Ordinance—an ordinance that was developed based on drug and policing activities in Charles and Bessie's old neighborhood. The case ruled that the city had the obligation to employ police power to protect the public good. Milton Dashiell, one of racial zoning's chief architects, reasoned that as *Rossberg* had allowed the city government to police its environs against the evils of cocaine through the criminalization of drug possession, so too could it empower that same government to protect its white residents against the evils of integration.[65]

Although somewhat persuasive from a legal standpoint, the drafters failed to make the ordinances airtight, leading some to be tossed for technical deficiencies and another to be invalidated by Maryland's high court. Despite these setbacks, the city council remained devoted to enacting a racial zoning ordinance that would pass muster with the courts. However, the movement was dealt a deathblow when, in 1917, the Supreme Court officially deemed racial zoning ordinances unconstitutional. Despite their short lifespan and relative inutility, Baltimore's racial zoning measures captured the spirit of segregationist fervor that animated the city's white citizenry. Undeterred, white people employed quasi-legal racial covenants, collusive grassroots efforts in the form of protective societies, and violence to move the cause of residential segregation forward.[66]

In the fall of 1913, as the ordinances shuffled between the city council and the courts, a series of violent confrontations erupted in West Baltimore's beleaguered Harlem Park. Roving white gangs tossed stones, pebbles, and marbles at homes that had been recently purchased by Black families. The next morning, police dispersed a gathering of twenty-five Black men and women after an unidentified gunman fired four shots at random. Later that day, a group of young Black men stoned a white home. Police quarantined the block to prevent further escalations of violence.[67] The quarantine, however, did not stop tensions from flaring in other parts of town. The *Sun* reported a series of scattered attacks that white vigilantes staged to throw the cops off their trails. The paper reported, "The whites feel that if they can but scatter their fire and draw out the line of police defense, they will make the system of fighting the negroes more effective."

184 · CHAPTER 6

All told, seven people—two white and five Black—were charged in connection to the hostilities in Harlem Park.[68] It is within this context that Charles and Bessie Williams settled into their new home on the predominately white block of 900 North Chapel Street. It is also within this context that tragedy struck the couple—at the hands of another Charles.

Charles Urban became a cop in 1917 (figure 15). Although born in Baltimore, he grew up in an immigrant household. His father, Anton, and his mother, Sophia, were Bohemian immigrants who came to the United States in 1882 and 1870, respectively. Anton worked as a tailor to provide for his eight children and maintain their home on 126 North Castle Street, an alley house that abutted a grammar school in a Bohemian-dominated part of East Baltimore.[69] In 1888, Anton and Sophia purchased the house from the latter's parents for $800.[70] As a teenager, Charles took up barbering to help around the house.[71] At age twenty, he married Mary Marsalek, a Bohemian immigrant who came to the United States in 1906 and became a naturalized citizen in 1913. The couple moved to an alley house on 914 North Port Street, the same year Charles and Bessie Williams moved to their alley house on North Chapel Street.[72] Their homes were separated by a few easily walkable blocks, and Charles Urban frequently made the trip to Charles and Bessie's block because his brother-in-law Joseph Marsalek lived across the street from the Black couple.[73] Although the visits began while he was a barber, in 1917, Urban became a police officer. From then on, every time he visited his brother-in-law, there existed the possibility that he came armed with his police-issued .32 caliber revolver. This possibility proved true on October 23, 1921.

By all accounts, Charles Williams valued thrift. He had made his way through life by working hard at every turn despite persistent anti-Black sentiment. Unsurprisingly, he applied this mindset to homeownership and made noticeable improvements to his house. According to the *Afro-American*, these improvements made the Williams abode a source of envy on the block. Across the way, Joseph Marsalek, perhaps jealous, complained to his brother-in-law Urban about the Williams family. He evidently "could not rest" because of their loud gramophone and habit of hosting parties. Marsalek also baselessly suspected the family of bootlegging whisky.[74] Although Urban and the police force did not address this preexisting animosity, the Black press made a point to emphasize what it learned from residents on the block regarding the neighborhood's dynamics. All told, on October 23, 1921, Charles Urban approached the Williams home animated by the knowledge of fervent citywide campaigns to exclude Black people from purchasing homes in white neighborhoods and alarmist narratives of "Negro invasion." He was also privy and party to a petty yet salient interpersonal conflict between

"Policemen Were the Biggest Liars" • 185

Central District Patrolman Who Shot And Killed Negro

CHARLES F. URBAN

Figure 15. Charles Urban was convicted for the unprovoked murder of Charles Williams. Source: "Central District Patrolman Who Shot and Killed Negro," *Baltimore Evening Sun*, October 25, 1921.

Williams and his brother-in-law Joseph. Finally, he carried the imperious expectation that Black men and women capitulate to the orders of police officers, even when they were off duty and even when they had no legal leg to stand on.[75]

Dressed in civilian clothing and armed with his police-issued revolver, Urban crossed the street and knocked on Charles Williams's door. The details surrounding this decision are murky at best and more likely the fabrications of a racist cop. In fact, Urban's inability to maintain a clear story made it difficult for the police department to defend the patrolman despite their every intention to do so. Initially, Urban alleged that he had been investigating Williams

186 · CHAPTER 6

on suspicions of bootlegging. This story was altogether unconvincing and easily disprovable upon searching the premises, so Urban switched his story and instead purported that he approached the Williams home after hearing cries of "Murder!"[76]

Hearing the knock, Williams opened the door. Based on eyewitness testimony from neighbors, the two exchanged words briefly before Williams closed the door in Urban's face. Urban then pulled out his revolver, blew a hole through the door, entered the premises, and shot Williams several times. This series of events characterized Urban's actions as what they most likely were—an aggressive response to a Black man who, well within his rights, refused to capitulate to a neighbor's harassment and retreated into his homestead. However, Urban spun the story to make it appear as though he acted in self-defense. According to the patrolman, "When the negro opened the door I displayed my badge and demanded to know the cause of the cries. The negro muttered something and kicked me in the abdomen. I saw him put his hand to his hip pocket, and as he did I fired several shots." This construction of events, while illustrative of expectations of deference, gestured toward Urban's manipulations. Urban indicated that Williams made a motion to perhaps reach for a gun. After police from the Northeastern District station house came to investigate the scene, they found no gun. Based on the bootlegging allegations, the police also searched the home for smoke whisky and found none.[77]

When all was said and done, Urban shot an unarmed Black man who had done nothing except exist inside of his house—the only place on earth where Charles Williams should have been able to reasonably expect a modicum of safety.

After suffering three bullet wounds, Williams, clinging to life, labored across the street to Joseph Marsalek's home and implored his neighbor, "God man, help me, I'm dying." Urban followed Williams and callously dragged him back across the street.[78] Williams died in the hospital later that day. He was survived by his wife, Bessie, and his mother, Mary. With Charles's death, Mary lost her final living child. As for Bessie, the widow realized the couple's dream of homeownership a year after Charles's death. In July 1922, she finished paying the mortgage on 929 North Chapel Street. Perhaps unable to bear living in the house in which her husband was murdered, Bessie sold it a few months later and moved out of the neighborhood.[79] Additionally, with the help of famed lawyer W. Ashbie Hawkins, Bessie filed a civil suit against Urban and Marsalek for $25,000.[80]

As for Urban, the press reported exhaustively on the patrolman's subsequent treatment and trial. After futilely surveying the Williams home for proof of bootlegging or weapons, Northeastern District police officers detained Urban

"Policemen Were the Biggest Liars" · 187

and brought him before Magistrate Frederick A. Rohleder, an infamously pro-cop judge.[81] Rohleder dismissed the charges and let Patrolman Urban go. He returned to active duty pending the results of an ongoing inquest spearheaded by Coroner J. Knox Insley who proved far less permissive. A few days after Rohleder freed Urban, Insley convened a jury of twelve to adjudge the matter. Over two hundred people attended the inquest.[82] Following a ten to two verdict against Urban, the city jail's warden detained and imprisoned the murderous cop. Urban's parents, Anton and Sophia, along with his mother-in-law, Justina, posted his $2,500 bail on October 28, 1921. After his release, Urban appealed to Police Commissioner Gaither for the police department's support by alleging that he acted in self-defense. Predictably, Gaither did not fire the patrolman. He defended his decision by expressing a desire to await the results of Urban's indictment. That news came a few weeks later when Charles Urban was indicted for the murder of Charles Williams. Despite the indictment, Commissioner Gaither did not fire Urban; rather, Gaither assigned Urban to desk duty and paid his full salary pending the results of the trial.[83]

Urban's trial began November 1922—a year after Charles Williams was murdered in cold blood.[84] Like Urban's sentencing, the press devoted ample resources to cover the trial. This publicity owed largely to widespread percep-tions of the police department's dysfunction. Amid the drama, the *Sun* ran a damning story that detailed how, in the seven months between September 1921 and March 1922, the police murdered six people, including Charles Williams. The *Afro-American* consistently criticized Police Commissioner Gaither and the police for failing to fulfill their obligation to protect Baltimore's citizenry. The paper took issue with the lack of accountability baked into the police de-partment's bureaucratic organization and the routine acts of harassment Black Baltimoreans faced at the hands of the all-white force.[85]

Gaither had long known that his police department was disordered and care-less. In a 1921 communication sent to his district captains, Gaither reprimanded them for allowing patrolmen to engage in "idle conversation," frequent recre-ational establishments during work hours, and for allowing them to "[perform] their duty in a very slovenly and slip-shod manner."[86] As this chaos became a matter of public record, Gaither responded to the cacophony of critiques in the press with a strongly worded yet seemingly empty gesture. Gaither threw the deputy marshal, George M. Henry, under the proverbial bus. He announced that Henry would be relieved of all office duties and assigned to street duty where he would closely monitor the actions of beat cops. The announcement came on the heels of the police murder of a saloonkeeper, the fatal bludgeoning of another man, a police joy ride that led to an accident, and complaints about the rampant intoxication that characterized the force's patrolmen who, in theory, should have been enforcing Prohibition. Considering these incidents, Gaither acknowledged, "The fact has been evident to me for some time that loose policing, instead of being the exception, was becoming the rule." Gaither stressed the need for superior officers to hold subordinates accountable—a value he publicly espoused and actively defied during Urban's trial.[87]

The court arraigned Charles Urban on November 27, 1922. He faced first- and second-degree murder charges. To ensure a fair trial, the court moved the case out of the city. Judge Frank Duncan of Baltimore County presided over the case which took place before an all-white jury.[88] The state prosecutors brought in several witnesses, including multiple police officers and many of Williams's neighbors. The defense brought in a similar assortment of witnesses, most central among them was Gaither.[89]

The trial lasted just two days. The defense's witnesses provided conflicting testimony that made for an extremely weak case. One witness, when confronted by the state's attorney regarding discrepancies in her testimony, alleged that she had been too afraid to tell the truth. According to the witness, "Negro residents of the neighborhood had threatened [my] life."[90] The *Afro-American's* coverage slammed this and similar testimony for cravenly relying on the "race question" to diminish Williams on moral grounds and stoke racist panic. The paper condemned one witness who brazenly commented, "Convict this white man for killing a drunken n——r. . . . You can't do it. Why if this shameful thing happens, n——s all over this section will rise up and defy white men."[91] Compounding this witnesses' transparent racism was the common paranoia—held by police and city leaders—that Black political and civic power menaced the city and state's racial hierarchy. It also brazenly echoed white expectations of Baltimore's Black citizenry during Jim Crow. Expectations of docility, submission, and subordination to white men typified social life and the criminal legal system. In contrast, Williams's insistence on the quiet enjoyment and use of his property was an expression of equality that flouted these expectations and undermined the authority of white men.[92]

By far the most damning testimony came from Commissioner Gaither. After admitting to the press that his police force was woefully deficient, particularly in maintaining order along the chain of command, Gaither took the stand and threw his full support behind Urban. Gaither testified that Urban was a good police officer and that the case should have never been tried.[93] His testimony met with criticism from diverse sectors. The *Afro-American*, which grew more critical of Gaither every day, reproached the commissioner for supporting a murderer (figure 16). The state's attorney reportedly agreed with this assessment, noting

"Policemen Were the Biggest Liars" • 189

White Wash Won't Cover It

Figure 16. After Patrolman Frank Picha was exonerated, the *Afro-American* satirized Charles Gaither and Charles Lastner, the Northwestern District captain, for their roles in providing cover to Picha, Urban, and other riotous patrolmen. Source: Fred B. Watson, "White Wash Won't Cover It," *Baltimore Afro-American*, August 29, 1925. Courtesy of the AFRO-American Newspapers Archives.

that Gaither's support for Urban lent credence to the idea that the police contributed to the lawlessness in the city just as much as the people they arrested, if not more.[94] An editorial in the *Sun* noted that Gaither's permissiveness in Urban's trial might embolden "other members of the Police Department to shoot other innocent citizens down in cold blood at the least provocation that might be given an officer by a citizen."[95] Gaither defended his actions by noting that juries inherently trusted police testimony more than civilian testimony. As such, he believed that testifying to Urban's character would not prejudice them either way.[96] This doublespeak belied the fact that if it were true that police testimony

190 · CHAPTER 6

was taken more seriously, by defending Urban, he prejudged the jury to support the murderous patrolman. However, given the disastrous defense and Urban's inconsistent story, the jury arrived at its decision relatively quickly.

On November 29, 1922, Charles Urban was found not guilty of murder in the first degree and guilty of murder in the second degree for killing Charles Williams. Judge Duncan denied Urban's motion for a new trial. Before levying his sentence, the judge asked Urban if he had any final words. Urban replied simply, "No sir."[97]

The court sentenced Urban to five years in the penitentiary. He served two years before receiving parole.[98] Gaither held firm behind Urban until the bitter end and only dismissed the officer after the court levied its sentence.[99] The trial and Gaither's actions emphasized beyond a doubt the insularity and imperiousness of the police department. Gaither valued the esprit de corps of his police platoons and sided with patrolmen whose heinous activities created noticeable disorder on the streets and in people's homes. While the legal system punished Urban for his actions, the punishment did not seem to fit the crime. In his "Day by Day" column, William Jones poignantly reflected on Urban's release and the disproportionate punishments levied against Black men and women. He wrote,

> Urban will have served but two years of his sentence. Over in a cell in the same prison where Urban has been there is a young colored criminal serving a sentence of 20 years for housebreaking. He stole a pair of pants and a few trinkets in an early morning burglary. There will be no pardon for him.[100]

Conclusion

Charles Williams's tragic murder encapsulated several key developments that typified—and continue to typify—racialized policing in Baltimore. First, Patrolman Urban's flagrant violation of Williams's privacy while off duty did not represent the unique actions of a rogue cop; rather, police during this decade grew increasingly emboldened to violate Black privacy, particularly when suspicious of signally legal behaviors. This dynamic materialized in systematized public order policing which cops exploited to arrest and discipline Baltimore's Black citizenry for activities that, while legal, presented a defiance of racial hierarchy and Jim Crow expectations. Police defended arrests targeted at discouraging consensual interracial sex by claiming that these acts "disgusted" or otherwise "disturbed" the white public. While Black lawyers challenged cops' legal ability to punish such behaviors, police power dictated that cops and city agencies uphold the public good. Armed with the vagaries of public order and a mandate to maintain the general welfare of the city, police suppression of potential miscegenation and their protection of the color line made their everyday acts of brutality and harassment relatively unassailable. Compounding that reality was the police commissioner's full-throated support of his police force, even in Charles Urban's blatant murder of a Black civilian in his own home. Gaither's support of Urban bolstered his reputation for routinely dismissing complaints regarding the police's consistent violations of Black privacy. These were not aberrant behaviors; they were structured expressions of police occupation in solidifying Black neighborhoods. Williams's murder provided an atrocious warning to Black Baltimoreans that they were not welcome in white neighborhoods, no matter how many racial zoning ordinances were deemed unenforceable.

Second, Williams's case demonstrated the centrality of the Black press both during the period and as an archival source. In the 1920s, the Black press used its platform to exhort police to do their jobs fairly. The police's records show that anti-Black policing became custom during the decade as they arrested Black people at historically unseen rates. However, as police hid the heinous infractions of their personnel behind nebulous disciplinary charges like "unofficerlike conduct," they also masked their racialized enforcement of Jim Crow behind public order charges like "disorderly conduct" and "disturbing the peace." The *Afro-American*, in its crusade to hold the police accountable, collected and published stories from victims of police brutality, sat in courtrooms and hearings, convened with lawyers, and publicized private communications from police officials to illuminate the true nature of policing. In doing so, the paper contextualized and clarified the range of deeds that constituted public disorder. From a woman demanding that an officer who profaned her be held to account, to a dentist driving his car home at night with a white-passing woman in the passenger seat, to men standing on sidewalks, to people seeming "suspicious," cops encountered and instigated this public disorder and responded with cuffs, clubs, and bullets.

Finally, Charles Williams's heartrending murder, as well as Urban's slap on the wrist, reaches from the past into the present to provide a sobering affirmation regarding the persistence of the police state. Williams's tragic fate conjures eerie associations to contemporary instances of police violence. Its grim familiarity shows that policing, while more sophisticated, has maintained a systematized and altogether routine reliance on lethality that cannot be explained away as the work of a few bad apples.

Conclusion

On March 20, 1909, the *Afro-American* published an editorial titled, "If We Are Children, We Ought to Be Treated like Children." The op-ed took aim at a popular political refrain that infantilized Black people and coded them as dependent, incapable, and impulsive.[1] Specifically, the editors took offense to high-ranking political and religious figures who had recently fed into this characterization. President William Taft remarked that Black Americans were "merely political children not having the mental stature of manhood."[2] A popular clergyman asserted that "the Negro is a child" to defend his broader position that racial equality was impossible.[3] Locally, disenfranchisement crusades hinged on the idea that Black men and women had not matured enough to exercise something as precious as the vote.[4] At the same time, white dailies routinely condemned Black men and women. The *Sun* once characterized them as "a bunch of overgrown children."[5]

While the *Afro-American* certainly rejected this infantilization, they questioned why, if whites believed Black people *were* children, they supported such horrendous treatment. For the editors, children should be set up for success. They should have access to a good education, secure housing, and quality medical treatment. They should not "receive the raw side of every side of every deal." Instead, they should be placed in safe environments, allowed equal opportunities, and furnished with the necessities of life. The editorial ended with a simple request:

194 · *Conclusion*

> Whether we are children or whether we are men, there is only one thing we ask, either treat us as children ought to be treated, or *let us alone* without placing any hinderances in our pathway and let us take our chances among the people of the communities in which we live.[6]

The editors wanted a fair shake—nothing more, nothing less. To be "let alone" meant to have the opportunity to build Baltimore's Black communities without an omnipresent and obstructive white political and legal establishment suppressing them at every turn. The editors echoed currents of Black political thought that animated movements to create Black-led institutions in American cities. Jeffrey O. G. Ogbar has dubbed this postbellum collective political orientation "Afro-self-determinism."[7]

In advocating for such determinism, Black Baltimore butted against a municipal apparatus that had congealed over more than half a century of struggle with the explicit intention to intervene in the lives of the city's discontents. After the Civil War, carceral facilities filled to the brim with poor men who sought desperately to be left alone. How did the liquid that coursed through their veins bear on their fellow citizens? Police, magistrates, and moral crusaders found these so-called bummers abhorrent. Their presence revolted passersby. They challenged who the streets belonged to and, in the process, expanded the police's use of public order enforcement. They packed the city jail, Bayview Asylum, and other facilities that struggled to stay afloat. At the same time, their incarceration provided opportunities for city agencies to generate revenue. Their detention lined magistrate pockets and filled station house coffers. Corruption prevailed, and while the poor suffered, the wealthy fought over who would guide processes of municipal development. The city jail revealed the degree to which Baltimore's elementary police state relied on retribution to reproduce its own conditions of existence by securing revenue from punishment and orienting incarceration around the production of economic subjects.

The late nineteenth century heralded the ascendance of a "silk stocking aristocracy" that, as a collective of powerful private citizens, reframed the nature of municipal governance and assumed the burden of reforming policing.[8] Led by the likes of Charles J. Bonaparte, Roger Cull, and John Rose, these reformers adopted police strategies to expose, dismantle, and reconstitute failing institutions. They watched the watchers during elections; they used avenues of civic participation to petition municipal bodies. When police proved obtrusive, they hired private detectives and commanded their agents to collect dirt to sling at the cops in the press. And while reformers established a firm foothold in city affairs, they fomented the condemnation of Black life. Machine politicians and

Conclusion • 195

loyalists contended that in reforming systems rooted in the delimitation of Black freedom, moral crusaders endorsed a fabricated wave of Black crime. Surely in attacking the police—the protectors of the color line—these reformers implicitly supported the threat of Black dysfunction that the cops kept in line. While Democrats benefited electorally from this moral panic in years to come, reformers were there to stay. Their advocacy expanded the powers of the police state in the reformation of city agencies and their insistence that policing extend to moral enforcement.

But they did not just appeal to city authorities to do their jobs. In some cases, reformers did their jobs for them. The charities movement constituted one spoke of the reform wheel of the late nineteenth century. They paid their own bills and operated with an autonomy that proved to be one of their greatest strengths. Charity groups pressured police to discontinue the age-old practice of providing asylum in station houses, particularly during the cold months. Instead, homeless Baltimoreans sought shelter in privately run facilities that forced them to work as a precondition of their lodging. At the behest of charity officers, patrolmen combed the city for habitual beggars and peddlers. These people, who made a modest living selling small wares, proved too annoying for genteel tastes. And while appeals to police constituted a significant facet of their advocacy, charity agents also desired to exercise police power themselves. Their greatest early success on this front was the establishment of an attendance officer program that deputized civilians to investigate, detain, and discipline truant children. Between 1904 and 1908, attendance officers brought 142 students before the juvenile court.[9] By 1913, these numbers ballooned to unanticipated heights. During that school year, attendance officers brought 266 cases before police magistrates, 85 cases before the juvenile court, and even brought a child before the criminal court.[10] Civilians entered the ranks of the police while city agencies, like the school board, became increasingly organized around punishment.

What is more, the reformers of the late nineteenth century either already were or eventually became cops. Joseph Packard, a Reform League leader, assumed the presidency of the school board in 1899 and oversaw the implementation of the school attendance officer program. The convention of white women spearheading the regulation of juvenile delinquency officially expanded to the police force when, in 1912, the state legislature empowered the police board to appoint five patrolwomen who would "look out for the physical and moral welfare of young folks." The city's first policewoman, Mary S. Harvey, participated in the Federated Charities for eleven years before accepting the appointment, while other appointees were similarly plucked from the charities movement.[11] John C. Rose went from secretary of Baltimore's Society for the Suppression of Vice

196 · *Conclusion*

to being a U.S. circuit judge. He would preside over Henry Brown's case and order the young man's execution. Finally, Charles Bonaparte went from being a civil service reformer and local leader to serving as the U.S. attorney general who organized the Bureau of Investigation (later the FBI). These and several other reformers, in their civic capacities and their careers, embodied the spirit of police power. They did not simply disappear after the political inflection points of the late nineteenth century; they graduated to bigger and more consequential offices where they maintained their moral investments in regulating what they considered troublesome population groups.

The twentieth century brought about a marked shift in the exercise of police power that built on these foundational precedents in incarceration, civic participation, and civilian policing. While the nineteenth century saw various public and private groups jockey for how to organize and use institutional resources, the twentieth century saw a turn toward more explicitly racialized policing. This is not to say that policing had not been racialized before. Indeed, after the Civil War, Black Baltimoreans accounted for a disproportionate number of public order arrests and jail commitments.[12] However, the twentieth century saw the ascendance of policing agendas rooted in explicit discourses of Black dysfunction. In 1901, the Democratic police board hosted public meetings to discuss and condemn the so-called "Negro rowdyism" that had gripped the city.[13] Such discourses materialized in targeted enforcement that resulted in monumental rates of Black confinement. The same year the police board condemned Negro rowdyism, Black men and women accounted for 56 percent of all city jail commitments despite comprising only 15 percent of the city's population.[14]

Subsequent street policing agendas took aim at regulating, suppressing, and eliminating such rowdyism. The early twentieth century introduced or saw an intensification of urban behaviors that the moral movements of the previous century compelled cops to eliminate. Drug use was chief among these behaviors. As cocaine popped up in cities around the country, legislators and police labored to regulate the novel drug. Sensationalized news coverage linked drug use to Negro rowdyism. Specifically, news stories fed into prevailing censures of Black womanhood. Coverage painted Black women as distinctly unable to control their supposed inherent impulses to use and abuse drugs which amplified their presumed erratic tendencies. Such moral panic opened the window for the police to draft and pass a local ordinance that criminalized the possession of narcotics. This ordinance provided both more discretion to surveil and detain Black people as well as a legal ruling that empowered the city to pass ordinances that were uniquely suited to address urban problems. The courts justified their rulings by appealing to police power provisions granted to the city in its 1898 home rule charter.[15] Baltimore's cocaine crusade trafficked in images of Negro rowdyism while helping the city free itself from state control. As such, police power was not just an assertion of police control by rank-and-file patrolmen or unseemly district captains. Policing, buttressed by legal doctrines that empowered local government, evolved the discretion, latitude, and affordances of the state and the municipal corporation.

By the 1920s, the Baltimore police, which continually gained more autonomy through appeals to the state legislature and courts, demonstrated unseen levels of corruption. Subsequent investigations would uncover this lawlessness, but in the meantime, Black men and women had to fend for themselves. The case of Henry Alfred Brown crystallized law enforcement's disregard for Black life, freedom, and political power. In 1921, naval officers and Baltimore police officers beat Henry Brown into confessing to a crime he did not commit. This practice, called the "third degree," broadly demonstrated how police could bend due process and how courts rewarded these constitutional violations by allowing compelled testimony to serve as admissible evidence. Brown's confession functioned as the only evidence connecting him to the murder of a Naval Academy nurse. A quick trial before an all-white jury condemned him to death. Activated by yet another instance of gross injustice, Black people banded together to exonerate Brown. They collected new evidence, petitioned the attorney general and the president, publicized their crusade, and made significant headway by securing multiple stays of execution. However, as Black people undermined the white legal establishment's ability to arrest, detain, and kill with impunity, a white public accustomed to swift and discriminatory justice pushed back. Brown's ultimate execution was a statement. Black people should know their place within the broader racial status quo. Guilty or not, Brown had to hang.

This attitude animated policing during the 1920s. What became clear during this decade was that police were not bound to the letter of the law. They could—and did—arrest anyone for anything. Under Baltimore's first police commissioner, Charles Gaither, Black Baltimoreans were arrested at historic rates. In 1929, Black people accounted for 46 percent of all arrests for disorderly conduct and 64 percent of arrests for disturbing the peace.[16] While these public order laws veiled the nature of police stops and arrests, the *Afro-American* revealed the actual character of police corruption in numerous instances where the charges disguised police harassment and brutality. Cops arrested men and women engaged in interracial sociality and charged them with these flexible misdemeanor offenses. On top of this intentional enforcement of the color line,

198 • Conclusion

police ransacked Black homes and brutalized Black people. The *Afro-American*, along with religious organizations and legal professionals, agitated for police accountability and publicized what was really going on.

In all, police power in post–Civil War Baltimore was incredibly adaptive. As the city grew, its obligations, duties, and powers did, too. If police power seems vague and capacious, it is. How do bummers, beggars, truant children, drug dealers, torture victims, and interracial lovers fit into the broader history of municipal development? At every turn, as these groups cropped up to challenge civic aspirations, new criminal statutes, buildings, government bodies, and policing orthodoxies emerged to regulate, detain, and neutralize them. Taken together, these strategies formed the seeds of Baltimore's police state which developed in distinct but complementary sites, including jails, meeting halls, schools, street corners, courts, and homes. And while Black Baltimoreans fought back at every turn, a system that steadily oriented itself around suppressing Black freedom, controlling Black movement, and cordoning Black neighborhoods in service of segregationist imperatives proved formidable. This battle continues in the present as organizers in Baltimore, and around the world, encounter the daunting challenges of police power. Like those before them, organizers face an overwhelming web of systems positioned around arbitrary and adaptable power. Also, like those before them, their resolve is steady and their cause righteous.

Notes

Abbreviations

BA	*Baltimore American*
BAA	*Baltimore Afro-American*
BCA	Baltimore City Archives
BOV	Board of Visitors
BPCCB	Board of Police Commissioners for the City of Baltimore
BPCP	Board of Police Commissioners Proceedings
BS	*Baltimore Sun*
CJBP	Charles Joseph Bonaparte Papers
CJR	City Jail Reports
EPFL	Enoch Pratt Free Library
JLAP	Joseph L. Arnold Papers
LOC	Library of Congress
MCHC	Maryland Center for History and Culture
MSA	Maryland State Archives
NAACP	National Association for the Advancement of Colored People
NARA II	National Archives at College Park, Maryland
ND	no date
NT	no title
RG 16	City Council
RG 29	Department of Legislative Reference
RG 31	Department of Education

200 · *Notes to Introduction*

RG 68	Agency Reports and Publications
SCRC	Special Collections Research Center, Temple University
TOP	Trustees of the Poor
UMD	University of Maryland, College Park Libraries
WP	*Washington Post*

Introduction

1. "Say They Intend to Kill Seven Police," *Baltimore Herald*, May 22, 1902.

2. "A Negro's Threat," *Baltimore Herald*, May 22, 1902; emphasis mine.

3. "Gives Police Hard Tussle," *BS*, May 23, 1902.

4. CJR, 1901, RG 29, Box 39, 23, BCA; *State of Maryland vs. Joseph Johnson*, Baltimore City Criminal Court Dockets, 122, MSA. See figure 2 for racialized incarceration trends.

5. My approach to the construction of Black life draws on philosophical and historical currents in Black studies that engage race as a set of political and hierarchizing relations that are reproduced symbolically and materially through disciplinary institutions and an array of other sites of articulation, including the "afterlife" or "wake" of enslavement. The latter must be considered in reference to the continued development of modern institutional structures—including the array of institutions that constitute American cities—to account for the residual and ever-present effects of enslavement in the United States. The following list of works have guided my thinking in this regard: Hartman, *Scenes of Subjection*; Sharpe, *In the Wake*; Weheliye, *Habeas Viscus*.

6. Constitutional professor Ernst Freund produced an exhaustive treatise on police power. Released in 1904, it serves both as a reference for the legal deployment of police power and a historical artifact that captures how such deployments responded to Gilded Age urbanization and new forms of social conflict that attended that process. Freund, *Police Power*. More recent treatments of the concept have described police power as a seemingly boundless legal doctrine that vests the state practically limitless power to detain and punish with impunity and lethality. A select group of texts include Dubber, *Police Power*; Jackson, "Police Power and Disorder"; Neocleous, *Critical Theory*; Neocleous, "'Original, Absolute, Indefeasible'"; Seigel, *Violence Work*; Wagner, *Disturbing the Peace*.

7. Dubber, *Police Power*, 122.

8. Several studies have emerged recently that engage the relationship between statecraft, policing, and racial capitalism. A few include Adler, *Murder in New Orleans*; Balto, *Occupied Territory*; Bardes, *Carceral City*; Czitrom, *New York Exposed*; Felker-Kantor, *Policing Los Angeles*; Fischer, *Streets Belong to Us*; Flowe, *Uncontrollable Blackness*; Gilfoyle, *Pickpocket's Tale*; Gross, *Colored Amazons*; Guariglia, *Police and the Empire City*; Hernández, *City of Inmates*; Jett, *Race, Crime, and Policing*; Kalifa, *Vice, Crime, and Poverty*; Mitrani, *Chicago Police Department*; Oller, *Rogues' Gallery*.

Notes to Introduction · 201

9. This discussion of the "state" as self-legitimizing owes largely to the following: Althusser, *Reproduction of Capitalism*; Deleuze and Guattari, *Anti-Oedipus*; Deleuze and Guattari, *Thousand Plateaus*.

10. Rothman, *Discovery of the Asylum*, 71–72; Foucault, *Discipline and Punish*, 297.

11. Several studies were published during the 1970s and 1980s that engage the rise of modern policing after the Civil War. A few include Fogelson, *Big-City Police*; Harring, *Policing a Class Society*; Monkkonen, *Police in Urban America*; Richardson, *Urban Police*; Richardson, "Police History"; Walker, *Critical History*.

12. Curtin, *Black Prisoners*; Haley, *No Mercy Here*; LeFlouria, *Chained in Silence*; Lichtenstein, *Twice the Work of Free Labor*.

13. McDougall, *Black Baltimore*, 1.

14. Crenson, *Baltimore*; Halpin, *Brotherhood of Liberty*; Hemphill, *Bawdy City*; Schley, *Steam City*; Terry, *Struggle*. For comprehensive engagements with policing in Baltimore, see Malka, *Men of Mobtown*; Shufelt, *Uncommon Case*.

15. For more on the racial demography of American cities between 1890 and 1950, see Terry, *Struggle*, table 1.

16. BPCCB, 1927, RG 68, Box 28, 38, BCA.

17. Chicago and Saint Louis both gave Baltimore a run for its money when adjusted to population. In 1929, Black Chicagoans accounted for 25 percent of all arrests while Black Saint Louisans accounted for 35 percent of all arrests. Chicago Police Department, Annual Report, 1929, 18; Board of Police Commissioners of the City of Saint Louis, Annual Report, 1929, 45.

18. Chicago Police Department, Annual Report, 1929, 8a; Board of Police Commissioners of the City of Saint Louis, Annual Report, 1929, 11; Police Department of the City of New York, Annual Report, 1929, 39; Police Department of the City of Los Angeles, Annual Report, 1929, 10; Fogelson, *Big-City Police*, 125.

19. For a detailed history of slave patrols in the U.S. South, see Haden, *Slave Patrols*.

20. Malka, *Men of Mobtown*, 11. Jeffrey S. Adler has recently detailed how such popular justice transformed professionalized police departments in the U.S. South. Adler, *Bluecoated Terror*.

21. M'Cullough and Scott, *Maryland Code*, 246.

22. "Charged with Being a Runaway," *BS*, September 29, 1859; "A Race for Liberty," *BS*, June 4, 1859; CJR, 1859–1865, RG 29, Box 39, BCA; Hynson, *Absconders*.

23. Brugger, *Maryland*, 306; Crenson, *Baltimore*, 259–63.

24. Shufelt, *Uncommon Case*, 4, 95.

25. Myers, *Self-Reconstruction of Maryland*, 125–31.

26. Fields, *Slavery and Freedom*, 135.

27. Fuke, *Imperfect Equality*, 127–31.

28. Scholars of Baltimore have written extensively about the postbellum period to examine how Reconstruction's meek implementation at the state and city levels led to concerted efforts aimed at both re-enslavement and the entrenchment of seemingly deracialized liberal ideologies that impeded Black citizens' integration into a hostile

202 • *Notes to Introduction*

and racist economic order. Richard Paul Fuke detailed the "apprenticeship" program that sprung up in several Maryland counties after the Civil War. Relying for legal cover on antebellum conventions, white slaveowners conscripted formerly enslaved Black children to remain on their property as laborers. Constant agitation and legal challenges by parents and lawyers led to a Supreme Court ruling in which the practice was deemed a civil rights violation and eventually abolished. Katie Hemphill and David Schley note how Reconstruction in Maryland gave way to abstract liberalist renderings of individualism that led to tighter interventionist approaches to economic and social life and the sedimentation of market orthodoxies rooted in wage work. Malka situates this broader liberalizing process within a history of policing to detail how the results of a largely absent Reconstruction movement flipped the racial orientation of policing drastically following the Civil War. Fuke, *Imperfect Equality*, chap. 4; Hemphill, *Bawdy City*, 9–10; Halpin, *Brotherhood of Liberty*; Malka, *Men of Mobtown*, 245; McDougall, *Black Baltimore*, 34–38; Olson, *Baltimore*, 183; Schley, *Steam City*, 199. For national discussions of Reconstruction, see Dubois, *Black Reconstruction*; Foner, *Reconstruction*; Litwack, *Trouble in Mind*; Mitchell, *Righteous Propagation*.

29. City Council of Baltimore, Ordinance No. 4, 1857, RG 16, 7–17, BCA; Shufelt, *Uncommon Case*, 19.

30. For more on street gangs in Baltimore, particularly the Plug Uglies, see Melton, *Hanging Henry Gambrill*.

31. This process referred to the imprisonment and provision of copious amounts of liquor to itinerant men who were then shepherded around precincts to cast votes. Rumor has it that Edgar Allan Poe's death resulted from the practice. Nevermore.

32. Shufelt, *Uncommon Case*, 87.

33. Lewis, "The Baltimore Police Case," 226; Monkkonen, *Local State*, 12.

34. Malka, *Men of Mobtown*, 82; Lewis, "The Baltimore Police Case."

35. Other cities in the United States organized in this way include Carson City, Nevada and Baltimore's "sister city," Saint Louis, Missouri. For more on this arrangement, see Annetta H. Gross, *Report on City County Consolidation with Special Reference to Philadelphia, San Francisco, Baltimore, St. Louis, and Denver*, 1928, Urban Archives and Pamphlets Collection, Box 73, Folder 453–16, SCRC.

36. Baum, *Brown in Baltimore*, 20.

37. Fogelson, *Big-City Police*, 15.

38. Katz, *Shadow of the Poorhouse*, 84.

39. Jessica Pliley's excellent book on the making of the FBI only mentions Bonaparte twice to contextualize the FBI's founding since, as attorney general, Bonaparte was empowered to create an investigative force within the Department of Justice. Pliley focuses more on President Theodore Roosevelt's part in the FBI's creation, though, as chapter 2 of this book details, Roosevelt and Bonaparte's relationship stemmed all the way back to their leadership within several municipal reform leagues during the late nineteenth century. In his history of the FBI, Rhodri Jeffreys-Jones provides a more thorough biographical sketch of Bonaparte in outlining his touch-and-go Pro-

gressivism as well as his participation in civil service reform. The author falls short of connecting the investigative ethos and morals-based nature of the newly minted Bureau of Investigation to Bonaparte's long and storied career of organizing private detectives in Baltimore's local haunts to uncover and regulate urban vice. See Pliley, *Policing Sexuality*, 76, 89; Jeffreys-Jones, *FBI*, 40–41.

40. *State of Maryland vs. William Rossberg*, Baltimore City Criminal Papers, Box 123, Indictment No. 1803, MSA.

41. For background on Baltimore's specific racial zoning laws and for racial zoning's broader legacies, see Connolly, *World More Concrete*; Power, "Apartheid Baltimore Style."

42. Crooks, *Politics & Progress*, 17.

43. For more on the inimitable legacy of the *Afro-American*, see Farrar, *Baltimore Afro-American*.

44. Carby, "Policing the Black Woman's Body"; Gross, *Colored Amazons*; Haley, *No Mercy Here*; Harris, *Sex Workers*; Hicks, *Talk with You*; LeFlouria, *Chained in Silence*.

45. The following studies guided my thinking around jails: Morris and Rothman, *Oxford History of the Prison*; Norton, Pelot-Hobbs, and Schept, *Jail Is Everywhere*; Newport, *This Is My Jail*. For a more general overview of incarceration, see Davis, *Are Prisons Obsolete?*; Alexander, *New Jim Crow*; Hirsch, *Rise of the Penitentiary*; McLennan, *Crisis of Imprisonment*.

46. For literature concerning the political, economic, and social changes that attended the Gilded Age and the Progressive era, see Beckert, *Monied Metropolis*; Brands, *American Colossus*; Cohen, *Reconstruction*; De Santis, *Shaping of Modern America*; Fronc, *New York Undercover*; Liazos, *Reforming the City*; Wiebe, *Search for Order.* With the notable exception of James Crooks's fantastic book, not much has been written regarding Charles Bonaparte's role in fostering Progressivism in Baltimore. Crooks, *Politics & Progress*.

47. Several studies proved useful in contextualizing Baltimore's charities movement within national currents of poverty relief. See Boyer, *Urban Masses*; Katz, *Shadow of the Poorhouse*; Komisar, *Down and Out*; McGerr, *Fierce Discontent*; O'Connor, *Poverty Knowledge*. Foundational and contemporary studies regarding juvenile delinquency that proved particularly useful include Agyepong, *Criminalization of Black Children*; Schneider, *Web of Class*; Platt, *Child Savers*; Schlossman, *Love and the American Delinquent*; Wolcott, "'The Cop Will Get You.'"

48. For studies of Jim Crow in Baltimore, see Fuke, *Imperfect Equality*; Halpin, *Brotherhood of Liberty*; Smith, *Here Lies Jim Crow*; Terry, *Struggle.* For grounded engagements with street policing, public order, and race, see Schweik, *Ugly Laws*; Shabbazz, *Spatializing Blackness*.

49. For more on early twentieth-century crime trends and police uses of third degree, see Adler, *Bluecoated Terror*; Jett, *Race, Crime, and Policing*; Niedermeier, *Color of the Third Degree*. Regarding the socialization of law and its manifestation in courtrooms during the Progressive era, see Willrich, *City of Courts.* Regarding Black political mo-

204 • *Notes to Introduction and Chapter 1*

bilization, particularly those campaigns headed by Black women during the early twentieth century, see Brown, "Woman Consciousness"; Harris, *"Commonwealth of Virginia vs. Virginia Christian"*; Higginbotham, *Righteous Discontent.*

50. For an overview of systematized police brutality during the early twentieth century, see Adler, *Bluecoated Terror*; Johnson, *Street Justice*. For studies engaging interracial sexuality and the policing thereof, see Blair, *I've Got to Make My Livin'*; Fischer, *Streets Belong to Us*; Gilfoyle, *City of Eros*; Harris, *Sex Workers*; Heap, *Slumming*; Hicks, *Talk with You*; Mumford, *Interzones.*

Chapter 1. "This Modern Hades"

1. "Discharge by Habeas Corpus," *BS*, June 9, 1879.

2. "Proceedings of the Court," *BS*, June 9, 1879.

3. CJR, 1862, RG 29, Box 39, 266, BCA.

4. Hemphill, *Bawdy City*, 172–73.

5. Monkkonen, *Local State*, 18.

6. Gilfoyle, "'America's Greatest Criminal Barracks,'" 526.

7. Seán McConville, "Local Justice: The Jail," in Morris and Rothman, *Oxford History of the Prison*, 297–327.

8. Monkkonen, *Police in Urban America*, 87–88.

9. Kargon, "Thomas Poppleton's Map," 194.

10. While Rothman's and Foucault's analyses capture a seemingly wholesale shift from corporal punishment to incarceration, historians like Sarah Haley and Talitha LeFlouria detail how public execution and state violence accompanied and formed part of the broader nineteenth-century carceral regime, particularly in the management of Black people. See Haley, *No Mercy Here*, 27–28 and LeFlouria, "'Under the Sting of the Lash,'" 370–71.

11. Ayers, *Vengeance and Justice*, 34–35; Rothman, *Discovery of the Asylum*, 61.

12. CJR, 1830, RG 29, Box 39, 54–55, BCA.

13. CJR, 1850, RG 29, Box 39, 46–47, BCA.

14. CJR, 1854, RG 29, Box 39, 340, BCA.

15. General Assembly of Maryland, Chapter 58, Session Laws, 1831, 50–55, MSA.

16. M'Cullough and Scott, *Maryland Code*, 450; emphasis mine.

17. Adam Malka details how popular and professional policing co-constituted the emergence of liberal policing in Baltimore. Malka, *Men of Mobtown*, 11. Jeffrey S. Adler has detailed how, in the postbellum American South, the aims and exercises of popular justice remained among white citizens up through the 1920s. During the interwar years, the goals and strategies of popular justice seeped into professional policing itself. Adler, *Bluecoated Terror*, 35.

18. CJR, 1845, RG 29, Box 39, 118–19, BCA; quote on 118.

19. "Interesting Municipal Dockets," *BS*, January 22, 1846.

20. CJR, 1854, RG 29, Box 39, 336, 339, BCA.

Notes to Chapter 1 · 205

21. CJR, 1845, RG 29, Box 39, 126–27, BCA.

22. For more on the Maryland Penitentiary, see Shugg, *Monument to Good Intentions*.

23. CJR, 1845, RG 29, Box 39, 127, BCA.

24. CJR, 1846, RG 29, Box 39, 121–23, BCA; quote on 122.

25. CJR, 1847, RG 29, Box 39, 162, BCA.

26. CJR, 1850, RG 29, Box 39, 42, BCA.

27. Crenson, *Baltimore*, 287–93.

28. Hirsch, *Rise of the Penitentiary*, 65.

29. CJR, 1859, RG 29, Box 39, 113–19, BCA; CJR, 1860, RG 29, Box 39, 107–12, BCA; Freedman, *Their Sisters' Keepers*, 9; Historic American Buildings Survey, "Baltimore City Jail," LOC.

30. CJR, 1866, RG 29, Box 39, 378, BCA.

31. Like other cities around the country, Baltimore's peak 1874 admissions were in part attributable to the panic of 1873. Edward Ayers details how this spike affected both Southern and Northern penal institutions around the United States. Ayers, *Vengeance and Justice*, 167–71.

32. For a discussion of tramps and their regulation vis-à-vis the burgeoning carceral state of the nineteenth century, see Hernández, *City of Inmates*, chap. 2.

33. Monkkonen, *Police in Urban America*, 89.

34. CJR, 1873, Reports of the City Officers, 819–22, UMD.

35. Friedman, *Crime and Punishment*, 24–27.

36. CJR, 1873, Reports of the City Officers, 815, UMD.

37. "Prisoners' Aid Society and the Justices of the Peace," *BS*, January 5, 1876.

38. BPCCB, 1868–73, RG 68, Box 27, BCA.

39. "The Cost of Bummers to the City," *BS*, January 14, 1874.

40. "A Sermon on Politics," *BS*, October 11, 1875.

41. General Assembly of Maryland, Chapter 28, Session Laws, 1876, 31–38, MSA.

42. BPCCB, 1878–79, RG 68, Box 27, 84–88, BCA.

43. "The May Term of the Courts," *BS*, May 8, 1876; CJR, 1875–80.

44. Poe, *Maryland Code*, 453, MSA.

45. "Judge Pinkney's Charge to the Grand Jury," *BS*, September 16, 1878.

46. CJR, 1870, Reports of the City Officers, 487–90, UMD.

47. CJR, 1871, Reports of the City Officers, 950–52, UMD.

48. For more on Kane's interesting biography, see Crenson, *Baltimore*, 302–3. Kane was perhaps most famous for being Baltimore's police marshal in 1861 when the Union Army arrested him and seized control of the local police.

49. George P. Kane, Mayor's Message, January 21, 1878, 6–9; quote on 8.

50. Both public schools and police received a paltry sum in comparison to debt service and temporary loans which constituted 40 percent of the city's total expenses. Register's Report, 1877, Reports of the City Officers, 105–6, UMD.

51. Johnson, *Policing the Urban Underworld*, 9–10.

52. BPCCB, 1880–81, RG 68, Box 27, 6–7, BCA.

206 · *Notes to Chapter 1*

53. BPCCB, 1878–79, RG 68, Box 27, 5–12, BCA; quote on 6.

54. General Assembly of Maryland, Chapter 24, Session Laws, 1880, 37, MSA.

55. "A Crowded Jail," *BS*, March 31, 1880; BPCCB, 1880–81, RG 68, Box 27, 29, BCA.

56. BOV, April 6, 1880, Baltimore City Jail, Proceedings of Visitors, MSA.

57. "Who Are the So-Called Bummers?" *BS*, February 4, 1884.

58. CJR, 1877, Reports of the City Officers, 488, UMD.

59. BOV, November 6, 1877, Baltimore City Jail, Proceedings of Visitors, MSA.

60. Ferdinand C. Latrobe, Mayor's Message, January 1, 1879, 33.

61. BOV, January 21, 1879, Baltimore City Jail, Proceedings of Visitors, MSA; BOV, January 23, 1879, Baltimore City Jail, Proceedings of Visitors, MSA; "Employment for Jail Prisoners," *BS*, February 15, 1879.

62. CJR, 1879, Reports of the City Officers, 927–29, UMD.

63. "Grand Jury Report," *BS*, January 13, 1879.

64. BOV, March 12, 1879, Baltimore City Jail, Proceedings of Visitors, MSA.

65. BOV, May 6, 1879, Baltimore City Jail, Proceedings of Visitors, MSA; "Local Matters," *BS*, May 2, 1879; "Surrender of Jail Bummers," *BS*, May 3, 1879.

66. For more on Morrison's fascinating political career, see Melton, "Power Networks."

67. Ferdinand C. Latrobe, Mayor's Message, January 1, 1881, 30.

68. CJR, 1880, Reports of the City Officers, 871, UMD; emphasis in original.

69. Griffith, *Report on the Penal and Reformatory Institutions*, 2. For more on the roots of these disparate forms of prison organization, see Davis, *Are Prisons Obsolete?*, 40–59.

70. CJR, 1880, Reports of the City Officers, 877–99, UMD.

71. CJR, 1880, Reports of the City Officers, 877–99, UMD.

72. CJR, 1880, Reports of the City Officers, 877–99, UMD.

73. Arnold, "Suburban Growth," 111–17.

74. On the development of the patrol wagon and signal box, see Harring, *Policing a Class Society*, chap. 3.

75. BPCCB, 1884–85, RG 68, Box 27, 5–31, BCA.

76. General Assembly of Maryland, Chapter 460, Session Laws, 1880, 727–29, MSA.

77. BPCCB, 1886–87, RG 68, Box 27, 5–16, BCA.

78. BPCCB, 1888–89, RG 68, Box 27, 45–46, BCA.

79. Lichtenstein, *Twice the Work*, 57–61.

80. CJR, 1881, Reports of the City Officers, 549–58, UMD.

81. CJR, 1882, Reports of the City Officers, 443–51, UMD.

82. "The Condition of the Jail," *BS*, January 10, 1885.

83. Gilfoyle, "'America's Greatest Criminal Barracks,'" 530–32.

84. "Overcrowding at the Jail," *BS*, January 22, 1885; "Condition of the City Jail," *BS*, January 24, 1885; "A University of Bummers," *BS*, January 31, 1885.

85. CJR, 1883, Reports of the City Officers, 1115–35, UMD.

Notes to Chapter 1 • 207

86. Kerson, "Almshouse," 213–14; Hemphill, *Bawdy City*, 183.

87. "Notes and Comments," *American Journal of Insanity*, April 1886, 539–41. For more on the role of insane asylums in the United States during the late nineteenth century, see Gonaver, *Peculiar Institution*; Segrest, *Administrations*; Summers, *Madness*.

88. Although there were very few such institutions, a comparable one could be found up the road in Philadelphia. John Bucknill, in *Notes on Asylums for the Insane in America*, regarded Blockley Almshouse as a disgraceful and overstuffed institution that violated both ethical standards and common human decency. Bayview would come to represent a similar inhumanity and mismanagement by the end of the nineteenth century. Bucknill, *Notes on Asylums*, 42–45.

89. Ferdinand C. Latrobe, Mayor's Message, January 1, 1889, 65; "The Law and the City's Street Beggars," *BS*, September 19, 1889.

90. Bayview Asylum, Rules of Order, RG 29, Box 16, 1866, 5–41, BCA.

91. Robert T. Banks, Mayor's Message, January 23, 1871, 25–27.

92. TOP, 1870–72, Annual Reports, Reports of the City Officers, UMD.

93. TOP, 1871, Annual Report, Reports of the City Officers, 887, UMD.

94. "Local Matters," *BS*, May 26, 1874. For more on the racialized history of physical restraints in asylums, see Gonaver, *Peculiar Institution*, 182–83. For more on the equally sordid history of Spring Grove, see Schoeberlein, "'Maryland's Shame.'"

95. TOP, 1874, Annual Report, Reports of the City Officers, 324–25, UMD.

96. Baltimore City Council, Ordinance No. 87, May 11, 1875, City Ordinances and Proceedings of the City Council, BCA; "The Insane Poor," *BS*, March 23, 1875; "Local Matters," *BS*, March 23, 1875; "Local Matters," *BS*, April 13, 1875.

97. Ferdinand C. Latrobe, Mayor's Message, January 1, 1879, 36–38.

98. TOP, 1878, Annual Report, Reports of the City Officers, 659–61, UMD; quote on 660.

99. Ferdinand C. Latrobe, Mayor's Message, January 1, 1881, 28.

100. Ferdinand C. Latrobe, Mayor's Message, January 1, 1885, 67–68.

101. "Dr. H. M. Hurd, Noted Teacher at JHU, Dies," *BS*, July 19, 1927.

102. TOP, 1890, Annual Report, Reports of the City Officers, 791, UMD.

103. Hurd, "Race and Insanity," 241–42.

104. "The Almshouse Investigation," *BS*, April 23, 1883.

105. Bayview Asylum, Rules of Order, RG 29, Box 16, 1882, 12, BCA.

106. "At the Poorhouse," *BS*, May 14, 1883.

107. TOP, Minutes, May 7, 1883, BCA.

108. "Report of the Grand Jury," *BS*, May 11, 1874.

109. "Half-Yearly Summary," *American Journal of Insanity*, January 1893, 525–27.

110. General Assembly of Maryland, Chapter 373, Session Laws, 1886, 601, MSA.

111. CJR, 1885, Reports of the City Officers, 686, UMD.

112. CJR, 1884–86, Reports of the City Officers, UMD.

113. "Warden of the Jail," *BS*, March 30, 1887.

Notes to Chapter 2

Chapter 2. "Silk Stocking Aristocracy"

1. Roger W. Cull, Instructions to Watchers, October 30, 1895, Box 195, CJBP, LOC.
2. Gilfoyle, *Pickpocket's Tale*, 253–54.
3. Bolin, *Bossism*; Fogelson, *Big-City Police*; Johnson, *Street Justice*; Link, *Paradox*; Oller, *Rogues' Gallery*; Wiebe, *Search for Order*; Yu, "'Boss Robert La Follette."
4. Crooks, *Politics & Progress*, 9–12; Kent, *Story of Maryland Politics*, 15–19.
5. *The Voters' Catechism*, ND, Box 195, CJBP, LOC.
6. Liazos, *Reforming the City*, 40–43.
7. Beisel, *Imperiled Innocents*, 49–57.
8. *BAA*, February 15, 1896.
9. Czitrom, *New York Exposed*, 69.
10. Muhammad, *Condemnation of Blackness*, 85–87.
11. Halpin, *Brotherhood of Liberty*, 93.
12. "Indecent Showbills," *BS*, February 23, 1886.
13. "Special Notices," *BS*, March 19, 1886.
14. "Anthony Comstock in Baltimore," *BS*, December 19, 1887.
15. Czitrom, *New York Exposed*, 1–4.
16. Friedman, *Crime and Punishment*, 152–53.
17. Charity Organization Society, Articles of Incorporation, Box 190, CJBP, LOC; De Santis, *Modern America*, 9.
18. "Civil-Service Reform," *BS*, June 11, 1881.
19. Crooks, *Politics & Progress*, 13.
20. Beisel, *Imperiled Innocents*, 51–53; Crooks, *Politics & Progress*, 14.
21. Bishop, *Charles Joseph Bonaparte*, chaps. 1–7.
22. "Vices of a City," *BS*, January 17, 1893.
23. Czitrom, *New York Exposed*, 94.
24. "To Suppress Vice," *BS*, May 28, 1888.
25. "For the Suppression of Vice," *BS*, June 12, 1888.
26. "To Suppress Vice," *BS*, December 19, 1888.
27. "Special Notices," *BS*, March 10, 1899.
28. "Liquor Licenses Refused," *BS*, May 7, 1896.
29. J. R. Slattery, Letter to Charles J. Bonaparte, April 1, 1895, Box 33, CJBP, LOC.
30. Crenson, *Baltimore*, 303.
31. "Procedure against Immoral Houses," *BS*, March 23, 1893.
32. "The Offenders' Parade," *BS*, July 1, 1893.
33. Fronc, *New York Undercover*, 27.
34. Czitrom, *New York Exposed*, 12.
35. McGerr, *Fierce Discontent*, 73. The quote is from James Weir Jr.
36. Czitrom, *New York Exposed*, 103–4; Brands, *American Colossus*, 513–15; Brands, *Reckless Decade*, 63.
37. Czitrom, *New York Exposed*, 132–34.

Notes to Chapter 2 · 209

38. Thomas Ralston Jr., Letter to Charles J. Bonaparte, January 26, 1895, Box 32, CJBP, LOC; Charles J. Bonaparte, Report of the Executive Committee of the Baltimore Reform League, April 27, 1895, CJBP, Box 188, LOC.

39. Liazos, *Reforming the City*, 34–35.

40. Charles J. Bonaparte, Letter to Roger W. Cull, March 23, 1895, Box 144, CJBP, LOC.

41. Liazos, *Reforming the City*, 40.

42. Good Government Club of Baltimore City, Constitution, Box 196, CJBP, LOC.

43. Charles J. Bonaparte, Letter to Joseph Packard, May 15, 1895, Box 145, CJBP, LOC.

44. Theodore Roosevelt, Letter to Charles J. Bonaparte, April 20, 1895, Box 32, CJBP, LOC; Theodore Roosevelt, Letter to Charles J. Bonaparte, April 25, 1895, Box 32, CJBP, LOC.

45. Johnson, *Street Justice*, 50–56.

46. Liazos, *Reforming the City*, 31–37.

47. Charles J. Bonaparte, Letter to Theodore Roosevelt, June 8, 1895, Box 145, CJBP, LOC.

48. Charles J. Bonaparte, Letter to Theodore Roosevelt, October 11, 1895, Box 146, CJBP, LOC.

49. Charles J. Bonaparte, Letter to Roger W. Cull, October 15, 1895, Box 146, CJBP, LOC.

50. "People En Masse!" *BA*, October 16, 1895.

51. Johnson, *Street Justice*, 56. Emily Brooks marks Tammany's fall with the election of Fiorello La Guardia in 1934. Brooks, *Gotham's War*, 30–31.

52. "People En Masse!" *BA*, October 16, 1895.

53. John C. Rose, Letter to Charles J. Bonaparte, July 30, 1895, Box 32, CJBP, LOC.

54. Charles J. Bonaparte, Letter to John C. Rose, October 19, 1895, Box 146, CJBP, LOC.

55. John C. Rose, Letter to Board of Supervisors of Elections, October 23, 1895, Box 32, CJBP, LOC; John C. Rose, Letter to Board of Supervisors of Elections, October 24, 1895, Box 195, CJBP, LOC.

56. John C. Rose, Letter to Board of Supervisors of Elections, October 24, 1895, Box 32, CJBP, LOC.

57. "Mr. Ahern Denies It," *BA*, October 29, 1895; "New Phase of Fraud," *BS*, October 29, 1895.

58. Charles J. Bonaparte, Letter to Roger W. Cull, October 26, 1895, Box 146, CJBP, LOC; Charles J. Bonaparte, Letter to Joseph Packard, October 28, 1895, Box 146, CJBP, LOC.

59. "The Transfer Frauds," *BS*, October 31, 1895; "Ahern, Jubb, and Jackson," *BS*, November 2, 1895.

60. "A Ring Agency," *BS*, October 28, 1895.

61. "'A Quiet Election,'" *BS*, November 5, 1895.

210 · *Notes to Chapter 2*

62. "Repeaters Shadowed," *BS*, November 5, 1895.

63. BPCCB, 1890–91 and 1894–95, RG 68, Box 27, BCA. It is important to note that in cases of fighting at the polls, which often happened, the station house magistrates frequently charged men with disorderly conduct rather than a specific election-related crime.

64. "Rowdyism Rampant," *BS*, November 6, 1895.

65. "What the Marshal Says," *BS*, November 6, 1895.

66. "Lowndes Elected," *BS*, November 6, 1895.

67. "Civic Patriotism," *BS*, November 6, 1895.

68. Charles J. Bonaparte, Letter to Theodore Roosevelt, November 6, 1895, Box 146, CJBP, LOC.

69. Czitrom, *New York Exposed*, 58; Fogelson, *Big-City Police*, 32.

70. For a more comprehensive discussion of the nuances of policy, see Vaz, *Running the Numbers*. For insight on the name "policy," in the film *Force of Evil*, the protagonist, Joe Morse, provides the following etymology: "They call this racket policy because people bet their nickels on numbers instead of paying their weekly insurance premium." See *Force of Evil*, directed by Alexander Polonsky (Metro-Goldwyn-Meyer, 1948), 13:38–13:43.

71. "Policy Playing," *BS*, June 8, 1897.

72. "Policy Playing," *BS*, June 8, 1897.

73. Kent, *Story of Maryland Politics*, 215.

74. Fogelson, *Big-City Police*, 7–8.

75. "Police Investigation," *BS*, June 17, 1897; "Police on the Rack," *BA*, June 17, 1897.

76. "Police Investigation," *BS*, June 17, 1897; "Police on the Rack," *BA*, June 17, 1897.

77. "Police Investigation," *BS*, June 17, 1897; "Police on the Rack," *BA*, June 17, 1897.

78. "Mr. Colton's View," *BS*, June 28, 1897.

79. "Police Marshal Frey," *BA*, June 29, 1897.

80. "Commissioner Johnson," *BS*, July 13, 1897; "The Police Shaken Up," *BA*, July 13, 1897.

81. "City Council Dots," *BAA*, November 30, 1895.

82. Halpin, *Brotherhood of Liberty*, 65–66.

83. Phelps, "Charles J. Bonaparte."

84. Halpin, *Brotherhood of Liberty*, 93.

85. While "law and order" is typically understood within the context of mid-twentieth century American politics, the term was exceedingly common in the late nineteenth century as "Law and Order Leagues" sprung up across the country. In Baltimore, one such league was established to protest saloons in the 1890s. "City News in Brief," *BS*, April 26, 1890.

86. Weeks, *New Charter*, iii–viii; Crenson, *Baltimore*, 322.

87. Vexler, *Baltimore*, 127–33.

88. Vexler, *Baltimore*, 131.

Notes to Chapters 2 and 3 · 211

89. "Forecast for Baltimore and Vicinity," *BS*, January 23, 1900; "City Legislation," *BS*, January 23, 1900.

90. Liazos, *Reforming the City*, 113.

91. "Mr. Hayes' Neighbors," *BS*, March 14, 1899.

92. Kent, *Story of Maryland Politics*, 245.

93. Kent, *Story of Maryland Politics*, 338.

94. "Col. Smith in Harford," *BS*, November 2, 1899.

95. "How the Police Are Helping the Machine," *Baltimore Herald*, October 23, 1901.

96. Litwack, *Trouble in Mind*, 224–27.

97. Halpin, *Brotherhood of Liberty*, 116. See also Perman, *Struggle for Mastery*.

98. "Democrats Gather at Hollins Hall," *BA*, October 29, 1901; Shufelt, *Uncommon Case*, 106.

99. Litwack, *Trouble in Mind*, 227.

100. "The Police Board," *BS*, October 29, 1901; emphasis in original.

101. "Democrats Gather at Hollins Hall," *BA*, October 29, 1901.

102. "Democrats Gather at Hollins Hall," *BA*, October 29, 1901.

103. Halpin, *Brotherhood of Liberty*, 100–101; Litwack, *Trouble in Mind*, 227.

104. Muhammad, *Condemnation of Blackness*, 35–39

105. Bruce, *Negro Problem*, 4–5.

106. Bruce, *Negro Problem*, 8.

107. Bruce, *Negro Problem*, 9.

108. Bruce, *Negro Problem*, 31–32.

109. Johnson, *Question of Race*, 4.

110. Johnson, *Question of Race*, 3.

111. "Shall the Negro Rule?" *BS*, October 29, 1901.

112. "Shall the Negro Rule?" *BS*, October 29, 1901.

113. Muhammad, *Condemnation of Blackness*, 35.

Chapter 3. "With the Power of the Law"

1. "Glass-House Boys," *Charities Record* 3, no. 6 (1898): 67, EPFL.

2. McGerr, *Fierce Discontent*, 109.

3. Platt, *Child Savers*, 127–28.

4. For more on the role of the wealthy upper crust in the administration of poverty relief, see Beisel, *Imperiled Innocents*, 51–53.

5. "Subscriptions for 1886," 1886, Box 190, CJBP, LOC.

6. Amos Warner, "The Charities of Baltimore," 1887, 13, Box 190, CJBP, LOC.

7. McGerr, *Fierce Discontent*, 73.

8. O'Connor, *Poverty Knowledge*, 8–9. Matthew Guariglia has recently coined the term "police intellectual," which encompasses individuals and groups who attempted to legitimize policing as an empirical practice in the early twentieth century. Charity agents fell in line with such aspirations and augmented the regulation of poor and

Notes to Chapter 3

working-class Black and foreign-born Americans. Guariglia, *Police and the Empire City*, 3.

9. The notion of "struggle" animated this social Darwinist position as the wealthy upper crust saw the industrial United States as a struggle over profit that would naturally go to the fittest and most capable. De Santis, *Modern America*, 9–10.

10. LeFlouria, *Chained in Silence*, 47; emphasis in original.

11. Cohen, *Reconstruction*, 5.

12. For more on the sociohistorical development of binary understandings of race in the United States, see Omi and Winant, *Racial Formation*.

13. Boyer, *Urban Masses*, 150–51.

14. Rothman, *Discovery of the Asylum*, 7–10. This conceit prevailed among the robber barons of the late nineteenth century, some of whom opted to voluntarily pass their ill-gotten wealth into public and private institutions.

15. Katz, *Shadow of the Poorhouse*, 60–66.

16. Clement, "Nineteenth-Century Welfare Policy"; Katz, *Shadow of the Poorhouse*; Komisar, *Down and Out*; Lewis, "Stephen Humphreys Gurteen"; McFadden, "'Frankenstein of Pauperism'"; Ziliak, "Self-Reliance."

17. Ziliak, "Self-Reliance," 440–42.

18. Katz, *Shadow of the Poorhouse*, 79.

19. Despite the scientific charity movement's ultimate failure, Baltimore's chapter retained an exceptional reputation as having started and maintained a comprehensive and influential friendly visiting program. Katz, *Shadow of the Poorhouse*, 84.

20. For more on Richmond's approach to charity, see Richmond, *Long View*.

21. Amos Warner, "The Charities of Baltimore," 1887, Box 190, CJBP, LOC.

22. Muhammad, *Condemnation of Blackness*, 6–7.

23. Muhammad, *Condemnation of Blackness*, 105.

24. "Absent from School 137 Times," *BS*, January 31, 1906; Roberts, *Infectious Fear*, 149.

25. Haley, *No Mercy Here*, 3.

26. Pendleton engaged in a common discursive consolidation of Black identity, especially Black women's identity, that established controlling images that prejudged Black women to conform to certain deterministic expectations around sexuality, labor, and exploitability. Historian Deborah Gray White has detailed the emergence of these controlling images, particularly the "mammy" and "jezebel," during enslavement. See White, *Ar'n't I a Woman?*, chap. 1. Samuel K. Roberts contends that Pendleton's prescriptions reinforced generalized perceptions of Black social disorder and disease. Roberts, *Infectious Fear*, 149–50.

27. Pendleton, "Negro Dependence," 55.

28. Pendleton, "Negro Dependence," 52.

29. Gross, *Colored Amazons*, 43; LeFlouria, *Chained in Silence*, 33–35.

30. Pendleton, "Negro Dependence," 55.

31. Pendleton, "Negro Dependence," 55.

Notes to Chapter 3 • 213

32. LeFlouria, *Chained in Silence*, 41–45; Haley, *No Mercy Here*, 18; Harris, *Sex Workers*, 30; Gonaver, *Peculiar Institution*, 129.

33. Benson, "Kowaliga," 22.

34. Crowe, "Racial Violence," 254.

35. In an oft-cited housing report, Janet Kemp, a COS official, condemned Black Baltimoreans who, in relation to their purportedly more dignified foreign-born white peers, supposedly failed to maintain clean homes because of deep-seated cultural mores. While Kemp's report is often regarded as an illuminating investigation into the social ills of housing inequality in Progressive-era Baltimore, the reformer regarded Black people with derision in ways that tinged her analysis in both explicit and oblique ways. See Kemp, *Housing Conditions*; Casiano, "'The Pot,'" in King, Davis, and Drabinski, *Baltimore Revisited*, 39–41.

36. Daniel Coit Gilman, "Baltimore Greeting to New Orleans," *Charities Record* 3, no. 1 (1897): 1–2, EPFL.

37. David Green, "The Library," *Charities Record* 1, no. 3 (1893): 32–34, EPFL, quote on 32–33.

38. McGerr, *Fierce Discontent*, 8.

39. Cohen, *Reconstruction*, 5; McGrerr, *Fierce Discontent*, 66–68.

40. David Green, "The Library," 33, EPFL.

41. Amos Warner, "The Library," *Charities Record* 1, no. 6 (1894): 68–69, EPFL.

42. For more on Kidd's theories of racial superiority, see Fog, *Cultural Selection*, 13–21.

43. "The Library," *Charities Record* 2, no. 5 (1896): 57–58, EPFL.

44. "The Library," *Charities Record* 2, no. 4 (1896): 44–45, EPFL; emphasis in original.

45. "First Principles," *Charities Record* 3, no. 5 (1898): 1, EPFL; emphasis in original.

46. McGerr, *Fierce Discontent*, 66–68.

47. McGerr, *Fierce Discontent*, 73.

48. Friedman, *Crime and Punishment*, 152–55.

49. BPCCB, 1892–93, RG 68, Box 27, 30, BCA.

50. BPCCB, 1894–95, RG 68, Box 27, 8–9, BCA.

51. Jacob Riis, "Police Lodging-Houses," *Christian Union*, January 14, 1893. For more on the decline of police welfare, see Monkkonen, *Police in Urban America*, 86–109.

52. McGerr, *Fierce Discontent*, 67.

53. Poe, *Maryland Code*, 565, MSA.

54. Poe, *Maryland Code*, 492, MSA.

55. Amos Warner, "The Charities of Baltimore," 1887, Box 190, CJBP, LOC.

56. Between 1886 and 1888, arrests increased from 103 to 140. BPCCB, 1886–89, RG 68, Box 27, BCA.

57. "Street Begging Must Stop," *BS*, May 19, 1897.

58. "Gathering in the Peddlers," *BS*, May 21, 1897. For more on the history of peddling, disability, and the right to the city, see Schweik, *Ugly Laws*, 210–14.

59. Charity Organization Society, Letter to Supporters, June 1, 1897, Box 190, CJBP, LOC.

214 · *Notes to Chapter 3*

60. "Editorial," *Charities Record* 2, no. 8 (1897): 88–89.

61. "Police Relief," *Charities Record* 3, no. 4 (1898): 37–38.

62. "Editorial," *Charities Record* 2, no. 8 (1897): 88.

63. "And This Is 'Charity,'" *BS*, January 7, 1901.

64. "Editorial," *Charities Record* 4, no. 8 (1901): 86–87, EPFL.

65. Katz, *Shadow of the Poorhouse*, 79.

66. "Cautionary List," *Charities Record* 1, no. 4 (1894): 46, EPFL.

67. "Cautionary List," *Charities Record* 3, no. 1 (1897): 10, EPFL.

68. "Cautionary List," *Charities Record* 3, no. 1 (1897): 10, EPFL.

69. "Cautionary List," *Charities Record* 3, no. 1 (1897): 10, EPFL.

70. A. L. Sears, Letter to Charles J. Bonaparte, June 7, 1895, Box 33, CJBP, LOC.

71. Katz, *Compulsory Education Laws*, 20. Anthony M. Platt's analysis of the "child-saving" movement of the late nineteenth century provides an excellent example of this circular logic that is broadly applicable to other population groups during this period. For Platt, administrators of juvenile delinquency took the existence of delinquency as a given with little to no recognition of their role in its production. As such, the laws governing juvenile delinquents and their implementation constructed juvenile delinquency in service of broader bourgeois and state imperatives during the Gilded Age. For Platt, analyzing the deficiencies of children deemed deviant missed one of the most consequential causes of juvenile delinquency: the rule makers who made it illegal in the first place. Platt, *Child Savers*, 36–43.

72. Katz, *Compulsory Education*, 19–20.

73. Brugger, *Maryland*, 363.

74. "Anti Child Labor Creed," ND, Box 190, CJBP, LOC.

75. Mary Willcox Brown, "Compulsory Education Laws," *Charities Record* 3, no. 7 (1898): 75–76, EPFL.

76. Rose Summerfeld, "Truancy," *Charities Record* 3, no. 7 (1898): 77–78, EPFL.

77. Board of School Commissioners, Annual Report, 1899, RG 31, Box 4, 71, BCA.

78. Board of School Commissioners, Annual Report, 1899, RG 31, Box 4, 69–72, BCA.

79. "'The Child at School,'" *BS*, March 16, 1900.

80. It is unclear whether this club bore any relationship to the Good Government Clubs chartered during the 1895 election.

81. "Education for All," *BS*, January 8, 1902; "To Arrest Truants," *BS*, January 10, 1902.

82. General Assembly of Maryland, Chapter 269, 1902, 377–81, Session Laws, MSA.

83. "Eight Ladies Named," *BS*, January 6, 1903.

84. Board of School Commissioners, Minutes, January 5, 1903, RG 31, Box 1, 138, BCA.

85. Board of School Commissioners, Minutes, January 14, 1903, RG 31, Box 1, 8–14, BCA.

86. Board of School Commissioners, Minutes, February 13, 1907, RG 31, Box 2, 28, BCA. For more on Jewish life in Baltimore, see Goldstein and Weiner, *On Middle Ground.*

Notes to Chapters 3 and 4 · 215

87. "To Compel Attendance," *BS*, January 15, 1903.

88. "For Parental School," *BS*, April 20, 1904.

89. Board of School Commissioners, Minutes, May 13, 1903, RG 31, Box 1, 59, BCA.

90. "Truant Officers Report," *BS*, April 9, 1903; "That Sunday Concert," *BS*, May 14, 1903.

91. "Hunted Up 2,772 Pupils," *BS*, February 12, 1903.

92. Board of School Commissioners, Annual Report, 1902, RG 31, Box 4, 39–42 BCA; quote on 40.

93. "Truant Officers' Report," *BS*, April 9, 1903.

94. Board of School Commissioners, Annual Report, 1903, RG 31, Box 4, 39–43, BCA; quote on 42.

95. Agyepong, *Criminalization*, 60–64; Barron, "History of the Chicago Parental School."

96. Board of School Commissioners, Annual Report, 1904, RG 31, Box 5, 5, BCA.

97. "The Law and the City's Street Beggars," *BS*, September 19, 1889.

98. Formally the Trustees of the Poor. "Truant Officers' Report," *BS*, April 9, 1903.

99. Baltimore City Council, Ordinance No. 89, June 6, 1904, City Ordinances and Proceedings of the City Council, BCA.

100. Board of School Commissioners, Annual Report, 1904, RG 31, Box 5, 5, BCA.

101. "They'll Have to Study," *BS*, November 17, 1904.

102. "Parental School Leased," October 19, 1906. Gilmor Lane is now called Vineyard Lane.

103. Bromley and Bromley, *Atlas*, 1906, Plate 18, BCA.

104. "Chicken for Bad Boys," *BS*, February 1, 1907.

105. Board of School Commissioners, Annual Report, 1906, RG 31, Box 5, 13, BCA.

106. Board of School Commissioners, Annual Report, 1907, RG 31, Box 5, 14, BCA.

107. "Conflicting Educational Ideals," *BS*, March 23, 1905.

108. "To Protest Once More," *BS*, July 28, 1903.

109. Board of School Commissioners, Minutes, April 27, 1904, RG 31, Box 1, 33, BCA.

110. "Dr. Buckler, Retired, Is Dead at 75," *BS*, November 29, 1949.

111. "Scores Public Schools," *BS*, October 10, 1907.

112. "For Enforced Bathing," *BS*, March 20, 1908.

113. Board of School Commissioners, Annual Report, 1903, RG 31, Box 4, 42, BCA.

114. Katz, *Shadow of the Poorhouse*, 79.

Chapter 4. "If I Had Told What I Know"

1. *State of Maryland vs. Alverta Bailey*, Baltimore City Criminal Papers, Box 122, Indictment No. 1169, MSA (hereafter *Bailey Indictment*).

2. 1900 U.S. Census, Baltimore City, Maryland, Population Schedule, Ward 3, Enumeration District No. 43, Sheet No. 11, 206 Halfmoon Alley, Alverta Bailey, accessed via ancestry.com (January 11, 2023); *Bailey Indictment*.

216 · *Notes to Chapter 4*

3. *Bailey Indictment*, 6.

4. *Bailey Indictment*, 9–15.

5. For more on the struggles to develop, realize, and execute efficient and continuous enforcement in civil service and other government activities, see Wiebe, *Search for Order*, chap. 6. For more on Baltimore's developing racialized police state, see Halpin, *Brotherhood of Liberty*, chap. 4; Shufelt, *Uncommon Case*, chap. 5. For more on white expectations of deference, particularly regarding law enforcement, see Terry, *Struggle*, 86–96.

6. Criminologists like Cesare Lombroso influenced American policing and provided academic heft to theories of cultural criminality in his influential texts. See Lombroso, *Criminal Man* and Lombroso and Ferrero, *Female Offender*. For more on housing segregation in Baltimore, see Glotzer, *How the Suburbs Were Segregated*; Power, "Apartheid."

7. Harris, *Sex Workers*, 27–28; Hunter, *To 'Joy My Freedom*, 57.

8. Baldwin, *In the Watches*, 172–75; Heap, *Slumming*, 76–77.

9. Hernández, *City of Inmates*, 30; emphasis in original.

10. Carby, "Policing the Black Woman's Body," 739–41.

11. Menika B. Dirkson charts a similar relationship between discursive constructions of Black criminality and policing practices in Philadelphia. Dirkson, *Hope and Struggle*, 15–16.

12. Paul Gootenberg details how cocaine, which was first synthesized in 1860 in Germany, underwent rapid regulation and criminalization between 1900 and the 1920s. Before its criminalization, the drug was used in scientific trials, botanical appraisals, and recreational activities in Germany, Britain, Peru, France, and North America. According to Gootenberg, the drug's use among the working class at the turn of the century provoked a mania that caused reformers and police departments to advocate for its illegalization. Gootenberg, *Cocaine*, 1–2.

13. "Druggist" is an anachronism for "pharmacist."

14. "Baltimore's Negroes Are in the Thrall of Cocaine," *BS*, December 16, 1906; "Cocaine an Open Trade in St. Louis; Woman Is Leader," *St. Louis Post-Dispatch*, November 20, 1910.

15. For a discussion of the "underworld" as a cultural construction, see Kalifa, *Vice*, introduction.

16. "Law Should Check Sale of Cocaine," *St. Louis Post-Dispatch*, July 24, 1903.

17. "Use of Cocaine among Negroes," *St. Louis Post-Dispatch*, November 2, 1902.

18. "Oklahoma Plans an Anti-Cocaine Law," *St. Louis Post-Dispatch*, December 18, 1904.

19. "Cocaine War on in Carr District; One Arrest of Dealer," *St. Louis Post-Dispatch*, August 14, 1905.

20. Musto, *American Disease*, xi.

21. "Physicians War against Cocaine," *St. Louis Post-Dispatch*, January 24, 1905.

22. Gilfoyle, *Pickpocket's Tale*, 82–90.

23. "'Cocaine Sniffing' Newest Excitement for New York's Jaded Thrill Seekers," *St. Louis Post-Dispatch*, September 6, 1908. For more on press coverage of interracial sex

in urban nightlife during the early twentieth century, see Gallon, *Pleasure in the News*, 112–18.

24. "Cocaine Habit Growing," *BS*, September 12, 1903, Box 45, Folder 3, JLAP.

25. "Drafts Anti-Drug Bill," *BS*, January 7, 1906, Box 45, Folder 3, JLAP; "Fighting the Cocaine Habit," *BS*, April 23, 1907; General Assembly of Maryland, Chapter 523, 1906, 1003–6, Session Laws, MSA

26. Cohen, *Contraband*, 315.

27. "Cocaine Crusade Continues," *BS*, October 21, 1906; "A Cocaine Route, It Is Said," *BS*, January 3, 1907; "Tilts in Morphine Case," *BS*, December 5, 1907, Box 45, Folder 3, JLAP.

28. "Fighting Cocaine Evil," *BS*, January 30, 1908, Box 45, Folder 3, JLAP.

29. "Takes Up Cocaine Cases," *BS*, January 1, 1907, Box 45, Folder 3, JLAP.

30. "Who the City Appointees Are," *BS*, February 20, 1908.

31. "'Eggs against Bullets,'" *BS*, May 23, 1908, Box 45, Folder 3, JLAP.

32. "The Atlanta Riot," *BS*, September 26, 1906.

33. Hunter, *To 'Joy My Freedom*, 124–29, 161–67; John Temple Graves, "He Blames Cocaine Habit for Negroes' Attacks on Women," *St. Louis Post-Dispatch*, September 24, 1906.

34. Hunter, *To 'Joy My Freedom*, 195.

35. "Baltimore's Negroes Are in the Thrall of Cocaine," *BS*, December 16, 1906.

36. CJR, 1908, RG 29, Box 39, 26, BCA.

37. "Drug Habit Growing," *BS*, September 14, 1902; "Baltimore's Negroes Are in the Thrall of Cocaine," *BS*, December 16, 1906.

38. "Cocaine & Beer Cause Trouble," *BS*, June 21, 1902.

39. Henrietta Woods, Baltimore City Police Department, Consolidated Criminal Docket, MSA.

40. For more on Black women's condemnation as "visual metaphors of female immorality," see Gross, *Colored Amazons*, 74.

41. "Cocaine Evil Grows: Nearly Every Negress Arrested Is a Victim of the Drug," *BS*, December 18, 1905; Benson, "Kowaliga," 22.

42. "The Police Board and the Charges against Members of the Force," *BS*, May 27, 1908.

43. "Dope," *BS*, July 23, 1906.

44. Carby, "Policing the Black Woman's Body," 739–41.

45. Now Mercy Hospital.

46. "Quiet Region of Homes, and Later a Resort of Bad Men, 'The Pot' Is Now the Center of the Cocaine Trade," *BS*, May 31, 1908.

47. "Quiet Region of Homes, and Later a Resort of Bad Men, 'The Pot' Is Now the Center of the Cocaine Trade," *BS*, May 31, 1908; LeFlouria, *Chained in Silence*, 47; Kendi, *Stamped from the Beginning*, 198–201.

48. "Quiet Region of Homes, and Later a Resort of Bad Men, 'The Pot' Is Now the Center of the Cocaine Trade," *BS*, May 31, 1908.

218 · *Notes to Chapter 4*

49. For more on the racial organization of Southern city space during Jim Crow, see Hanchett, *Sorting Out*, 3–8.

50. Pietila, *Not in My Neighborhood*, 7–8.

51. "'Big Dan's' Safe Opened," *BS*, May 29, 1908.

52. Harris, *Sex Workers*, 96, 104.

53. Alverta Bailey, Baltimore City Police Department, Criminal Docket, Central District, MSA; *State of Maryland vs. Alverta Bailey*, Baltimore City Criminal Papers, Box 121, Indictment No. 935, MSA.

54. *State of Maryland vs. Daniel Waters*, Baltimore City Criminal Papers, Box 121, Indictment No. 936, MSA.

55. "'Cocaine Queen' Talks," *BS*, May 31, 1908.

56. For a comprehensive overview of Black women's domestic work in the first half of the twentieth century, see Clark-Lewis, *Living in, Living Out*.

57. "'Cocaine Queen' Talks," *BS*, May 26, 1910.

58. Brandon T. Jett has argued that during the early twentieth century, Black men and women in the American South routinely resorted to the criminal legal system to advocate for their own self-interests. See Jett, *Race, Crime, and Policing*, 5.

59. Haley, *No Mercy Here*, 205–6.

60. "'Big Dan' Sent to Jail," *BS*, May 7, 1908.

61. "Four Policemen Are Suspended," *BA*, May 26, 1908; "Fifth Officer Is Suspended," *BA*, May 26, 1908.

62. "Police Accused in 'Coke' Cases," *BA*, May 26, 1908. Regarding municipal police's sponsorship of vice during this period, see Fogelson, *Big-City Police*, 32.

63. "'Coke' Vendors Accuse Police," *BA*, June 7, 1908.

64. "Concluding Testimony: Witnesses Tell of Cocaine Selling in 'the Pot,'" *BS*, June 9, 1908.

65. "Police Officers Stand Acquitted," *BA*, June 9, 1908; "Policemen Acquitted: All Declared Not Guilty without Defense Being Heard," *BS*, June 9, 1908.

66. Sherlock Swann, NT, Sherlock Swann Papers, Box 1, MCHC.

67. City Council of Baltimore, Ordinance No. 156, 1908, RG 16, 364–68, BCA.

68. Massachusetts General Court, Chapter 387, 1910, State Library of Massachusetts; "Twelve Taken in Raids," *Boston Daily Globe*, June 15, 1911; "New Cocaine Bill Adds to Penalties," *New York Times*, January 17, 1913.

69. BPCCB, 1908–10, RG 68, Box 27, BCA.

70. "Cocaine Evil Grows," *BS*, December 18, 1905. For more on this ordeal, see Casiano, "'The Pot,'" in King, Davis, and Drabinski, *Baltimore Revisited*, 41–48.

71. "Given One Day in Jail," *BS*, April 2, 1909; BPCP, 1910, Baltimore City Police Department, Box 2, Vol. 32, 129–30, MSA.

72. *State of Maryland vs. William Rossberg*, Baltimore City Criminal Papers, Box 123, Indictment No. 1803, MSA (hereafter *Rossberg Indictment*).

73. "Swann Cocaine Law Up," *BS*, January 17, 1909; "Swann Law in Balance," *BS*, January 20, 1909.

Notes to Chapter 4 • 219

74. *Rossberg Indictment.*

75. "Swann Law Sustained," *BS*, March 27, 1909.

76. "Strong for West Plan," *BS*, October 11, 1910. For more on racial zoning, see Power, "Apartheid."

77. Sherlock Swann, NT, Sherlock Swann Papers, Box 1, MCHC.

78. "Shortage in City Hall," *BS*, March 31, 1909.

79. BPCP, Baltimore City Police Department, Box 2, Vol. 30, 420–21, 437–38, MSA.

80. New York police detective Thomas Byrnes was the father of criminal identification in the United States. He developed thorough criminal typologies in the late nineteenth century. See Byrnes, *Professional Criminals of America*; Czitrom, *New York Exposed*; Oller, *Rogues' Gallery*.

81. Fronc, *New York Undercover*, 6–7, 29–30.

82. Oller, *Rogues' Gallery*, 240–41.

83. BPCCB, 1900–1901, RG 68, Box 27, 11, BCA.

84. Cole, *Suspect Identities*, 81.

85. McCabe, *History of the Baltimore Police*, 45–46.

86. George League, "Lookout Sheet," January 25, 1911, Baltimore City Police Department, Police Commissioner Reports, MSA.

87. Fred L. Ford, "Persons Wanted," August 11, 1956, Baltimore City Police Department, Police Commissioner Reports, MSA.

88. Hunter, *To 'Joy My Freedom*, 27–28, 59–65.

89. In 1910, the police board began reporting demographic information on suspects subjected to Bertillon classification. Black people accounted for almost half of those identified through the invasive Bertillon procedure. Black women were twice as likely as white women to experience the procedure. BPCCB, 1910, RG 68, Box 27, 72, BCA.

90. "Hattie Woodbridge" and "Kate Vincent," Baltimore City Police Department, Arrestees Physical Description, MSA.

91. *State of Maryland vs. Kate Vincent and Hattie Woodbridge*, Baltimore City Criminal Papers, Box 120, Indictment No. 162, MSA.

92. BPCCB, 1908–9, RG 68, Box 27, 14–15, 100, BCA.

93. Baltimore City Police Department, "Information for Citizens," March 1909, Sherlock Swann Papers, Box 1, MCHC.

94. For more on Theodore Bingham's xenophobic reign as New York's police commissioner, see Guariglia, *Police and the Empire City*, 124–34.

95. "Colonel Swann 'At School,'" *BS*, March 14, 1908.

96. "Col. Swann Returns," *BS*, March 16, 1908.

97. This type of looking has been theorized as "sousveillance." For more on the concept, see Browne, *Dark Matters*, 18–19.

98. "Must 'Face the Masks,'" *BS*, May 6, 1908.

99. "Sleuths Have Mask System," *BS*, July 29, 1908.

100. "Police 'Mugg' the Governor," *BS*, December 6, 1908.

101. Folsom, *Our Police*, 462–85; Baldwin, *In the Watches*, 24.

220 · *Notes to Chapters 4 and 5*

102. For more on this patrol box system, see Harring, *Policing a Class Society*, chap. 3

103. BPCP, Baltimore City Police Department, Box 2, Vol. 30, 339, MSA.

104. BPCCB, 1908–9, RG 68, Box 27, 77, BCA.

105. BPCP, Baltimore City Police Department, Box 2, Vol. 30, 215–16, 229–30, MSA; "Leigh Bonsal Scores President Swann," *BAA*, April 17, 1909.

106. BPCP, 1909–10, Baltimore City Police Department, Box 2, Vol. 31, 49, 78, 348, MSA.

107. For a detailed overview of how private and public interests, including the Baltimore police, collaborated to systematically shut down Baltimore's red light districts during this period, see Hemphill, *Bawdy City*, 276–92.

108. BPCCB, 1908–9, RG 68, Box 27, 45–46, 65–66, BCA.

109. BPCP, 1909–10, Baltimore City Police Department, Box 2, Vol. 31, 157–58, MSA.

110. BPCP, 1909–10, Baltimore City Police Department, Box 2, Vol. 31, 324, 362–63, 393, MSA; *State of Maryland vs. Sadonia Young*, Baltimore City Criminal Papers, Box 122, Indictment No. 1157, MSA; "Negress Accuses Policeman," *BS*, June 17, 1908.

111. BPCP, 1909–10, Baltimore City Police Department, Box 2, Vol. 31, 286–87, 312–23, MSA. Hemphill, *Bawdy City*, 275–76.

112. Sherlock Swann, "Speech Made by S. Swann to Police Department," May 31, 1908, Sherlock Swann Papers, Box 1, MCHC.

113. Sherlock Swann, NT, Sherlock Swann Papers, Box 1, MCHC.

114. Baltimore journalist H. L. Mencken received an early promotion to cover the Central District, which, for him, represented "the premier Baltimore district, journalistically speaking, for it included the busiest of the police courts, a downtown hospital, police headquarters, the city jail, and the morgue." Mencken, *Days*, 224.

115. McCabe, *History of the Baltimore Police*, 88.

116. For more on the history of suburbanization during the early twentieth century, see Glotzer, *How the Suburbs Were Segregated*, 80–82.

117. BPCCB, 1910, RG 68, Box 27, 97, BCA.

Chapter 5. "I Ask Mercy at Your Hands"

1. *Stenographic Transcript in the Case of United States of America v. Henry A. Brown*, March 28, 1921, Criminal Case No. 3158, U.S. District Court for the District of Maryland Records, National Archives at Philadelphia (hereafter NAP), 63–75 (hereafter *Transcript*); Robert Carman, Letter to James Finch, June 8, 1921, Pardon Case Files, Box 940, NARA II.

2. *Transcript*, 79–85.

3. "Bury Slain Nurse in Navy Cemetery," *Evening Star*, January 17, 1921.

4. "Henry A. Brown," Criminal Docket, Northwestern District, 130, MSA.

5. BPCCB, 1921, 34.

6. The master-at-arms is the senior law enforcement official on a naval ship.

Notes to Chapter 5 • 221

7. *Transcript*, 248.

8. "Bury Slain Nurse in Navy Cemetery," *Evening Star*, January 17, 1921.

9. Adler, *Murder in New Orleans*, 9.

10. Flowe, *Uncontrollable Blackness*, 18.

11. The two most impactful assertions of this genealogy include Rothman, *Discovery of the Asylum* and Foucault, *Discipline and Punish*. Although their frameworks are indispensable to understanding the emergence of the modern carceral state, scholars, especially Black feminist scholars, have problematized their elision of public torture, particularly in the U.S. context in which lynching, third degree, and violent brutality were integral to racialized modes of policing and incarceration. Haley, *No Mercy Here*, 27–28.

12. Seigel, *Violence Work*, 10–11.

13. National Commission on Law Observance and Enforcement, *Lawlessness in Law Enforcement*, 20.

14. Czitrom, *New York Exposed*, 43; Oller, *Rogues' Gallery*, 51–55. Regarding the prevalence of third-degree torture before Byrnes's reign, Timothy Gilfoyle notes that New York law enforcement, as early as the 1850s, isolated and starved prisoners in dark cells to elicit confessions. Gilfoyle, *Pickpocket's Tale*, 251.

15. "Victim of 'Third Degree,'" *BAA*, May 28, 1910.

16. Frederic Haskin, "The Third Degree," *WP*, March 10, 1910.

17. "National—'The Third Degree' by Charles Klein," *WP*, January 10, 1909.

18. "'Atrocious Institution,'" *WP*, June 27, 1909; "Danger to Body Politic," *WP*, June 27, 1909.

19. "What the 'Third Degree' Is," *WP*, January 30, 1910.

20. Adler, *Bluecoated Terror*, chaps. 3 and 4.

21. These numbers were culled from a series of criminal dockets and represent cases in which defendants were charged with murder and found guilty, either of murder or manslaughter. Baltimore City Criminal Court Dockets, 1917–23, MSA.

22. Terry, *Struggle*, 44.

23. "Scores the 'Third Degree,'" *BS*, February 11, 1910.

24. "Senseless on the Floor," *BS*, August 29, 1903; "Think Miss Link Fell," *BS*, August 30, 1903; "All Point to Murder," *BS*, September 1, 1903; "Miss Link Killed by Boy," *BS*, September 9, 1903; "Jones Gets 15 Years," *BS*, November 11, 1903.

25. See figures 1, 2, and 10.

26. Friedman, *Crime and Punishment*, 273–76; Johnson, *Street Justice*, 133–42.

27. National Commission on Law Observance and Enforcement, *Lawlessness in Law Enforcement*, 4.

28. Friedman, *Crime and Punishment*, 295–304.

29. National Commission on Law Observance and Enforcement, *Lawlessness in Law Enforcement*, 1.

30. Willrich, *City of Courts*, xxvi–xxvii.

31. Willrich, *City of Courts*, 242–43.

222 • *Notes to Chapter 5*

32. McCabe, *History of the Baltimore Police*, 114; BPCCB, 1904–5, RG 68, Box 27, 52, BCA.

33. "P. B. Bradley, Master Detective of City's Force, Dies Suddenly," *BS*, July 28, 1921.

34. "Detectives Are Accused," *BS*, November 1, 1902; "Drops Hammersla Case," *BS*, December 3, 1902.

35. "Hammersla Is Dismissed," *BS*, May 9, 1903.

36. McCabe, *History of the Baltimore Police*, 121–23; "'Stole, but Didn't Kill,'" *BS*, January 11, 1905; "Jones Admits Murder," *BS*, January 12, 1905; "Murder in First Degree," *BS*, January 20, 1905.

37. BPCP, 1910, Baltimore City Police Department, Box 2, Vol. 32, 376, MSA.

38. Flowe, *Uncontrollable Blackness*, 9.

39. Walter Johnson has detailed how forced confessions can be read to understand the "prejudices, fears, and fantasies" of white populations and law enforcement. Johnson, *Broken Heart*, 91–99; quote on 94.

40. "Religious Talk Wrings Confession after the Third Degree Fails," *BAA*, January 28, 1921.

41. "Nurse's Slayer to Be Brought Here for Trial," *Evening Sun*, January 20, 1921; "Nurse's Slayer Held Prisoner in Navy Brig," *Evening Sun*, January 20, 1921; "Suspect Awaits Trial in the 'Brig,'" *Evening Star*, January 20, 1921; "Slayer of Nurse Is in City Jail," *BA*, January 22, 1921.

42. J. Frank Supplee, *Final Mittimus*, February 2, 1921, Case File, NAP.

43. "Brown Now Lodged in City Jail Here," *Evening Sun*, January 21, 1921; "Naval Nurse's Slayer to Be Rushed to Trial," *BS*, January 21, 1921.

44. "Declares Hanging Forced Confession," *BA*, February 3, 1921; "Deny Forcing Negro to Confess Murder," *Evening Sun*, February 3, 1921; "Brown Denies Slaying Nurse," *Washington Times*, February 3, 1921; "Negro Now Denies Murdering Nurse," *WP*, February 3, 1921; "Negro Denies Slaying Nurse at Annapolis," *Evening Star*, February 3, 1921; "Negro Recants Confession of Killing Nurse," *BS*, February 3, 1921; Henry A. Brown, Petition for Executive Clemency, May 30, 1921, Pardon Case Files, Box 940, NARA II.

45. *United States of America vs. Henry A. Brown*, Case File, NAP.

46. "Deny Forcing Negro to Confess Murder," *Evening Sun*, February 3, 1921.

47. "Brown Denies Slaying Nurse," *Washington Times*, February 3, 1921.

48. "Negro Now Denies Murdering Nurse," *WP*, February 3, 1921; "Negro Denies Slaying Nurse at Annapolis," *Evening Star*, February 3, 1921; "Negro Recants Confession of Killing Nurse," *BS*, February 3, 1921.

49. "Naval Nurse's Slayer to Be Rushed to Trial," *BS*, January 21, 1921.

50. Rose's record as a public servant and noble reformer was relatively unimpeachable. Three years before Brown's trial, he oversaw a municipally sponsored and sweeping study on the causes of poverty in the city. See Alliance of Charitable and Social Agencies, *Poverty in Baltimore and Its Causes* (Baltimore: McCoy Hall, 1918), Urban Archives and Pamphlets Collection, Box 58, Folder 374–20, SCRC.

Notes to Chapter 5 • 223

51. Warner T. McGuinn, "The Late Federal Judge Rose Dared Smite Segregation," *BAA*, April 9, 1927.

52. "Brown Murder Trial Monday," *BS*, March 26, 1921; "Prepare Case against Alleged Nurse Slayer," *Evening Star*, March 27, 1921.

53. "A. W. Schnepfe Funeral Set," *BS*, October 28, 1969.

54. *Transcript*, 11–19, 122–23.

55. *Transcript*, 19–25, 45–63; quote on 266.

56. *Transcript*, 138–79.

57. *Transcript*, 140–43; quote on 141.

58. *Transcript*, 141.

59. *Transcript*, 175.

60. House, a key figure in the ordeal, accompanied Green on patrol duty the night of the murder. He had fallen ill and could not testify during the trial.

61. *Transcript*, 179–91; quote on 191.

62. *Transcript*, 140 ("Get it straight"), 193 ("For the purpose . . . ").

63. *Transcript*, 131; "Nurse's Slayer to Be Brought Here for Trial," *Evening Sun*, January 20, 1921.

64. *Transcript*, 133.

65. *Transcript*, 144–52.

66. *Transcript*, 228–54.

67. *Transcript*, 258–64.

68. "Negro Slayer of Navy Nurse Found Guilty," *BA*, March 29, 1921; "All White Jury Convicts Brown," *BAA*, April 1, 1921; "Nurse's Slayer to Hang," *BS*, April 2, 1921.

69. "The Police Department and Negroes," *BAA*, May 31, 1902; emphasis mine.

70. Murphy, *Jim Crow Capital*, 2–3.

71. 1860 U.S. Census, Marion County, Kentucky, Slave Schedule, 15, Phillip Cooper, Slave Owner, accessed via ancestry.com (January 11, 2023); 1870 U.S. Census, Jefferson County, Kentucky, Population Schedule, 32, 217 Two Mile House, Henry Dickerson, accessed via ancestry.com (January 11, 2023); 1880 U.S. Census, Saint Louis, Missouri, Population Schedule, Enumeration District No. 61, Sheet No. 8, 1015 Orchard Street, Laura F. Dickerson, accessed via ancestry.com (January 11, 2023); 1900 U.S. Census, Jefferson County, Kentucky, Population Schedule, Ward 10, Enumeration District No. 92, Sheet No. 13, 1202 Walnut Street, Laura Dickerson, accessed via ancestry.com (January 11, 2023); 1910 U.S. Census, Baltimore City, Maryland, Population Schedule, Ward 17, Enumeration District No. 292, Sheet No. 2, 1230 Druid Hill Avenue, Laura F. Wheatley, accessed via ancestry.com (January 11, 2023); 1920 U.S. Census, Baltimore City, Maryland, Population Schedule, Ward 17, Enumeration District No. 298, Sheet No. 5, 1230 Druid Hill Avenue, Laura F. Wheatley, accessed via ancestry.com (January 11, 2023).

72. Laura Wheatley, Letter to Mary White Ovington, November 5, 1920, NAACP, Branch Files, Series I, Box G-84, Folder 10, LOC; "The Deadly Parallel," *BAA*, November 12, 1920.

224 · *Notes to Chapter 5*

73. Laura Wheatley, Letter to James Weldon Johnson, July 8, 1921, NAACP, Legal Files, Series I, Box D-2, Folder 2, LOC.

74. Laura Wheatley, Letter to James Weldon Johnson, February 9, 1921, NAACP, Branch Files, Series I, Box G-84, Folder 11, LOC.

75. "Murderer Sought Mrs. Harding's Aid," *BA*, June 1, 1921.

76. Emma Truxon, Letter to O. E. Weller, May 18, 1921, Pardon Case Files, Box 940, NARA II.

77. Laura Wheatley, Letter to James Weldon Johnson, June 14, 1921, NAACP, Legal Files, Series I, Box D-2, Folder 2, LOC.

78. Henry A. Brown, Petition for Executive Clemency, May 30, 1921, Pardon Case Files, Box 940, NARA II; J. Steward Davis, Letter to Warren G. Harding, June 3, 1921, Pardon Case Files, Box 940, NARA II.

79. Laura Wheatley, Letter to Warren G. Harding, May 31, 1921, Pardon Case Files, Box 940, NARA II.

80. Zachariah Jackson, Affidavit, May 30, 1921, Pardon Case Files, Box 940, NARA II.

81. J. Steward Davis, Letter to Harry Daugherty, ND, Pardon Case Files, Box 940, NARA II; Annie Rhuebottom, Affidavit, June 10, 1921, Pardon Case Files, Box 940, NARA II; Rhoda Simms, Affidavit, June 10, 1921, Pardon Case Files, Box 940, NARA II.

82. "Negro within Shadow of Gallows Reprieved," *Evening Sun*, May 31, 1921.

83. "President Stays Hanging of Condemned Murderer," *BS*, June 1, 1921; "President Gives Brown Thirty Days Respite," *BAA*, June 3, 1921.

84. "Ignorance of Rights Wins Negro Reprieve," *Evening Sun*, June 30, 1921; "Brown Gets Second Respite," *BS*, June 30, 1921.

85. Laura Wheatley, Letter to James Weldon Johnson, June 14, 1921, NAACP, Legal Files, Series I, Box D-2, Folder 2, LOC.

86. Wells, *Light of Truth*.

87. Executions, Baltimore City Jail, Execution and Punishment Notes, MSA. This record is somewhat disorganized but broadly captures execution trends at the city jail where, until 1923, people sentenced to death were hanged. Given the city's penchant for removing cases to the county courts to mitigate bias, some high-profile executions were not recorded because the sentences were levied in Baltimore County, not Baltimore City. I have reintegrated some of these into the dataset, including the executions of James West, Howard Cooper, and John Devine. These men were all Black and accused of assaulting or murdering a white person—in Devine's case, a white police officer. "Gallows Scenes in Maryland," *BS*, August 23, 1873; "The Lynching of Howard Cooper," *BS*, July 14, 1885; "Devine Hanged at the City Jail," *Baltimore Herald*, September 20, 1902. For more on racialized execution trends in the South see Kotch, *Lethal State*.

88. "Hanging Brown," *BS*, July 10, 1921.

89. "Slayer of the Buffalo Nurse," *Buffalo Morning Express*, July 12, 1921.

Notes to Chapter 5 • 225

90. "A Stay of Execution," *BA*, June 2, 1921.

91. "A Ray of Hope," *Negro Star*, July 15, 1921.

92. "Fund Being Raised to Aid Negro Slayer," *BA*, July 12, 1921; "Colored People Meet to Save Henry Brown," *BS*, July 12, 1921.

93. Baltimore Branch of the NAACP, Constitution and By-Laws, July 15, 1915, NAACP, Branch Files, Series I, Box G-84, Folder 9, LOC.

94. NAACP, "The Branch Bulletin" 5:11 (December 1921), NAACP, Administrative Files, Series I, Box C440, LOC.

95. Laura Wheatley, Letter to James Weldon Johnson, August 1, 1921, NAACP, Legal Files, Series I, Box D-2, Folder 2, LOC.

96. "Ritchie Urges Action in Case of Murderer," *BA*, July 7, 1921; Albert C. Ritchie, Letter to Harry Daugherty, July 5, 1921, Pardon Case Files, Box 940, NARA II.

97. "People Resent Second Respite Granted Brown," *BS*, July 6, 1921; "An Unfortunate Delay," *Evening Sun*, July 6, 1921.

98. Harry Daugherty, Letter to Albert C. Ritchie, July 6, 1921, Pardon Case Files, Box 940, NARA II.

99. "U.S. Pardon Agent Seeks Third Stay for Negro Slayer," *BA*, July 28, 1921.

100. "U.S. for Care, Not Speed, in Brown Case," *BS*, July 7, 1921.

101. "Brown Likely to Get Additional Respite," *BS*, July 28, 1921.

102. "Brown's Third Respite Is Regarded as Certain," *BS*, July 29, 1921; "Brown Is Granted Respite by Harding," *BA*, July 30, 1921; "Reprieve Is Asked," *Evening Star*, July 30, 1921; "Respite Received for Brown," *BS*, July 31, 1921.

103. Albert C. Ritchie, Letter to Harry Daugherty, July 7, 1921, Pardon Case Files, Box 940, NARA II.

104. Laura Wheatley, Letter to James Weldon Johnson, August 1, 1921, NAACP, Legal Files, Series I, Box D-2, Folder 2, LOC; emphasis in original; Ritchie quote in "New Probe of Murder Case Governor Ritchie Opposes," *BA*, July 8, 1921.

105. "Linthicum Submits New Data in Brown Case to U.S. Agents," *BA*, August 5, 1921; J. Charles Linthicum, Letter to James A. Finch, August 1, 1921, Pardon Case Files, Box 940, NARA II; Laura Wheatley, Letter to J. Charles Linthicum, August 31, 1921, Pardon Case Files, Box 940, NARA II.

106. J. Charles Linthicum, Letter to James A. Finch, August 1, 1921, Pardon Case Files, Box 940, NARA II.

107. "Linthicum Letter Brings out Protest," *Evening Sun*, August 5, 1921.

108. Strauss, a Democrat, did write a letter. After his review, Strauss believed that the compelled confession should have been thrown out and that Rose made a grave error keeping the confession Brown made before the board of inquiry since Brown was still obviously shaken from the abuse he received. Isaac Lobe Strauss, Letter to Harry Daugherty, August 8, 1921, Pardon Case Files, Box 940, NARA II.

109. "Henry Brown's Counsel Disclaims Any Responsibility for Asking Congressman Linthicum's Political Influence to Aid the Convicted Negro Murderer," *Evening Sun*, August 8, 1921; "Brown's Counsel Denounces Mrs. Wheatley's Acts," *BAA*, August

226 • *Notes to Chapter 5*

12, 1921; J. Steward Davis, Letter to James Finch, August 6, 1921, Pardon Case Files, Box 940, NARA II.

110. James Weldon Johnson, Letter to Laura Wheatley, August 10, 1921, NAACP, Branch Files, Series I, Box G-84, Folder 11, LOC.

111. James A. Finch, Report of the Pardon Attorney on Application for Pardon of Henry A. Brown, August 8, 1921, Pardon Case Files, Box 940, NARA II (hereafter *Finch Report*); "Report on Brown Case Filed," *BS*, August 13, 1921.

112. Laura Wheatley, Letter to James A. Finch, July 6, 1921, Pardon Case Files, Box 940, NARA II; emphasis in original.

113. *Finch Report*, 39.

114. *Finch Report*, 19–23.

115. *Finch Report*, 34.

116. Sadie Bolden, Affidavit, August 8, 1921, Pardon Case Files, Box 940, NARA II; John T. Bolden, Affidavit, August 8, 1921, Pardon Case Files, Box 940, NARA II.

117. *Finch Report*, 39.

118. *Finch Report*, 47.

119. *Finch Report*, 47.

120. *Finch Report*, 48.

121. Harry Daugherty, Report of Attorney General, August 20, 1921, Pardon Case Files, Box 940, NARA II, 2.

122. Harry Daugherty, Report of Attorney General, August 20, 1921, Pardon Case Files, Box 940, NARA II, 11; emphasis mine.

123. "Harding Denies Pardon Appeal Filed by Brown," *BS*, August 21, 1921.

124. "President Refuses to Halt Sentence," *BA*, August 21, 1921.

125. "Brown Tells a Reporter—'I Am Innocent,'" *BAA*, August 26, 1921.

126. "Brown Hears Fate without Comment," *BA*, August 23, 1921.

127. Laura Wheatley, Letter to James Weldon Johnson, August 23, 1921, NAACP, Branch Files, Series I, Box G-84, Folder 11, LOC.

128. Laura Wheatley, Letter to James Weldon Johnson, August 23, 1921, NAACP, Branch Files, Series I, Box G-84, Folder 11, LOC.

129. NAACP, Minutes, February 14, 1921, NAACP, Board of Directors Reports, Series I, Box A-15, Folder 2, LOC; NAACP, Minutes, April 7, 1921, NAACP, Board of Directors Reports, Series I, Box A-15, Folder 2, LOC.

130. Peter Corosh, Affidavit, ND, Pardon Case Files, Box 940, NARA II.

131. Laura Wheatley, Emma Truxon, and Boston Allen, Letter to the NAACP, August 23, 1921, NAACP, Branch Files, Series I, Box G-84, Folder 11, LOC.

132. James Weldon Johnson, Letter to Laura Wheatley, September 10, 1921, NAACP, Branch Files, Series I, Box G-84, Folder 11, LOC.

133. James Weldon Johnson, Letter to Harry Daugherty, September 10, 1921, NAACP, Branch Files, Series I, Box G-84, Folder 11, LOC.

134. Henry A. Brown, Letter to Warren G. Harding, August 28, 1921, Pardon Case Files, Box 940, NARA II

Notes to Chapters 5 and 6 • 227

135. "Dies Protesting Innocence," *BS*, September 2, 1921; block quote from "Brown Dies on Gallows," *BA*, September 2, 1921.

136. Niedermeier, *Color of the Third Degree*, 10.

Chapter 6. "Policemen Were the Biggest Liars"

1. "N. W. Police Cursed and Insulted Her, Girl Says," *BAA*, March 9, 1929.

2. BPCCB, 1929, RG 68, Box 28, 34, BCA.

3. For more on the growth of Black West Baltimore, see Orser, *Blockbusting*.

4. For more on residential segregation in Baltimore, see Power, "Apartheid."

5. Hernández, *City of Inmates*, 4.

6. The degree to which police during the 1920s violated the sanctity of Black homes expanded on the city's policing conventions. As Adam Malka has demonstrated, cops and the criminal court often protected Black householders in antebellum Baltimore. Both institutions sought to uphold and promote the patriarchal liberal values associated with homeownership. Malka, *Men of Mobtown*, 124–38. However, as Gordon Shufelt has detailed, Black privacy came under the scrutiny of police upon their organization in 1857 as they relied on city ordinances to exercise "legally authorized intrusions into the private lives of African Americans." Shufelt, *Uncommon Case*, 19. The 1920s saw a blatant disregard for Black homesteads and Black privacy as the intimacy of sex, sociality, and even homeownership itself became subject to police scrutiny.

7. Shabazz, *Spatializing Blackness*, 26–27.

8. Pietila, *Ghosts of Johns Hopkins*, 180.

9. Johnson, *Street Justice*, 133–42.

10. Arnold, "Suburban Growth," 117–25.

11. Walsh, *Baltimore Prohibition*, 60–61.

12. Farrar, *Baltimore Afro-American*, xv.

13. General Assembly of Maryland, Chapter 15, 1900, 11–13, Session Laws, MSA.

14. "To Fix Police Control," *BS*, November 21, 1919.

15. General Assembly of Maryland, Chapter 559, 1920, 1146–47, Session Laws, MSA; "One-Man Board June 1," *BS*, April 1, 1920.

16. "One-Man Board June 1," *BS*, April 1, 1920.

17. "Police Change Feared," *BS*, November 22, 1919.

18. "Question of Police Control," *BS*, October 1, 1920.

19. General Assembly of Maryland, Chapter 113, 1920, 183–84, Session Laws, MSA.

20. "Returns in Baltimore City," *BS*, November 3, 1920.

21. "Gen. Gaither Chosen Police Commissioner," *BS*, May 24, 1920; Guariglia, *Police and the Empire City*, 73; Seigel, *Violence Work*, 52–58.

22. General Assembly of Maryland, Chapter 429, 1920, 730–31, Session Laws, MSA.

23. BPCCB, 1920, RG 68, Box 27, 12–13, BCA; BPCP, 1920–21, Baltimore City Police Department, Box 7, Vol. 59, 203, 224, 258, 326, 339, and 340, MSA.

24. BPCP, 1923–25, Baltimore City Police Department, Box 8, Vol. 63, 493, MSA.

228 • *Notes to Chapter 6*

25. In 1921, the total police force numbered 1,359. In 1929, it numbered 1,893. BPCCB, 1921, 9; BPCCB, 1929, RG 68, Box 28, 12, BCA.

26. Statistics compiled from BPCCB, 1920–29, RG 68, Boxes 27–28, BCA.

27. "Gaither Backs Up McLain," *BAA*, July 23, 1920.

28. BPCP, 1921–22, Baltimore City Police Department, Box 8, Vol. 60, 96, MSA; "Cop Sought Social Equality after Dark," *BAA*, July 22, 1921.

29. "Police Used Club on Woman's Head," *BAA*, October 17, 1925.

30. "Raise Protest over Police Brutality," *BAA*, April 30, 1927; "Light Fine for Cop Who Used Nightstick," *BAA*, May 14, 1927.

31. BPCP, 1920–21, Baltimore City Police Department, Box 7, Vol. 59, 317, MSA.

32. BPCP, 1921–22, Baltimore City Police Department, Box 8, Vol. 60, 298, MSA.

33. "Cowardly Whites Stone His Home," *BAA*, January 17, 1925. Brandon T. Jett has detailed how such a request was relatively common among Southern police departments. Because police were abysmal at solving crimes, Black people often took it upon themselves to investigate crimes for which they desired police redress. Jett, *Race, Crime, and Policing*, 126.

34. "Says Police Invaded Sanctity of Home," *BAA*, April 18, 1925.

35. Fischer, *Streets Belong to Us*, 27; Mumford, *Interzones*, 17.

36. William N. Jones, "Day by Day," *BAA*, April 13, 1923.

37. William N. Jones, "Day by Day," *BAA*, April 13, 1923.

38. Innumerable studies have detailed the role of sexuality in shaping broader social agendas of the early twentieth century, including Blair, *I've Got to Make My Livin'*; Gilfoyle, *City of Eros*; Harris, *Sex Workers*; Hicks, *Talk with You*; Mumford, *Interzones*; Pliley, *Policing Sexuality*.

39. Fischer, *Streets Belong to Us*, 5.

40. 1920 U.S. Census, Baltimore City, Maryland, Population Schedule, Ward 17, Enumeration District No. 295, Sheet No. 4, 1038 Pennsylvania Avenue, James White, accessed via ancestry.com (January 11, 2023).

41. "Arrests Dentist and Companion Whom He Thot to Be 'White,'" *BAA*, August 8, 1925.

42. "271 Policeman to Get Medals for Services," *BS*, December 29, 1924.

43. "Arrests Dentist and Companion Whom He Thot to Be 'White,'" *BAA*, August 8, 1925.

44. "Arrests Dentist and Companion Whom He Thot to Be 'White,'" *BAA*, August 8, 1925.

45. "Police Hearing Awaits Return of Gaither," *BAA*, August 15, 1925.

46. "Police Hearing Awaits Return of Gaither," *BAA*, August 15, 1925.

47. "Police Hearing Awaits Return of Gaither," *BAA*, August 15, 1925.

48. "Police Hearing Awaits Return of Gaither," *BAA*, August 15, 1925.

49. "Brutality of the Police," *BAA*, August 15, 1925.

50. "Nothing to Be Done Says Gen. Gaither," *BAA*, August 22, 1925.

51. "Nothing to Be Done Says Gen. Gaither," *BAA*, August 22, 1925.

Notes to Chapter 6 · 229

52. William Jones, "Day by Day," *BAA*, August 29, 1925; emphasis in original; "Police Law," *BAA*, August 29, 1925.

53. "Gaither and N. W. Police Are Scored," *BAA*, August 29, 1925.

54. BPCCB, 1925, RG 68, Box 28, 39, BCA.

55. Terry, *Struggle*, 87.

56. 1880 U.S. Census, Baltimore City, Maryland, Population Schedule, Ward 5, Enumeration District No. 45, Page No. 10, 34 Little McElderry Street, Charles E. Williams, accessed via ancestry.com (January 11, 2023); Bromley and Bromley, *Atlas*, 1887, Plate 9, BCA.

57. 1910 U.S. Census, Baltimore City, Maryland, Population Schedule, Ward 5, Enumeration District No. 54, Sheet No. 1, 502 North Eden Street, Charles E. Williams, accessed via ancestry.com (January 11, 2023).

58. Olson, *Baltimore*, 324–28.

59. Fairbanks and Hamill, *Statistical Analysis*, 110–11.

60. Fairbanks and Hamill, *Statistical Analysis*, 116.

61. Bromley and Bromley, *Atlas*, 1906, Plate 1, BCA; Charles E. Williams, Baltimore City Directory, 1914, 2079.

62. For more on the social and economic history of alley housing in Baltimore, see Hayward, *Baltimore's Alley Houses*.

63. Bromley and Bromley, *Atlas*, 1906, Plate 7, BCA.

64. For more on these racial zoning ordinances, see Power, "Apartheid"; Connolly, *A World More Concrete*, 39; Terry, *Struggle*, 34–37.

65. "Strong for West Plan," *BS*, October 11, 1910.

66. Halpin, *Brotherhood of Liberty*, chap. 6.

67. "Negro Homes Stoned; Four Persons Hurt," *BS*, September 26, 1913.

68. "One Shot; One Stabbed," *BS*, September 27, 1913.

69. 1900 U.S. Census, Baltimore City, Maryland, Population Schedule, Ward 7, Enumeration District No. 92, Sheet No. 2, 126 North Castle Street, Urban Family, accessed via ancestry.com (January 11, 2023).

70. Baltimore City Superior Court, Block Book, Joseph and Mary Musel and Anton and Josephine Urban, Deed Assignment, May 1, 1888, 104; Baltimore City Superior Court, Block Book, Anton and Josephine Urban and Joseph and Mary Musel, Mortgage, May 1, 1888, 104, MSA; Baltimore City Superior Court, Block Book, Joseph and Mary Musel and Anton and Josephine Urban, Mortgage Release, September 10, 1890, 106, MSA.

71. 1910 U.S. Census, Baltimore City, Maryland, Population Schedule, Ward 6, Enumeration District No. 62, Sheet No. 7, 126 North Castle Street, Charles F. Urban, accessed via ancestry.com (January 11, 2023).

72. 1920 U.S. Census, Baltimore City, Maryland, Population Schedule, Ward 7, Enumeration District No. 93, Sheet No. 8, 914 North Port Street, Charles F. and Mary Urban, accessed via ancestry.com (January 11, 2023).

73. Joseph Marsalek, Baltimore City Directory, 1909, 1346.

230 · *Notes to Chapter 6*

74. "Race Question Injected into Trial of White Policeman," *BAA*, December 8, 1922.

75. For more on the expectations of deference held by Baltimore police, see Terry, *Struggle*, 86–96.

76. "Negro Killed in Own House by Policeman," *BS*, October 24, 1921.

77. "Negro Killed in Own House by Policeman," *BS*, October 24, 1921; "Race Question Injected into Trial of White Policeman," *BAA*, December 8, 1922.

78. "Extra!!!! Police Kill Two in Their Own Homes," *BAA*, October 28, 1921.

79. Baltimore City Superior Court, Block Book, Goetze Building and Loan Association to Bessie Williams, Deed Assignment, July 25, 1922, 72, MSA; Baltimore City Superior Court, Block Book, Bessie Williams to Louis Levin, Deed Assignment, October 16, 1922, 73, MSA.

80. "Sues Husband's Slayer to Be Tried for Murder," *BS*, November 28, 1922; "Suits Filed," *BS*, November 28, 1922.

81. Rohleder served as the presiding magistrate over James White's ordeal, too.

82. For more on coroner's inquests, see Friedman, *Crime and Punishment*, 208–9; Shufelt, *Uncommon Case*, chap. 3.

83. "Accused Patrolman on Duty," *BS*, October 25, 1921; "Coroner Holds Policeman for Causing Negro's Death," *BS*, October 28, 1921; "Urban Released on Bail," *BS*, October 29, 1921; "Patrolman Urban Indicted," *BS*, November 16, 1921; "Charles F. Urban," Baltimore City Criminal Court, Criminal Papers, Box 207, MSA.

84. *State of Maryland vs. Charles F. Urban*, Baltimore City Criminal Court Dockets, 652, MSA.

85. "Question of Police Control," *BAA*, October 1, 1920; "Cop Sought Social Equality after Dark," *BAA*, July 22, 1921.

86. BPCP, 1921–22, Baltimore City Police Department, Box 8, Vol. 60, 106, MSA.

87. "Shake-Up Hits High Official among Police," *BS*, February 18, 1922; "6 Killed by Policemen since September," *BS*, March 19, 1922.

88. "Urban Gets Change of Venue," *BS*, June 9, 1922.

89. *State of Maryland vs. Charles F. Urban*, Baltimore County Criminal Docket, Removals, 104, MSA.

90. "Witness for Urban Tells of Threats," *BS*, November 29, 1922.

91. "Race Question Injected into Trial of White Policeman," *BAA*, December 8, 1922.

92. Adam Malka persuasively argues that this authority ungirded the emergence of Baltimore's nascent police state in the antebellum period. Malka, *Men of Mobtown*.

93. "Race Question Injected into Trial of White Policeman," *BAA*, December 8, 1922.

94. "Race Question Injected into Trial of White Policeman," *BAA*, December 8, 1922.

95. Mary E. Pollheim, "Criticizes Mr. Gaither," *BS*, December 4, 1922.

96. "Gaither Explains Department's Action in the Urban Case," *BAA*, December 22, 1922.

97. *State of Maryland vs. Charles F. Urban*, Baltimore County Criminal Docket, Removals, 104, MSA; "Urban Found Guilty of Killing Negro," *BS*, November 30, 1922; "The Urban Case," *BAA*, December 8, 1922.

Notes to Chapter 6 and Conclusion • 231

98. "Ritchie Gives Stays in Two Sentences," *BS*, December 20, 1924.
99. BPCP, 1922–23, Baltimore City Police Department, Box 8, Vol. 62, 34, MSA.
100. William N. Jones, "Day by Day," December 20, 1924.

Conclusion

1. "If We Are Children We Ought to Be Treated like Children," *BAA*, March 20, 1909.
2. "Tuskegee Celebrates," *BS*, April 5, 1906.
3. "Another Prophet Has Arisen in Israel," *BAA*, March 13, 1909.
4. Between 1905 and 1911, the General Assembly put forth several plans to disenfranchise Black voters. These efforts were ultimately defeated through a combination of Black advocacy and fears that literacy requirements and grandfather clauses would inhibit foreign-born whites from participating in elections. Crenson, *Baltimore*, 336–40; Halpin, *Brotherhood of Liberty*, chap. 5.
5. "Quiet Region of Homes, and Later a Resort of Bad Men, 'The Pot' Is Now the Center of the Cocaine Trade," *BS*, May 31, 1908.
6. "If We Are Children We Ought to Be Treated like Children," *BAA*, March 20, 1909; emphasis mine.
7. Ogbar, *America's Black Capital*, 4–5.
8. NT, *BAA*, February 15, 1896.
9. Board of School Commissioners, Annual Report, 1903–1908, RG 31, Boxes 4 and 5, BCA.
10. Board of School Commissioners, Minutes, September 24, 1913, Box 1, 285, BCA.
11. "Women on Police Force," *BS*, June 20, 1912.
12. Malka, *Men of Mobtown*, 235–45.
13. "The Police Board," *BS*, October 29, 1901.
14. CJR, 1901, RG 29, Box 39, 23, BCA. See figure 1 for more on racialized rates of incarceration.
15. *Rossberg Indictment*.
16. BPCCB, 1929, RG 68, Box 28, 34, BCA.

Bibliography

Archives and Manuscript Collections

ALBIN O. KUHN LIBRARY SPECIAL COLLECTIONS, UNIVERSITY OF MARYLAND, BALTIMORE COUNTY, CATONSVILLE, MARYLAND

Joseph L. Arnold Papers, 1970–2003

BALTIMORE CITY ARCHIVES, BALTIMORE, MARYLAND

Agency Reports and Publications
Baltimore City Jail
Cartographic Records
City Ordinances and Proceedings of the City Council
Department of Education
Department of Legislative Reference
Minutes, Trustees of the Poor for Baltimore City and County

ENOCH PRATT FREE LIBRARY, BALTIMORE, MARYLAND

Periodicals Department

LIBRARY OF CONGRESS, WASHINGTON, D.C.

Charles J. Bonaparte Papers, 1760–1921
Harry S. Cummings Papers, 1890–1916
National Association for the Advancement of Colored People Records, 1842–1999
Newspapers and Current Periodicals

234 · *Bibliography*

MARYLAND STATE ARCHIVES, ANNAPOLIS, MARYLAND

Baltimore City Courts, Petitions of Inebriates
Baltimore City Jail, Proceedings of Visitors
Baltimore City Criminal Court, Criminal Papers
Baltimore City Criminal Court Dockets
Baltimore City Jail Execution and Punishment Notes
Baltimore City Jail Runaway Docket
Baltimore City Police Department Criminal Record
Baltimore County Criminal Docket, Removals
Board of Police Commissioner Proceedings
Codes, Compilation of Laws, Rules and Regulations
Maryland Land Records
Police Casualties
Police Commissioner Reports
Session Laws

MARYLAND CENTER FOR HISTORY AND CULTURE, BALTIMORE, MARYLAND

Hughes Collection, 1910–46
Sherlock Swann Papers, 1884–1924

NATIONAL ARCHIVES AND RECORDS ADMINISTRATION, WASHINGTON, D.C.

United States Census Records

NATIONAL ARCHIVES AT COLLEGE PARK, COLLEGE PARK, MARYLAND

Records of the Office of the Pardon Attorney

NATIONAL ARCHIVES AT PHILADELPHIA, PHILADELPHIA, PENNSYLVANIA

Records of U.S. District and Other Courts in Maryland, 1790–1972

TEMPLE UNIVERSITY SPECIAL COLLECTIONS RESEARCH CENTER, PHILADELPHIA,
PENNSYLVANIA

Charles L. Blockson Afro-American Collection
Free Library of Philadelphia Pamphlets Collection
Urban Archives and Pamphlets Collection

UNIVERSITY OF MARYLAND, COLLEGE PARK SPECIAL COLLECTIONS, COLLEGE PARK, MARYLAND

Baltimore City Directories
Maryland Manuscripts Collections
University Libraries

Newspapers and Periodicals

American Journal of Insanity
Baltimore Afro-American

Baltimore American
Baltimore American and Commercial Advertiser
Baltimore Bee
Baltimore Evening Sun
Baltimore Morning Herald
Baltimore Sun
Baltimore Sunday Herald
Buffalo Morning Express
Charities
Charities Record
Chicago Defender
Evening Star (Washington, D.C.)
Journal of Nervous and Mental Disease
National Police Journal
Negro Star (Wichita, Kansas)
New York Times
Saturday Evening Post
Scientific American
St. Louis Post-Dispatch
The Century
The Nation
Washington Post
Washington Times

Online Archives

Ancestry (ancestry.com)
HathiTrust Digital Library (hathitrust.org)
Internet Archive (archive.org)

Published Primary Sources

Benson, William E. "Kowaliga: A Community with a Purpose: What One Alabama Town Is Doing to Counteract the Movement of Negroes from Country to City." *Charities* 15, no. 1 (1905): 22–24.

Bishop, Joseph B. *Charles Joseph Bonaparte, His Life and Public Services.* New York: Scribner's, 1922.

Black, Henry C. *Black's Law Dictionary: Definitions of the Terms and Phrases of American and English Jurisprudence, Ancient and Modern.* Saint Paul: West Publishing, 1968.

Bromley, George W., and Walter S. Bromley. *Atlas of the City of Baltimore, Maryland.* Philadelphia: Bromley, 1887.

Bromley, George W., and Walter S. Bromley. *Atlas of the City of Baltimore, Maryland.* Philadelphia: Bromley, 1906.

Bruce, William C. *The Negro Problem.* Baltimore: John Murphy, 1891.

236 · Bibliography

Bucknill, John. *Notes on Asylums for the Insane in America.* London: Churchill, 1876.

Byrnes, Thomas. *Professional Criminals of America.* New York: Press of Hunter & Beach, 1886.

Folsom, De Francias. *Our Police: A History of the Baltimore Force from the First Watchman to the Latest Appointee.* Baltimore: Ehlers & Co. and Guggenheimer, Weil, & Co., 1888.

Hall, Clayton C. *Baltimore: Its History and Its People, Volume I—History.* New York: Lewis Historical Publishing, 1912.

Hall, Clayton C. *Baltimore: Its History and Its People, Volume II—Biography.* New York: Lewis Historical Publishing, 1912.

Hall, Clayton C. *Baltimore: Its History and Its People, Volume III—Biography.* New York: Lewis Historical Publishing, 1912.

Hurd, Henry M. "Race and Insanity." *Journal of Nervous and Mental Disease* 12, no. 2 (1885): 241–42.

Hurd, Henry M. *The Institutional Care of the Insane in the United States and Canada.* Baltimore: Johns Hopkins University Press, 1916.

Goldman, Eric F. *Charles J. Bonaparte, Patrician Reformer: His Earlier Career.* Baltimore: Johns Hopkins University Press, 1943.

Griffith, G. S. *Report on the Penal and Reformatory Institutions of the State of Maryland Made to the International Penitentiary Congress of London.* London: Spottiswoode, 1872.

Johnson, Harvey. *The Question of Race: A Reply to W. Cabell Bruce, Esq.* Baltimore: Printing Office of J. F. Weishampel, 1891.

Kemp, Janet. *Housing Conditions in Baltimore: Report of a Special Committee.* Baltimore: Federated Charities, 1907.

Kent, Frank R. *The Story of Maryland Politics.* Baltimore: Thomas and Evans Printing, 1911.

Lombroso, Cesare. *Criminal Man.* New York: Putman, 1911.

Lombroso, Cesare, and William Ferrero. *The Female Offender.* New York: Appleton, 1898.

McCabe, Clinton. *History of the Baltimore Police Department, 1774–1907.* Baltimore: Fleet-McGinley, 1907.

M'Cullough, Hiram, and Otho Scott, eds. *The Maryland Code: Public General Laws and Public Local Laws.* Baltimore: John Murphy, 1860.

Mencken, H. L. *The Days Trilogy.* Exp. ed. New York: Library of America, 2014.

National Commission on Law Observance and Enforcement. *Report on Lawlessness in Law Enforcement.* Washington, D.C.: U.S. Government Printing Office, 1931.

Pendleton, Helen. "Negro Dependence in Baltimore." *Charities* 15, no. 1 (1905): 50–58.

Poe, John P. *Supplement to the Code of Public General Laws of Maryland, Containing the Public General Laws Passed at the Sessions of the General Assembly of 1890, 1892, 1894, 1896, 1898.* Baltimore: King, 1898.

Poe, John P. *The Maryland Code.* Baltimore: King, 1904.

Poe, John P. *The Maryland Code, Public Local Laws.* Baltimore: King, 1888.

Richmond, Mary. *The Long View.* Philadelphia: Russell Sage Foundation, 1930.

Vexler, Robert I. *Baltimore: A Chronological and Documentary History.* Dobbs Ferry: Oceana Publications, 1975.

Bibliography • 237

Waring, J. H. N. "Some Causes of Criminality." *Charities* 15, no. 1 (1905): 45–49.
Waring, J. H. N. *Work of the Colored Law and Order League: Baltimore, Md.* Cheyney, PA: Committee of Twelve for the Advancement of the Interests of the Negro Race, 1908.
Weeks, Henry W., ed. *The New Charter of Baltimore City, Enacted by the Acts of 1898, Ch. 123.* Baltimore: Baltimore City Printing and Binding, 1923.

Secondary Sources

Adler, Jeffrey S. *Bluecoated Terror: Jim Crow New Orleans and the Roots of Modern Police Brutality.* Los Angeles: University of California Press, 2024.
Adler, Jeffrey S. *First in Violence, Deepest in Dirt: Homicide in Chicago.* Cambridge, MA: Harvard University Press, 2006.
Adler, Jeffrey S. *Murder in New Orleans: The Creation of Jim Crow Policing.* Chicago: University of Chicago Press, 2019.
Agee, Christopher L. *The Streets of San Francisco: Policing and the Creation of a Cosmopolitan Liberal Politics, 1950–1972.* Chicago: University of Chicago Press, 2014.
Agyepong, Tera Eva. *The Criminalization of Black Children: Race, Gender, and Delinquency in Chicago's Juvenile Justice System, 1899–1945.* Chapel Hill: University of North Carolina Press, 2018.
Alexander, Michelle. *The New Jim Crow: Mass Incarceration in the Age of Colorblindness.* New York: New Press, 2010.
Althusser, Louis. *On the Reproduction of Capitalism: Ideology and Ideological State Apparatuses.* New York: Verso, 1970.
Anderson, Benedict. *Imagined Communities: Reflections on the Origin and Spread of Nationalism.* Rev. ed. New York: Verso, 2006.
Argersinger, Jo Ann E. *Toward a New Deal in Baltimore: People and Government in the Great Depression.* Chapel Hill: University of North Carolina Press, 1988.
Arnold, Joseph L. *History of Baltimore, 1729–1920.* Baltimore: University of Maryland, Baltimore County, 2015, unfinished manuscript.
Arnold, Joseph L. "Suburban Growth and Municipal Annexation in Baltimore, 1745–1918." *Maryland Historical Magazine* 73, no. 2 (1978): 109–28.
Ayers, Edward L. *Vengeance and Justice: Crime and Punishment in the 19th-Century American South.* Oxford: Oxford University Press, 1984.
Baldwin, Davarian L. *Chicago's New Negroes: Modernity, the Great Migration, and Black Urban Life.* Chapel Hill: University of North Carolina Press, 2007.
Baldwin, Peter C. *In the Watches of the Night: Life in the Nocturnal City, 1820–1930.* Chicago: University of Chicago Press, 2012.
Balto, Simon. *Occupied Territory: Policing Black Chicago from Red Summer to Black Power.* Chapel Hill: University of North Carolina Press, 2019.
Barclay, Jennifer. *The Mark of Slavery: Disability, Race, and Gender in Antebellum America.* Urbana: University of Illinois Press, 2021.
Bardes, John K. *The Carceral City: Slavery and the Making of Mass Incarceration in New Orleans, 1803–1930.* Chapel Hill: University of North Carolina Press, 2024.

238 · Bibliography

Bardes, John K., and K. Stephen Prince. "'There Is No God in Heaven': Black Religion, Resistance, and the Police Power in Jim Crow New Orleans." *Journal of African American History* 108, no. 2 (2023): 220–43.

Barron, Cynthia K. "History of the Chicago Parental School, 1902–1975." PhD diss., Loyola University Chicago, 1993.

Baum, Howell S. *Brown in Baltimore: School Desegregation and the Limits of Liberalism.* Ithaca: Cornell University Press, 2010.

Beckert, Sven. *The Monied Metropolis: New York City and the Consolidation of the American Bourgeoisie, 1850–1896.* Cambridge: Cambridge University Press, 2001.

Beisel, Nicola K. *Imperiled Innocents: Anthony Comstock and Family Reproduction in Victorian America.* Princeton: Princeton University Press, 1998.

Berg, Manfred. *"The Ticket to Freedom": The NAACP and the Struggle for Black Political Integration.* Gainesville: University Press of Florida, 2005.

Blair, Cynthia M. *I've Got to Make My Livin': Black Women's Sex Work in Turn-of-the-Century Chicago.* Chicago: University of Chicago Press, 2010.

Bolin, James D. *Bossism and Reform in a Southern City: Lexington, Kentucky, 1880–1940.* Lexington: University Press of Kentucky, 2000.

Boyer, Paul. *Urban Masses and Moral Order in America, 1820–1920.* Cambridge, MA: Harvard University Press, 1978.

Brands, H. W. *American Colossus: The Triumph of Capitalism, 1865–1900.* New York: Anchor, 2010.

Brands, H. W. *The Reckless Decade: America in the 1890s.* Chicago: University of Chicago Press, 1995.

Brooks, Emily. *Gotham's War within a War: Policing and the Birth of Law-and-Order Liberalism in World War II–Era New York City.* Chapel Hill: University of North Carolina Press, 2023.

Brown, Elsa B. "Woman Consciousness: Maggie Lena Walker and the Independent Order of Saint Luke." *Signs* 14, no. 1 (1989): 186–87.

Brown, Elsa B. "'What Has Happened Here': The Politics of Difference in Women's History and Feminist Politics." *Feminist Studies* 18, no. 2 (1992): 295–312.

Brown, Lawrence T. *The Black Butterfly: The Harmful Politics of Race and Space in America.* Baltimore: Johns Hopkins University Press, 2021.

Browne, Gary L. *Baltimore in the Nation, 1789–1861.* Chapel Hill: University of North Carolina Press, 1980.

Browne, Simone. *Dark Matters: On the Surveillance of Blackness.* Durham, NC: Duke University Press, 2015.

Brugger, Robert J. *Maryland: A Middle Temperament, 1634–1980.* Baltimore: Johns Hopkins University Press, 1988.

Burns, Rebecca. *Rage in the Gate City: The Story of the 1906 Atlanta Race Riot.* Rev. ed. Athens: University of Georgia Press, 2009.

Carby, Hazel V. "Policing the Black Woman's Body in an Urban Context." *Critical Inquiry* 18, no. 4 (1992): 738–55.

Bibliography · 239

Clark-Lewis, Elizabeth. *Living in, Living Out: African American Domestics in Washington, D.C., 1910–1940.* Washington, D.C.: Smithsonian Books, 2010.

Clement, Priscilla F. "Nineteenth-Century Welfare Policy, Programs, and Poor Women: Philadelphia as a Case Study." *Feminist Studies* 18, no. 1 (1992): 35–58.

Cohen, Andrew W. *Contraband: Smuggling and the Birth of the American Century.* New York: Norton, 2015.

Cohen, Nancy. *The Reconstruction of American Liberalism, 1865–1914.* Chapel Hill: University of North Carolina Press, 2002.

Cole, Simon. *Suspect Identities: A History of Fingerprinting and Criminal Identification.* Cambridge, MA: Harvard University Press, 2002.

Collins, Patricia H. *Black Feminist Thought: Knowledge, Consciousness, and the Politics of Empowerment.* London: Routledge, 2000.

Connolly, N. D. B. *A World More Concrete: Real Estate and the Remaking of Jim Crow South Florida.* Chicago: University of Chicago Press, 2014.

Crenson, Matthew A. *Baltimore: A Political History.* Baltimore: Johns Hopkins University Press, 2019.

Crooks, James B. *Politics & Progress: The Rise of Urban Progressivism in Baltimore, 1895 to 1911.* Baton Rouge: Louisiana State University Press, 1968.

Crowe, Charles. "Racial Violence and Social Reform: Origins of the Atlanta Riot of 1906." *Journal of Negro History* 53, no. 3 (1968): 234–56.

Curtin, Mary E. *Black Prisoners and Their World, Alabama, 1865–1900.* Charlottesville: University of Virginia Press, 2000.

Czitrom, Daniel. *New York Exposed: The Gilded Age Police Scandal that Launched the Progressive Era.* Oxford: Oxford University Press, 2016.

Davis, Angela Y. *Are Prisons Obsolete?* New York: Seven Stories Press, 2003.

De Santis, Vincent P. *The Shaping of Modern America, 1877–1920.* 3rd ed. Wheeling, IL: Harlan Davidson, 2000.

Delany, David. *Race, Place, and the Law, 1836–1948.* Austin: University of Texas Press, 1998.

Deleuze, Gilles, and Félix Guattari. *A Thousand Plateaus: Capitalism and Schizophrenia.* Minneapolis: University of Minnesota Press, 1987.

Deleuze, Gilles, and Félix Guattari. *Anti-Oedipus: Capitalism and Schizophrenia.* New York: Penguin, 1972.

Dirkson, Menika B. *Hope and Struggle in the Policed City: Black Criminalization and Resistance in Philadelphia.* New York: New York University Press, 2024.

Dorr, Linda L. *White Women, Rape, and the Power of Race in Virginia, 1900–1960.* Chapel Hill: University of North Carolina Press, 2004.

Drake, St. Clair, and Horace R. Clayton. *Black Metropolis: A Study of Negro Life in a Northern City.* Chicago: University of Chicago Press, 1945.

Dubber, Markus D. *The Police Power: Patriarchy and the Foundations of American Government.* New York: Columbia University Press, 2005.

DuBois, W. E. B. *Black Reconstruction in America, 1860–1880.* New York: Free Press, 1935.

240 · *Bibliography*

DuBois, W. E. B. *The Philadelphia Negro: A Social Study.* Philadelphia: University of Pennsylvania Press, 1899.

DuBois, W. E. B. "The Shape of Fear." *North American Review* 223, no. 831 (1926): 291–304.

DuBois, W. E. B. *The Souls of Black Folks: Essays and Sketches.* Chicago: McClurg, 1903.

Elfenbein, Jessica, John R. Breihan, and Thomas L. Hollowak, eds. *From Mobtown to Charm City: New Perspectives on Baltimore's Past.* Baltimore: Maryland Historical Society, 2002.

Elfenbein, Jessica, Thomas J. Hollowak, and Elizabeth M. Nix, eds. *Baltimore '68: Riots and Rebirth in an American City.* Philadelphia: Temple University Press, 2011.

Ezratty, Harry A. *Baltimore in the Civil War: The Pratt Street Riot and a City Occupied.* Charleston, SC: History Press, 2010.

Fairbanks, W. L., and W. S. Hamill. *A Statistical Analysis of the Population of Maryland.* Baltimore: Maryland Development Bureau of the Baltimore Association of Commerce, 1931.

Farrar, Hayward. *The Baltimore Afro-American, 1892–1950.* Westport, CT: Greenwood, 1998.

Fee, Elizabeth, Linda Shopes, and Linda Zeidman, eds. *The Baltimore Book: New Views of Local History.* Philadelphia: Temple University Press, 1991.

Felker-Kantor, Max. *Policing Los Angeles: Race, Resistance, and the Rise of the LAPD.* Chapel Hill: University of North Carolina Press, 2018.

Fernández-Kelly, Patricia. *The Hero's Fight: African Americans in West Baltimore and the Shadow of the State.* Princeton: Princeton University Press, 2015.

Fields, Barbara J. *Slavery and Freedom on the Middle Ground: Maryland during the Nineteenth Century.* New Haven: Yale University Press, 1985.

Fischer, Anne Gray. *The Streets Belong to Us: Sex, Race, and Police Power from Segregation to Gentrification.* Chapel Hill: University of North Carolina Press, 2022.

Flowe, Douglas. "'Drug-Mad Negroes': African Americans, Drug Use, and the Law in Progressive Era New York City." *Journal of the Gilded Age and Progressive Era* 20, no. 4 (2021): 503–22.

Flowe, Douglas. *Uncontrollable Blackness: African American Men and Criminality in Jim Crow New York.* Chapel Hill: University of North Carolina Press, 2020.

Fog, Agner. *Cultural Selection.* Dordrecht: Kluwer, 1999.

Fogelson, Robert M. *Big-City Police.* Cambridge, MA: Harvard University Press, 1977.

Foner, Eric. *Reconstruction: America's Unfinished Revolution, 1863–1877.* New York: Harper Perennial, 1988.

Foucault, Michel. *Discipline and Punish: The Birth of the Prison.* New York: Vintage, 1975.

Freedman, Estelle B. *Their Sisters' Keepers: Women's Prison Reform in America, 1830–1930.* Ann Arbor: University of Michigan Press, 1981.

Freund, David M. P. *Colored Property: State Policy and White Racial Politics in Suburban America.* Chicago: University of Chicago Press, 2007.

Freund, Ernst. *The Police Power: Public Policy and Constitutional Rights.* Chicago: University of Chicago Press, 1904.

Bibliography · 241

Friedman, Lawrence M. *Crime and Punishment in American History*. New York: Basic Books, 1993.

Fronc, Jennifer. *New York Undercover: Private Surveillance in the Progressive Era*. Chicago: University of Chicago Press, 2009.

Fuentes, Marisa J. *Dispossessed Lives: Enslaved Women, Violence, and the Archive*. Philadelphia: University of Pennsylvania Press, 2016.

Fuke, Richard P. "Blacks, Whites, and Guns: Interracial Violence in Post-Emancipation Maryland." *Maryland Historical Magazine* 92, no. 3 (1997): 327–47.

Fuke, Richard P. *Imperfect Equality: African Americans and the Confines of White Racial Attitudes in Post-Emancipation Maryland*. New York: Fordham University Press, 1999.

Gallon, Kim. *Pleasure in the News: African American Readership and Sexuality in the Black Press*. Urbana: University of Illinois Press, 2020.

Garb, Margaret. *City of American Dreams: A History of Home Ownership and Housing Reform in Chicago, 1871–1919*. Chicago: University of Chicago Press, 2005.

Gilfoyle, Timothy J. *A Pickpocket's Tale: The Underworld of Nineteenth-Century New York*. New York: Norton, 2007.

Gilfoyle, Timothy J. "'America's Greatest Criminal Barracks': The Tombs and the Experience of Criminal Justice in New York City, 1838–1897." *Journal of Urban History* 29, no. 5 (2003): 525–54.

Gilfoyle, Timothy J. *City of Eros: New York City, Prostitution, and the Commercialization of Sex, 1790–1920*. New York: Norton, 1992.

Gilmore, Ruthie W. *Golden Gulag: Prisons, Surplus, Crisis, and Opposition in Globalizing California*. Berkeley: University of California Press, 2007.

Ginzburg, Carlo, John Tedeschi, and Ann C. Tedeschi. "Microhistory: Two or Three Things I Know about It." *Critical Inquiry* 20, no 1. (1993): 10–35.

Glotzer, Paige. *How the Suburbs Were Segregated: Developers and the Business of Exclusionary Housing, 1890–1960*. New York: Columbia University Press, 2020.

Goldstein Eric L., and Deborah R. Weiner. *On Middle Ground: A History of the Jews of Baltimore*. Baltimore: Johns Hopkins University Press, 2018.

Gonaver, Wendy. *The Peculiar Institution and the Making of Modern Psychiatry, 1840–1880*. Chapel Hill: University of North Carolina Press, 2019.

Gootenberg, Paul. *Andean Cocaine: The Making of a Global Drug*. Chapel Hill: University of North Carolina Press, 2008.

Gootenberg, Paul, ed. *Cocaine: Global Histories*. New York, Routledge, 1999.

Gross, Kali N. *Colored Amazons: Crime, Violence, and Black Women in the City of Brotherly Love, 1880–1910*. Durham, NC: Duke University Press, 2006.

Gruber, Aya. "Policing and 'Bluelining.'" *Houston Law Review* 58, no. 2 (2021): 867–936.

Guariglia, Matthew. *Police and the Empire City: Race and the Origins of Modern Policing in New York*. Durham, NC: Duke University Press, 2023.

Haden, Sally E. *Slave Patrols: Law and Violence in Virginia and the Carolinas*. Cambridge, MA: Harvard University Press, 2003.

Haley, Sarah. *No Mercy Here: Gender, Punishment, and the Making of Jim Crow Modernity*. Chapel Hill: University of North Carolina Press, 2016.

242 · *Bibliography*

Halpin, Dennis P. *A Brotherhood of Liberty: Black Reconstruction and Its Legacies in Baltimore, 1865–1920.* Philadelphia: University of Pennsylvania Press, 2019.

Hanchett, Thomas W. *Sorting Out the New South City: Race, Class, and Urban Development in Charlotte, 1875–1975.* Chapel Hill: University of North Carolina Press, 1998.

Hanhardt, Christina B. *Safe Space: Gay Neighborhood History and the Politics of Violence.* Durham, NC: Duke University Press, 2013.

Harring, Sidney L. *Policing a Class Society: The Experience of American Cities, 1865–1915.* 2nd ed. Chicago: Haymarket, 2017.

Harris, Cheryl I. "Whiteness as Property." *Harvard Law Review* 106, no. 8 (1993): 1707–91.

Harris, Jacqueline L. *History and Achievement of the NAACP.* New York: African-American Experience, 1992.

Harris, LaShawn. *Sex Workers, Psychics, and Numbers Runners: Black Women in New York City's Underground Economy.* Urbana: University of Illinois Press, 2016.

Harris, LaShawn. "The '*Commonwealth of Virginia vs. Virginia Christian*': Southern Black Women, Crime, and Punishment in Progressive Era Virginia." *Journal of Social History* 47, no. 4 (2014): 922–42.

Hartman, Saidiya. *Scenes of Subjection: Terror, Slavery, and Self-Making in Nineteenth-Century America.* Oxford: Oxford University Press, 1997.

Hartman, Saidiya. "Venus in Two Acts." *Small Axe* 12, no. 2 (2008): 1–14.

Hartman, Saidiya., *Wayward Lives, Beautiful Experiments: Intimate Histories of Riotous Black Girls, Troublesome Women, and Queer Radicals.* New York: Norton, 2020.

Hayward, Mary E. *Baltimore's Alley Houses: Homes for Working People since the 1780s.* Baltimore: Johns Hopkins University Press, 2008.

Hayward, Mary E., and Charles Belfoure. *The Baltimore Rowhouse.* New York: Princeton Architectural Press, 1999.

Heap, Chad. *Slumming: Sexual and Racial Encounters in American Nightlife, 1885–1940.* Chicago: University of Chicago Press, 2009.

Hemphill, Katie M. *Bawdy City: Commercial Sex and Regulation in Baltimore, 1790–1915.* Cambridge: Cambridge University Press, 2020.

Hernández, Kelly L. *City of Inmates: Conquest, Rebellion, and the Rise of Human Caging in Los Angeles, 1771–1965.* Chapel Hill: University of North Carolina Press, 2017.

Hicks, Cheryl D. *Talk with You like a Woman: African American Women, Justice, and Reform in New York, 1890–1935.* Chapel Hill: University of North Carolina Press, 2010.

Higginbotham, Evelyn B. *Righteous Discontent: The Women's Movement in the Black Baptist Church, 1880–1920.* Cambridge, MA: Harvard University Press, 1994.

Hinton, Elizabeth. *America on Fire: The Untold History of Police Violence and Black Rebellion since the 1960s.* New York: Liveright, 2021.

Hinton, Elizabeth. *From the War on Poverty to the War on Crime: The Making of Mass Incarceration in America.* Cambridge, MA: Harvard University Press, 2016.

Hinton, Elizabeth, and DeAnza Cook. "The Mass Criminalization of Black Americans: A Historical Overview." *Annual Review of Criminology* 4 (2021): 261–86.

Bibliography · 243

Hirsch, Adam J. *The Rise of the Penitentiary: Prisons and Punishment in Early America*. New Haven: Yale University Press, 1992.

Hirsch, Arnold. *Making the Second Ghetto: Race & Housing in Chicago, 1940–1960*. Chicago: University of Chicago Press, 1998.

Hong, Grace K. "Existentially Surplus: Women of Color Feminism and the New Crises of Capitalism." *GLQ* 18, no. 1 (2012): 87–106.

Hunter, Tera W. *To 'Joy My Freedom: Southern Black Women's Lives and Labors after the Civil War*. Cambridge, MA: Harvard University Press, 1997.

Hynson, Jerry M. *Absconders, Runaways and Other Fugitives in the Baltimore City and County Jail*. Westminster, MD: Willow Bend Press, 2004.

Jackson, Will. "Police Power and Disorder: Understanding Policing in the Twenty-First Century." *Social Justice* 47, no. 3–4 (2020): 95–114.

Jacobson, Matthew F. *Whiteness of a Different Color: European Immigration and the Alchemy of Race*. Cambridge, MA: Harvard University Press, 1998.

James, C. L. R. *The Black Jacobins: Toussaint L'Ouverture and the San Domingo Revolution*. New York: Vintage Books, 1963.

Jeffreys-Jones, Rhodri. *The FBI: A History*. New Haven: Yale University Press, 2007.

Jett, Brandon T. *Race, Crime, and Policing in the Jim Crow South: African Americans and Law Enforcement in Birmingham, Memphis, and New Orleans, 1920–1945*. Baton Rouge: Louisiana State University Press, 2021.

Johnson, David R. *Policing the Urban Underworld: The Impact of Crime on the Development of the American Police, 1800–1887*. Philadelphia: Temple University Press, 1979.

Johnson, Jessica M. *Wicked Flesh: Black Women, Intimacy, and Freedom in the Atlantic World*. Philadelphia: University of Pennsylvania Press, 2020.

Johnson, Marilynn S. *Street Justice: A History of Police Violence in New York City*. Boston: Beacon, 2003.

Johnson, Walter. *The Broken Heart of America: St. Louis and the Violent History of the United States*. New York: Basic Books, 2020.

Jonas, Gilbert. *Freedom's Sword: The NAACP and the Struggle against Racism in America, 1909–1969*. New York: Routledge, 2004.

Jones, Martha S. *Birthright Citizens: A History of Race and Rights in Antebellum America*. Cambridge: Cambridge University Press, 2018.

Joyner, Charles W. *Shared Traditions: Southern History and Folk Culture*. Urbana: University of Illinois Press, 1999.

Kaba, Mariame, and Andrea Ritchie. *No More Police: A Case for Abolition*. New York: New Press, 2022.

Kalifa, Dominique. *Vice, Crime, and Poverty: How the Western Imagination Invented the Underworld*. New York: Columbia University Press, 2019.

Kargon, Jeremy. "Thomas Poppleton's Map: Vignettes of a City's Self Image." *Maryland Historical Magazine* 104, no. 2 (2009): 185–207.

Katz, Michael B. *In the Shadow of the Poorhouse: A Social History of Welfare in America*. New York: Basic Books, 1986.

244 · Bibliography

Katz, Michael S. *A History of Compulsory Education Laws.* Bloomington: Phi Delta Kappa Educational Foundation, 1976.

Kendi, Ibram X. *Stamped from the Beginning: The Definitive History of Racist Ideas in America.* New York: Nation Books, 2016.

Kerson, Toba S. "Almshouse to Municipal Hospital: The Baltimore Experience." *Bulletin of the History of Medicine* 55, no. 2 (1981): 203–20.

King, P. Nicole, Joshua Clark Davis, and Kate Drabinski, eds. *Baltimore Revisited: Stories of Inequality and Resistance in a U.S. City.* New Brunswick, NJ: Rutgers University Press, 2019.

Komisar, Lucy. *Down and Out in the USA: A History of Social Welfare.* New York: New Viewpoints, 1974.

Kotch, Seth. *Lethal State: A History of the Death Penalty in North Carolina.* Chapel Hill: University of North Carolina Press, 2019.

Lefebvre, Henri. *Marxist Thought and the City.* Minneapolis: University of Minnesota Press, 2016.

LeFlouria, Talitha L. *Chained in Silence: Black Women and Convict Labor in the New South.* Chapel Hill: University of North Carolina Press, 2015.

LeFlouria, Talitha L. "'Under the Sting of the Lash': Gendered Violence, Terror, and Resistance in the South's Convict Camps." *Journal of African American History* 100, no. 3 (2015): 366–84.

Lewis, H. H. Walker. "The Baltimore Police Case of 1860." *Maryland Law Review* 26, no. 3 (1966): 215–28.

Lewis, Verl S. "Stephen Humphreys Gurteen and the American Origins of Charity Organization." *Social Service Review* 40, no. 2 (1966): 190–201.

Liazos, Ariane. *Reforming the City: The Contested Origins of Urban Government, 1890–1930.* New York: Columbia University Press, 2019.

Lichtenstein, Alex. *Twice the Work of Free Labor: The Political Economy of Convict Labor in the New South.* Chicago: Haymarket, 1996.

Link, William A. *The Paradox of Southern Progressivism, 1880–1930.* Chapel Hill: University of North Carolina Press, 1992.

Litwack, Leon F. *Trouble in Mind: Black Southerners in the Age of Jim Crow.* New York: Vintage Books, 1998.

Malka, Adam. *The Men of Mobtown: Policing Baltimore in the Age of Slavery and Emancipation.* Chapel Hill: University of North Carolina Press, 2018.

Marable, Manning. *How Capitalism Underdeveloped Black America: Problems in Race, Political Economy, and Society.* Cambridge, MA: South End Press, 1983.

Marx, Karl. *Capital: A Critique of Political Economy, Vol. 1.* London: Penguin, 1990.

McDougall, Harold A. *Black Baltimore: A New Theory of Community.* Philadelphia: Temple University Press, 1993.

McFadden, James J. "'Frankenstein of Pauperism': The Early Years of Charity Organization Case Recording, 1877–1907." *Social Service Review* 88, no. 3 (2014): 469–92.

McGerr, Michael. *A Fierce Discontent: The Rise and Fall of the Progressive Movement in America, 1870–1920.* Oxford: Oxford University Press, 2005.

McKittrick, Katherine. *Demonic Grounds: Black Women and the Cartographies of Struggle.* Minneapolis: University of Minnesota Press, 2006.

McKittrick, Katherine, and Clyde Woods, eds. *Black Geographies and the Politics of Place.* Cambridge, MA: South End Press, 2007.

McLennan, Rebecca M. *The Crisis of Imprisonment: Protest, Politics, and the Making of the American Penal State, 1776–1941.* Cambridge: Cambridge University Press, 2008.

Melton, Tracy M. *Hanging Henry Gambrill: The Violent Career of Baltimore's Plug Uglies, 1854–1860.* Baltimore: Maryland Center for History and Culture, 2006.

Melton, Tracy M. "Power Networks: The Political and Professional Career of Baltimore Boss J. Frank Morrison." *Maryland Historical Magazine* 99, no. 4 (2004): 455–79.

Mitchell, Michele. *Righteous Propagation: African Americans and the Politics of Racial Destiny after Reconstruction.* Chapel Hill: University of North Carolina Press, 2004.

Mitrani, Sam. *The Rise of the Chicago Police Department: Class and Conflict, 1850–1894.* Urbana: University of Illinois Press, 2013.

Monkkonen, Eric H. *Police in Urban America, 1860–1920.* Cambridge: Cambridge University Press, 1981.

Monkkonen, Eric H. *The Local State: Public Money and American Cities.* Stanford: Stanford University Press, 1995.

Morris, Norval, and David J. Rothman, eds. *The Oxford History of the Prison: The Practice of Punishment in Western Society.* Oxford: Oxford University Press, 1998.

Muhammad, Khalil G. *The Condemnation of Blackness: Race, Crime, and the Making of Modern Urban America.* Cambridge, MA: Harvard University Press, 2010.

Mumford, Kevin. *Interzones: Black/White Sex Districts in Chicago and New York in the Early Twentieth Century.* New York: Columbia University Press, 1997.

Murphy, Mary-Elizabeth B. *Jim Crow Capital: Women and Black Freedom Struggles in Washington, D.C., 1920–1945.* Chapel Hill: University of North Carolina Press, 2018.

Mustakeem, Sowande' M. "'Armed with a Knife in Her Bosom': Gender, Violence, and the Carceral Consequences of Rage in the Late 19th Century." *Journal of African American History* 100, no. 3 (2015): 385–405.

Musto, David F. *The American Disease: Origins of Narcotic Control.* 3rd ed. Oxford: Oxford University Press, 1999.

Myers, William S. *The Self-Reconstruction of Maryland, 1864–1867.* Baltimore: Johns Hopkins University Press, 1909.

Neocleous, Mark. *A Critical Theory of Police Power: The Fabrication of Social Order.* New York: Verso, 2021.

Neocleous, Mark. "'Original, Absolute, Indefeasible': Or, What We Talk about When We Talk about Police Power." *Social Justice* 47, no. 3–4 (2020): 9–32.

Neverdon-Morton, Cynthia. *Afro-American Women in the South and the Advancement of the Race, 1895–1925.* Knoxville: University of Tennessee Press, 1989.

Newport, Melanie D. *This Is My Jail: Local Politics and the Rise of Mass Incarceration.* Philadelphia: University of Pennsylvania Press, 2022.

Ngai, Mae M. *Impossible Subjects: Illegal Aliens and the Making of Modern America.* Princeton: Princeton University Press, 2004.

246 · *Bibliography*

Niedermeier, Silvan. *The Color of the Third Degree: Racism, Police Torture, and Civil Rights in the American South, 1930–1955.* Chapel Hill: University of North Carolina Press, 2019.

Norton, Jack, Lydia Pelot-Hobbs, and Judah Schept, eds. *The Jail Is Everywhere: Fighting the New Geography of Mass Incarceration.* New York: Verso, 2024.

O'Connor, Alice. *Poverty Knowledge: Social Science, Social Policy, and the Poor in Twentieth-Century U.S. History.* Princeton: Princeton University Press, 2001.

Ogbar, Jeffrey O. G. *America's Black Capital: How African Americans Remade Atlanta in the Shadow of the Confederacy.* New York: Basic Books, 2023.

Oller, John. *Rogues' Gallery: The Birth of Modern Policing and Organized Crime in Gilded Age New York.* New York: Dutton, 2021.

Olson, Sherry H. *Baltimore: The Building of an American City.* Baltimore: Johns Hopkins University Press, 1997.

Omi, Michael, and Howard Winant. *Racial Formation in the United States.* 3rd ed. New York: Routledge, 2014.

Ordaz, Jessica. *The Shadow of El Centro: A History of Migrant Incarceration and Solidarity.* Chapel Hill: University of North Carolina Press, 2022.

Orser, W. Edward. *Blockbusting in Baltimore: The Edmonson Village Story.* Lexington: University of Kentucky Press, 1994.

Parsons, Anne E. *From Asylum to Prison: Deinstitutionalization and the Rise of Mass Incarceration after 1945.* Chapel Hill: University of North Carolina Press, 2018.

Perman, Michael. *Struggle for Mastery: Disenfranchisement in the South, 1888–1908.* Chapel Hill: University of North Carolina Press, 2003.

Phelps, Jane L. "Charles J. Bonaparte and Negro Suffrage in Maryland." *Maryland Historical Magazine* 54, no. 4 (1959): 331–52.

Phillips, Christopher. *Freedom's Port: The African American Community of Baltimore, 1790–1860.* Urbana: University of Illinois Press, 1997.

Pietila, Antero. *Not in My Neighborhood: How Bigotry Shaped a Great American City.* Chicago: Ivan R. Dee, 2010.

Pietila, Antero. *The Ghosts of Johns Hopkins: The Life and Legacy that Shaped an American City.* Lanham: Rowman & Littlefield, 2018.

Platt, Anthony M. *The Child Savers: The Invention of Delinquency.* Chicago: University of Chicago Press, 1969.

Pliley, Jessica R. *Policing Sexuality: The Mann Act and the Making of the FBI.* Cambridge, MA: Harvard University Press, 2014.

Polanyi, Karl. *The Great Transformation: The Political and Economic Origins of Our Time.* Boston: Beacon, 1944.

Power, Garrett. "Apartheid Baltimore Style: The Residential Segregation Ordinances of 1910–1913." *Maryland Law Review* 42, no. 2 (1983): 289–328.

Power, Garrett. "The Unwisdom of Allowing City Growth to Work Out Its Own Density." *Maryland Law Review* 47, no. 3 (1988): 626–74.

Richardson, James F. "Police History: The Search for Legitimacy," *Journal of Urban History* 6, no. 2 (1980): 231–46.

Richardson, James F. *Urban Police in the United States.* Port Washington, NY: Kennikat Press, 1974.

Richie, Beth E. *Arrested Justice: Black Women, Violence, and America's Prison Nation.* New York: New York University Press, 2012.

Roberts, Dorothy. *Killing the Black Body: Race, Reproduction, and the Meaning of Liberty.* 20th anniv. ed. New York: Vintage, 2017.

Roberts, Samuel K. *Infectious Fear: Politics and the Health Effects of Segregation in the Urban South.* Chapel Hill: University of North Carolina Press, 2009.

Robinson, Cedric J. *Black Marxism: The Making of the Black Radical Tradition.* Chapel Hill: University of North Carolina Press, 1983.

Rockman, Seth. *Scraping By: Wage Labor, Slavery, and Survival in Early Baltimore.* Baltimore: Johns Hopkins University Press, 2009.

Roediger, David R. *The Wages of Whiteness: Race and the Making of the American Working Class.* New York: Verso, 1999.

Rothman, David J. *The Discovery of the Asylum: Social Order and Disorder in the New Republic.* Rev. ed. New York: Aldine de Gruyter, 2002.

Ryan, Mary P. *Taking the Land to Make the City: A Bicoastal History of North America.* Austin: University of Texas Press, 2019.

Sartain, Lee. *Borders of Equality: The NAACP and the Baltimore Civil Rights Struggle, 1914–1970.* Jackson: University of Mississippi Press, 2013.

Schley, David. *Steam City: Railroads, Urban Space, and Corporate Capitalism in Nineteenth-Century Baltimore.* Chicago: University of Chicago Press, 2020.

Schlossman, Steven L. *Love and the American Delinquent: The Theory and Practice of "Progressive" Juvenile Justice, 1825–1920.* Chicago: University of Chicago Press, 1977.

Schneider, Eric C. *In the Web of Class: Delinquents and Reformers in Boston, 1810s–1930s.* New York: New York University Press, 1992.

Schoeberlein, Robert W. "'Maryland's Shame': Photojournalism and Mental Health Reform, 1935–1949." *Maryland Historical Magazine* 98, no. 1 (2003): 35–72.

Schweik, Susan M. *The Ugly Laws: Disability in Public.* New York: New York University Press, 2009.

Segrest, Mab. *Administrations of Lunacy: Racism and the Haunting of American Psychiatry at the Milledgeville Asylum.* New York: New Press, 2020.

Seigel, Micol. "Objects of Police History." *Journal of American History* 102, no. 1 (2015): 152–61.

Seigel, Micol. "On the Critique of Paramilitarism." *Global South* 12, no. 2 (2018): 166–83.

Seigel, Micol. "The Dilemma of 'Racial Profiling': An Abolitionist Police History." *Contemporary Justice Review* 20, no. 4 (2017): 474–90.

Seigel, Micol. *Violence Work: State Power and the Limits of Police.* Durham, NC: Duke University Press, 2018.

Shabazz, Rashad. *Spatializing Blackness: Architectures of Confinement and Black Masculinity in Chicago.* Urbana: University of Illinois Press, 2015.

Sharpe, Christina. *In the Wake: On Blackness and Being.* Durham, NC: Duke University Press, 2016.

Shufelt, Gordon H. *The Uncommon Case of Daniel Brown: How a White Police Officer Was Convicted of Killing a Black Citizen, Baltimore, 1875.* Kent, OH: Kent State University Press, 2021.

Shugg, Wallace. *A Monument to Good Intentions: The Story of the Maryland Penitentiary, 1804–1995.* Baltimore: Maryland Historical Society, 2000.

Skotnes, Andor. *A New Deal for All? Race and Class Struggles in Depression-Era Baltimore.* Durham, NC: Duke University Press, 2013.

Smith, C. Fraser. *Here Lies Jim Crow: Civil Rights in Maryland.* Baltimore: Johns Hopkins University Press, 2008.

Suddler, Carl. *Presumed Criminal: Black Youth and the Justice System in Postwar New York.* New York: New York University Press, 2019.

Sugrue, Thomas J. *The Origins of the Urban Crisis: Race and Inequality in Postwar Detroit.* Princeton: Princeton University Press, 1996.

Summers, Martin. *Madness in the City of Magnificent Intentions: A History of Race and Mental Illness in the Nation's Capital.* Oxford: Oxford University Press, 2019.

Terry, David T. *The Struggle and the Urban South: Confronting Jim Crow in Baltimore before the Movement.* Athens: University of Georgia Press, 2019.

Thompson, Heather A. "Rethinking Working-Class Struggle through the Lens of the Carceral State: Toward a Labor History of Inmates and Guards." *Labor* 8, no. 3 (2011): 15–45.

Thompson, Heather A. "Why Mass Incarceration Matters: Rethinking Crisis, Decline, and Transformation in Postwar American History." *Journal of American History* 97, no. 3 (2010): 703–34.

Thompson, Heather A., and Donna Murch. "Rethinking Urban America through the Lens of the Carceral State." *Journal of Urban History* 41, no. 5 (2015): 751–55.

Vaz, Matthew. *Running the Numbers: Race, Police, and the History of Urban Gambling.* Chicago: University of Chicago Press, 2020.

Wagner, Bryan. *Disturbing the Peace: Black Culture and the Police Power after Slavery.* Cambridge, MA: Harvard University Press, 2009.

Walker, Samuel. *A Critical History of Police Reform: The Emergence of Professionalism.* Lexington, MA: Lexington Press, 1977.

Walsh, Michael T. *Baltimore Prohibition: Wet and Dry in the Free State.* Charleston, SC: American Palate, 2017.

Washington, Booker T. *Up from Slavery: An Autobiography.* New York: Doubleday, Page, 1906.

Weheliye, Alexander G. *Habeas Viscus: Racializing Assemblages, Biopolitics, and Black Feminist Theories of the Human.* Durham, NC: Duke University Press, 2014.

Wells, Ida B. *The Light of Truth: Writings of an Anti-Lynching Crusader.* New York: Penguin, 2014.

White, Deborah G. *Ar'n't I a Woman?: Female Slaves in the Plantation South*. New York: Norton, 1999.

Wiebe, Robert H. *The Search for Order, 1877–1920*. New York: Hill and Wang, 1967.

Williams, Rhonda Y. *The Politics of Public Housing: Black Women's Struggles against Urban Inequality*. Oxford: Oxford University Press, 2004.

Willrich, Michael. *City of Courts: Socializing Justice in Progressive Era Chicago*. Cambridge: Cambridge University Press, 2003.

Wolcott, David. "'The Cop Will Get You': The Police and Discretionary Juvenile Justice, 1890–1940." *Journal of Social History* 35, no. 2 (2001): 349–71.

Wolcott, Victoria W. *Race, Riots, and Roller Coasters: The Struggle over Segregated Recreation in America*. Philadelphia: University of Pennsylvania Press, 2012.

Woloson, Wendy A. *In Hock: Pawning in America from Independence through the Great Depression*. Chicago: University of Chicago Press, 2009.

Woloson, Wendy A. "'Fence-ing Lessons: Child Junkers and the Commodification of Scrap in the Long Nineteenth Century." *Business History* 61, no. 1 (2019): 38–72.

Woods, Clyde. *Development Arrested: The Blues and Plantation Power in the Mississippi Delta*. New York: Verso, 1998.

Woodward, C. Vann. *The Strange Career of Jim Crow*. Oxford: Oxford University Press, 1974.

Yu, Wang. "'Boss Robert La Follette and the Paradox of the U.S. Progressive Movement." *Journal of American History* 108, no. 4 (2022): 726–44.

Ziliak, Stephen T. "Self-Reliance before the Welfare State: Evidence from the Charity Organization Movement in the United States." *Journal of Economic History* 64, no. 2 (2004): 433–61.

Index

Note: Page numbers in *italics* denote figures.

accountability, 55, 59, 65, 118, 171, 173–75, 178–79, 187, 191, 198
activism, 2, 10, 14, 69, 83; Black, 148–51, 163, 173, 183. *See also* Citizens Committee (Baltimore); National Association for the Advancement of Colored People (NAACP)
addiction, 59, 88, 103–4, 106, 108–10, 118, 121, 172
Adler, Jeffrey S., 204n17
Afro-American, 12, 16, 46–47, 165–68, 171–79, *182,* 184, 187–91, 193, 197–98; and Brown case, 141, 147, 149, 152, 156, *159*
Afro-Southern migrants, 137, 148, 167, 181
Agyepong, Tera Eva, 94
Ahern, John F., 56–57
alcohol, 14, 33, 40, 51, 55–57, 67, 70–72, 77, 182, 202n31; and policing, 121–22, 127, 188; and racialized policing, 102, 106, 108, 110–11, 118, 182. *See also* intoxication, public; Liquor Board; Prohibition
Allen, Boston, 149, 152, 156
almsgiving, 74, 76–77, 82, 85, 87

almshouses, 4, 10, 18–19, 23, 37, 41–42, 49, 76, 207n88
American Academy of Political and Social Science, 70
American North, 6, 8, 77, 137, 205n31
American Psychiatric Association (APA), 37
American South, 6, 8, 15, 55–56, 68–69, 71, 78–79, 181, 204n17, 205n31; and racism, 102, 105, 108, 112, 141, 162, 204n17, 205n31, 218n58, 228n33. *See also* Afro-Southern migrants
Annapolis, MD, 11, 65, 169–70; and Brown case, 131–32, 138–40, 142–43, 145, 149, 153–54, 160
Anniston, AL, 169
annoyances, 5, 18, 34, 84, 88, 195
anonymity, 36, 102, 107, 119, 121, 123–24
anti-Blackness, 4, 9, 65, 70, 109, 156, 175, 184, 191; and policing, 2, 5, 7, 12, 102
Anti-Saloon League, 138
anti-vice politics, 14–15, 26, 50–52, 59, 203n39; and commerce, 59, 106, 175; and drugs, 108, 116, 121; and policing, 121, 176; and poverty relief, 77, 79–80

252 • Index

arrests, 1, 14, 16, *136*, 177, 184, 196, 205n48;
and Brown case, 132, 134–37, 150–51,
162; and children, 91–92, 97; citizens',
22; and data, 121–23, 125; and disorderly
conduct, 17, *30*, 164–65, 171–73, 176–80,
189–90, 197–98; and drugs, 101, 103,
106, 110, 114, 116, 118; and interraciality,
172; and poverty, 26–27, 29, 36, 84–86;
and racialization, 66–68, 70–71, 119,
128–29; rates of, 7–9, 12, 34, 151, 169–
70, 175, 191, 201n17, 213n56; and reform,
51, 55, 57–58, 60, 63

assault, 58, 68, 84, 108, 110–11, 116, 151,
162, 173, 224n87

Associated Negro Press (ANP), 152

Association for Improving the Condition of
the Poor (New York), 75

Association for the Improvement of the
Condition of the Poor (Baltimore), 85

asylums, 4–5, 13, 18–19, 37–38, 40–43, 76,
83, 98, 207n87. *See also* Bayview Asylum;
Sheppard Asylum

attorneys, 33, 58, 60, 62, 66, 68, 100–101,
119, 125, 202n28; Black private life, 173,
177, 179–80, 186, 190–91; and Brown
case, 141, 149, 154, 156. *See also* attorneys
general; Office of the Pardon Attorney;
state's attorneys

attorneys general, 46, 106, 137, 196, 202n39;
and Brown case, 149–50, 152–58, 160–
62, 197

Auburn system, 24

Aunt Sarah figure, 78–79

Austrian immigrants, 112

authority, 4, 14, 29, 69–70, 72, 93–95, 146;
city, 11, 120, 195; expert (supposed), 108,
113; police, 55, 63, 93–95, 116, 175, 179–
80, 186, 230n92; state, 15, 46, 129; white,
133, 156, 188

autonomy, 11, 19, 52, 65, 74, 101, 106, 152,
195, 197

bail, 57, 60–61, 115, 140, 164, 187

Bailey, Alverta "Sweetie," 100–101, 103–4,
113–16, 118, 128

Baldwin, Summerfield, 50

Baltimore Health Department, 96

Bayview Asylum, 19, 36–43, 84, 94,
207n88; and poverty, 86–88, 98, 194

beatings, police, 134, 144, 146, 171, 178. *See
also* third degree; torture, police

Beebe & Co., 32

begging, 49, 74, 77, 80, 83–88, 98, 102, 195,
198

behaviors, 17–18, 20, 23, 27, 29, 32; and
disorderly conduct, 166, 171; and drugs,
109, 111, 196; of police, 178–79, 191; and
poverty, 76, 78–80; private, 173, 190; and
reform, 47, 70

Bergman, Henry, 125

Bertillon system, 122, 124, 219n89

Bethel AME Church, 152

Bingham, Theodore, 123

biological essentialism, 39, 42, 68–69,
81. *See also* cultural evolution; eugenics;
heredity

biometric data, 98, 102, 121–24, 129, 135.
See also fingerprinting

Black adolescents, 15, 139, 160, 162. *See also*
Brown, Henry Alfred

Black advancement, 1, 15, 47, 64–71, 79,
99–101, 151, 178, 188, 194

Black criminality, 11, 15, 99, 216n11; and
drugs, 101, 103, 105–6, 113; and judicial
inequality, 140, 150, 154; and reform, 35,
47, 57, 64, 67–68, 71, 195. *See also* criminal classes; criminalization

Black dysfunction, 182, 195–96

Black feminism, 12, 221n11; and refusal,
115–16

Black men, 1, 4–5, 9–11, 40, 60, 78; and
arrests, 170–71, 173, 180, 196; and
criminalization, 12–16, 34–35, 68, 71,
84, 116, 163–64, 218n58; and drugs,
100–101, 103, 105–7, 109, 111–16,
118–20, 129; and elections, 56–58, 66,
193; and execution, 151, 154, 163; and
justice, 125–26, 147, 151, 154–55, 160;
and police expansion, 164, 172, 197–98;
and police torture, 132, 137, 139; and
private lives, 176–79, 183, 185–86, 190;
and reform, 46–47, 51, 78; and surveillance, 34, 125–26. *See also* Brown,
Henry Alfred

Black neighborhoods, 1, 7, 11, 120, 128, 133,
141, 174; and privacy, 165, 171, 181–83,
191, 198. *See also* interraciality; racial
zoning; white neighborhoods

Blackness, 47, 98, 162; and drugs, 105–6, 111, 113; as threat, 71, 74, 101, 104, 151

Black people, 91, 108, 125, 156, 167, 193–94, 198, 201n28; and criminalization, 15, 23, 57, 64–71, 130, 162, 204n10; and demographics, 6–7, 10; and disorderly conduct, 165–66, 168, 178–80; and drugs, 101–12, 116, 118, 129, 196; and justice, 147, 149–50, 152, 155, 160; and police identification, 219n89; and police torture, 132–33, 135, 137, 197; and police violence, 173, 176; and poverty, 73–74, 77–78, 213n35; and private lives, 170–72, 175, 177, 187–91, 197–98, 227n6; and reform, 141, 194–95. *See also* Afro-Southern migrants; Black men; Black women

Black women, 1, 4–5, 9, 78, 156, 193, 212n26; and arrests, 35, 116, 170–71, 173, 179, 196; and criminalization, 12–13, 16, 71, 101, 112, 122–23, 129, 163–64, 218n58; and drugs, 101–5, 109–11, 113–15, 118–20, 129, 196; and execution, 151, 154; and justice, 147, 160; and policing, 12, 172, 197, 219n89; and poverty, 78–79, 88; and private lives, 183, 185, 190; and surveillance, 34, 126–28

Blood Tubs, 9

Board of Election Supervisors, 56

board of visitors (BOV), 22–24, 26, 28, 30–32, 35–36

Boas, Franz, 77

Bohemian immigrants, 181, 184. *See also* Czech immigrants

Bolden, Samuel, 174

Bolivian immigrants, 112

Bonaparte, Charles J., 10, 14, 45–46, 49–59, 62, 64, 71, 141, 194, 202n39; and poverty relief, 73, 83, 87–88, 196, 203n46

Bonaparte, Jérôme, 49–50

Bonaparte, Napoleon, 49

Bonsal, Leigh, 58, 125

bootlegging, 171, 184, 186

Bosanquet, Bernard, 81

Bosanquet, Helen, 81

bossism, 4, 32, 44, 46–47, 49–50, 53–55, 65, 71, 83

Boston, George, 17

Boteler, John, 142, 145

bourgeoisie, 36, 46, 71, 113, 214n71; Black, 156

Bradley, Peter, 138, 140, 144–46

Brennan, Annie E., 95

Broening, William F., 169

brothels, 45, 48, 50–51, 55, 60, 67, 149, 152, 176; and drug enforcement, 102, 126, 128

Brown, Frank, 68

Brown, Henry Alfred, 15, 132–33, 137–49, 151–56, 158–60, 162–63, 177–78, 196–97, 222n50

Brown, John, 69

Brown, John Young, 104

Brown, Laura, 127

Brown, Mary Wilcox, 90, 96

Brown, Robert and Cornelius, 125

Brown, Ruth Virginia, 148

Brown, Stella, 149–50

Brown communities, 5

Bruce, William Cabell, 68–70, 87, 91

Brush, E. N., 41

brutality, police, 5, 16, 36–38, 44, 116, 119, 179–80, 191, 197–98, 221n11; and Brown case, 133, 135, 141, 143–44, 147, 150–51, 163; and expansion, 165–67, 171–73, 175, 179–80

Bryan, William S., 100–101

Buckler, H. Warren, 96–97

bummers, 13, 17–19, 21, 25–37, 42–43, 77, 81, 194, 198

bureaucracies, 2–4; and asylums, 38, 43; and policing, 121, 187; and poverty, 18–20, 23, 27, 75; and reform, 45–47, 53, 55, 65, 70

Bureau of Identification (BOI), 121–23

burglary, 68, 190. *See also* robbery

Burke, Alvin, 172

Burke, Mary J., 122

businesses, 28, 30–32, 34, 42, 73, 104; and education, 91–92; and policing, 126–28, 149; and reform, 52–53, 61–62

Byrnes, Thomas, 134, 219n80

Callis, James A. B., 148

Camp McClellan, 169

capitalism, 2–4, 18, 25–27; and incarceration, 19, 30, 32, 42; industrial, 37, 84–85; and poverty, 81–82, 88; racial, 23, 156, 200n8

254 · *Index*

Carby, Hazel, 12
carceral facilities, 12, 22–23, 29, 41–43, 194, 205n31; and capacities, 18–20, 25, 27, 36. *See also* detention; jails; penitentiaries; prisons
carceral history, 3–7, 13
carceral state, 5, 34, 76, 80, 94, 129, 133, 204n10, 205n32, 221n11
Cargill, J. M., 64
Carman, Robert R., 141, 144, 155–56
Carroll, Charles, 40
Carter, Bernard, 63
Casey, Roland, 157–58
Catholicism, 45, 50–51
Central District, Baltimore, 60, 62–63, 110, 128, 181, *185*, 220n14
Chancellor, C. W., 38
Chandler, Rose, 172
charities, 10, 73, 75–76, 81–83, 89–90, 195, 203n47, 212n19; and agents, 3, 10, 14, 75–77, 86–88, 98, 102, 195, 211n8; and policing, 85, 98, 108. *See also* Charity Organization Society (COS)
Charities Record, 72, 75, 77, 80, 82, 85–87
Charity Organization Society (COS), 10, 14, 49, 71–88, 90–91, 98–99, 112, 213n35
Chicago Parental School, 94
children, 4, 63, 78, 94, 102, 181, 186; Black, 68, 94, 96, 99, 137, 202n28; Black people as, 111–12; and Black women, 78–79; and criminalization, 10, 14–15, 22–23, 72–74, 102; and education, 93–99, 195, 198, 214n71; and labor, 72–74, 89–93, 95–97; and poverty, 85–86, 184; white, 95, 99. *See also* juvenile delinquency; schools, Baltimore public; truancy
Children's Aid Society, 90, 95
Chinese communities, 67, 128
citizen policing, 22, 34, 50, 89, 93–94, 97–98, 123, 166, 176, 195
Citizens Committee, Baltimore, 148–51, 153–60
citizenship, 22, 78–80, 91, 96–97
city agencies, 3–5, 12–13, 41–43; and asylums, 41, 194; and bummers, 27, 29, 36; and poverty, 18–19, 23, 82–83, 85; and racializing crime, 69, 190; and reform, 45, 48–49, 53, 56, 65, 69–71, 195. *See also*

civil services; schools, Baltimore public; social welfare
city agents, 16–19, 32, 45, 48, 64–65, 94, 104, 120, 167
city charters, 3, 14, 45–47, 64–65, 70, 107, 120, 197
city council (Baltimore), 15, 18, 26, 30, 35, 95; and Bayview, 38–39; and Blackness, 64–65, 183; and drugs, 101, 103; and reform, 53, 58, 71, 90, 92
city governance, 2, 5–6, 9–15, 18–19, 43, 194, 198; and Blackness, 46–47, 70, 176; and drugs, 120, 129, 196–97; and education, 93, 97; and incarceration, 18, 20, 24, 37; and policing, 101–2, 121, 168–69, 175; and poverty, 42, 71, 76, 83, 98; and Reconstruction, 201n28; and reform, 43, 47–50, 53, 70
City Hospital (Saint Louis), 104
City Vigilance League, 44
civic life, 8, 14, 43, 194; and Blackness, 47–48, 64, 66, 68–70, 101, 112, 147, 188; and poverty, 73–74, 80, 86; and reform, 52, 56, 59, 196, 198. *See also* elections
civilian policing, 22, 34, 93–94, 97–98
civil rights, 9, 64, 66, 69, 147, 202n28
Civil Service Reform Association (CSRA), 49, 54, 71
civil services, 14, 19, 83, 98, 121, 141, 196, 202n39, 216n5; and reform, 45–47, 50
Civil War, 2, 4–9, 13, 17, 19, 25–26, 34, 105, 201n11, 202n28; and Black privacy, 194, 196, 198; and Brown case, 147, 151, 154, 162; and reform, 47, 52. *See also* Confederacy; Reconstruction; Union, the
cocaine, 100–111, 113–21, 129, 183, 196–97, 216n12. *See also* Swann's Cocaine Ordinance
Cohen, Andrew W., 106
Colgate, Samuel, 48–49
color line, 5, *7,* 11, 104, 126, 133; and Black privacy, 165, 167, 177, 180–81, 191, 195, 197
Colton, William, *61,* 61–63
Comstock, Anthony, 48–49
Confederacy, 6, 8–9, 45
confessions, 132, 134–35, 137–38, 140–41, 145–47, 151–54, 157, 162, 197, 225n108

convictions, 135, 146–47, 162, 178, 188, 190, 197, 221n21; and drugs, 101, 103, 106; rates of, 12, 15, 134–36; and reform, 61–63

Corosh, Peter, 142, 160

corruption, 4, 9, 26, 43, 66, 70–71, 79, 97, 194; and Blackness, 103, 105, 111–12; police, 10, 54–55, 60–67, 83, 115, 119, 127–28, 150, 166–68, 180, 197; and reform, 46–50, 52–54, 56, 59

Court of Common Pleas, 17, 45

courts, 2–4, 10–12, 15, 18, 24, 36, 188, 191, 198, 220n14, 224n87; of appeals, 11, 107, 120–21, 183; juvenile, 92, 94, 195. *See also* courts, criminal; Superior Court; Supreme Bench; U.S. Supreme Court

courts, criminal, 27, 29, 32, 52, 57, 84, 195–96, 227n6; and Bayview, 38, 41; and Brown case, 147, 162–63, 197; and drugs, 101, 103, 119–20; and police in, 178, 188–90, 220n114; and police torture, 133, 135, 137–39, 191; and surveillance, 121, 123, 128, 130, 198. *See also* criminal legal system

crime prevention, 4–5, 28–29, 34, 44, 183

criminal classes, 19–21, 25, 68, 117, 122, 138

criminalization, 13, 42–43, 133, 176, 216n6, 216nn11–12; and Black drug use, 101, 103, 105–6, 108–9, 111, 113–16, 118–19, 196; and Black men, 139, 177, 190; and Black people, 7, 12, 35, 47, 57, 64–71, 74, 78, 140, 154, 216n11; and drug possession, 11, 183, 196, 216n12; and poverty, 12, 17–20, 22–24, 28, 36, 77, 79–85, 87; and reform, 48, 51–52, 54; and surveillance, 121–30; and truancy, 10, 72–73, 90–94, 97, 99. *See also* Black criminality; criminal classes; identification, police

criminal legal system, 15, 18–19, 97, 115, 218n58; and Black people, 101, 123, 134, 177, 188; and Brown case, 134, 141, 147, 150–51, 153, 156, 163; and police, 59, 139, 190; and poverty, 24, 30; and reform, 26, 35–36, 198. *See also* courts; courts, criminal

criminal typologies, 121–22, 176, 219n80

criminology, 18, 32–33, 47, 216n6

Cromwell, Amelia, 88

Crooks, James, 49, 203n46

Crothers, Austin, 117–18, 124

Crowe, Charles, 79

Cuban immigrants, 112

Cull, Roger, 44, 54, 56–58, 60, 71, 194

cultural evolution, 14, 48–49, 69, 73, 82, 88, 98, 101, 112. *See also* biological essentialism; eugenics; heredity

Cummings, Harry S., 64

Czech immigrants, 103. *See also* Bohemian immigrants

Czitrom, Daniel, 46

Dashiell, Milton, 120, 183

databases, 87, 121–22, 129

Daugherty, Harry, 150, 153–55, 158–59

Davis, J. Steward, 149, 153, 156, 159, 173, 177–78

Davis, Bob, 57

Delaware: Wilmington, 57

Democratic State Central Committee, 154

Democrats, 8–10, 12, 15, 86; and Brown, 153–55, 225n108; and drugs, 101, 121; and policing, 168–70, 195–96; and racializing crime, 64–71; and reform, 44–49, 52–53, 55–58, 60, 63, 141, 195

Department of Justice (DOJ), 139–40, 156, 202n39

dependent populations, 4, 18, 71, 74, 78–79, 98, 104, 193

desertion, military, 132, 139–40, 142–43, 145, 149

detectives, 102, 119–24, 126, 129, 162, 178, 194, 219n80; and Brown case, 134, 137–41, 144–46, 158; bureaus, 29, 107, 135; private, 10, 14–15, 52, 176, 194, 203n39

detention, 2–3, 12, 14, 16, 72, 132, 194, 198; and bummers, 81; and children, 92–93, 95; facilities, 8, 19, 21, 24–25, 36, 137; long-term, 23, 27, 32; and runaway slaves, 22–23; short-term, 13, 28, 31–32, 42. *See also* carceral facilities; jails; penitentiaries; prisons

deviance, 4, 39, 42, 78, 80, 98, 121, 214n71

Dickerson, Bertha, 148

Dickerson, Henry and Mollie, 147

Dirkson, Menika B., 216n11

disability, 84–85, 88, 97

256 · Index

discipline, 2–5, 9, 11–12, 200n5; and asylums, 38, 40; and Black people, 101, 113, 126, 163, 175–76, 190; and Brown case, 133, 143; and institutions, 20, 23, 32–33, 74, 200n5; and police misconduct, 125–27, 173, 180, 191; and poverty, 76, 87, 98–99; and reform, 52, 58; and truancy, 72, 90–92, 94, 96–97, 195

discretion, police, 1, 5, 15–17, 26, 29, 34, 40, 42, 196–97; and Black privacy, 165–67, 176, 180; and Brown case, 132–35, 138, 162–63; and drugs, 103, 121, 129; and reform, 55, 64, 66

disenfranchisement, 64, 66, 101, 160, 193, 231n4

disorderly conduct, 16–17, 26–27, 29, 34, 36, 126, 210n63; and Black people, 164–66, 176–80, 191, 197

Dixon, Thomas and James, 24–25, *25*

domestic labor, 78, 100–101, 114–15, 122–23, 127, 147

Downs, William F., 121

downtown Baltimore, 100, 111, *117*, 127–28, 131, 139, 176, 181–82, 220n114; and reform, 51, 54, 60–61

drugs, 11, 109, 196; and dealing, 100–104, 106–7, 110, 113–16, 118–19, 129–30, 172; and druggists, 100–101, 104, 106–7, 110, 113–14, 118–20, 216n13; and enforcement, 103–4, 106–7, 133, 183, 196; and possession, 11, 106–7, 118–20, 183, 196; and trafficking, 114–15, 127; and use, 59, 67, 102–8, 110–11, 118–19, 182, 196

DuBois, W. E. B., 77

due process, 132–33, 135, 137–38, 150, 157, 174, 180, 197

Dull, Will, 100–101, 114–16, 118

Duncan, Frank, 188, 190

Dyer, Leonidas, 160

East Baltimore, 184

Eastern Michigan Asylum (Pontiac), 39

economics, 5–6, 80, 85, 167, 194, 202n28; and Black people, 78, 91, 96, 105, 167, 177–78, 202n28; and education, 91, 96; and informal economies, 48, 52, 70, 102–3, 105, 114; and jails, 18, 22–25, 28;

and migration, 9–10; and poverty relief, 42, 73, 75–77, 80, 194; and reform, 44–45, 53, 61. *See also* poverty

education, 8, 48–49; and Black people, 65, 78, 108, 113, 157, 193; and truancy, 10, 14–15, 72–74, 76, 80, 88–99, 195, 198

efficiency, 2, 70, 121, 138, 216n5; and police, 11, 14, 67, 125, 130, 170; and poverty, 10, 81; and reform, 19, 22, 24, 40, 42–43, 45–46, 55, 59, 64, 121

Elaine massacre, 152

elections, 9, 14, 34, 44–46, 49–50, 98, 101, 116, 169, 194; and reform, 53–59, 61, 63–66, 70–71, 194–95. *See also* voting

employment, 56, 148, 181, 184; and Black people, 9, 78, 112, 177; and bummers, 25–26, 28, 30–32; and education, 89, 91, 96; and policing poverty, 86, 88. *See also* children; labor

England, 39, 76, 81; London, 75

epidemics, 37–38, 102, 109, 121

ethics, 14, 36, 40, 43, 45–46, 96, 145, 162, 207n88

eugenics, 82, 138. *See also* biological essentialism; cultural evolution; heredity; pseudoscience; social Darwinism

evidence, legal, 27, 40, 51, 60–63, 106, 119, 126, 166, 179, 197; and Brown case, 135, 137, 139–40, 145–46, 150, 152–61, 197

executions, 15, 148–54, 156–57, 159–60, 162–63, 196–97, 204n10, 224n87

Farnan, Marshal, 120

Farrar, Hayward, 167

Faulkner, Sherman, 144–45

Fawcett, Robert, 96

Federal Bureau of Investigation (FBI), 10, 46, 196, 202n39, 203n39

Federated Charities, 195

fee-based systems, 20, 23, 26–27

Fields, Barbara Jeanne, 9

Fighting Mag figure, 78–79

Finch, James A., 154, 156–59

fines, 18, 26, 29–30, 127, 173; and drugs, 106–7, 119; and poverty, 52, 91

fingerprinting, 121–23, 130

Fischer, Anne Gray, 176

Fischer, William A., 73

Flowe, Douglas, 15, 132
Fogelson, Robert M., 59
Foggy, Ray, 146
Foucault, Michel, 4, 204n10
France, 75, 216n12
freedoms, 3, 66, 110, 174–75; Black, 2, 47,
  68–70, 79, 115–16, 118, 147, 175, 195,
  197–98
Freund, Ernst, 200n6
Frey, Marshal Jacob, 57–58, 62–63
Friedman, Lawrence, 83
Friendly Inn, 83
Friendly Inn Association, 83
Fronc, Jennifer, 52, 122
Fuke, Richard Paul, 9, 202n28

Gaither, Charles, 138, 166, 169–74, 177–80,
  187–91
gambling, 14, 34, 48, 80–81, 98, 103, 122;
  and reform, 48, 50–51, 55, 57, 59–60,
  62, 67, 70
Garrett, Robert S., 73
gender, 2, 5, 12, 20, 78, 123, 126; and drugs,
  105, 108–10, 115; and education, 94, 96;
  and race, 78–79. See also Black men;
  Black women; mothers; white men;
  white women
Georgia: Atlanta, 45, 107–8
German immigrants, 91, 112
German Society, 85
Germany, 75, 216n12
Gilbert, J. J., 60–63
Gilded Age, 18, 49, 200n6, 214n71
Gilman, Daniel Coit, 73, 79
Good Government Clubs (GGCs), 53–54,
  71, 91
Gootenberg, Paul, 216n12
Gorman, Arthur Pue, 45, 54–55
Great Britain, 73, 216n12. See also England
Green, Stewart, 142–44, 146, 223n60
Griffith, G. S., 31, 35, 73
Gross, Kali, 12
Guariglia, Matthew, 211n8
Gurteen, Stephen Humphreys, 76
Guthrie, Charles E., 67

Haiti, 153, 160
Haley, Sarah, 5, 12, 115, 204n10

Hall, Thad, 31
Hammersla, Henry, 138–40, 145–46
harassment, police, 1, 30, 36, 125, 165–66,
  171, 177, 180, 186–87, 191, 197
harbor police, 34
Hardesty, James, 127
Hardesty, Samuel, 142
Harding, Florence, 148
Harding, Warren G., 150–52, 154, 158–60,
  197
Harlem Park (Baltimore), 183–84
Harpers Ferry, 69
Harris, LaShawn, 12, 113
Harris, Sadie, 114
Harrison, Helen, 164
Harrison Act (1914), 118
Harvard University, 50
Harvey, Mary S., 195
Hawkins, George, 84
Hawkins, W. Ashbie, 186
Hayes, Thomas G., 65
Hebrew Benevolent Society, 85
Heddinger, D. C., 60, 62–63
Hemphill, Katie, 202n28
Henderson, Charles Richmond, 80–81
Henry, George M., 187
Henry classification system, 122
Henry Watson Children's Aid Society, 90,
  95
heredity, 14, 77, 80, 90, 98, 101, 138. See also
  biological essentialism; cultural evolu-
  tion; eugenics
Hernández, Kelly Lytle, 102, 165
Hibernian Club, 127
Hicks, Cheryl, 12
Hinks, Samuel, 9
Hisley, George W., 127
Hodges, James, 73
Hollins Hall (Baltimore), 66–67
Hollins Market (Baltimore), 56
home rule, 3, 10–11, 14, 65, 70, 197; and
  drugs, 103, 120
homes, 2, 14, 16, 42, 47, 51–52, 86, 100,
  148, 213n35; Black, 112–14, 127, 166–67,
  171–76, 181–91, 198, 227n6, 228n33. See
  also truancy; visiting programs
Hooper, Alcaeus, 54
Hoover, Herbert, 137

258 · *Index*

hospitals, 4, 39, 41–43, 76, 88, 104, 131–32, 186, 220n14, 220n114; mental, 18, 37–38. *See also* Bayview Asylum; Johns Hopkins Hospital; Maryland Hospital for the Insane

House, Samuel, 143, 223n60

House of Corrections (Jessup, MD), 36, 150

House of Refuge, 23, 92

Hurd, Henry M., 39

identification, police, 72–73, 121–22, 124–26, 129–30, 133, 135, 219n80. *See also* Bertillon system; databases; fingerprinting

idleness, 21, 38, 72, 80–82, 105

Illinois, 127; Chicago, 7–8, 94, 134, 201n17; General Assembly, 94

immigrants, 4, 14, 39, 176, 181–82, 184, 212n8, 231n4; and drugs, 103, 111, 119, 125, 128; and education, 89, 91, 99; and poverty, 72–73, 76–77, 79, 112; and reform, 47, 52, 55, 67, 71

incarceration, 1, 4–5, 52, 150, 187, 202n31, 204n10; and Bayview, 37–42; and Black people, 70, 132, 221n11; and bummers, 26–28, 30–31; and drugs, 107, 110, 116; and jails, 24–25, 27, 32–33; and poverty, 18–21, 74, 84, 194; and profit, 22–23, 28; rates of, 9, 12, 34–35, 151. *See also* jail, Baltimore city; jails; penitentiaries; prisons

Indiana: Indianapolis, 76

Indian Territory, 123

indigence, 37–42, 65

Indigenous people, 40

insanity, 18–19, 25, 36–39, 41–43, 81, 109, 111. *See also* Bayview Asylum; Maryland Hospital for the Insane; mental health

Insley, J. Knox, 187

institutionalization, 2, 4–6, 10–14, 194, 196, 200n5, 205n31; and Bayview, 37–43, 98, 207n88; and city jail, 23–25, 28, 32–33; and education, 89–90, 92, 94–95, 97, 99; and police forces, 55, 71, 132, 165, 170, 176; and poverty relief, 72, 74–76, 78, 80, 82–88, 98, 212n14; and

profit, 19–20, 22, 194; and racialized policing, 99, 101–2, 104, 163, 181. *See also* carceral facilities

interraciality, 160; and couples, 174–75, 181, 198; and neighborhoods, 15, 103, 105, 109–12, 119, 128–29, 133, 182, 184, 186; and sex, 165–66, 174, 176, 179–80, 190–91, 204n50, 216n23; and sociality, 16, 67, 99, 105–6, 172–73, 177, 180, 197, 227n6

interrogation, police, 134–35, 137, 139, 143–45, 162. *See also* torture, police

intimidation, 45, 55, 58, 112, 125–26, 137, 149–50, 165, 172

intoxication, public, 5, 9, 15–17, 21–23, 26–30, 34, 36, 42–43, 84; and police, 121–22, 127, 134, 188; and racialized policing, 102–3, 108, 128. *See also* alcohol

investigations, 70, 147, 202n39; and Black people, 128–29, 174, 176, 178, 180, 185–86; and Brown case, 131, 137–41, 147, 150–60; and education, 89, 91–93; of police, 44–46, 54, 59–61, 125, 187, 197; and poverty, 83–84, 213n35; private, 10, 14, 48, 52–53, 122, 138–39, 151, 195, 228n33

Irish immigrants, 39–40, 127

Italian immigrants, 103, 112–13

Jackson, Zachariah, 149

Jacobs, Randal, 146

Jeffreys-Jones, Rhodri, 202n39

jail, Baltimore city, 13, 17–25, 42, 52, 121, 140, 146, 220n14, 224n87; and Black people, 71, 108–9, 151, 160, 196; and bummers, 26–27, 29–37, 194; and drugs, 110, 115, 120. *See also* Auburn system

jails, 1–2, 4–5, 18–20, 43, 60, 76, 98, 198; and commitments, 17, 20–21, 24–27, 35, 196; and officials, 3, 19–24, 27, 30–31, 33, 36, 99; and wardens, 32–33, 43, 187; and workers, 18, 27, 31. *See also* carceral facilities; detention; jail, Baltimore city

Jewish communities, 92

Jim Crow era, 2, 5, 15, 66, 68, 71, 74, 113; and drugs, 101–4, 116, 119, 129; and

Index · 259

housing, 181, 183; and policing, 165–66, 170, 175–78, 188, 190–91
Johns Hopkins Hospital, 39, 182
Johns Hopkins University, 73, 79
Johnson, Harvey, 69
Johnson, James Weldon, 148, 152–54, 157, 159, 160
Johnson, Joseph, 1–2
Johnson, W. W., 60, 63
Jones, Annie, 127–28
Jones, Charles, 137
Jones, William Henry, 139, 174, 179, 190
Jubb, William, 56–57
judges, 52, 56, 101, 141–42, 144, 155, 162, 178, 188, 196; and drugs, 108–9, 120
juries, 15, 32, 36, 41, 101, 189–90; and Brown case, 134, 140–41, 144–45, 150, 157–58; and drugs, 107, 118; and police misconduct, 187; and reform, 52, 57, 62–63; and whiteness, 79, 123, 135, 140, 142, 146–47, 188, 197
Just Government League, 155
justice, 18–19, 29, 50, 155; and Brown case, 147–48, 150, 152, 156, 159; popular, 132–35, 137–38, 147, 162, 201n20, 204n17; and racism, 15, 22, 101, 115, 125, 175, 179, 197. *See also* white popular justice
juvenile delinquency, 14, 25, 72, 89, 94, 99, 195, 203n47, 214n71

Kane, George P., 28–29, 31, 205n48
Katz, Michael B., 10, 76, 89, 98
Kavanaugh, Harriet M., 131, 139–40, 142–43, 146, 149, 151, 154–55, 157, 160, 162–63
Keating-Owen Act (1916), 90
Kemp, Janet, 213n35
Kentucky, 20; Louisville, 147
Kidd, Benjamin, 81
Kieffner, George W., 141
Klein, Charles, 134
Know Nothing Party, 9, 168
Ku Klux Klan, 15, 153

labor, 4, 9, 53, 97, 102, 114–15, 147, 181, 202n28, 212n26; penal, 5, 13, 18–28,

30–32, 35–36, 38–39, 42–43; and policing poverty, 83–84, 86–88; and poverty relief, 72–74, 76, 78, 80–82, 195. *See also* children; employment
Lastner, Charles, *189*
Latrobe, Ferdinand C., 31, 38–39, 41, 94
law enforcement, 3, 6, 14, 22, 31, 103, 107–8, 115, 166, 220n6; and Black people, 166, 177, 180–81, 196; and education, 89, 94; and morality, 83–84; and poverty, 26–27, 29, 36, 84; and private citizens, 50, 123; and racism, 141, 171, 174–75, 197; and reform, 48, 65, 67; and trials, 134, 144, 146, 221n14, 222n39. *See also* drugs; morality; police forces
LeFlouria, Talitha, 5, 12, 74, 204n10
legal proceedings, 79, 122, 196–97, 202n28; and Brown, 138–49, 154–62, 197, 222n50, 223n60; and drug enforcement, 100–101, 116–21, 127; and police, 62–64, 134, 179, 186–91; and reform, 56–57, 60–64. *See also* confessions; convictions; judges; testimony
legislation, city, 3, 11, 14, 28–29, 42, 74; and charity, 83, 89–92, 94, 97; and drugs, 103, 106–7, 118, 197; and race, 66, 112, 183; and reform, 44, 48, 53, 116; and surveillance, 121–22
legislation, state, 10–11, 14, 22, 28, 56; and drugs, 106–7, 119–20
leisure, 4, 45, 70, 104–5, 121, 128–29, 172, 176, 180
Lewis, Verl S., 76
Lexow Committee, 44, 53–54, 59
Liazos, Ariane, 46
liberalism, 8, 74, 80, 87, 98, 201n28, 204n17, 227n6
Lincoln, Abraham, 58
Link, Caroline, 135
Linthicum, J. Charles, 155–57, 159–60
Liquor Board, 48, 51. *See also* alcohol
Lombroso, Cesare, 216n6
Long, Robert Cary, Sr., 20
Lowell, Josephine Shaw, 76
Lowndes, Lloyd, 54–55, 68
lynching, 132, 140, 145, 148, 152–54, 160, 163, 221n11

260 · *Index*

Madison Square Presbyterian Church (New York City), 49

magistrates, 3, 13, 18, 23, 26–30, 34–35, 110, 195, 230n81; and Black privacy, 176, 178–80, 187, 194

Malka, Adam, 8, 202n28, 204n17, 227n6, 230n92

Marsalek, Joseph, 184–86

Marsalek, Mary, 184

Maryland, 2, 5, 8–10, 15, 21, 36, 55, 89, 181, 202n28; and alcohol, 174–75; and drug enforcement, 100–101, 103, 106, 113, 118–20; Jessup, 36; and justice, 147, 149–51, 163, 183; and racism, 65, 69, 153, 156, 160, 163, 177; and reform, 45, 55, 58, 68–69; Towson, 41

Maryland Conference of Charities and Correction, 90

Maryland Constitution, 8, 119

Maryland General Assembly, 22, 167, 231n4

Maryland Hospital for the Insane, 38

Maryland Penitentiary, 20, 23–24, 41, 101, 123, 137, 190

Maryland Prisoners' Aid Association (MPAA), 26, 35

Massachusetts, 89, 118; Boston, 10, 91

mayors, 9, 18, 168; and asylums, 38–39, 41; and drugs, 101, 103; and policing, 28–29, 31, 169; and poverty, 73, 84, 90; and reform, 18, 45, 54, 58, 65–66, 71, 168. *See also individual names*

McCahan, John E., 92–95, 97

McConville, Seán, 20

McDougall, Harold, 6

McGerr, Michael, 52

McGuinn, Warner T., 141

McKinley, William, 58

Meadow Gang (Baltimore), 56–57, 111–12

media coverage, 1, 12, 36, 62; and asylums, 37–38, 40; Black, 165–68, 171–79, *182,* 184, 186–91, 193, 197–98; and Blackness, 74, 193, 196; and Brown case, 140–41, 144–45, 148–57, 159, 163; and drugs, 102–16, 118–19, 129; and police power, 12, 220n14; and poverty, 17, 26, 29–30, 73, 75, 77, 80, 82–83, 85–87; and racializing crime, 66, 68, 70, 147; and reform, 44, 46, 51, 55–58, 60; and truancy,

95–96; and violence, 132, 134, 183. See also *Afro-American;* Associated Negro Press (ANP)

medical treatment, 22, 37–38, 40, 43, 104–5, 129, 131, 193; and cocaine, 107, 109. *See also* prescriptions

Meehan, Edward F., 60, 63

Mencken, H. L., 220n14

mental health, 37–39, 43, 97. *See also* insanity

Merchant's National Bank, 63

methodology of book, 11–16

Mexican Border War, 169

Meyers, David, 84

Michigan: Detroit, 8, 10

Miles, Alonzo J., 66–68

militarism, 2–4, 55, 107, 131–33, 149, 157, 169–70, 173

Ministerial Union of Baltimore, 48, 67

Ministry to the Poor (Boston), 75

Mississippi, 105

Missouri: Saint Louis, 8, 104–5, 147, 201n17, 202n35

Monkkonen, Eric, 25–26

Monumental Literary and Scientific Association, 69

morality, 11–12, 14, 32; and Blackness, 65, 71, 74, 79, 83, 112–13, 175, 188; bourgeois, 36; and drugs, 102, 104–5, 111, 120, 196; and education, 93–94, 96–97; and jails, 20, 35; and police torture, 138, 140; and policing poverty, 86, 88; and poverty, 18, 28, 72, 75, 79, 82, 84, 194; public, 4, 19, 34, 46, 49, 52, 54–55, 59, 167; and reform, 44, 47–48, 50–51, 67, 71, 195–96; and surveillance, 122, 126–27. *See also* anti-vice politics

Morrison, J. F., 32–33, 35–37, 42

mothers, 79, 86–88, 147, 181, 184–87

Muhammad, Khalil, 71, 77

murder, 1, 16, 68, 81, 221n21; of Black people, 2, 27, 162–63, 166, 171, 175, 181–182, *182,* 185–91; and Brown case, 132, 134–35, 137, 139–46, 149–50, 152–55, 157, 160, 197; and racialized cases, 15, *136. See also* executions

Musto, David, 105

Mutual United Brotherhood of Liberty, 64

Index · 261

National Association for the Advancement of Colored People (NAACP), 148–49, 152–53, 155, 160–61, 163
National Civil Service Reform League, 46
National Commission on Law Observance and Enforcement, 137
National Conference of Charities and Correction, 79–80
National Cordage Company, 53
National Guard, 166, 169
National Municipal League, 46
National Prison Association, 80
National Rifle Association, 170
Naval Academy, 131–32, 139, 142–43, 145–46, 157–58, 160, 197
naval board of inquiry, 130, 132, 139, 143, 146, 157–58, 225n108
Nelson, Howard, 119
Nevada: Carson City, 202n35
New Albert Auditorium, 164
New Jersey, 20; Jersey City, 148
New York, Lake Erie, and Western Railroad, 53
New York City, 7–8, 10, 36, 44, 91, 105; and policing, 123–24, 134, 219n80; and poverty, 75–76, 83; and reform, 48–49, 53–55
New York City police, 59
New York State, 20, 118; Albany, 86; Buffalo, 76, 141
North Carolina, 176
Northeastern District (Baltimore), 186
Northwestern District (Baltimore), 1, 78, 127, 149–50, 164–65, 173, 176–81, *189*

Oblender, Susan, 160
O'Connor, Alice, 73
Office of the Pardon Attorney, 150, 153–54, 156–59
Ohio: Cleveland, 10
Ogbar, Jeffrey O. G., 194
Oklahoma, 105
Old Town Merchants and Manufacturers Association, 126
opiates, 105, 109, 111, 118
overcrowding, institutional, 21, 26, 28, 30, 35–36, 38–39, 42
Ovington, Mary White, 77

Owens, Albert, 100–101, 119–20

Packard, Joseph, 54, 57, 90, 195
Pan-African Congress, 153
Parker, John, 173
Parkhurst, Charles H., 44, 49
patrolling, 2, 5, 8, 17, 26, 29, 66, 142–43, *189*, 195; and Black privacy, 166–67, 171, 174, 176–81, *182*, 185–90; and drugs, 102–3, 107, 110, 116, 119, 197; and expansion, 34, 164–65, 169–70, 172–73, 175; and misconduct, 127–29; and poverty, 85; and reform, 57–58, 66; and surveillance, 125–26; and truancy, 92, 98
patronage systems, 22, 46–47, 49–50, 53
Patterson, Elizabeth, 49–50
Patterson, William, 50
pauperism, 19, 36, 38, 76–77, 79–82, 84–88, 102
peace arrests, 13, 21, 23–24, 26–27, 29, 34, 68; and Black people, 165, 172, 191, 197–98; and drugs, 110, 120, 126
peddling, 74, 84, 88–89, 102, 172, 195
Peirce, Florence E., 91–92, 96
Pendleton, Helen, 77–79, 212n26
penitentiaries, 4, 18, 20–21. *See also* carceral facilities; jails; Maryland Penitentiary; prisons
Pennsylvania, 20; Philadelphia, 7, 45, 57, 75, 207n88
Philadelphia and Reading Railroad, 53
Phillips, Myrtle, 176–77, 179–80
Picha, Frank, 176, 178–80, *189*
Pinkney, Robert, 142–43
plainclothes officers, 85, 102, 107, 119, 121, 126, 129–30
Platt, Anthony, 14, 73, 214n71
Plessy v. Ferguson, 64
Pliley, Jessica, 202n39
Plug Uglies, 9
Plum, Frank, 128
Poe, Edgar Allan, 202n31
Poe, John Prentiss, 66
police abuses, 26, 43, 53–54, 57, 137, 172, 175, 225n108; and misconduct, 44, 118, 127–28, 130, 135, 168, 173, 178–80, 187, 191. *See also* torture, police; violence
police administrators, 27, 128

262 · Index

police boards, 28–29, 34, 167–68, 219n89; and drugs, 101, 103, 107, 116–18; and misconduct, 123–30, 139; and politics, 170, 195–96; and poverty, 83–85; and reform, 54, 58, 60–63, 65–68

police captains, 60, 62–63, 127–28, 135, 170, 187, 189, 197

police chiefs, 123

police commissioners, 12, 16, 54, 60–63, 138, 187–88, 191, 197; and drugs, 115, 123, 125, 128; and expansion, 164, 166–74, 179–80. *See also* Gaither, Charles

police departments, 4–5, 8, 10, 13, 30, 83, 135; and Black privacy, 167–68, 170, 173, 176, 178–80, 185, 187, 189–90; and drugs, 120–23, 125, 127–28, 134; and reform, 55, 59, 61–62, 64

police forces, 8–15, 17, 101, 116, 198, 204n17, 205n50, 220n107; and Black private life, 166, 170–72, 174, 177, 179–80, 182–91, 197–98, 227n6, 228n33; and Brown case, 150, 156–58; and drugs, 105–7, 110, 115–17, 119–21, 126, 216nn11–12; and expansion, 29, 34, 168–71, 187–88, 228n25; and misconduct, 116–18, 128, 130, 135, 139, 190; and poverty relief, 74–75, 80, 82–83, 87, 98, 194; and reform, 4, 44, 48, 50, 53, 55, 59, 62–64, 194–95; and surveillance, 121–29; and torture, 132–35, 138, 145, 221n11, 225n108. *See also* citizen policing; discretion, police; harbor police; law enforcement; plain-clothes officers

police marshals, 28, 59, 63–64, 173, 205n48

police power, 2–3, 5–6, 10–16, 19, 200n6; and Black private life, 163, 166, 171, 173–77, 190; and drugs, 99, 101–3, 107, 116, 120, 129, 183, 197; and education, 72, 91, 93–95, 98–99; and poverty, 17, 28, 36, 74, 83, 85, 98–99; and reform, 43, 47–48, 50–52, 59, 64, 70, 195–98; and surveillance, 121–22, 126, 129–30; and torture, 132–33, 162

police raids, 51, 60–62, 106, 113–114, 114, 126–27, 138, 176

police states, 2, 6, 9, 11, 13, 43, 123, 194–95, 198, 230n92; and Black privacy, 170, 175,

191; and Brown case, 133, 137, 141, 156, 162; and city jail, 18, 194; and poverty, 75, 83, 98

police station houses, 10, 18, 26, 30, 34, 60, 83, 194–95, 210n63; and Black privacy, 172, 176, 179–80, 186; and drugs, 110, 122–23, 125; and reform, 49, 58; and torture, 132–33, 162

policy (game), 59–64, 210n70

political machines, 9, 14–15, 20, 26, 36, 121, 141, 175, 194; and reform, 43–58, 66–67, 71

politics, 2–5, 8–12, 14–16, 193–94, 196–97, 200n5; and Black privacy, 168, 170, 183, 188; and Brown case, 133, 138, 141, 147, 151–52, 154–56, 159, 162–63; and drugs, 101–3, 105, 107, 110–11, 118, 121; and incarceration, 18, 26, 29, 32, 34–35, 39, 42–43; and poverty, 73–74, 78, 80–81, 83, 96, 99; and reform, 44–50, 52–55, 59–61, 63–71, 196

Potters, 116–18

poverty, 4, 10, 12–14, 19, 65, 152, 161; and criminalization, 17–20, 23–24, 26–28, 30; and drugs, 105, 112–13, 116, 118; and education, 89–99; and incarceration, 18–20, 24–30, 36–37, 41, 41–43, 194; and reform, 48–49, 52, 55, 57, 63, 65, 222n50; and relief, 46, 49, 71–88, 98–99, 203n47, 211n8. *See also* begging; Charity Organization Society (COS); insanity; pauperism; vagrancy

power, 104, 121; Black political, 69, 168, 178, 188; city vs. state, 52, 65–66, 107, 168–69, 197; political, 9, 15, 70–71, 101, 197; and poverty relief, 73, 81, 83, 86, 88; and reform, 45, 47, 53; state, 4, 14, 34, 43, 74, 95–99, 102, 108, 122–24, 133, 162, 200n6. *See also* police power

prescriptions, 70, 106–8, 114–15, 119, 121, 212n26

prisons, 4–5, 13, 19–24, 26–36, 38, 41, 73, 76, 94, 98; and policing, 123–24, 127, 134–35. *See also* Bayview Asylum; carceral facilities

private citizens, 3–4, 70, 194–95; and policing, 22, 34, 89–90, 93–94, 97–98, 123–25, 147, 166, 176, 195; and poverty relief,

36, 73–74, 85, 87; and reform, 9–10, 14, 48–52, 54, 56

profanity, 14, 48, 68, 72, 165, 191

Progress Club, 91

Progressivism, 14, 79, 202n39, 203n46, 213n35; and drugs, 116, 121, 129; and education, 73–74, 77, 80, 82–83, 88, 91, 98; and justice, 138, 147, 162; and racism, 175–76

Prohibition, 55, 71, 166–67, 174–75, 188

property, 3, 122; and drugs, 103, 112; protection of, 17–19, 22, 29, 34, 126, 128–29, 134, 173–74; and race, 15, 67–68, 188, 202n28; and reform, 50–51, 63

protection, police, 15, 45, 59–60, 116, 128, 162, 174, 187

protests, 2, 16, 26, 50, 56, 70, 95, 125, 210n85

pseudoscience, 39, 47–48, 71, 73–74, 97, 129. See also biological essentialism; charities; cultural evolution; eugenics; social Darwinism

public disturbance, 16, 21, 111, 171, 179

public good, 3, 13, 19, 27, 36, 126

public order, 1, 7, 128, 194, 196; and Black privacy, 171, 175–77, 180, 190–91, 197; and drugs, 101–2, 108, 110–11, 119–20, 126, 128–29; and incarceration, 13, 16, 18, 20, 24–25; and policing, 27–28, 30, 34–35, 138, 164–67; and reform, 43, 55, 64

Pumphrey, A. J., 135, 137

punishment, 2–5, 8, 15, 80, 138, 151, 162, 200n6, 204n10; and drugs, 101, 107, 119–21, 123, 126; of police, 44, 127–28, 130, 168, 172–73, 177–80, 187, 190–91; and poverty, 23–24, 30, 32, 35–36, 43, 78, 82, 88, 98; and profit, 17–19, 194; and reform, 48, 50–52, 54; and truancy, 74, 89, 92, 94–95, 97–98, 195. See also labor

Pure Food and Drug Act, 106

race riots, 1, 107–8, 111

racialization, 6, 9, 11, 22, 145; and Black privacy, 162–63, 178–79, 201n28; and Brown case, 135, 137–38, 141, 147, 151, 163; and drugs, 101–2, 104–5, 107, 109, 118, 129; and education, 90–91, 96–97;

and poverty, 74–75, 78, 82, 98; and punishment, 34, 123, 200n4; and reform, 53, 57. See also interraciality; racialized policing; racial zoning; segregation

racialized policing, 1–2, 5–8, 11–15, 34, 99, 136, 196; and Black privacy, 170–72, 175–77, 190; and Brown case, 135, 137, 163, 221n11; and drugs, 101, 126, 129; and reform, 47, 64–71

racial zoning, 11, 103, 112, 120, 181, 183, 191

racism, 12, 39, 68–69, 129, 139–41, 147–48, 180, 188, 202n28; and police, 118, 155, 185; and poverty, 77, 79; and reform, 175–76; and whiteness, 1, 69–70, 99, 116, 150–54, 160, 163, 177, 180, 193. See also Black advancement; Black criminality; Black dysfunction; white supremacy; white vigilantism

Ragan, Bridget, 86–87

rape, 68, 81, 108, 119, 148, 151, 162

Rasin, Isaac Freeman, 45

Raywick, KY, 147

Reconstruction, 2, 8–9, 55, 201n28

Reddick, Thomas, 173–74

reform, 4–5, 10–16, 18, 42, 44–53, 141, 196, 202n39; and coalitions, 46, 49, 52–53, 70; and drugs, 108, 111, 118, 121–22, 216n12; and education, 89–93, 95–97; and elections, 53–59; and incarceration, 20–23, 26–29, 31–32, 35–36, 42–43; and justice, 138, 147, 163; and policing, 59–64, 122, 125–26, 167–68, 170, 194; and poverty, 72–74, 77–80, 82–86, 88, 98–99, 213n35, 222n50; and racializing crime, 64–71, 101–2, 104, 194–96; and racism, 99, 173, 175–76

Reform League, 44–46, 49, 54–64, 71, 83–85, 90, 141, 195, 202n39

rehabilitation, 18, 20, 28, 41, 76

Republicans, 9, 12, 15, 121, 149; and policing, 168–69; and racializing crime, 64–68, 70–71, 101; and reform, 44–47, 52–54, 56, 58, 60, 63, 71, 141

Rhuebotton, Annie, 150

Richardson, Frank, 65

Richmond, Mary, 10, 76–77, 87

Riis, Jacob, 83

Riley, Kenneth W., 131, 160

264 · *Index*

Riley's Hotel, 127
Rip Raps, 9
Ritchie, Albert C., 153–55, 158, 168–69, 171
robbery, 40, 51, 81, 134, 139, 174, 190. *See also* burglary
Rohleder, Frederick A., 176–78, 187, 230n81
Roosevelt, Theodore, 46, 54–55, 59, 202n39
Rose, John C., 51–52, 56–58, 71, 141–47, 150, 155, 162, 194–95, 222n50, 225n108
Rossberg, William, 119–21, 129
Rossberg v. State of Maryland, 120–21, 129, 183
rowdyism, 15, 35, 47, 64–71, 78, 99, 196; and drugs, 101, 104, 108–9, 112–13, 126, 129, 197; and violence, 151, 163
rule of law, 18–19, 27, 43
Russia, 75
Russian immigrants, 181; Jewish, 92, 112–13

Sabbatarianism, 121
safety, public, 67, 153
Saint Vincent de Paul Society, 85
Saint Vincent's Catholic Church, 50
saloons, 45, 48–52, 55–57, 60, 84, 176, 187, 210n85; Black, 108, 112–14, 141; and surveillance, 126, 128, 138, 182. *See also* Anti-Saloon League
Schley, David, 202n28
Schnepfe, August W., 141–42, 144–46, 149
schools, Baltimore public, 2, 4–5, 12, 29, 65, 100, 112, 147, 198, 205n50; and attendance officers, 3, 14, 89–94, 97–98, 195; and commissioners, 65; and criminalization, 72–73, 89–99; and school board, 78, 195; and superintendents, 91–94
Schryver, E. M., 60
Scott, James, 173
Sears, A. L., 88
segregation, 8, 13, 38, 78, 99, 156, 160, 167; and drugs, 101, 103, 108–9, 112–13, 119; and housing, 120, 141, 183, 198; and policing, 129, 133, 165, 174, 176; and reform, 46, 50, 64, 68–69, 141. *See also* racial zoning
Seigel, Micol, 133
self-incrimination, 101, 137–38, 149

sex, 78–79, 106, 127, 165, 176, 212n26, 227n6, 228n38
sex work, 34, 50, 59, 70, 102, 110, 121–22, 126–30, 149, 175–76, 182, 220n107. *See also* brothels
Shabazz, Rashad, 166
Sheppard Asylum, 41
shootings, 58, 105–6, 171–73, 175, 183, *185,* 185–186, 189
Shufelt, Gordon, 227n6
Sickle, James H. Van, 91
Simms, Rhoda, 150
Simuels, Henry, 172–73
Slattery, J. R., 51
slavery, 6–9, 68–70, 147, 151, 200n5, 201n28, 212n26; and emancipation, 9, 78–79; and freedmen, 22, 151; and jails, 21–23, 42; and poverty, 42, 74, 78–79; and runaway slaves, 8, 21–23, 85
Smith, James F., 60, 63
Smith, John W., 65
Smith, Raymond, 142–45, 160
social Darwinism, 69, 73, 81, 212n9. *See also* biological essentialism; cultural evolution; eugenics
social order, 3, 5–6, 11, 13, 24, 46, 127; and Blackness, 47, 106, 212n26
social science research, 76–77, 80, 97–99, 101, 112
social welfare, 19, 76, 83, 98, 102, 191
social work, 10, 75–77, 99, 149
Society for the Prevention of Crime, 44
Society for the Suppression of Vice (BSSV), 48–52, 59–61, 63, 67, 71, 90, 141, 195
Sommerfeld, Rose, 90
South Carolina: Charleston, 148
Southern District (Baltimore), 173
Spanish-American War, 169
Spring Grove, Maryland, 38
state government, 4, 6, 8–14, 49, 70, 89, 97, 201n28, 214n71; and agencies, 3, 5, 65, 71, 174; and drugs, 101, 103; and officials, 132–33, 167, 174; and policing, 66, 168
state legislature, 8, 107, 167, 169, 195, 197; and education, 89, 91, 94; and incarceration, 17, 22, 26–27, 29, 34; New York, 53; and reform, 48, 66. *See also* legislation, state

state's attorneys, 100–101, 119–20, 188
Stephen, Leslie, 81
Straus, Isaac Lobe, 156
Strawbridge Methodist Episcopal Church, 67
street gangs, 9
street policing, 2–3, 5, 10, 14–15, 28–29, 187, 196, 198; and drugs, 101–3, 107, 112, 118–19, 121, 129; and expansion, 166–67, 172–74, 180; and misconduct, 132–33, 135; and poverty, 87–88; and surveillance, 125–26, 130
Sunday laws, 34
Superior Court, 56
Supervisors of Charities, 95
Supplee, J. Frank, 140
Supreme Bench, 120
surveillance, 2, 10, 14, 16, 29, 130, 219n97; and drugs, 102–3, 107–8, 115, 196; and elections, 57, 97, 194; and jails, 24, 28; and poverty, 49, 73, 75–78, 82, 86–87, 98; private, 46, 50, 59; and racialization, 15, 34, 121–29
suspects, 8, 22–23, 115, 121–25, 130, 133–35, 137, 147, 178, 219n89; and Brown case, 132, 138, 141, 154, 157, 162
suspicion, police, 17, 34, 141, 165, 171–72, 175, 177, 180–81, 186, 191
Swann, Sherlock, 11, 107, 116–21, 123, 125, 127–28, 135, 162, 168
Swann, Thomas, 9, 116
Swann's Cocaine Ordinance, 118–20, 129, 183

Taft, William, 193
Talbott, J. Frederick, 45
Tammany Hall (New York City), 44, 49, 54–55, 59
Tennessee: Memphis, 104
Tennessee Parties, 105
Terry, David Taft, 180
testimony, 12, 52, 62–63, 100–101, 116–18, 128, 178, 186–89, 197; and Brown case, 142–50, 154, 157–58, 160, 197
theft, 9, 20, 22, 40, 78, 81, 122–23
third degree, 15, 133–40, *159*, 162, 178, 197, 221n11, 221n14. *See also* torture, police
Thomas, Douglas H., 63

Tombs (New York), 36
torture, police, 15, 36, 132–37, 140, 142–44, 162–63, 198, 221n11, 221n14
traffic policing, 167, 169–70, 179–80
truancy, 10, 14–15, 72–74, 80, 89–99, 195, 198
Trustees of the Poor, 23, 37–38, 40
Truxon, Emma, 149, 152–53, 156
Tubman, Harriet, 69
Tulsa race massacre, 152, 160
Turner, Nat, 69

Underground Railroad, 69
unemployment, 37, 53, 78, 86, 91
Union, the, 6, 8–9, 205n48
Union Benevolent Association (Philadelphia), 75
Union for Public Good, 53
United Irish League, 127
University of Chicago, 80
Urban, Anton and Sophia, 184, 187
Urban, Charles, 184–91
urban sociology, 73–74, 77, 80–81
U.S. Civil Service Commission, 54
U.S. Congress, 45, 155–56
U.S. Constitution, 8–9, 101, 119, 129, 138, 183; Fifteenth Amendment, 66, 137; Fourth Amendment, 174
U.S. District Court, 15, 140–41
USS *Cumberland*, 140, 142–44, 146–47, 154–55, 157, 160. *See also* Brown, Henry Alfred
U.S. Supreme Court, 3, 51–52, 64, 183, 202n28

vagrancy, 19, 21–22, 28, 38, 77, 108, 150, 195, 202n31
vandalization, 173–74
Vermont, 89
Vincent, Kate, 122–23
violence, 9, 57–58, 94, 116, 131, 151, 154; and crime, 15, 64, 68, 134–35, 137, 151; and drugs, 102, 105, 110, 129; police, 9, 59, 125, 133–35, 138, 166–67, 171–73, 175–79, 191, 221n11; and racism, 12, 79, 132–33, 173, 183; state, 3, 204n10. *See also* assault; beatings, police; brutality, police; harassment, police; shootings; torture, police
Virginia, 20

266 · *Index*

visiting programs, 75, 87, 212n19
volunteerism, 21, 50, 73, 75–76
voting, 8–9, 160, 168–69, 193, 202n31; fraud, 50, 56–59, 61, 202n31; and racialization, 66, 70, 101, 116, 154, 231n4; and reform, 45, 54–55, 65, 69. *See also* disenfranchisement

wages, 9, 78, 88, 115, 122, 202n28
Ward, Bernard J., 128
wards, Baltimore: and housing, 181–82; and reform, 44–45, 50, 53–54, 56
Warner, Amos, 77, 81
War of Southern Aggression, 13. *See also* Civil War
Washburn, Edward, 146
Washington, Booker T., 77
Washington, D.C., 89, 132, 141, 149
Washington, Fred, 148
Waters, Daniel "Big Dan," 113–16
Watson, Henry, 90
Wayfarer's Lodge, 83
W. B. A. Electric Railway, 142
wealth, 14, 26, 36, 42, 96, 105, 112, 194; and policing, 125–26, 128, 139; and poverty relief, 73, 75, 81, 87–88, 98, 194, 212n9, 212n14; and reform, 46, 49–50, 52, 63, 71
Weller, Ovington, 149
West Baltimore, 174, 182–83
West Virginia, 78
Wheatley, Edward J., 148
Wheatley, Laura, 147–48, 150, 152–57, 159–60, 163, 177
White, Deborah Gray, 212n26
White, Francis, 73
White, James A., 176–80, 230n81
White, Mary, 176
white flight, 181
white men, 8, 60, 66, 83, 170; and drugs, 105, 109; and racism, 67, 69, 140, 174, 188; and reform, 48, 56, 58
white neighborhoods, 11, 15, 103, 112, 119–20, 181, 183–84, 191. *See also* Black neighborhoods; racial zoning
white people, 13, 16, 39, 112, 148–49, 156, 176, 194, 202n28; and arrests, 7, 16,

34–35, 137, 170; and Brown case, 156–57, 160, 197; and drugs, 102–8, 110, 113, 118; as immigrants, 111, 119, 181; and juries, 79, 123, 135, 140, 142, 145–47, 188, 197; and policing, 22, 60, 125, 128–29, 168, 172–74, 178, 187; and poverty, 73, 77–78; and property, 15, 134; and racism, 1, 69–70, 99, 116, 150–54, 160, 163, 177, 180, 193; and reform, 45–48, 54, 56–58, 66; and segregation, 113, 183, 190. *See also* white men; white women
white popular justice, 8, 15, 22, 204n17. *See also* white vigilantism
white supremacy, 5, 8–9, 47, 64–70, 96, 145, 147, 156, 163; and policing, 129, 166, 171, 176; and poverty, 73–74, 81. *See also* racism; white vigilantism
white vigilantism, 2, 8, 22, 50, 183. *See also* white popular justice
white women, 67–68, 127–28, 155, 170; and drugs, 105, 108–9; and murder, 135, 138, 141, 145, 151; and policing, 195, 219n89; and poverty relief, 73, 76; and private lives, 176–80; and safety, 153, 162–63, 191
Wickersham Commission, 137, 153, 166
Williams, Bessie, 181–84, 186
Williams, Charles Edward, 181–90
Williams, Codger, 31
Williams, Emanuel, 171–72
Willrich, Michael, 138
women, incarcerated, 33, 42
Woodbridge, Hattie, 122–23
Woods, Henrietta, 110–11, 113
workhouses, 5, 18, 30
working classes, 3–4, 10, 19, 42, 112, 125, 167, 212n8; Black, 78–79, 101, 110, 114–15, 123; and criminalization, 12, 72, 74, 88, 126; and drugs, 109, 111, 119, 129, 216n12; and neighborhoods, 5, 128; and reform, 46–47, 52, 55, 70–71
World War I, 25, 52, 169

Yeggmen, 138
YMCA (Baltimore), 48
Young, Sadonia, 127–28

MICHAEL CASIANO is an assistant professor of American Studies at the University of Maryland, Baltimore County.

The University of Illinois Press
is a founding member of the
Association of University Presses.

Composed in 10.25/13 Marat Pro
with Trade Gothic LT Std display
by Lisa Connery
at the University of Illinois Press

University of Illinois Press
1325 South Oak Street
Champaign, IL 61820-6903
www.press.uillinois.edu